DODD–FRANK WALL STREET REFORM AND CONSUMER PROTECTION ACT

Purpose, Critique, Implementation Status and Policy Issues

World Scientific–Now Publishers Series in Business

ISSN: 2251-3442

Vol. 1 Games and Dynamic Games
by Alain Haurie, Jacek B. Krawczyk and Georges Zaccour

Vol. 2 Dodd–Frank Wall Street Reform and Consumer Protection Act: Purpose, Critique, Implementation Status and Policy Issues
edited by Douglas D. Evanoff and William F. Moeller

Vol. 3 The History of Marketing Science
edited by Russell S. Winer and Scott A. Neslin

World Scientific–Now Publishers Series in Business: **Vol. 2**

DODD-FRANK WALL STREET REFORM AND CONSUMER PROTECTION ACT

Purpose, Critique, Implementation Status and Policy Issues

Douglas D Evanoff
William F Moeller

Federal Reserve Bank of Chicago, USA

now

World Scientific

Published by

World Scientific Publishing Co. Pte. Ltd.

5 Toh Tuck Link, Singapore 596224

USA office: 27 Warren Street, Suite 401-402, Hackensack, NJ 07601

UK office: 57 Shelton Street, Covent Garden, London WC2H 9HE

and

now publishers Inc.
PO Box 1024
Hanover, MA 02339
USA

Library of Congress Cataloging-in-Publication Data
Dodd–Frank Wall Street reform and consumer protection act: purpose, critique, implementation status and policy issues / [edited] by Douglas D. Evanoff and William F. Moeller (Federal Reserve Bank of Chicago, USA).
pages cm. -- (World scientific-now publishers series in business, ISSN 2251-3442 ; volume 2)
Includes bibliographical references and index.
ISBN 978-9814590037 (alk. paper)
1. United States. Dodd-Frank Wall Street Reform and Consumer Protection Act 2. Financial institutions--Law and legislation--United States. 3. Financial services industry--Law and legislation--United States. 4. Consumer protection--Law and legislation--United States. I. Evanoff, Douglas Darrell, 1951– editor of compilation. II. Moeller, William F., editor of compilation.
KF969.58201.A2 2014
346.73'082--dc23

2014004396

British Library Cataloguing-in-Publication Data
A catalogue record for this book is available from the British Library.

Cover Illustration by Robert Dlotkowski

In-House Editors: Sutha Surenddar/Philly Lim

Typeset by Stallion Press
Email: enquiries@stallionpress.com

Dedications

This collection is dedicated to the women in my family who have put up with my musings/reflections/arguments about my work and profession throughout the years. They have provided support in my research efforts, and in life more generally. That would include: Mary Ann, Rachel, Kathryn and Othia.

Doug

This work is dedicated to my mom, Kitty, dad, Bill, and all of my grandparents for the unrelenting support and encouragement throughout my life; to my brother, Carl, and sister, Kathryn, for keeping me on my toes; to my nephew Finley for bringing the joy out of any situation; and to my girlfriend Marnie for making me smile during these busy few years.

Will

Preface

The Dodd–Frank Wall Street Reform and Consumer Protection Act (Dodd–Frank) was signed into law on July 21, 2010 following the financial crisis and the onset of the Great Recession. It introduced significant regulatory reform aimed at protecting consumers, investors and taxpayers. Most agree that it will have far-reaching implications for how financial services firms will conduct business in the future.

The act has been praised for positioning the financial industry to support the U.S. economy in a more stable manner than seen in the past. It has also been criticized for being unnecessary (since many of the 'new' regulations could arguably have been enforced in the pre-Dodd–Frank environment) and excessively burdensome without really addressing the issues that generated the financial crisis of the 2000s.

The new regulation requires significant effort from regulators. For example, the act requires the development and implementation of some 398 new regulatory rules, various mandated studies, and the need to introduce a number of new bureaus, offices and councils with responsibility to study, evaluate, and promote consumer protection and financial stability. Additionally, and perhaps most challenging, there is a mandate for regulators to identify and increase regulatory scrutiny of systemically important institutions and introduce new macroprudential regulations aimed at increased financial market stability. Three plus years into the implementation of the act, much has been done, but much remains to be done. It continues to be a work in progress.

This volume serves as a practitioner's guide to recent financial regulatory reform. What are thought to be some of the more important aspects of the Dodd–Frank Act are discussed in a non-technical manner and from a number of perspectives: including that of industry scholars who have been actively involved in evaluating financial regulation, regulators who are responsible for implementing the reform, financial policy experts representing think tanks and banking trade associations, congressmen and congressional staff involved with developing the legislation, and legal scholars. The purpose of this volume is to summarize and critique the act, evaluate how the act is being implemented and how the implementation process is progressing, and discuss modifications that, in the views of the authors, might be needed to more effectively achieve the stated goals of the legislation.

Versions of some of the articles in this volume were previously published and credit for the original publications is provided in each article. The editors thank the various agencies and publications for allowing the works to be reproduced in this volume. They particularly thank the Federal Reserve Bank of Chicago for allowing articles from its' *Economic Perspectives* and various *Proceedings of a Conference on Bank Structure and Competition* to be reprinted. Representatives from the FDIC were also most cooperative and made a significant contribution to the volume.

As an aside, the articles included often come from very different sources — scholarly finance and economic journals, speeches, legal journals, congressional committee reports, and regulatory agency releases describing how new regulations are to be implemented — and, as a result, differ significantly in style. This results in some inconsistencies in reference listings and footnote formats across the various reprinted sources. Nevertheless, we willingly accept these inconsistencies as the articles included seem to be the relevant pieces to achieve the goals of the volume.

Finally, the editors thank the individual authors for taking the time to address the issues and being willing to share their views. They would also like to thank colleagues at the Chicago Federal Reserve for numerous discussions about the act; Rita Molloy and Han Choi for editorial assistance; Ella Dukes, Sue Parren and Pam Suarez for helping with formatting issues; Bob Dlotkowski for developing the cover design; and Zac Rolnik from now publishers Inc. for being flexible and helpful in bringing this publication to fruition. The views expressed in this volume should be recognized as those of the authors and may not reflect the views of the Federal Reserve Bank of Chicago, the Federal Reserve System, or the organizations with which the individual authors are affiliated.

Contents

PART I

Introduction and Summary of The Act

Part I of this volume serves to provide an overview of the major elements of financial regulatory reform introduced in Dodd–Frank. This overview is provided in an article by Douglas Evanoff and William Moeller, both from the Federal Reserve Bank of Chicago. Instead of taking a title by title approach, Evanoff and Moeller introduce and summarize what are thought to be the major components of the act, highlight what problems are being addressed and provide insight on the economic reasoning behind the regulatory changes. The major regulatory changes include efforts to improve financial stability via macroprudential regulation, greater supervisory coordination, new failure resolution procedures, limits to proprietary trading by insured depository institutions, new requirements for over-the-counter (OTC) derivative markets (particularly clearing and settlement requirements), and new consumer protections. The goal for this part is to take a 'positive' approach and discuss the new regulations resulting from the act, rather than providing a comprehensive appraisal of them. That appraisal comes in the forthcoming chapters; most formally in Chapter 2.

Chapter 1

The Dodd–Frank Act: An Overview

Douglas D. Evanoff and William F. Moeller[1]

As financial regulation evolved over the past 80 years, it became common to introduce new legislation with the claim that "this is the most significant regulatory reform since the Great Depression and the Banking Act of 1933." On July 21, 2010, following the 2008–2009 financial crisis, President Barack Obama signed into law the Dodd–Frank Wall Street Reform and Consumer Protection Act (hereafter Dodd–Frank). In the view of many in the industry, Dodd–Frank became the new standard against which all future reforms should be compared.[2] The stated goals of the act were to provide financial regulatory reform, to protect consumers and investors, to put an end to the too-big-to-fail (TBTF) problem, to regulate the over-the-counter (OTC) derivatives markets, and to prevent future financial crises. The act has far-reaching implications for industry stability and how financial services firms will conduct business in the future.

The implementation of Dodd–Frank requires the development of some 398 new regulatory rules and various mandated studies.[3] There is also the need to introduce and staff a number of new entities (bureaus, offices, and councils) with responsibilities to study, evaluate, and promote consumer protection and financial

[1]Douglas D. Evanoff is senior financial economist and vice president at the Federal Reserve Bank of Chicago and is an adjunct professor at DePaul University. William F. Moeller is a senior associate economist in the Economic Research Department of the Federal Reserve Bank of Chicago. The material in this chapter draws from, and builds on, Evanoff and Moeller (2012).

[2]More details and the full text of the act are available at http://www.gpo.gov/fdsys/pkg/PLAW-111publ203/html/PLAW-111publ203.htm.

[3]A number of law firms and consulting firms provide periodic updates as to the status of Dodd–Frank implementation. See, for example, Davis Polk & Wardwell LLP (2013) and various issues.

stability. Additionally, there is a mandate for the regulators to identify and increase regulatory scrutiny of systemically important financial institutions (SIFIs). As a result, macroprudential regulation (aimed at mitigating risk to the financial system as a whole) will play a much more important role than it has in the past (see Bernanke, 2011). More than three years into the implementation of the act, much has been done, but much remains to be done.[4]

Dodd–Frank continues to be debated in the political, business, and public arenas. Were the right lessons learned from the recent crisis? Were the appropriate reforms introduced in the new regulations?[5] Did the act go far enough — or too far? Were regulators given too much discretion in implementing the act? How burdensome are the new regulations and how will the intermediation process be affected? Will financial innovation be affected? Might regulatory reform induce some current financial activities to shift toward the less-regulated shadow financial sector?[6] Are banks finding ways to effectively avoid or cushion the impact of the new rules? These issues will be touched on in this chapter and will be critiqued more fully in later chapters of this volume.

In this overview chapter, we summarize the major components of Dodd–Frank. We also discuss the economic rationale behind many of the reforms. It should be emphasized, however, that this is not an attempt to cover every aspect of the act — as with any legislation, there were certain issues amended to the act late in the drafting process that are well outside the realm of financial regulation.[7] Rather, we summarize what we consider the major components of the act: namely, financial stability via macroprudential regulation, supervisory coordination, new failure resolution procedures, limits to proprietary trading by insured depository institutions, new requirements for OTC derivatives markets (particularly clearing and settlement requirements), and new consumer protection oversight. We also outline the purpose of the reforms and the tools available to regulators to achieve the desired outcomes.

---

[4]The implementation process has preceded too slowly for some industry observers; see Volcker (2013). As of July 15, 2013, Davis Polk & Wardwell (2013) report that of the 398 new rules, only 158 (40%) had been finalized.

[5]This topic is addressed in Part VII of this book. See, for example, Financial Crisis Inquiry Commission (2011), which is accompanied by dissents.

[6]See, for example, Duffie (2012). For a discussion of issues associated with regulation of the shadow financial markets see Claessens *et al.* (2014).

[7]In the case of Dodd–Frank, this includes issues such as "disclosures relating to conflict minerals originating in the Democratic Republic of the Congo" and "reporting requirements regarding coal or other mine safety."

Background

While there have been a number of modifications to the U.S. financial regulatory environment over the past 80 years, the reform in Dodd–Frank is different. It takes a much more aggressive and comprehensive approach than did past reforms, with an emphasis on consumer protection and financial market stability via enhanced prudential regulation. Many recent proposals were mostly concerned with restructuring the regulatory agencies than altering prudential regulation and allowable financial activities. For example, the U.S. Department of the Treasury (2008) proposed the phase out of the thrift charter, the transition of thrifts toward a bank charter, and the elimination of the Office of Thrift Supervision (OTS).[8] It also recommended a federal regulator for insurance companies. However, there were few proposed changes to product powers or prudential regulation as in Dodd–Frank.

Dodd–Frank also differs from reforms put in place in recent years in that it reverses the deregulatory trend that started in the early 1980s. For example, bank and bank holding company (BHC) product powers had been expanded with the 1980 Monetary Control Act, the 1982 Garn–St. Germain Act, and the 1999 Gramm–Leach–Bliley Act. The 1980 and 1982 acts also eased deposit pricing restrictions on the industry. Limitations to geographic expansion were lifted with the 1994 Interstate Banking and Branching Efficiency Act (the Riegle–Neal Act) and numerous state laws aimed at increasing banks' ability to operate across state borders. Dodd–Frank reverses this trend and reimposes some of the restrictions that were lifted during this period — see the Volcker Rule discussion.

Another way in which Dodd–Frank differs from other recent regulatory reforms is in the flexibility it gives regulators. This approach contrasts significantly with that of the Federal Deposit Insurance Corporation (FDIC) Improvement Act of 1991, for example. The 1991 act was passed in the aftermath of the savings and loan crisis when Congress was frustrated with bank regulators over the large number of bank failures and the resulting large losses to the bank insurance fund — for details, see Kane (1989a,b), Benston and Kaufman (1994), and Young (1993). By contrast, many aspects of Dodd–Frank lack specificity as to how they

---

[8]Under Dodd–Frank, the OTS has been eliminated and chartered thrifts will be supervised (depending on the charter type) by the national regulator or state bank regulator. Thrift holding companies will be supervised by the Federal Reserve. There have been proposals for additional changes to the financial regulatory structure — see, for example, Volcker (2013) and U.S. General Accounting Office (1994). These proposals often result from concerns about inefficiencies and distortions in the current regulatory construct — see, for example, Rosen (2003).

are to be implemented, giving the regulators significant discretionary authority to develop and implement rules — for details, see Casey (2011) and Van Der Weide (2012). However, while giving regulators discretion in the act's implementation, in many cases Dodd–Frank explicitly imposed deadlines by which reforms needed to be in place or studies needed to be completed. This placed significant pressure on regulators to meet rulemaking deadlines and implement the reforms while considering the potential regulatory burden that might be imposed on the industry; a burden that the industry argues may adversely impact its effectiveness in carrying out its basic role in financial and economic markets. With that description of the rather trying regulatory environment created by Dodd–Frank (for both the regulators and regulatees), we next turn to the major issues addressed in the act.

Financial stability

Perhaps the most important objective of Dodd–Frank is to ensure a safe and stable financial system.[9] Toward that goal, the act shifts from exclusively concentrating on microprudential regulation, which focuses on risk at individual institutions, to include macroprudential regulation, which focuses on overall market stability and systemic risk. During the financial crisis, it became obvious that the assumption that the financial system as a whole could be kept safe by regulating individual institutions was unsound. A purely microprudential approach ignores interconnections and externalities, whereby the actions of a single financial institution can induce spillover effects that adversely affect general market conditions, other financial institutions, and ultimately the economy as a whole. In contrast, macroprudential regulatory approaches attempt to manage overall financial system risk.[10] Ideally, macroprudential tools can be used to induce financial institutions to internalize the costs of their actions on society, including externalities where costs are generated and shifted to others.[11] With the increased reliance on macroprudential regulation, there was also a realization that regulators need to anticipate forthcoming industry problems.

[9]A discussion of alternative regulatory efforts to ensure financial stability is included in Part III of this volume.

[10]One of the first to stress this need was Borio (2003). For a more thorough discussion of macroprudential regulation, see Hanson *et al.* (2011).

[11]Pollution is the classic example of a negative externality. The polluting firm imposes costs on others that are not accounted for in the production process and in determining the prices and quantities of outputs. Regulation should induce the polluters to internalize the costs they are imposing on others. Systemic risk is the externality addressed in Dodd–Frank.

These challenges were addressed in Title I of Dodd–Frank, which created the Financial Stability Oversight Council (FSOC) and the Office of Financial Research (OFR), which is housed in the U.S. Treasury Department and serves to support the FSOC. FSOC is structured as a consultative group of financial regulators. Its role is to identify risks that pose a threat to the stability of financial system, promote market discipline, and respond to emerging threats. To accomplish this, FSOC has the authority to make recommendations about appropriate macroprudential regulation, to collect information about market activities, and, perhaps most importantly, to designate systemically important institutions or activities that will come under the oversight of the Federal Reserve, which is empowered as the new systemic risk regulator.[12] The consultative format of FSOC allows the individual agencies not only to continue to handle the substantive supervision of their industry-specific institutions but also to share insights and keep the other agencies aware of the developments across the financial industry. By design, this consultative format avoids the creation of another regulatory bureaucracy, but brings the key regulatory agencies together in a formal way to contribute to public policy.

FSOC consists of 10 voting members and 5 nonvoting members, combining the expertise of the federal and state regulators and an insurance expert appointed by the President.

The voting members are as follows:

- Secretary of the Treasury, who serves as the chairman of the Council,
- Chairman of the Board of Governors of the Federal Reserve System,
- Comptroller, Office of the Comptroller of the Currency,
- Director of the Consumer Financial Protection Bureau (CFPB),
- Chairman of the Securities and Exchange Commission (SEC),
- Chairman of the FDIC,
- Chairman of the Commodity Futures Trading Commission (CFTC),
- Director of the Federal Housing Finance Agency,
- Chairman of the National Credit Union Administration Board, and
- An independent member with insurance expertise, appointed by the President and confirmed by the Senate for a 6-year term.

The nonvoting members, who serve in an advisory capacity, are as follows:

- Director of the OFR,
- Director of the Federal Insurance Office,

[12]The other regulators will also be involved in the regulation of SIFIs through their role in the Council and the continuation of their previous regulatory authorities.

- A state insurance commissioner designated by the state insurance commissioners,
- A state banking supervisor designated by the state banking supervisors, and
- A state securities commissioner (or officer) designated by the state securities commissioners.

FSOC's success will hinge on its ability to maintain a comprehensive view of the workings of the financial system. Given the vast, complex, and changing nature of the system, this is a monumental task. FSOC has the authority to request information from a number of sources, including the member agencies, financial institutions (if the information is not readily available from primary regulators), and the new OFR. The breadth and quality of this information will be critical in helping FSOC to meet its objective of anticipating threats to financial stability, such as emerging asset bubbles.[13] The OFR could play an integral role in this process as it collects, organizes, and analyzes financial data in its role of supporting FSOC and its member agencies. In addition, FSOC's member agencies could also conduct more targeted analysis aimed at their particular industry sectors.

Perhaps most importantly, FSOC can also designate a nonbank institution as systemically important if the material distress or failure of the institution would pose a risk to financial stability. These nonbank SIFIs would then be combined with bank SIFIs, which are explicitly defined in Dodd–Frank as BHCs with assets greater than $50 billion, and made subject to enhanced prudential standards. In deciding on the nonbank SIFI designations, FSOC will consider the firm's size, leverage, liquidity profile, interconnectedness, mix of activities, and importance as a source of credit and liquidity to the financial system. To facilitate the designation process, FSOC can obtain information from the firm in question, the firm's primary regulator, and the OFR. FSOC may also ask the Federal Reserve to conduct examinations of the financial institution to facilitate the designation process. If, after the evaluation processes, the company is designated as systemically important, it will be subject to supervision by the Federal Reserve and subject to additional regulatory scrutiny.

FSOC can also make recommendations to the Federal Reserve regarding the form that the enhanced regulatory scrutiny should take. The act requires that the standards be more stringent than those applicable to other nonbank financial companies. In addition, the standards and requirements are likely to increase in

[13] For a discussion of asset bubbles and their impact on financial regulation and the implementation of monetary policy, see Evanoff *et al.* (2012).

stringency with the size of the company's systemic footprint. The enhanced prudential standards could apply to any or all of the following[14]:

- Risk-based capital requirements,
- Leverage limits,
- Liquidity requirements,
- Resolution plan and credit exposure reports,
- Concentration and credit exposure limits,
- Contingent capital requirements,
- Enhanced public disclosures,
- Short-term debt limits, and/or
- Overall risk-management requirements.

In addition to recommendations concerning nonbank SIFIs, FSOC may also recommend that the Federal Reserve apply enhanced prudential standards to institutions designated by FSOC as financial market utilities (FMUs) — that is, institutions primarily involved in payment, clearing, or settlement activities that facilitate the completion of financial transactions. Again, the concern is that problems at these institutions could have systemic implications for the effectiveness of the broader financial system. Title VIII of the act requires the Federal Reserve to develop risk-management standards, incorporating relevant international standards, for the operations of these systemically important FMUs with respect to credit, liquidity, settlement, operational and legal risks. The designation of these systemically important FMUs has proceeded more quickly than has the designation of nonbank SIFIs. In July 2012, FSOC designated eight FMUs as systemically important and subject to Federal Reserve oversight.[15] The list was composed of the following:

- The Clearing House Payments Company, LLC (on the basis of its role as operator of the Clearing House Interbank Payments System, or CHIPS),
- CLS Bank International,
- Chicago Mercantile Exchange, Inc.,

[14]The nonbank SIFI designation process has proceeded slowly. As of June 2013, three companies reported that they had heard from the Council that they would be designated as nonbank SIFIs. The three companies were American International Group (AIG), Prudential Financial, and GE Capital. There is a formal process for the companies to challenge the designation, which will likely play out over the second half of 2013 — see Noked (2013).

[15]The reasoning for the designation and a brief discussion of the activities of each designated FMU are included in Financial Stability Oversight Council (2012a), Appendix A, available at www.treasury.gov/initiatives/fsoc/Documents/2012%20Appendix%20A%20Designation%20of%20Systemically%20Important%20Market%20Utilities.pdf.

- The Depository Trust Company,
- Fixed Income Clearing Corporation,
- ICE Clear Credit LLC,
- National Securities Clearing Corporation, and
- The Options Clearing Corporation.

It is obvious that each designee is involved in large dollar financial transactions or payments settlement/clearing, has significant counterparty exposures, and would likely have a significant adverse impact on critical financial markets if they encountered financial difficulties. That is, each is systemically important to the financial system. In addition, FSOC may issue similar recommendations for financial firms that are not designated as FMUs, but play an important role in payment, clearing, and settlement activities. For example, FSOC could make recommendations to impose restrictions on banks that act as agents in the tri-party repo market.

Furthermore, FSOC may provide recommendations to primary regulators to apply new or more stringent regulation on the *activities and practices* undertaken by financial institutions, even if these financial institutions have not been designated as FMUs or SIFIs. Such recommendations can also be applied to specific financial instruments that are used or sold by these institutions. These recommendations may be made if a specific practice, activity, or financial instrument could create or increase the risk of significant liquidity, credit, or other problems in the financial markets.[16]

Finally, if the Federal Reserve determines that a SIFI poses a significant threat to the financial stability of the United States, it can impose restrictions on the institution's activities upon getting approval from FSOC. This is yet another action that can be taken to limit potential market upheaval. The tools available to the Federal Reserve to mitigate such risks include the following:

- Limiting the ability of the company to merge with, acquire, consolidate with, or otherwise become affiliated with another company,
- Restricting the ability of the company to offer a financial product or products,
- Requiring the company to terminate one or more activities,
- Imposing conditions on the manner in which the company conducts activities, and
- Requiring the company to sell or otherwise transfer assets or off-balance-sheet items to unaffiliated entities.

---

[16] For example, see the Council's proposed reforms to address the "structural vulnerabilities" of money market mutual funds; see Financial Stability Oversight Council (2012b).

Arguably, many institutions and specific areas of the financial system were not subject to adequate supervision and regulation prior to the financial crisis. Possible examples include operating units of insurance giant American International Group, Inc. (AIG) and global investment bank Lehman Brothers, the OTC derivatives markets, and consumer mortgage lending. The new oversight structure and SIFI designation processes mandated under Dodd–Frank are an effort to better capture and regulate institutions and activities that can threaten the stability of the financial system. The success of that effort will depend critically on the ability of the regulatory agencies to collectively target current and potential sources of systemic risk and put in place the appropriate safeguards to address that risk.

Orderly liquidation authority

Since the failure, and subsequent rescue, of Continental Illinois National Bank in 1984, there has been a general outcry against the use of a TBTF policy and the resulting means by which large, complex financial institutions are resolved — typically with government support.[17] The general argument against such policies — which result in an implicit government guarantee — is that they reduce market discipline and result in moral hazard, allowing systemically important firms to take on excessive risk.[18] In addition, these firms obtain a comparative advantage in the marketplace as a result of their perceived TBTF status, which lowers the risk premiums on their debt instruments (deposits, senior debt, and subordinated debt).[19] The practice of preferential treatment for any company goes against the philosophical underpinnings of a capitalist society. Moreover, in times of financial crisis, the financial industry appears to be favored by the government. It might

[17]While TBTF has been the term commonly used in the past, in recent years "too-systemic-to-fail" (TSTF) has come into vogue, since size is not the only determining factor of whether a failing financial firm could cause significant market disruption. Means to generate financial stability via improved failure resolution processes are discussed in Part IV of this volume. Questions about the effectiveness of the new resolution process are discussed in Part V.

[18]For more on Continental Illinois and the means to address the TBTF issue, see Wall and Peterson (1990), Evanoff and Wall (2001), Evanoff *et al.* (2011), Bliss and Kaufman (2011), and Brewer and Jagtiani (2013).

[19]The literature on this topic is quite extensive. See, for example, Flannery and Sorescu (1996), Evanoff and Wall (2002), DeYoung *et al.* (2001), and Kwast *et al.* (1999). For an alternative view of the possible reasons for larger, complex financial institutions to have a cost advantage see Strongin *et al.* (2013). For a discussion of the value of the financial sector to society, particularly the positives and negatives associated with TBTF banks, see Acharya *et al.* (2014).

seem reasonable, therefore, to argue that financial firms, like other firms, should be resolved through the standard bankruptcy process. However, when Lehman Brothers failed, was not bailed out, and filed for bankruptcy in 2008, the consequences for the financial markets were severe, putting further strain on an already stressed system. For policymakers, this experience underscored the need to develop a more efficient resolution process for financial institutions that would reduce the risk of market disruption without making taxpayers accountable for the resolution costs.

U.S. law, like that in most other major jurisdictions, provides for liquidation (Chapter 7) and rehabilitation (Chapter 11) procedures upon bankruptcy. When firms enter the bankruptcy process, the objective is to maximize the value for creditors and create an orderly process for distributing that value in order of priority. However, with a systemically important firm, an *optimal* resolution process also needs to account for the potential impact on parties other than the creditors of the firm — that is, the spillover effects on other financial sector participants and the overall economy. These are the externalities mentioned earlier. In an effort to address this need, the existing bankruptcy process provides special treatment for "qualified financial contracts." These contracts — particularly repurchase agreements and derivatives — are insulated from typical bankruptcy provisions that would prevent creditors from terminating their contracts or seizing and selling collateral. Therefore, particular creditors of the failing financial firm are able to terminate, accelerate, or net contracts, as well as acquire and sell collateral associated with these contracts to close out their positions. While these creditors avoid the bankruptcy process, other creditors are prevented from closing out their positions and must enter the process as a general or senior creditor, depending on their contractual priority.

However, these "safe harbor provisions" for qualified financial contracts can also have unintended consequences. Given the interconnectedness of financial firms, there are still concerns about adverse spillover effects; and new concerns about the over-utilization of qualified contracts and inconsistent or inequitable treatment of creditors. The safe harbor provisions, and the associated rush to close out positions or obtain access to collateral, could actually lead to significant market disruption as parties move quickly to replace the contracts or sell collateral into what may be very illiquid markets resulting in fire sales. That is, it is argued that there could still be adverse systemic effects; in fact, some could actually be exacerbated. During the financial crisis, one 'solution' for these concerns was to bailout the troubled financial institutions to eliminate the spillover effects. However, as discussed above, this was also seen as a suboptimal solution (see also, Ayotte and Skeel). Thus, when Dodd–Frank was being written, there was a perceived need for a new means to avoid bankruptcy procedures and avoid bailouts for large, complex financial institutions.

The orderly liquidation authority (OLA) in Dodd–Frank is intended for this purpose.[20] Title II of Dodd–Frank spells out the role of the FDIC, in certain limited cases, as the new OLA for institutions deemed to be systemically important.[21] In that process, the bankruptcy courts are avoided, the safe harbor provisions are eliminated and the FDIC manages the resolution process. The use of such authority, however, is expected to be extraordinary and employed only when the stability of the whole U.S. financial system is in jeopardy. In most cases, the standard bankruptcy process, or traditional FDIC bank resolution process, will continue to apply.

To initiate the orderly liquidation process, the Secretary of the Treasury will decide if the financial firm is in default or in danger of default, if the firm is systemically important, and whether it would be in the interest of the stakeholders of the firm to enter into the orderly resolution process. The Secretary of the Treasury would typically initiate the process and recommend that the FDIC be made receiver of the troubled company. Depending on the type of financial institution, others on FSOC could make a similar recommendation.

Dodd–Frank, however, imposes significant restrictions on the new resolution process. First, the management and board of directors who were responsible for the failure of the firm must be removed from the organization. Second, the priority of claims in the resolution process should be adhered to in allocating firm losses — that is, equity holders will not receive anything until all the other creditors, including the FDIC, have been repaid according to their priority. Third, the FDIC will not take an equity position with the failing firm. Finally, no taxpayer funds are to be used to prevent the firm from being liquidated. Instead, creditors, and the industry, perhaps through special assessments, will incur any losses from the resolution process.

---

[20] Some argue that instead of the new OLA, the existing bankruptcy code should be utilized for financial firm failures (Skeel, 2014) or that the code only need be slightly modified to better handle systemic financial firm failures (Scott, 2012). For a discussion of the advantages and disadvantages of using the bankruptcy code to resolve systemically important firms, see Bliss and Kaufman (2011) and Board of Governors (2012a). For a discussion of the problems associated with safe harbor provisions, see Skeel and Jackson (2012).

[21] The decision to use the OLA would be made on a case-by-case basis. Bank holding company and nonbank SIFIs would qualify for consideration by the authorities to enter the orderly resolution process. The status of designated FMUs is currently unclear.

An important element of the new resolution process is the requirement that SIFIs provide supervisors with a document indicating how they could most efficiently be resolved should they encounter financial problems — the so-called *living will* (see Avgouleas *et al.*, 2010; Bernanke, 2010).[22] One of the major problems with resolving a large financial institution is the complex interconnectedness of the various elements of the organization. Affiliates and subsidiaries may be legally structured in a manner to achieve certain corporate objectives, such as tax avoidance or regulatory arbitrage that may make the resolution process more difficult. The living will is intended to provide the resolution authority with critical information on the firm's organizational structure to aid in the resolution process. With a living will in place, regulators can work with the SIFIs to better understand the details of the organizational structure and possibly to modify that structure to avoid potential difficulties should resolution become necessary.[23] The first submission of living wills for the largest SIFIs (those with nonbank assets of $250 billion or more) was in July 2012. Smaller SIFIs had to submit their wills in 2013 — see Board of Governors (2012b) for a more complete submission schedule.

Based on the requirements in Dodd–Frank, the FDIC has put in place plans to accomplish the twin goals of eliminating the TBTF problem and eliminating taxpayer-funded bailouts. In the orderly resolution process, the FDIC will act as receiver and the failing firm will be removed from the bankruptcy process.[24] In Part IV of this volume, additional details are provided concerning the procedures that have been developed by the FDIC, as well as other foreign central banks, to carry out this orderly resolution.[25]

---

[22]It has been suggested that FMUs also be required to develop living wills.

[23]Indeed, one of the recommendations in the 2012 FSOC annual report was to use information from the living wills to simplify financial firms' organizational structure. See Financial Stability Oversight Council (2012a).

[24]Some remain skeptical of whether the law will succeed in making TBTF a thing of the past and protecting taxpayers from having to fund bailouts — for example, see Wilmarth (2011) and several chapters in Part V of this volume. However, Moody's, a credit ratings agency, recently said they would reconsider their ratings for large U.S. banks in light of the "reduced government support" they will receive with the introduction of the new resolution authority. This aligns with a potential decline in the value of the subsidy resulting from the perceived TBTF status — see Moody's (2013).

[25]As this publication went to press, the FDIC was awaiting public comment on a proposal describing how it would, in practice, resolve a SIFI under its new "Single Point of Entry" process. This strategy has the FDIC being appointed receiver for the SIFI's top-level U.S. holding company. Importantly, it would allow the various operating entities within the holding company to continue operations and, hopefully, limit market disruptions. For additional details on the FDIC proposal see FDIC (2013). For a somewhat critical assessment see Rehm (2013).

Limits on proprietary and speculative trading: The "Volcker Rule"

Title VI of Dodd–Frank strives to improve the prudential regulation of financial institutions and their respective depository subsidiaries, with a goal of removing threats to market stability. One means to accomplish this is by placing restrictions on firms' trading activities. Supported strongly by former Federal Reserve Chairman Paul Volcker, the new restrictions generally preclude these institutions and their subsidiaries from proprietary trading of financial instruments and from significant investment in hedge funds or private equity funds. The new rules have garnered significant attention from both the industry participants and regulators because of the difficulty in carrying out the intent of the statute.

More formally, Section 619 of Title VI amends the 1956 Bank Holding Company Act to prohibit banking entities from:[26]

- engaging in proprietary trading, defined as the purchase and sale of securities, derivatives and other financial instruments with the intent to profit in the near-term,[27] and
- acquiring or retaining an ownership interest in sponsoring or maintaining certain relationships with hedge funds or private equity funds.

Exemptions from these prohibitions include the following:

a. Trading in obligations or instruments issued by the U.S. government, government-sponsored enterprises (GSEs), Federal Home Loan Banks, Farm Credit System and of any state or municipality,
b. trading for the purpose of, or in connection with, underwriting or market-making (so long as it does not exceed demands of clients, customers, or counterparties),
c. engaging in risk-mitigating hedging activities for individual or aggregated positions, contracts, or other holdings,
d. trading on behalf of clients in a brokerage capacity,
e. investing in Small Business Investment Companies and qualified public welfare expenditures,

---

[26] Banking entities are defined as insured depository institutions, as defined by Section 3 of the Federal Deposit Insurance Act, and companies that control insured depository institutions, including bank holding companies (BHCs), financial holding companies (FHCs), savings and loan holding companies (SLHCs), and their associated affiliates.

[27] See Board of Governors' Proposed Rules (November 7, 2011) for a definition of "near-term."

f. trading by regulated insurance affiliates for the bank's own insurance account, subject to certain restrictions,
g. organizing, offering, and having a *de minimis* investment[28] in these restricted funds (subject to certain restrictions),
h. trading conducted outside of the United States by non-U.S. banking entities, and
i. investments in foreign covered funds by non-U.S. banking entities.

However, these exemptions are also subject to limits. Overall, no transaction, activity, or relationship will be permitted under these exemptions if the relevant regulatory agency determines that it would result in a material conflict of interest between the banking entity and its clients, customers, or counterparties; expose the banking entity, directly or indirectly, to high-risk assets or high-risk trading strategies; pose a threat to the safety and soundness of the banking entity; or pose a threat to the financial stability of the United States.

The Volcker Rule prohibitions do not apply to nonbank financial companies supervised by the Board of Governors of the Federal Reserve System — that is, companies designated (as discussed earlier) as nonbank SIFIs by the FSOC. However, if such companies engage in any of these prohibited activities, the Board can impose additional capital requirements, quantitative limits, and other restrictions. Moreover, the aforementioned exemptions (and limits on the exemptions) also apply to nonbank SIFIs.

The legislation allows banking entities two years from the date that the prohibitions become effective to conform to the restrictions; similarly, it gives nonbank SIFIs two years after the firms are designated as such to adhere to the restrictions.[29] This allows firms time to adjust to the Volcker Rule. Additionally, there is a special provision to address difficulties that banking entities may have exiting certain activities because of market illiquidity — for example, a private equity or hedge fund may be principally invested in illiquid assets making the position difficult to liquidate. These provisions are intended to minimize market disruptions as banking entities and nonbank SIFIs attempt to conform to the new prohibitions.

The general reasoning behind the Volcker Rule is the belief that the prohibited activities are speculative, nonessential for bank customers, and high-risk.[30] Additionally, financial institutions are likely to over utilize these activities

[28]This is defined as an investment that does not exceed 3% of Tier 1 capital.

[29]Banking entities can request up to three 1-year extensions.

[30]See, for example, the Paul Volcker interview with Bill Moyers available at http://billmoyers.com/segment/paul-volcker-on-the-volcker-rule/. Others argue that such activities were unrelated to the

because of moral hazard resulting from government support via FDIC deposit insurance, Federal Reserve lending facilities, and an expected backing for TBTF firms during periods of market distress.[31] These backstops and support mechanisms, which are meant to promote financial stability, actually create valuable *put options* for certain banking entities, limiting their exposure to downside risk and distorting (weakening) market discipline mechanisms. In effect, there is incentive to increase risk taking because expected payoffs are higher, funding costs are lower, and both are less volatile than they would be without the support mechanisms. Restrictions on proprietary trading and investments partially address these *moral hazard* problems by limiting risk taking, thus reducing potential losses of taxpayer funds. The provisions are also intended to promote financial stability by reducing risk profiles, as well as complexity and interconnectedness at both bank and nonbank SIFIs — which should reduce potential systemic effects.

Defining specific criteria with which to implement the Volcker Rule has proven to be a monumental task. The difficulty stems from a number of different factors. First, it can be difficult to distinguish proprietary trading from hedging or market-making activity and all these activities must be identified and monitored by regulators. Similarly, Dodd–Frank contains language that is somewhat subjective and difficult to define. For instance, how does one define the short-term? Is it a fixed time period or is it a relative concept, that is, one based on the type of asset? For example, it might be rational to define the short term as 5 minutes for a very liquid asset (for instance, exchange-traded stocks) and five days for a relatively illiquid asset (for instance, collateralized-debt-obligations). Finally, there is also a concern that developing specific definitions may lead to unintended consequences and inefficiencies in financial markets, perhaps reducing market liquidity and raising the cost and availability of credit. The Federal Reserve, along with the other relevant regulatory agencies, is taking into account these issues and incorporating comments from the public in the final rulemaking process, so as to carry out the intent of the legislation while minimizing adverse effects on the financial system.[32]

---

financial crisis, which was the impetus for the Dodd–Frank Act and, as such, need not be restricted — for example, see White (2010).

[31]As discussed earlier, the new failure resolution authority was introduced to eliminate distortions resulting from the government backing of TBTF firms.

[32]As this article goes to press, regulators are finalizing the Volcker Rule. On December 10, 2013, the regulatory agencies issued the "final rule." Compliance will be required by July 21, 2015, however, the regulatory reporting requirements of the rule will be required by June 30, 2014. This "final rule" was an updated version based on over 18,000 comments to the original rule initially issued in October 2011. Finally, on January 14, 2014, in response to significant push-back by small banks, including a

OTC derivative markets

Title VII of Dodd–Frank establishes a framework for the regulation of previously unregulated OTC derivatives.[33] Even before the financial crisis, there were concerns that the OTC derivatives market represented a risk to the financial system because it lacked the oversight and risk management tools typically associated with clearing house and exchange arrangements (see Born, 1998). The legislation brings the swap market under a joint SEC–CFTC regulatory regime (the joint regulators) to improve transparency, governance, and regulatory oversight. Broadly speaking, the legislation imposes new requirements for the instruments (swaps and security-based swaps[34]), the market participants (swap dealers (SDs) and major swap participants (MSPs)), and the facilities on which the trades will be executed and cleared (designated contract markets, swap execution facilities, and derivatives clearing organizations). The regulatory responsibilities are then split between the SEC and the CFTC, with the SEC regulating security-based swaps and the CFTC regulating all other swaps.[35]

A swap is an agreement between counterparties to exchange the cash flows of two distinct reference items. Often, one of the reference items has a fixed rate and one a floating rate. The contracts can be based on various interest rates, exchange rates, currencies, commodities, securities, indexes, and other reference items. OTC swaps are customized bilateral contracts negotiated between counterparties; this customization is often of significant value to the buyer of the contract. However, buyers of OTC swaps are exposed to liquidity risk — the inability to sell

law suit by a banking trade association, the regulatory agencies addressed an unintended consequence of the "final rule" and slightly modified it to allow banks to retain collateralized debt obligations (CDOs) backed by trust preferred securities — securities used by community banks as a regulatory capital source. Absent this modification, the market for trust preferred securities could have been adversely affected and community banks would have been required to sell these securities and to immediately recognize losses incurred on them. This would have significantly affected a segment of the industry that few thought the Volcker Rule (generally thought to be concerned with speculative trading at larger institutions) was aimed at. See Hamilton and Hopkins, 2014.

[33] Discussions on the regulation of derivatives markets with a goal of improving financial market stability are in Part III of this volume.

[34] Security-based swaps are broadly defined as swaps based on a single security, or a loan, or a narrow-based group, or an index of securities, or events relating to a single issuer or issuers of securities in a narrow-based security index.

[35] Forward contracts on commodities that are guaranteed for physical delivery, foreign exchange swaps, and foreign exchange forwards are exempt from the definition of a swap; the latter two being exempted by the Secretary of the Treasury, by authority granted in Dodd–Frank. See www.treasury.gov/initiatives/wsr/Documents/FX%20Swaps%20and%20Forwards%20NPD.pdf.

an asset when necessary — and counterparty risk — the possibility that the seller will default on the contract's obligations. Interest rate swaps make up the largest segment of the swaps market by notional value of contracts outstanding — approximately $400 trillion as of December 2011.[36]

The credit default swap (CDS) was considered by many to be a significant factor in the financial crisis of 2008.[37] These instruments were originally designed to provide lenders and market participants with a method to hedge against the credit risk of a particular company, institution, or industry. The buyer of a CDS pays a pre-negotiated fixed premium to the seller for the life of the contract in return for a guarantee that the seller will make a payment if a prespecified credit event occurs on the reference security. If the buyer of the CDS owned the reference security, the CDS would be a hedge against losses on that security. If the buyer of the CDS did not own the reference security, the CDS would be an indirect hedge or a speculative short; in this scenario, the CDS is called a *naked CDS* contract.[38] In either case, the seller takes a long position on the reference security, collecting premiums in exchange for providing credit protection to the buyer. The market for CDS (and the synthetic securities derived from pools of CDS contracts) was initially concentrated in corporate credit — that is, the underlying reference securities were typically corporate loans or bonds. However, the market expanded into consumer and commercial credit as CDS contracts were written on residential/commercial mortgage-backed securities and consumer/commercial asset-backed securities.

When asset prices deteriorated leading into the financial crisis, problems in the OTC derivatives market became apparent. Information on prices, quantities, and firm-specific exposures was limited. In addition, the lack of central counterparty clearing house (CCP) arrangements, which serve to better manage risk and guarantee the fulfillment of the contracts, increased the complexity and uncertainty around counterparty risks. This lack of transparency intensified the withdrawal of liquidity during the crisis, because financial institutions were reluctant to enter into lending or OTC derivatives contracts without the ability to properly assess their counterparties' risk profiles. For example, prior to the crisis, AIG and other institutions had sold large amounts of credit protection in the form of CDS

[36] See Table 19 in www.bis.org/statistics/otcder/dt1920a.pdf.

[37] Such contracts are typically associated with AIG, leading up to its rescue during the crisis. However the issue with the AIG contracts may have had more to do with the collateralization "hair triggers" and the sudden need to meet these calls.

[38] In the case of naked CDS contracts, the notional amount of the contracts can become greater than the notional amount of the assets on which the contracts are written.

contracts.[39] As margin calls and payments were triggered, the insuring institutions were unable to fulfill their obligations and there was no CCP backing to cover payments to the owners of the credit protection.

To see the value of the CCP mechanism, contrast the situation in the CDS market to one with this clearing and settling mechanism. During this same period leading up to the financial crisis, approximately 50% of the global OTC interest rate swap market was cleared by an independent CCP, the SwapClear service of LCH.Clearnet. This market functioned relatively well during the crisis, even when Lehman Brothers failed with a $9 trillion portfolio. The risk-management procedures performed as planned and the collateral that Lehman held covered all defaults; additionally, the portfolio was successfully unwound and auctioned off by the CCP (see LCH.Clearnet, 2008). Without such a mechanism in the CDS market, significant market disruption occurred as providers of the credit protection were unable to perform on their contracts.[40]

As a result of Dodd–Frank, the joint regulators will have the power to determine which types of swaps will have to be cleared through a CCP and which swaps will be exempt from such clearing requirements. The joint regulators will also determine the appropriate margin and collateral requirements for swap transactions cleared on CCPs, taking into account systemic risk considerations. These requirements are powerful tools to control risk levels in the financial system.[41] Additionally, CCPs that clear any non-security-based swaps (for

---

[39]Many financial institutions owned CDS contracts and other credit derivatives as hedges against their exposure to structured assets or to other financial institutions.

[40]While agreeing that aspects of central counterparty clearing provide undoubted financial stability benefits, Steigerwald (2014) argues that it is not necessarily a panacea. Central clearing does not completely eliminate opacity or complexity, and the effectiveness of CCPs depends extensively on services provided by financial facilities; e.g., settlement banks, custodians, liquidity providers, etc. Clearing members will participate in those facilities and, as a result, the CCP is connected to and dependent on a variety of counterparties, some of them serving in multiple capacities. Thus, the financial stability benefits of central counterparty clearing are somewhat offset by these interdependencies created with central clearing. The key question for policymakers, then, is whether the benefits of central counterparty clearing dominate, or whether they are in part or whole offset by systemic costs that are both pervasive and perhaps even expanded by the centralization and concentration of risk at the CCP. The push toward more extensive use of CCPs in Dodd–Frank inherently assumes that the benefits of CCPs dominate. Steigerwald argues that while this may be correct, it is not obvious. We need a better understanding and analysis of the costs and benefits of central counterparty clearing — and, in particular, the implications of mandatory central clearing. To date, that detailed analysis has not been undertaken.

[41]If one of the entities involved in a nonexempt swap transaction is a nonfinancial commercial end-user, then the trade is exempt from any clearing requirement.

example, interest rate swaps) must register with the CFTC as a derivatives clearing organization (DCO) and will be subject to reporting, recordkeeping, and operational guidelines.[42] Many DCOs will also register as swap data repositories and perform the functions prescribed in Dodd–Frank, which include making data and information on market participants' open swap positions readily available to regulators.[43] The goal is for all swaps that are mandated to be cleared centrally to be executed as standardized products on a designated contract market (for example, CME Group) or a newly created swap execution facility, both of which will be required to follow reporting, recordkeeping, and operational guidelines set by the joint regulators. These execution requirements are intended to provide market participants and regulators with more transparent price and volume data.

Dodd–Frank requires that any entity substantially involved in making a market for swaps be designated as a SD, and any non-dealer substantially involved in trading swaps be designated as a MSP. In general, if an entity is a commercial enterprise using swaps to hedge its activities, it will be exempt from these definitions. Both SDs and MSPs must register as such with the joint regulators and must adhere to the regulators' reporting, recordkeeping, and operational guidelines, even if the entity is a bank or BHC. If the SD or MSP does not have a prudential regulator, the joint regulators can impose capital requirements and margin requirements for non-cleared swap transactions. Otherwise, the prudential regulators will impose these requirements. However, the joint regulators can prescribe rules that limit the activities of nonbank SDs and MSPs, even if these entities have prudential regulators. These rules may include position limits and limitations on the involvement with certain types of swaps.

The goal of Title VII is to enable the CFTC and the SEC to regulate their markets comprehensively. The legislation imposes new restrictions and requirements on the instruments, market participants, and trading platforms. The implementation process is very difficult but of critical importance, especially given the enormous size and scope of the OTC derivatives market in the financial system.

Consumer Financial Protection

In addition to reforms that address the safety of financial institutions and markets, Title X and title XIV of Dodd–Frank focus on improving consumer

[42] CCPs that only clear security-based swaps are not subject to the same requirements.

[43] See www.cftc.gov/ucm/groups/public/@newsroom/documents/file/sdr_qa.pdf.

financial protection.[44] Title X (*Consumer Financial Protection Act of 2010*) establishes the independent CFPB, housed in the Board of Governors of the Federal Reserve System, and empowers it with broad authorities to enforce relevant laws, issue new regulations and supervise institutions. Generally, the act consolidated rule-making and oversight activities that had previously been spread across seven regulatory agencies. The consolidation was aimed at achieving a consistency in enforcement and introducing a cross-market perspective (for example, bank versus nonbanks) aimed at eliminating regulatory arbitrage.[45] Title XIV of Dodd–Frank (*Mortgage Reform and Anti-Predatory Lending Act*) amends the Truth in Lending Act and establishes new standards for mortgage lending activity. The broad goal is to ensure borrowers are fully aware of the obligations and the risks associated with their mortgages. It also limits certain (predatory) lending tactics, establishes provisions for loan modifications, and imposes guidelines that should reduce or eliminate mortgages that significantly exceed the borrower's ability to repay.

More specifically, the objective of the CFPB under Title X is to ensure that consumers have access to fair and competitive markets for consumer financial products and services, including mortgages, credit cards, and student loans. It will regulate the offering of these products by enforcing federal consumer protection laws such as the Fair Debt Collection Practices Act, the Fair Credit Reporting Act, and the Truth in Lending Act.

Under Title X, the CFPB is granted certain authority to achieve this objective. For instance, it is given primary enforcement authority for depository institutions with assets over $10 billion. It will have the exclusive authority to request reports and conduct examinations for the purposes of assessing such depository institutions' compliance with laws, the efficacy of their compliance systems, and the potential risks to consumers from their lending practices. With regard to smaller depository institutions, the CFPB's authority is more limited. However, it may still request reports (after other resources are exhausted) and participate in a sampling of examinations for the purposes of assessing compliance with laws and procedures. Finally, the CFPB will supervise nonbank institutions that provide the origination of, or servicing of, consumer loans secured by real estate, private education loans, or payday loans. Importantly, across the broad array of consumer product markets, the CFPB is generally responsible for restricting deceptive,

---

[44]The goals, advantages, and disadvantages of the new agency are discussed more fully in Part VI of this book. For an alternative summary of the consumer protection aspects of the Dodd–Frank Act, see Cadwalader, Wickersham & Taft LLP (2012).

[45]See Katz (2013) and Cordray (2013).

abusive, and discriminatory practices; processing and addressing consumer complaints; promoting financial education; and researching consumer and institutional behavior.

The CFPB will also be responsible for enforcing most of the mortgage reform provisions within Title XIV of Dodd–Frank. This includes a new "ability-to-repay" standard, whereby lenders must make a reasonable and good faith determination of a consumer's ability to repay a mortgage along with all applicable taxes, insurance, and assessments. This determination must be made by using verified and documented information, such as the consumer's credit history, current and expected income, current obligations, debt-to-income ratio (and similar measures), current assets that can secure repayment of the loan, and employment status. Additionally, lenders must make this determination based on a payment schedule that fully amortizes the principal and interest over the full term of the loan.[46]

Title XIV also creates a safe harbor provision for lender compliance with the ability-to-repay standard by defining a specific type of loan called a *qualified mortgage*. This is an important component of the new regulation because lenders can assume that a loan is in conformance with the ability-to-repay requirement if it meets the definition of a qualified mortgage. From Dodd–Frank, to be considered a qualified mortgage, the following general criteria must be met[47]:

- Regular periodic payments may not result in an increase of principal balance or allow the consumer to defer repayment of principal,
- Contract terms cannot result in a balloon payment that is more than twice as large as the average of earlier scheduled payments,
- Income and financial information relied upon must be verified and documented,
- For fixed rate loans, the underwriting process must be based on a payment schedule that fully amortizes the principal and interest over the term of the loan (adjustable rate mortgages should use the maximum permitted rate within the first five years of the loan),
- The loan must comply with all guidelines and regulations related to measures of ability to repay (e.g., debt to income thresholds determined by regulators),

---

[46]This rule applies to nonstandard loans with features such as interest-only or negative amortization. In the past, certain borrowers were sometimes qualified for loans based only on the loan terms in the early years of the loan; for example, an adjustable-rate mortgage with some of the abovementioned characteristics. This provision requires the comprehensive terms of the loan be taken into account.

[47]Although some of these criteria are relatively specific, additional specificity was to be added by regulators. Additionally, there are some exceptions in the act to these general rules.

- The total points and fees payable do not exceed 3% of the total loan amount, and
- The term of the loan does not exceed 30 years.

After significant interaction with market participants, on May 29, 2013, the CFPB issued a final rule detailing the specific criteria to implement the ability-to-repay and qualified mortgage standards.[48]

In addition to these reforms, Title XIV also addresses certain lending practices considered potentially abusive to consumers. It bans prepayment penalties on residential mortgages that do not meet the qualified mortgage criteria — an attempt to protect consumers from being trapped in a high cost mortgage. It also prohibits mortgage originators from paying loan officers (or brokers) compensation that varies based on the terms of the loan, except the amount of the principal — an attempt to protect consumers from being steered toward products that they are overqualified for, but that may handsomely compensate mortgage brokers. Additionally, originators may not arrange for a consumer to finance any fees unless they are paid to unrelated third parties for items such as closing costs -- an attempt to protect consumers from being gouged with excessive, in-house fees. Finally, the legislation directly prohibits originators from steering borrowers into less attractive mortgage contracts when they qualify for more standard, lower-risk contracts. Examples of prohibited actions would include steering borrowers from qualified to nonqualified mortgages to a loan that the consumer lacks the ability to repay or to a loan with certain predatory characteristics (such as equity stripping, excessive fees, and other abusive terms).

The primary justification for these reforms is to address problems that arose in consumer mortgage lending markets just prior to the recent financial crisis. The goal is to limit irresponsible and predatory lending practices, thereby protecting consumers and supporting financial stability. It is argued that the new consumer protections were needed because in the buildup to the crisis, large volumes of risky mortgages were originated with characteristics such as high loan-to-value ratios, minimal documentation on the borrower, and high-risk payment structures (for example, negative amortization). Such practices led many borrowers to purchase mortgages they simply could not afford. Further problems ensued as home prices declined and borrowers could not refinance at affordable levels and/or had to come up with cash for larger down payments.

Before the onset of the financial crisis, Elizabeth Warren, the current U.S. Senator from Massachusetts and longtime consumer advocate, argued vigorously

---

[48] See http://files.consumerfinance.gov/f/201305_cfpb_final-rule_atr-concurrent-final-rule.pdf.

for improved regulation of consumer finance markets. While "nearly every product sold in America has passed basic safety regulations well in advance of reaching store shelves," she noted that "credit products, by comparison, are regulated by a tattered patchwork of federal and state laws that have failed to adapt to changing markets" (Warren, 2007). She contended that more effort was put into "ensuring the safety of toaster ovens than the safety of mortgage loans" and proposed that a "financial product safety commission" similar to those in other industries be introduced to better protect consumers. Given that the failure of consumer regulation was considered by many to be a major cause of the financial crisis, Warren's idea of a consumer financial protection agency became the template for financial product regulatory reform under Dodd–Frank.[49]

Overall, many market participants argue that the recent financial crisis revealed that borrowers were not sufficiently informed to make proper financial decisions and were often misled by lending institutions in the lending heyday leading up to the crisis. The consumer protection aspects of Dodd–Frank were intended to address these concerns. However, the new consumer protection regulation, as well as the role of the CFPB, has been one of the more controversial aspects of the act. Dodd–Frank has received significant praise from consumer advocates who argue the reforms were necessary to address the abuses overlooked prior to the crisis. Others argue that the resulting new powers of the CFPB are too far-reaching and it has too little accountability — as a result it can generate market inefficiencies and adverse unintended consequences.[50] The debate will no doubt continue as markets continue to recover from the financial crisis.

Conclusion

On July 21, 2010, the Dodd–Frank Wall Street Reform and Consumer Protection Act became law. The purpose of this chapter has been to summarize some of the major regulatory changes resulting from the act, describe the reasons for the changes, and set the stage for the analysis of Dodd–Frank that appears in the chapters that follow. We are particularly interested in the implementation

[49]See U.S. Senate (2010) at 166 and Cordray (2013). Soucy (2013) provides a discussion of Warren's involvement in setting up the CFPB, including expectations that she would be appointed its initial chairperson. For a discussion of efforts to quantify the role of predatory lending and securitization in the financial crisis, see Agarwal *et al.* (2014) and Agarwal *et al.* (2011), respectively.

[50]For views in favor of the CFPB, see Warren (2007) and Center (2012); for counterviews, see Katz (2013) and Soucy (2013).

issues.[51] The treatment in this chapter is not comprehensive. We have chosen to focus on specific aspects of the reform and discuss the reasons for the proposed changes. However, it should be noted that these particular aspects have dominated the debate about Dodd–Frank and will dominate the discussion in the remaining chapters in this volume. In fact, it will be the discussion of these issues that will most likely dominate the financial regulatory landscape in the foreseeable future.

References

Abernathy, Wayne A., 2012, "Dodd–Frank Act Implementation: Well Into It and No Further Ahead," *Economic Perspectives*, Federal Reserve Bank of Chicago, Vol. 36, Third Quarter, pp. 103–107. Reprinted in this volume.

Acharya, Viral, Thorsten Beck, Douglas Evanoff, George Kaufman and Richard Portes (eds.), 2014, *The Social Value of the Financial Sector: Too Big to Fail or Just Too Big?* Hackensack, NJ: World Scientific Publishing Co. Pte. Ltd.

Agarwal, Sumit, Eugene Amromin, Itzhak Ben-David, Souphala Chomsisengphet and Douglas Evanoff, 2011, "The role of securitization in mortgage renegotiation," *Journal of Financial Economics,* 102(3), December, pp. 559–578.

Agarwal, Sumit, Eugene Amromin, Itzhak Ben-David, Souphala Chomsisengphet and Douglas Evanoff, 2014, "Predatory lending and the subprime crisis," *Journal of Financial Economics,* forthcoming.

Avgouleas, Emilios, Charles Goodhart and Dirk Schoenmaker, 2010, "Living Wills as a Catalyst for Action," Duisenberg School of Finance, DSF policy paper, No. 4, May.

Ayotte, Kenneth and David Skeel, 2010, "Bankrupcy or Bailouts?" *Journal of Corporate Law*, Vol. 35, pp. 469–498.

Benston, George and George Kaufman, 1994, "Improving the FDIC Improvement Act," in *Reforming Financial Institutions and Markets in the United States*, George Kaufman (ed.), Boston: Kluwer Academic Publishers.

Bernanke, Ben, 2011, "Implementing a Macroprudential Approach to Supervision and Regulation," *Implementing Dodd–Frank: Progress to Date and Recommendations for the Future*, Proceedings of the 47th Annual Conference on Bank Structure and Competition, Federal Reserve Bank of Chicago, pp. 1–8.

Bernanke, Ben, 2010, "The Squam Lake report: Fixing the Financial System," speech delivered at the Squam Lake Conference, New York, June 16.

Bliss, Robert and George Kaufman, 2011, "Resolving insolvent large complex financial institutions: A better way," *Banking Law Journal*, Vol. 128, No. 4, April, pp. 339–363.

[51]Which are more comprehensively considered in Abernathy (2012), Van Der Weide (2012), O'Malia (2012), and Tarullo (2012).

Board of Governors of the Federal Reserve System, 2012a, "Study on the Resolution of Financial Companies Under the Bankruptcy Code," report, Washington, DC: Board of Governors of the Federal Reserve System, available at: www.federalreserve.gov/publications/other-reports/bankruptcy-financial-study-01107.htm.

Board of Governors of the Federal Reserve System, 2012b, "Resolution plans," Washington, DC: Board of Governors of the Federal Reserve System, July 2, available at: http://www.federalreserve.gov/bankinforeg/resolution-plans.htm.

Borio, Claudio, 2003, "Towards a macroprudential framework for financial supervision and regulation?" *CESifo Economic Studies*, Vol. 49, No. 2, pp. 181–216. Reprinted in Douglas Evanoff, George Kaufman, and A.G. Malliaris (ed.), 2012, *New Perspectives on Asset Price Bubbles: Theory, Evidence, and Policy*, New York: Oxford University Press, pp. 243–270.

Born, Brooksley, 1998, *Testimony Before the U.S. House of Representatives, Committee on Banking and Financial Services*, Washington, DC, July 24, available at: www.cftc.gov/opa/speeches/opaborn-33.htm.

Brewer, Elijah and Julapa Jagtiani, 2013, "How much did banks pay to become too-big-to-fail and to become systemically important?" *Journal of Financial Services Research*, Vol. 43, No. 1, February, pp. 1–35.

Cadwalader, Wickersham & Taft LLP, 2012, "The Consumer Financial Protection Bureau: The New, Powerful Regulator of Financial Products and Services," memo, March 6, available at: www.cadwalader.com/assets/client_friend/030612consumerfinancialprotectionbureau.pdf.

Casey, Kathleen L., 2011, "The Regulatory Implementation and Implications of Dodd–Frank," speech at the Corporate Directors Forum conference: Directors, Management & Shareholders in Dialogue, University of San Diego, Joan B. Kroc Institute for Peace & Justice, San Diego, January 23.

Center for Responsible Lending, 2012, "Consumer Financial Protection Bureau (CFPB)," available at: http://www.responsiblelending.org/other-consumer-loans/consumer-financial-protection-bureau/#.

Claessens, Stijn, Douglas Evanoff, George Kaufman and Luc Laeven, 2014, *Shadow Banking Within and Across National Borders*, Hackensack, NJ: World Scientific Publishing Co. Pte. Ltd., forthcoming.

Cordray, Richard, 2013, "Remarks to the Exchequer Club" Speech before the Exchequer Club, June 19, Washington, DC.

Davis Polk & Wardwell LLP, 2013, *Dodd–Frank Progress Report*, July (see also various issues), available at: http://www.davispolk.com/Dodd-Frank-Rulemaking-Progress-Report/.

DeYoung, Robert, Mark Flannery, William Lang and Sorin Sorescu, 2001, "The information content of bank exam ratings and subordinated debt prices," *Journal of Money, Credit, and Banking*, Vol. 33, No. 4, November, pp. 900–925.

Duffie, Darrell, 2012, "Market Making Under the Proposed Volcker rule," Stanford University, Graduate School of Business, report to the Securities Industry and

Financial Markets Association and submission to the Office of the Comptroller of the Currency, the Board of Governors of the Federal Reserve System, the Federal Deposit Insurance Corporation, and the Securities and Exchange Commission, January 16, available at: www.darrellduffie.com/uploads/policy/DuffieVolckerRule.pdf.

Evanoff, Douglas, George Kaufman and A.G. Malliaris (ed.), 2012, *New Perspectives on Asset Price Bubbles: Theory, Evidence, and Policy,* New York: Oxford University Press, Inc.

Evanoff, Douglas, Julapa Jagtiani and Taisuke Nakata, 2011, "Enhancing market discipline in banking: The role of subordinated debt in financial regulatory reform," *Journal of Economics & Business,* Vol. 63, No. 1, January–February, pp. 1–22.

Evanoff, Douglas and Larry Wall, 2001, "Sub-debt yield spreads as bank risk measures," *Journal of Financial Services Research*, Vol. 20, Nos. 2–3, October, pp. 121–145.

Evanoff, Douglas and Larry Wall, 2002, "Measures of the riskiness of banking organizations: Subordinated debt yields, risk-based capital, and examination ratings," *Journal of Banking & Finance*, Vol. 26, No. 5, May, pp. 989–1009.

Evanoff, Douglas and William Moeller, 2012, "Dodd–Frank: Content, Purpose, Implementation Status and Issues," *Economic Perspectives,* Federal Reserve Bank of Chicago, Vol. 36, pp. 75–84.

FDIC, 2013, "Resolution of Systemically Important Financial Institutions: The Single Point of Entry Strategy," *Federal Register*, Vol. 78, No. 243, December 18.

Financial Crisis Inquiry Commission, 2011, *The Financial Crisis Inquiry Report: The Final Report of the National Commission on the Causes of the Financial and Economic Crisis in the United States*, Washington, DC: U.S. Government Printing Office, January, available (with dissents) at: http://fcic.law.stanford.edu/report.

Financial Stability Oversight Council (FSOC), 2012a, *2012 Annual Report*, Washington, DC: U.S. Government Printing Office, available at: www.treasury.gov/initiatives/fsoc/Pages/annual-report.aspx.

Financial Stability Oversight Council (FSOC), 2012b, *Proposed recommendations regarding money market mutual fund reform,* November, available at: http://www.treasury.gov/initiatives/fsoc/Documents/Proposed%20Recommendations%20Regarding%20Money%20Market%20Mutual%20Fund%20Reform%20%20November%2013,%202012.pdf.

Flannery, Mark and Sorin Sorescu, 1996, "Evidence of bank market discipline in subordinated debenture yields: 1983–1991," *Journal of Finance*, Vol. 51, No. 4, September, pp. 1347–1377.

Hamilton, Jesse and Cheyenne Hopkins, 2014, "Volcker Rule Curbs on Banks Owning CDOs Eased in U.S." *Bloomberg Politics*, January 14, available at: http://www.bloomberg.com/news/2014-01-14/u-s-regulators-said-ready-to-ease-volcker-cdo-limits-for-banks.html.

Hanson, Samuel G., Anil K. Kashyap and Jeremy C. Stein, 2011, "A macroprudential approach to financial regulation," *Journal of Economic Perspectives*, Vol. 25, No. 1, Winter, pp. 3–28.

Kane, Edward, 1989a, "Changing incentives facing financial-services regulators," *Journal of Financial Services Research*, Vol. 2, No. 3, September, pp. 265–274.

Kane, Edward, 1989b, *The S&L Insurance Mess: How Did it Happen?* Washington, DC: The Urban Institute Press.

Katz, Diane, 2013, "The CFPB in Action: Consumer Bureau Harms Those It Claims To Protect," *Heritage Foundation Report*, #2760, January 22.

Kwast, M., D. Covitz, D. Hancock, J. Houpt, D. Adkins, N. Barger, B. Bouchard, J. Connolly, T. Brady, W. English, D. Evanoff and L. Wall, 1999, "Using Subordinated Debt As an Instrument of Market Discipline," Board of Governors of the Federal Reserve System, staff study, No. 172, December.

LCH.Clearnet, 2008, "$9 Trillion Lehman OTC Interest Rate Swap Default Successfully Resolved," press release, London, October 8, available at www.lchclearnet.com/images/2008-10-08%20swapclear%20default_tcm6-6506.pdf.

Moody's Investors Service, 2013, "Moody's Reviews U.S. Bank Holding Company Ratings to Consider Reduced Government Support, *Moody's Global Credit Research,* August 22.

Noked, Noam, 2013, "FSOC Proposes the First Three Nonbank SIFIs," *The Harvard Law School Forum on Corporate Governance and Financial Regulation*, June 8.

O'Malia, Scott D., 2012, "Implementing Dodd–Frank: Progress to Date and Recommendations for the Future," *Economic Perspectives*, Federal Reserve Bank of Chicago, Vol. 36, Third Quarter, pp. 113–116. Reprinted in this volume.

Rehm, Barbara, 2013, FDIC's Own Experts Skeptical of Resolution Plan, *American Banker*, December 12. Available at: http://www.americanbanker.com/bankthink/fdics-own-experts-skeptical-of-resolution-plan-1064259-1.html.

Rosen, Richard J., 2003, "Is three a crowd: Competition among regulators in banking," *Journal of Money, Credit, and Banking*, 35(6 Part 1), 967–998.

Scott, Kenneth, 2012, "A Guide to the Resolution of Failed Financial Institutions: Dodd–Frank Title II and proposed Chapter 14," Resolution Project, Stanford University, Hoover Institute, paper, February 29, available at: www.hoover.org/taskforces/economic-policy/resolution-project/publications.

Skeel, David A., Jr., 2014, "Real and Imaginary Resolution Options for Large Financial Institutions," in *The Role of Central Banks in Financial Stability: How Has It Changed?* Douglas Evanoff, Cornelia Holthausen, George Kaufman, and Manfred Kremer (eds), Hackensack, NJ: World Scientific Publishing Co. Pte. Ltd.

Skeel, David A., Jr. and Thomas Jackson, 2012, "Transaction consistency and the new finance in bankruptcy," *Columbia Law Review*, Vol. 112, No. 1, January, pp. 152–202.

Soucy, Brenden D., 2013, "The Consumer Financial Protection Bureau: The solution or the problem?" *Florida State University Law Review*, 40(3), 691–720. Reprinted in this volume.

Steigerwald, Robert, 2014, "Central Counterparty Clearing and Systemic Risk Regulation," forthcoming in Anastasios G. Malliaris and William T. Ziemba (eds.), *The WSPC Handbook of Futures Markets*, Hackensack, New Jersey: World Scientific Publishing Company.

Strongin, Steven, Amanda Hindlian, Sandra Lawson, Jorge Murillo, Koby Sadan and Balakrishna Subramanian, 2013, *Measuring the 'Too Big to Fail' Effect on Bond Pricing*, Goldman Sachs Report, New York: http://www.goldmansachs.com/our-thinking/public-policy/regulatory-reform/measuring-tbtf.html.

Tarullo, Daniel, 2012, "Financial Stability Regulation," speech presented at the University of Pennsylvania Law School, Philadelphia, PA, October 10, 2012. Reprinted in this volume.

U.S. Department of the Treasury, 2008, *Blueprint for a Modernized Financial Regulatory Structure*, report, Washington, DC: Government Printing Office, March.

U.S. General Accounting Office, 1994, *Bank Regulation: Consolidation of the Regulatory Agencies*, Washington, DC: Government Printing Office, Publication No. T-GGD-94-106.

U.S. Senate, 2010, *Report on The Restoring American Financial Stability Act of 2010*, Washington, DC: Report 111176, April 30.

Van Der Weide, Mark, 2012, "Implementing Dodd–Frank: Identifying and Mitigating Systemic Risk," *Economic Perspectives*, Federal Reserve Bank of Chicago, Vol. 36, Third Quarter, pp. 108–112. Reprinted in this volume.

Volcker, Paul A., 2013, "Central Banking at a Crossroads," Remarks Before the Economic Club of New York, May 29, 2013: New York City.

Wall, Larry and David Peterson, 1990, "The effect of Continental Illinois' failure on the financial performance of other banks," *Journal of Monetary Economics*, Vol. 26, No. 1, August, pp. 77–99.

Warren, Elizabeth, 2007, "Unsafe at Any Rate," *Democracy Journal*, Issue #5, Summer.

White, Lawrence J., 2010, "The Gramm–Leach–Bliley Act of 1999: A bridge too far? Or not far enough?" *Suffolk University Law Review*, Vol. 43, No. 4, pp. 937–956.

Wilmarth, Arthur E., Jr., 2011, "The Dodd–Frank Act: A flawed and inadequate response to the too-big-to-fail problem," *Oregon Law Review*, Vol. 89, No. 3, pp. 951–1057.

Young, Harrison, 1993, "The meaning of FDICIA," in *FDICIA: An Appraisal — Renaissance, Requiem or Just Another Acronym?* Proceedings of the 29th Annual Conference on Bank Structure and Competition, Federal Reserve Bank of Chicago, pp. 520–533.

PART II

Critical Assessment of the Act

Part II of this volume will provide a critique of what Dodd–Frank was attempting to accomplish, as well as an assessment of what its successes and shortcomings are. While Part I of this book describes the content of the regulatory reform, this part delves more deeply into an analysis of the changes. This part consists of a study by Matthew Richardson, Charles E. Simon Professor of Applied Economics at New York University, which summarizes a more thorough evaluation of the legislation by his colleagues at the Stern School of Business at New York University.

Richardson highlights what he considers many beneficial aspects of the act — such as efforts to measure and regulate systemic risk; expansion of the regulatory reach to systemically important financial institutions (SIFIs) that are nonbanks; and efforts to introduce a new resolution process for SIFIs. He also addresses what he terms "missed opportunities" in the regulatory reform effort, as well as the potential for unintended adverse consequences. He concludes that the true impact of Dodd–Frank will depend critically on the implementation process, which relies heavily on the discretion of regulatory agencies. Accordingly, he states that "the rules, for the most part, are still being written, so it remains an open question as to how effective the legislation will be."

Chapter 2

Regulating Wall Street: The Dodd–Frank Act

Matthew Richardson[1]

In this chapter, I review some of the main findings described in *Regulating Wall Street: The Dodd–Frank Act and the New Architecture of Global Finance*, which I co-edited.[2] As such, this chapter is based on the work of 40 or so faculty members and PhD students at New York University's Stern School of Business (NYU Stern); I especially draw on the work in the volume of my co-editors, Viral V. Acharya, Thomas Cooley, and Ingo Walter. Moreover, in this chapter, where appropriate, I also mention and describe some of the updates to the implementation of the Dodd–Frank Wall Street Reform and Consumer Protection Act being performed by the various government agencies since passage of the act.

Because the financial crisis of 2007–2009 started with a "bubble" in housing prices and was global in nature, the first narrative from analysts and academics focused on the low interest rate policy of the Federal Reserve in the years preceding the crisis and the global imbalance of payments due to the growth of emerging economies (see, for example, Taylor, 2009; Caballero and Krishnamurthy, 2009; and Portes, 2009). While these factors may have played a role in the formation of the crisis, it is generally understood that these factors were not the entire story. Rather, when analysts and academics peeled back the financial architecture of the

---

[1]Matthew Richardson is the Charles E. Simon Professor of Applied Economics in the Finance Department at the Leonard N. Stern School of Business at New York University. The material in this chapter was originally published in the Federal Reserve Bank of Chicago's *Economic Perspectives*, Volume 36, 3rd quarter, 2012. The views expressed are the author's and do not necessarily reflect the views of the Leonard N. Stern School of Business at New York University.

[2]Acharya *et al.* (2010a).

United States and that of the global system, especially in Europe, they found gaping holes and noted that considerable parts of the architecture were broken (see, for example, Acharya and Richardson, 2009a).

So, with the financial architecture in need of much improvement, the Dodd–Frank Act attempts to make the appropriate updates and repairs. Indeed, the Dodd–Frank Act reaches far and wide: In particular, the act consists of 849 pages, 16 titles, and 225 new rules across 11 agencies.[3] No one can accuse the act of not being all-encompassing. The fact the act is written this way, however, is not without some justification.

That said, one can also argue it is not well thought out in this regard. In a now infamous exchange between Federal Reserve Chairman Ben Bernanke and JPMorgan Chase CEO Jamie Dimon on June 7, 2011, the latter described a litany of changes to the financial system and asked whether any policymakers or regulators had studied the accumulated costs of such a buildup in financial regulations. Bernanke replied that there were many things wrong with the financial system, so many of these changes were needed; however, he did admit that no such analysis of the aggregate costs had been performed.[4]

Let me consider just one example of many to illustrate this point. One of the widely accepted fault lines of the financial crisis of 2007–2009 was the poor quality of loans, especially nonprime residential mortgages. How does the Dodd–Frank Act deal with this issue? Here lies the problem.

First, the act sets up the Consumer Finance Protection Bureau in Title X to deal with misleading products and, more generally, predatory lending practices (see also Title XIV, Subtitles A and C). Second, in Title XIV, Subtitle B and Title IX, Subtitle D, the act imposes particular underwriting standards for residential mortgages and focuses on the residential mortgage market, creating preferential treatment for a new brand of mortgages, notably qualified residential mortgages. Third, in Title IX, Subtitle D, the act requires firms performing securitization to retain at least 5% of the credit risk, the motivation being that these firms had no "skin in the game." Fourth, in Title IX, Subtitle C, the act increases regulation of the rating agencies — with a focus on their underlying conflicts of interests with issuers of asset-backed securities, as well as on the reduction of regulatory reliance on their ratings — in an attempt to increase the transparency of the credit risk of the underlying pool of loans. Yet, with all of these new provisions, the act does

[3]The entirety of the Dodd–Frank Act (Public Law 111–203) is available at www.gpo.gov/fdsys/pkg/PLAW-111publ203/pdf/PLAW-111publ203.pdf. Excerpts from this source are quoted throughout this chapter.

[4]A video of the June 7, 2011, exchange is available at http://video.cnbc.com/gallery/?video=3000026289.

not even address what we at NYU Stern consider to be a primary fault for the poor quality of loans — namely, the mispriced government guarantees in the system that led to price distortions and an excessive buildup of leverage and risky credit.

Of course, all of these provisions are aimed at improving the underlying quality of the loans. While one can make the argument that the underlying benefits overlap and the act's provisions are therefore substitutable (albeit with varying degrees of success), one cannot make the same argument with respect to the unintended costs of these provisions. These costs add up across all these enacted provisions, possibly drowning out the main benefit of improving loan quality. I think this is the point that JPMorgan Chase CEO Dimon was making to Fed Chairman Bernanke.

For example, consider some of the unintended consequences of the aforementioned provisions. First, the act abolishes the use of negative amortization loans, prepayment penalties for residential mortgages, and steering incentives for mortgage brokers (that is, payments to brokers for selling specific types of loans), among other items. The implied reason for these prohibitions is that these are standard tools and strategies used by predatory lenders. In some respects, this reasoning is justifiable. Yet, young urban professionals with substantial incomes in the future (such as lawyers, doctors, etc.) might find a negative amortization loan the most efficient way to buy a significant house; prepayment penalties are quite common elsewhere in the system, such as with commercial mortgages, and allow lenders to share in some of the upside of the underlying properties; and mortgage brokers who know the neighborhood well might be able to put together the best packages for borrowers. There are clear costs to imposing such restrictions.

Second, Title XIV of the Dodd–Frank Act applies minimum underwriting standards for mortgages. One of its more important clauses is that "in accordance with regulations prescribed by the Board [of Governors of the Federal Reserve System], no creditor may make a residential mortgage loan unless the creditor makes a reasonable and good faith determination based on verified and documented information that, at the time the loan is consummated, the consumer has a reasonable ability to repay the loan, according to its terms, and all applicable taxes, insurance (including mortgage guarantee insurance), and assessments." While most would agree that higher lending standards would improve the securitization process, it is not clear that a presumption of loan repayment is realistic. Surely, some loans, even mortgages, may be economically viable, even if there is a significant chance of default. Of course, the interest rate underlying the loan should reflect the probability of default. Indeed, this is the basis for the market's pricing of credit risk. Loan originators might be straitjacketed by the direct stipulation of underwriting standards — that is, those precluding the origination of loans that could be made inherently less risky through innovative contractual and monitoring mechanisms or simply different credit terms, such as requiring a higher down payment. In other words, such a provision may restrict worthwhile mortgage credit from being provided to the marketplace.

Third, the guiding principle behind Title IX, Subtitle D — namely, that securitizers should have skin in the game — appears to be reasonable and is a natural outcome of aligning incentives between investors and the securitizers. That said, to my knowledge, there has been no empirical study of the extent to which securitizers had skin in the game before the crisis. The legislation therefore may be based on a generally false premise, though it may have been true in some specific cases. Forcing all securitizers to have skin in the game for the majority of pooled assets clearly pushes securitization to the larger firms that have better access to funding. Given the problems that emerged in the recent financial crisis, is this a good thing? Moreover, one would suspect that many innovative, custom-made securitizations that would have normally taken place will now fall by the wayside.

And even if a lack of skin in the game was a source for the failure of securitization markets, there needs to be a well-constructed argument for why the private sector cannot solve the issue. I would argue that the best line of reasoning in this respect is the existence of mispriced government guarantees in the financial system, such as deposit insurance, too-big-to-fail (TBTF) subsidies, and government-sponsored enterprise (GSE) debt subsidies. Of course, a more direct attack of the problem would call for either the dismantling or appropriate pricing of government guarantees. This issue is further discussed in the next section of this chapter.

Fourth, Title IX, Subtitle C of the Dodd–Frank Act introduces some much-needed reform of the rating agencies. These reforms include the removal of regulatory reliance on ratings; some possible mechanisms to explicitly deal with the conflict of interest between raters and issuers of asset-backed securities; the increased likelihood of litigation damages; and a much-heavier-handed approach to the supervision of rating agencies. The purpose of such reforms is to improve the quality of the ratings for loans and asset-backed securities, which regulators and investors consult. This, in theory, would then lead to higher-quality loan standards overall. In other words, the goal is the same as the other parts of the Dodd–Frank Act. Of course, there are consequences to the act's provisions for rating agencies. For example, with the removal of regulatory reliance on the ratings, the act comes squarely up against capital regulation being put forth in the new international banking supervision accord Basel III.[5] Moreover, this point aside, the

[5]For details on Basel Committee on Banking Supervision and the Basel Accords, see www.bis.org/bcbs/about.htm.

Securities Exchange Commission (SEC) suggested new rules on April 11, 2011, to deal with the new provision to remove regulatory reliance on ratings — namely, to put more of an onus on the financial institutions to demonstrate their creditworthiness. But hasn't this been argued as one of the leading problems with Basel II and its application in the recent financial crisis? That is, it has been argued that self-regulation does not work well given the misaligned incentives of the financial sector.

I hope the point comes across that the accumulation of the Dodd–Frank Act's provisions might be overkill in a respective cost–benefit analysis. The question we need to ask is, which of the provisions best improves underwriting standards at the lowest cost to the system?

The rest of this chapter will focus on three major aspects of the Dodd–Frank Act, which my colleagues and I argue in our *Regulating Wall Street* book are positives. These parts of the act are (1) the measurement and regulation of systemic risk; (2) the resolution of failing large, complex financial institutions (LCFIs); and (3) the regulation of some major and very systemically important markets, in particular over-the-counter (OTC) derivatives markets. That said, after briefly describing the positives, I will focus the majority of my analysis on some missed opportunities for the Dodd–Frank Act to have addressed these important issues, as well as on some of the unintended consequences stemming from the legislation.

Systemic risk

The economic theory of regulation is very clear. Regulate where there is a market failure. It is apparent that a major market failure in this crisis was the emergence of systemic risk. More specifically, systemic risk emerged when aggregate capitalization of the financial sector became low. The intuition for why this is a problem is straightforward. When a financial firm's capital is low, it is difficult for that firm to perform financial services; and when capital is low in the aggregate, it is not possible for other financial firms to step in and address the breach. This breakdown in financial intermediation is the reason that severe consequences occurred in the broader economy. When financial firms therefore ran aground during the crisis period, they contributed to the aggregate shortfall, leading to consequences beyond the individual firms. Individual firms had no incentive to manage the systemic risk.

Therefore, it is a big positive that the Dodd–Frank Act focuses on the market failure of systemic risk. The negative externality associated with such risks implies that private markets cannot efficiently solve the problem, so government intervention is required. Prior to the financial crisis, the U.S. financial system and the regulatory apparatus of the Basel Accords were focused too much on individual institutional risk and not enough on system-wide risk. In other words, regulators now need to focus *not just* on the losses of individual financial institutions, but also on the cost that their failure would impose on the system.

The Dodd–Frank Act now emphasizes macroprudential regulation as an important component of the financial regulatory system. For the first time in U.S. financial regulatory history, the act requires such regulation — that is, (1) to measure and provide tools for measuring systemic risk, (2) to then designate firms and even sectors as those that pose systemic risk, and (3) to provide enhanced regulation of such firms and sectors. While arguably this type of regulation was always in the purview of the central bank and regulators, the recent crisis has shown the importance of writing it into law.

Specifically, the Dodd–Frank Act creates a supporting research organization within the U.S. Department of the Treasury — namely, the Office of Financial Research (OFR) — to measure and provide tools for measuring systemic risk. The Dodd–Frank Act assigns new responsibilities to a new body, the Financial Stability Oversight Council (FSOC), which will use the data provided by the OFR to identify systemically important financial institutions (SIFIs). FSOC and the other relevant agencies are then given the power to provide enhanced regulation of these SIFIs — such as levels of capital and liquidity necessary to withstand major shocks to asset markets. In addition, the act also gives the power for prompt corrective action of SIFIs through the orderly liquidation authority (OLA), which is to be run and modeled by the Federal Deposit Insurance Corporation (FDIC). This is the focus of the next section of this chapter.

Of course, the devil is in the details, and there are plenty of things in the Dodd–Frank Act that do not coincide with my thinking on macroprudential regulation (or with that of many of my colleagues at NYU Stern). In the Dodd–Frank Act, large banks (that is, those with over $50 billion in assets) are designated as SIFIs. Subsequent to the passage of the Dodd–Frank Act, FSOC published its final rule (and interpretative guidance), detailing the potential criteria for nonbank financial companies to also be SIFIs.[6] These criteria involve a three-stage process. The final FSOC rule states that "the first stage of the process ("Stage 1") is designed to narrow the universe of nonbank financial companies to a smaller set of nonbank financial companies," which is completed "by applying uniform

[6]FSOC initially issued a report for designating nonbank financial companies as SIFIs in October 2011. The final official document, which was based on that report was published in the April 11, 2012, *Federal Register*; see Financial Stability Oversight Council (2012).

quantitative thresholds that are broadly applicable across the financial sector to a large group of nonbank financial companies." Next, according to the rule, "in the second stage of the process ("Stage 2"), the Council [FSOC] will conduct a comprehensive analysis … of the potential for the nonbank financial companies identified in Stage 1 to pose a threat to U.S. financial stability." And finally, the rule explains that "the Council will send a notice of consideration to each nonbank financial company that will be reviewed in Stage 3," which "will build on the Stage 2 analysis using quantitative and qualitative information collected directly from the nonbank financial company." In addition, the rule states that "based on the analysis performed in Stages 2 and 3, the Council may consider whether to vote to subject a nonbank financial company to a proposed determination [of SIFI status]."[7]

The FSOC rule narrowed the Dodd–Frank Act's criteria to six factors: size, interconnectedness, substitutability, leverage, liquidity risk and maturity mismatch, and existing regulatory scrutiny.[8] Each of these factors would then be applied to the process described previously to come up with a possible SIFI designation. As Title I of the Dodd–Frank Act states, once SIFIs have been determined, then FSOC will provide "the establishment and refinement of prudential standards" for them that "are more stringent than those applicable to other nonbank financial companies and bank holding companies that do not present similar risks to the financial stability of the United States." Moreover, these stricter standards may include "(A) risk-based capital requirements; (B) leverage limits; (C) liquidity requirements; (D) resolution plan and credit exposure report requirements; (E) concentration limits; (F) a contingent capital requirement; (G) enhanced public disclosures; (H) short-term debt limits; and (I) overall risk management requirements."

Rather than provide a long list of criticisms of the Dodd–Frank Act's approach to systemic risk, I will mention just a few important ones. The six factors mentioned in the FSOC rule are reasonable descriptions of the failure risk of financial institutions. However, these factors may not be adequate for addressing this point: It is not the individual institution's risk *per se*, but its contribution to system-wide risk that matters. What we care about is whether a financial firm will falter when other firms are struggling. In other words, systemic risk is about codependence — that is, how much leverage a firm has and how correlated its assets are with those of other institutions in the bad state of nature, as well as whether its failure increases the

---

[7]That is, the nonbank firm can be regulated differently because of its systemic importance. See Financial Stability Oversight Council (2012), pp. 21641–21642, 21646.

[8]Financial Stability Oversight Council (2012), p. 21641.

likelihood of other firms failing. There is no mention in the Dodd–Frank Act or subsequent revisions about the co-movement of a financial firm's asset returns with aggregate factors and tail risk. Of course, this does not preclude FSOC from making codependence an important component of systemic risk measurements in the future, but at present FSOC does not require this.

For example, it is looking increasingly likely that capital regulation will be the blunt instrument to deal with SIFIs. Analysis by a number of us at NYU Stern makes clear that higher capital requirements resulting from systemic risk do not have to coincide with larger financial institutions (see http://vlab.stern.nyu.edu/welcome/risk/). For a variety of reasons, it may well be the case that large financial institutions deserve heightened prudential regulation. But if the criterion is that they need sufficient capital to withstand a crisis, it does not follow that size necessarily is the key factor unless it adversely affects a firm's marginal expected shortfall, that is, a firm's expected losses in a financial crisis.

The fact that this simple point about codependence is missed by both the Dodd–Frank Act and subsequent FSOC rulings is worrying. This problem is exacerbated by the added concern that a collection of small firms, such as money market funds, can have a systemic impact on the financial system and the overall economy, yet may not be detected by FSOC's three-stage evaluation of the six identified factors. This issue is discussed in more detail later.

That said, the financial crisis was primarily caused by the existence of incentives of LCFIs to take excess risk and leverage. The primary source of this misalignment of incentives was two-fold: (1) the fact that systemic-risk costs do not get internalized by individual institutions and (2) the existence of a conflict of interest between firms' shareholders and the taxpayers via mispriced government guarantees of debt (for example, deposit insurance and TBTF subsidies).

With respect to individual institutions not internalizing systemic risk, the Dodd–Frank Act creates incorrect incentives by charging *ex post* rather than *ex ante* for systemic risk (an issue discussed in greater detail in the next section). The act misses the opportunity to fix the negative externality of systemic risk by imposing the standard economic solution of taxing such an externality. In other words, there should be an additional fee or premium that is tied specifically to the systemic risk of LCFIs as their failures impose costs on the rest of the financial sector and the real economy (for example, Acharya *et al.*, 2010c). The issues underlying the development and implementation of such a systemic fee structure are, however, nontrivial. This point aside, in order to avoid these fees, LCFIs would organically become less systemic by choosing less leverage and holding assets that have less aggregate tail risk. It is interesting to note that in the House of Representatives' version of the precursor bill to the Dodd–Frank Act, such a provision was included.

But this is not the approach taken by the Dodd–Frank Act. As mentioned previously, it is looking increasingly likely that the result will be to follow Basel III's lead. With respect to Basel III, there are certainly improvements to Basel II, most notably the addition of a liquidity requirement for financial firms, a simple leverage ratio as a supplementary measure to risk-based capital, and higher capital requirements overall for SIFIs. All of these are included in the Dodd–Frank Act.

Unfortunately, however, Basel III continues the risk weights that are tied to credit ratings both within and across asset classes, as well as the internal ratings approach that many have forcefully argued against as a result of the crisis. Remarkably, the Basel III approach and, therefore, that of Dodd–Frank, are still focused on the risk of individual banks as opposed to system-wide risks. Indeed, Basel III continues the focus of the previous Basel Accords on risk-weighted capital measures of individual firms as the main indicator.

This approach is a core problem of the new financial regulation. Basel's approach to systemic risk weights seem arbitrary and is not based on objective criteria. Thus, across-the-board higher capital requirements, as are being proposed for SIFIs, may actually exacerbate the problem. Regulation should not be about more capital *per se* but about more capital for systemically riskier financial firms. One of the problems that emerged in the financial crisis was the preferred capital treatment provided to certain asset-backed securities, such as AAA-rated mortgage-backed securities (MBS). With simply higher capital requirements for SIFIs, it cannot be ruled out that the preference for AAA-rated MBS or other similarly rated securities will be even greater, causing an even bigger buildup in aggregate systemic risk. Granted, the Dodd–Frank Act does provide some mitigating solutions, such as the Volcker Rule,[9] that still need to be played out.

Moreover, whatever is being proposed for the banking sector in terms of capital requirements should have comparable regulation for the "shadow" banking system,[10] lest the activities simply be shifted from one part of financial markets to another. The result of such a shift could actually lead to an increase in systemic risk. This issue is not directly covered in the Dodd–Frank Act. But I discuss it in greater detail later in this chapter.

Finally, the problem of mispriced government guarantees (and resulting moral hazard) gets little coverage in the Dodd–Frank Act other than in the OLA

---

[9]See http://lexicon.ft.com/Term?term=volcker-rule.

[10]The shadow banking system represents the network of financial firms (for example, hedge funds and insurance companies) that are outside the traditional banking system.

in Title II. There is little analysis of what it means for the ability to regulate the financial sector when many financial institutions can finance their activities at below-market rates, which we know can lead to excessive risk. These distortions occurred not only at banks with access to FDIC insurance, but also at Fannie Mae and Freddie Mac (the two major GSEs) and the TBTF LCFIs. And such distortions remain a big issue. With regard to this point, there is a 2002 study by economists at the Federal Reserve Bank of Richmond that found about 45% of all financial liabilities in 1999 fell under the U.S. safety net (Walter and Weinberg, 2002); a similar study performed more recently by the Richmond Fed found that a decade later almost 60% of all financial liabilities were covered by the safety net (see Malysheva and Walter, 2010).

It is hard to imagine how systemic risk can be addressed without simultaneously dealing with the mispriced safety net of the U.S. financial sector. Thus, it seems necessary that financial firms be charged fees commensurate with the explicit or implicit government insurance they enjoy on a continuous basis. If one looks at the act itself, it does make some changes to FDIC insurance premiums in Title III. For example, FDIC premiums are expanded beyond the insured deposit base to most liabilities, and the upper limit for the ratio of the FDIC-insured fund to total deposits is removed. That said, the GSEs are ignored in the act. For the insurance sector, there's a national office to look into these issues, but the sector is, for the most part, ignored and thus left to rely on small state guarantee funds. Most problematic is the fact that no significant changes to risk-based pricing have been made since the FDIC Improvement Act of 1991. Some 20 years later, both the nature of the risks and our understanding of those risks have changed greatly.

Resolving LCFIs

There is almost universal agreement that there needs to be a solvency regime to deal with LCFIs. One might prefer the receivership approach of the Dodd–Frank Act; changes to the U.S. bankruptcy code, in the form of Chapter 11F for financial institutions (see, for example, Jackson, 2010); or "bail-in" alternatives, which I explain more later (see, for example, Acharya *et al.*, 2010). But nearly all agree that the regulatory system must be powerful enough to be able to take prompt corrective action — in other words, it must have enough authority to deal with troubled institutions prior to default. The financial crisis of 2007–2009 illustrated the problems that can arise when an LCFI, such as Lehman Brothers, fails without adequate planning and safeguards. At least from 30,000 feet above, the fact that Title II of the Dodd–Frank Act puts such liquidation authority in place appears to be a positive. The Case I make here, however, is that there remain several important questions about the implementation of this authority, as well as concerns about the systemic risk that can emerge from it.

The Dodd–Frank Act describes the following process. FSOC would have previously made a determination that a financial company (that is, a bank holding company, insured depository institution, nonbank financial company, or insurance company) is systemically risky — that is, it is a SIFI. The FDIC and the Fed (or, for insurance companies, the Federal Insurance Office) must report to the Treasury Secretary that the SIFI is in danger of default and then explain how this default would affect overall financial stability, why normal bankruptcy proceedings are not appropriate, and why a private sector solution is not available. Under these circumstances, the Treasury Secretary seeks appointment of the FDIC as receiver. If the company does not consent to be placed into receivership, then a petition by the Treasury Secretary must be filed at the U.S. District Court for the District of Columbia. The court's only determination is whether the decision was "arbitrary and capricious." This determination must be made within 24 hours of the receipt of petition.

If the Treasury Secretary's petition succeeds in court, the FDIC assumes complete control over the company and its liquidation process. Most important, the FDIC has unilateral authority to review and pay claims. The principle of priority should be followed; however, in contrast to normal bankruptcy proceedings, the FDIC has latitude to deviate from this principle under the Dodd–Frank Act's OLA process. Some examples of the FDIC tools are: (1) advanced planning enhanced by living wills of SIFIs, (2) prompt distribution of proceeds upon the sales of assets, (3) the authorization to provide "going concern" support via a bridge financial company, (4) the authorization to borrow from the Treasury to provide such funding (eliminating the uncertainty of debtor-in-possession (DIP) funding), and (5) the ability to transfer qualified financial contracts (for example, swaps, repurchase agreements, and other types of securities contracts) to the bridge company via a brief automatic stay.

The last tool highlights the benefits and costs of providing safe harbors for qualified financial contracts. On the one hand, safe harbors allow counterparties to terminate, liquidate, or net out their contracts immediately, potentially causing fire sales, which might propagate systemic risk. On the other hand, automatic stays tie up the contracts and reduce liquidity, making runs on the financial system more likely. The Dodd–Frank Act provides a compromise between these two unfortunate outcomes.

The main problem with the Dodd–Frank Act's approach to the failure of a financial institution, however, mirrors its problems with respect to managing systemic risk described earlier. The OLA of Title II provides the regulator legal power to act in the case of a failure of a SIFI, but it does not set up the appropriate regime to deal specifically with banking crises — that is, with multiple SIFI failures occurring simultaneously.

The problem is that the Dodd–Frank Act really puts a heavy reliance on the creation of the OLA to solve financial crises. Resolution by its nature is a balancing act between two forces that (potentially) work against each other. The first force is that ideally the act should mitigate moral hazard and therefore bring back market discipline. The countervailing force is that the act should also help manage systemic risk when it emerges. So, how well does the Dodd–Frank Act do this? Not that well, from my perspective.

It seems to me that the act is, for the most part, focused on the orderly liquidation of an individual institution and not on the system as a whole. What is unique about a financial firm's failure, however, is its impact on the rest of the financial sector and the broader economy. In other words, losses to SIFI creditors can wipe out the capital of other SIFIs, which in turn can cause the economy to falter. This suggests that we need an *ex ante* orderly liquidation fund.

To put this into perspective, consider Federal Reserve Chairman Ben Bernanke's oft-cited analogy for why bailouts, however distasteful, are sometimes necessary.[11] Bernanke has described a hypothetical neighbor who smokes in bed and, through his carelessness, starts a fire and begins to burn down his house. You could teach him a lesson by refusing to call the fire department and letting the house burn to the ground. However, you would risk the fire spreading to your home and other homes. So first, the fire has to be put out. Only later should you deal with reform and retribution. This is how I would describe legislation prior to the Dodd–Frank Act.

In terms of Bernanke's analogy, the Dodd–Frank Act's approach would be to not call the fire department and to let the neighbor's house burn down. The act would forbid the fire department from initially coming to the scene. Given the costs of such a policy, the Dodd–Frank Act would police the neighborhood to try and make sure no one smokes, and if a fire results, it would charge the neighbors eventually for costs associated with a fire. I suppose the hope is that these neighbors would therefore also police each other.

Instead, I would argue that (again, in terms of the Chairman's analogy) you should call the fire department, but instead of saving the neighbor's house, the firefighters should stand in protection of your house and those of your other neighbors. If the fire spreads, they are ready to put it out. This is what the role of

[11] Bernanke (2009).

the orderly liquidation fund should be. And by the way, because a fire department is expensive to keep, I would charge all the smokers in the neighborhood the cost. And over time, the neighborhood would have fewer smokers. This is what I mean by balancing moral hazard mitigation and systemic risk management.

The Dodd–Frank Act clearly does not do this. Here is one example. As mentioned before, the act creates incorrect incentives by charging *ex post* rather than *ex ante* for systemic risk. In particular, if firms fail during a crisis and monies cannot be fully recovered from creditors, the surviving SIFIs must make up the difference *ex post*. This actually increases moral hazard because there is a free-rider problem — prudent firms are asked to pay for the sins of others. It also increases systemic risk in two important ways. First, firms will tend to herd together, so a race to the bottom could ensue. Second, it requires the surviving firms to provide capital at the worst possible time.

Another important issue is the question of how to deal with liquidity. As Tirole (2010) points out, the approach for the prudential regulation of liquidity can be very similar to that for the prudential regulation of capital; that is, this approach can be micro-based, by protecting taxpayers, and macro-based, by managing systemic risk. The Dodd–Frank Act does not apply a macro-based approach to the prudential regulation of liquidity, and it arguably hinders a solution — namely, the Fed's role as a credible lender of last resort (LOLR).

As past crises have shown, in particular during the Panic of 1907, liquidity crises can quickly turn into solvency crises. In fact, in the wake of the Panic of 1907, Congress passed the Aldrich–Vreeland Act, resulting in a final report on the crisis some three years later. This report in turn led Congress to pass the Federal Reserve Act on December 22, 1913, creating the Federal Reserve System. While the Federal Reserve has clearly evolved over time, it still serves its original purpose as a credible LOLR, as it did in the most recent financial crisis. The underlying principle of the LOLR is based on Walter Bagehot's (1873) famous work *Lombard Street: A Description of the Money Market*, which suggested that in order to prevent the failure of solvent but illiquid banks, the central bank should lend freely on good collateral at a penalty rate.

While there is substantial disagreement among policymakers, analysts, and academics as to whether the Fed stretched this principle to insolvent firms, there is little disagreement that the LOLR was used widely throughout the crisis. At the very least, as the recent financial crisis has shown, solvency crises can be greatly amplified by liquidity funding problems. From my perspective, it is clear that the architecture of the financial system should be built around this point.

Title XI of the Dodd–Frank Act now changes the Fed's role in dealing with a liquidity crisis. Specifically, Title XI restricts the Fed's LOLR ability — established under Section 13(3) of the Federal Reserve Act — to deal with nonbanks unless a system-wide crisis emerges. In particular, emergency lending can no longer be applied to any "individual, partnership, or corporation," but only to "participants in any program or facility with broad-based eligibility." Moreover, according to Title XI of the Dodd–Frank Act, "any emergency lending program or facility is for the purpose of providing liquidity to the financial system, and not to aid a failing financial company." Further, these actions have been politicized to the extent that any Fed programs that allow for the efficient distribution of liquidity in a crisis to solvent financial institutions with acceptable collateral would now require approval of the Treasury Secretary.

The most recent financial crisis illustrates the importance of the Fed's role as the LOLR, whether it be for nonbanks — like Bear Stearns, American International Group (AIG), or Lehman Brothers (which was not supported) — or the money market fund sector. The Panic of 1907 taught us something, namely, that the financial system can collapse without a corresponding large aggregate economic shock, like other crises. It is indeed troubling that when the financial system is weak, temporary liquidity problems at a particular firm can now trigger a full-blown crisis because the Fed's LOLR ability has been restricted.

Specifically, the problem is that without an LOLR for "shadow banks" and other nonbank institutions, systemically important institutions will be put through the OLA process, even if it is just for a liquidity event. But of course once this happens, similar institutions will also suffer runs as lenders try to avoid the OLA process, paradoxically triggering regulators to place them into the OLA process. From a relatively minor crisis, such as the Panic of 1907, the system could now face a severe financial crisis and systemic event. This is precisely why the LOLR was created following the Panic of 1907. In the modern world, there may be no functional difference between a bank and some other financial institution, so why restrict the Fed's ability to act?

As a final comment on resolving LCFIs, it is reasonable to question the Dodd–Frank Act's choice of the FDIC receivership approach. To the FDIC's credit, subsequent to the Dodd–Frank Act being passed, the FDIC produced a white paper outlining how it would have used its authority under Dodd–Frank to deal with Lehman Brothers.[12] It is an interesting document because it highlights the tools now available to the FDIC as a result of Title II of the Dodd–Frank Act.

That said, there are reasons to question the analysis of the FDIC authors. Their argument is based on several key assumptions, such as (1) market discipline,

---

[12]Federal Deposit Insurance Corporation (2011).

because Lehman management and staff would no longer believe the firm was too-big-to-fail; (2) advanced liquidation plans, especially in light of Bear Stearns's troubles; (3) the ability to provide sufficient liquidity to operate as a going concern; and (4) an open bidding process to sell assets and operations. A few observations are in order. First, aside from the third point, the FDIC document is arguably too optimistic on these points. For example, the authors assume Barclays could have been persuaded to buy Lehman's derivatives business — even though its value would have been in question. Second, one of the main issues related to Lehman's collapse was not just the rapid unwinding of derivative and swap positions not granted a stay in bankruptcy, but also how this signaled to other LCFIs, in particular the other major investment banks, that these firms would not be bailed out, triggering runs on their liabilities. Third, it would have to be the case that the unintended consequences of Lehman's failure — such as the Reserve Primary Fund (a large money market fund with exposures to Lehman Brothers debt securities) "breaking the buck" and the resulting run on money market funds and the rehypothecation[13] and freezing of hedge fund assets at Lehman's U.K. prime brokerage unit — could have been identified *a priori*. Fourth, there is a presumption that international coordination would have taken place that somewhat relies on the false premise of a uniform legal framework across different jurisdictions.

As an alternative to the OLA process, Jackson (2010) has argued for a more standard bankruptcy model with adjustments for financial institutions — the so-called Chapter 11F. The basic notion is that the bankruptcy code has been around in some form for 200 years, so given our lengthy experience with it, there is much more certainty with respect to how it would operate. Jackson concedes that adjustments would need to be developed — such as (1) a prompt corrective trigger possibly by involuntary petition; (2) an "experienced" judiciary court focused on LCFIs; (3) qualified financial contracts being divided into two types — illiquid (subject to the stay) and liquid (exempt); and (4) a role for government through DIP financing, albeit subject to rules of strict priority. While this model alone would not solve all the issues mentioned previously, its implementation might be smoother.

In Acharya *et al.* (2010a), my colleagues and I argue that based on the academic concept of a living will from the corporate finance literature (for example, Adler, 1993), it may be possible to impose discipline on creditors without even relying on bankruptcy. This idea is typically called a "bail-in" and is close in spirit to the concept of contingent capital (which, to the Dodd–Frank Act's credit, is

[13]Rehypothecation refers to the practice of an institution lending securities that its clients have pledged as collateral.

discussed as a possible tool to be used by FSOC for SIFIs). The idea is to divide a financial firm's capital structure into a hierarchy of priority tranches. In the event of a default on a debt obligation, equity would be eliminated, and the lowest-priority debt tranche would be converted to equity. If this is not sufficient, then the process is repeated until all defaults are cured or the highest tranche is converted to equity. Only at this point would senior debtholders have reason to foreclose on collateral. There are a number of issues surrounding the implementation of a bail-in that would need to be addressed; however, in the purest form of a bail-in, creditors pay for the firm's failure, but the cost of financial distress is avoided.

Shadow banks and regulation by form, not function

As of the summer of 2007, just prior to the start of the financial crisis, the short-term liabilities of the U.S. financial system were approximately $15.3 trillion in size; however, just $4.8 trillion of this amount was insured by the FDIC. Of the rest, $2.7 trillion represented uninsured deposits, $3.1 trillion money market mutual funds, $2.5 trillion broker–dealer repo agreements, $1.2 trillion asset-backed commercial paper (ABCP), $0.6 trillion securities lending, and $0.4 trillion old-fashioned financial institution commercial paper.[14]

The shadow banking system performs functions like banks but takes the form of other financial firms or entities. These financial institutions borrow short term in rollover debt markets, leverage significantly, and lend and invest in longer-term and illiquid assets. The growth of shadow banking over the past 25 years has been extraordinary relative to the growth in traditional bank deposits. The SEC aside, the shadow banking system is, for the most part, unregulated. It is also unprotected from bank-like runs (that is, there are no explicit guarantees provided by the government). Of course, the financial crisis of 2007–2009 showed that much of the shadow banking system — investment banks through repos, money market funds, and ABCP conduits in particular — ended up being run on and eventually bailed out. This part of the financial system, considered in whole, was TBTF.

Does history tell us anything about how to regulate the shadow banking system? Early in the 20th century, for example, during the aforementioned Panic of 1907 and the various banking panics that occurred in 1930–1932 in the Great Depression, uncertainty and lack of information about which financial institutions were insolvent led to system-wide bank runs. In response to these systemic runs, the government created the Federal Reserve with its LOLR facility, the

[14]Ricks (2010).

FDIC and deposit insurance, and a number of banking and investment acts. Arguably, the most important part of the legislation was that depositors no longer had to run on banks because the government guaranteed the funds. Of course, it is well understood that this safety net creates a moral hazard, that is, an incentive for banks to undertake greater risk than they would without this insurance. Over time, regulators and policymakers therefore set up a number of countervailing barriers: (1) banks would have to pay to be a part of the deposit insurance system, so, at least, on an *ex ante* basis, regulators took into account the cost of the insurance; (2) the risk-taking activities of banks were ring-fenced to the extent that there was a separation of the commercial and the riskier investment banking activities; and (3) enhanced supervision (generally in the form of capital requirements and prompt corrective action) and winding-down provisions of individual banks were established.

So how does the Dodd–Frank Act address the regulation of the shadow banking system? For the most part, the act is silent on the shadow banking system. This is unfortunate, since the size and nature of the shadow banking system produced obvious systemic risk effects and, at a minimum, amplified the severity of the crisis. Hence, broadly speaking, the Dodd–Frank Act falls into the trap of regulating by form not function.

This is a problem for two major reasons. First, the experience of the most recent financial crisis showed the importance of capital requirements being consistently set across markets and institutions. In other words, if the risk of the underlying loans is the same, it should not matter how those loans are sliced and diced through securitization in terms of determining the required capital buffer of banking institutions. Second, institutions performing similar tasks (for example, depository institutions *and* money market funds) should be regulated similarly. Without such treatment, regulatory arbitrage is likely to occur at the cost of creating systemic risk. Next, I provide a few examples from the most recent crisis illustrating these points.

First, the exploitation of the capital regulatory rules of the Basel Accords and the U.S. regulatory structure was a major problem contributing to the financial crisis of 2007–2009 (for example, Acharya *et al.*, 2010b). While the Dodd–Frank Act plugs some of the loopholes, the overall general approach is unchanged. One striking illustration relates to Fannie Mae and Freddie Mac, the two major GSEs. Starting in the mid-1980s, they held about 7% of the market share of the mortgage market. By the time of the crisis, the number had become almost 50%, representing $5 trillion of credit risk. How did the two GSEs become so dominant? If a bank made a portfolio of mortgage loans, the bank was required to hold 4% capital. If the same bank took that portfolio of mortgage loans, sold it to Fannie Mae or

Freddie Mac, and bought it back as MBS, the bank only had to hold 1.6% capital; since Fannie and Freddie were only required to hold 0.45% capital on their mortgage guarantees, the financial system as a whole only needed 2.05% capital. So for the exact same risks and exact same loans, the financial system could have about twice the leverage (see, for example, Acharya *et al.*, 2011). All that was required was that the GSEs had to be involved and the banks held the securities. Not surprisingly, a significant fraction of the mortgage risk — approximately 40% — never left the systemically riskier parts of the financial system. These problems still persist under the Dodd–Frank Act.

Second, the development of a parallel banking sector that used wholesale funding and OTC derivatives to conduct identical banking activities as commercial banks — even though that sector's activities were not subject to the same rules and regulations — is perfectly illustrated by the behavior of the Reserve Primary Fund, the large money market fund that "broke the buck" when Lehman Brothers failed. Kacperczyk and Schnabl (2010), NYU Stern professors, analyze the risk-taking behavior and incentives of money market funds during the crisis. The Reserve Primary Fund was one of the oldest money market funds, and historically, it had been operated as a very safe fund. Going into the summer of 2007, its $15 billion fund yielded spreads of around 7–8 basis points above Treasury securities. Then, all of a sudden, in mid-August 2007, the fund started offering spreads of 20 basis points and its assets more than doubled in value. Before the financial crisis went pandemic with Lehman's collapse in September 2008, the fund's assets had accumulated to over $60 billion and the fund had been offering spreads of 40 basis points. So what was the Reserve Primary Fund doing? It had loaded up on ABCP, raising the share of its holdings in ABCP from essentially 0% to over 50%; it did this by reducing the U.S. government securities and repo exposures of its holdings from 40% to 10%. Of course, the fund did this by taking a big bet on ABCP. The first major run in the shadow banking system was on ABCP, with yield spreads widening from 10 to 100 basis points after August 7, 2007.[15]

Why is this relevant? The answer lies in the following question: What is the likelihood, either before or after the passage of the Dodd–Frank Act, that if a bank was behaving in this manner, regulators would not intervene? The problem is that shadow banks by definition operate in the "shadows" and are thus not subject to the regulation or capital requirements that traditional banks are. Granted, these shadow banking firms may not have access to the safety net, but the fact they may need it confirms the systemic level of their activities.

---

[15]The numbers cited here are from the original Kacperczyk and Schnabl (2010) working paper. In a 2011 version (available at: http://pages.stern.nyu.edu/~pschnabl/public_html/KacperczykSchnabl2011.pdf), the authors report industry-adjusted numbers.

That said, proponents of the Dodd–Frank Act will argue that a number of titles in the act are relevant for shadow banking. Title I of the act allows nonbanks — possibly shadow banks — to be designated as SIFIs and therefore fall under the regulatory umbrella. Title VIII (which can be cited as the Payment, Clearing, and Settlement Supervision Act of 2010) can also be interpreted as dealing with some issues related to shadow banking. Title IV calls for registration of hedge funds; Title V, for a study of insurance companies; and Title IX, Subtitle D, for greater transparency of the securitization process (a main vehicle for shadow banks). That said, of the 16 titles in the Dodd–Frank Act, there is no specific title on shadow banking. Analysis of shadow banking and corresponding regulation of these entities, therefore, are left to working groups and task forces at the various regulatory agencies. Without the full support of the Dodd–Frank Act, it remains to be seen what these new rules will look like.

Of course, Title VII of the Dodd–Frank Act did bring one of the major and very systemically important markets, OTC derivatives, operating in the "shadows" back into the regulatory fold. From my perspective, we can quibble about whether we like every aspect of how the act treats OTC derivatives markets, but I think the fact that it is now part of the regulatory environment is a net positive.

OTC derivatives account for a significant proportion of overall banking and intermediation activity — for example, notional amounts of OTC derivatives went from $60 trillion in 1998 to almost $600 trillion within just a decade.[16] On the one hand, they enable end-users like corporations, including industrial and financial firms, to hedge their underlying risk exposures in a customized manner. On the other hand, they enable banks and other financial intermediaries — the providers of hedging services to end-users — to earn profits, as they, in turn, hedge the customized OTC products they sell, either by diversifying the risk across different end-users or by shedding the risk to other intermediaries via liquid markets for standardized derivatives. It is clear that there is value to the economy from derivative products, which enable users to hedge and transfer risk by altering the patterns of their cash flows.

The financial crisis of 2007–2009, however, exposed two aspects of the OTC derivatives market that deserved reform (see, for example, Acharya *et al.*, 2010d). The first aspect is that banks can use OTC derivatives to tailor their own risk-taking and leverage buildup, since some of these positions are not reflected on their balance sheets, from either a regulatory or statutory disclosure perspective.

[16]Author's calculations based on data from various issues of the *BIS Quarterly Review* and Bank for International Settlements' Semiannual Over-The-Counter (OTC) Derivatives Markets Statistics, available at: www.bis.org/statistics/derstats.htm.

In other words, regulatory capital requirements had not been suitably adjusted to reflect all aspects of OTC derivative exposures. Consider the following illustration. In AIG's 2007 annual report, published in mid-March 2008, well before the firm was brought down, AIG describes its now infamous $527 billion of credit default swap (CDS) positions by its subsidiary AIG Financial Products Corporation (AIGFP). As stated in the document, "approximately $379 billion ... of the $527 billion in notional exposure of AIGFP's super senior CDS portfolio as of December 31, 2007, represents derivatives written for financial institutions, principally in Europe, for the purpose of providing them with regulatory capital relief rather than risk mitigation."[17] If financial institutions held AAA-rated securities and bought protection on those securities from AA- or AAA-rated insurance companies, then these institutions would have 0% capital reflected on their balance sheets for such positions. Such rules possibly explain the huge leverage positions of UBS, ABN AMRO, and Merrill Lynch, among others, prior to the crisis.

The second aspect that deserves attention concerns the opacity of exposures in OTC derivatives. By definition, an OTC derivatives market does not have a central marketplace, where all trades occur. This is in contrast to exchange-traded derivatives, which are both traded on an exchange and cleared through a clearinghouse. Unlike cleared derivatives, where the clearinghouse monitors the risk of the positions of the various participants and imposes margins and other risk-mitigating devices, the risk-monitoring function in OTC markets is left to the individual counterparties. Going into the crisis, neither market participants nor regulators had accurate knowledge of the full range of the exposures and interconnections of the various market participants. This leads to a counterparty risk externality, where each trade's counterparty risk is affected by other trades that are being done by other counterparties, although this information is not visible (see Acharya and Engle, 2009). The systemic risk arising from the collapse of Lehman Brothers is but one example of a counterparty risk externality. The government support provided to AIG during the crisis is another.

The Dodd–Frank Act, in theory, addresses these two problems through enhanced regulation and increased transparency of derivatives markets. In particular, the act calls for (1) central clearing of standardized derivatives, (2) regulation of complex ones that can remain OTC, in particular by imposing capital requirements, (3) transparency of all positions (that is, price/volume information for the public and position-level information for regulators), and (4) the separation of nonstandardized derivative positions (other than those for interest rate, foreign exchange, and single-name credit derivatives) into

[17] American International Group Inc. (2008), p. 122.

well-capitalized subsidiaries. As with other parts of the act, the implementation of the regulation is complicated by trying to define commercial hedging transactions (which are exempt) and standardized derivatives. The rules, for the most part, are still being written, so it remains an open question as to how effective the legislation will be.

That said, there are potential unintended consequences of the Dodd–Frank Act's reform of the derivatives market. Note that the act relies heavily on margin requirements as the first line of defense against leverage buildup through derivatives. In particular, a clearinghouse is required to charge margins such that it can withstand the failure of its largest exposure among the various members. Assuming that it is highly unlikely that two single members of a clearinghouse will default in the same day, this would mean the clearinghouse is reasonably well protected most of the time, and yet offers substantial collateral efficiency to its members. The problem, of course, arises during a systemic event when there might be multiple exposure failures. Tremendous amounts of systemic risk are housed within clearinghouses, with potentially catastrophic consequences for the financial system. Scrutiny of the clearinghouse system will be necessary; but if, as it looks likely, there are multiple clearinghouses, then a race to the bottom is possible, as they institute laxer standards to gain more members. Moreover, for derivative positions outside clearinghouses, there may be a clear cost to dealers and noncommercial users in making markets and trading these derivatives. To the extent that derivatives are useful tools to mitigate aggregate risk, they can potentially lower the systemic risk of SIFIs. This risk reduction role can warrant regulatory capital relief. That said, depending on how the margin rules are written under the Dodd–Frank Act, SIFIs might be pushed away from using derivatives.

References

Acharya, Viral V., Barry Adler, Matthew Richardson and Nouriel Roubini, 2010, "Resolution authority," in *Regulating Wall Street: The Dodd–Frank Act and the New Architecture of Global Finance*, Viral V. Acharya, Thomas Cooley, Matthew Richardson, and Ingo Walter (eds.), Hoboken, NJ: John Wiley and Sons, pp. 213–240.

Acharya, Viral V., Thomas Cooley, Matthew Richardson and Ingo Walter (eds.), 2010a, *Regulating Wall Street: The Dodd–Frank Act and the New Architecture of Global Finance*, Hoboken, NJ: John Wiley and Sons.

Acharya, Viral V., Thomas Cooley, Matthew Richardson and Ingo Walter, 2010b, "Manufacturing tail risk: A perspective on the financial crisis of 2007–2009," *Foundations and Trends in Finance*, Vol. 4, No. 4, pp. 247–325.

Acharya, Viral V. and Robert Engle, 2009, "Derivatives trades should all be transparent," *Wall Street Journal*, May 15, available at: http://online.wsj.com/article/SB124234528710721693.html.

Acharya, Viral V., Lasse Pedersen, Thomas Philippon and Matthew Richardson, 2010c, "Taxing systemic risk," in *Regulating Wall Street: The Dodd–Frank Act and the New Architecture of Global Finance*, Viral V. Acharya, Thomas Cooley, Matthew Richardson, and Ingo Walter (eds.), Hoboken, NJ: John Wiley and Sons, pp. 121–142.

Acharya, Viral V. and Matthew Richardson (eds.), 2009a, *Restoring Financial Stability: How to Repair a Failed System*, Hoboken, NJ: John Wiley and Sons.

Acharya, Viral V., Matthew Richardson, Stijn Van Nieuwerburgh and Lawrence J. White, 2011, *Guaranteed to Fail: Fannie Mae, Freddie Mac, and the Debacle of Mortgage Finance*, Princeton, NJ: Princeton University Press.

Acharya, Viral V., Or Shachar and Marti Subrahmanyam, 2010d, "Regulating OTC derivatives," in *Regulating Wall Street: The Dodd–Frank Act and the New Architecture of Global Finance*, Viral V. Acharya, Thomas Cooley, Matthew Richardson, and Ingo Walter (eds.), Hoboken, NJ: John Wiley and Sons, pp. 367–425.

Adler, Barry E., 1993, "Financial and political theories of American corporate bankruptcy," *Stanford Law Review*, Vol. 45, No. 2, January, pp. 311–346.

American International Group Inc., 2008, *2007 Annual Report*, New York, March 14, available at: www.ezodproxy.com/AIG/2008/AR2007/images/AIG_AR2007.pdf.

Bagehot, Walter, 1873, *Lombard Street: A Description of the Money Market*, 3rd ed., London: Henry S. King.

Bernanke, Ben S., 2009, "Ben Bernanke's greatest challenge," interview by Scott Pelley, *60 Minutes*, CBS, March 15 (updated on June 4, 2009), available at: www.cbsnews.com/8301-18560_162-4862191.html.

Caballero, Ricardo J. and Arvind Krishnamurthy, 2009, "Global imbalances and financial fragility," *American Economic Review*, Vol. 99, No. 2, May, pp. 584–588.

Federal Deposit Insurance Corporation, 2011, "The orderly liquidation of Lehman Brothers Holdings Inc. under the Dodd–Frank Act," *FDIC Quarterly*, Vol. 5, No. 2, pp. 31–49, available at: www.fdic.gov/bank/analytical/quarterly/2011_vol5_2/Article2.pdf.

Financial Stability Oversight Council, 2012, "Authority to require supervision and regulation of certain nonbank financial companies," *Federal Register*, Vol. 77, No. 70, April 11, pp. 21637–21662, available at: www.gpo.gov/fdsys/pkg/FR-2012-04-11/pdf/2012-8627.pdf.

Jackson, Thomas H., 2010, "Chapter 11F: A proposal for the use of bankruptcy to resolve financial institutions," in *Ending Government Bailouts as We Know Them*, Kenneth E. Scott, George P. Shultz, and John B. Taylor (eds.), Stanford, CA: Hoover Institution Press, pp. 217–251.

Kacperczyk, Marcin and Philipp Schnabl, 2010, "Implicit guarantees and risk taking: Evidence from money market funds," New York University, Stern School of Business, Department of Finance, working paper, September.

Malysheva, Nadezhda and John R. Walter, 2010, "How large has the federal financial safety net become?" *Economic Quarterly*, Federal Reserve Bank of Richmond, Vol. 96, No. 3, Third Quarter, pp. 273–290.

Portes, Richard, 2009, "Global imbalances," in *Macroeconomic Stability and Financial Regulation: Key Issues for the G20*, Mathias Dewatripont, Xavier Freixas, and Richard Portes (eds.), London: Centre for Economic Policy Research, pp. 19–26.

Ricks, Morgan, 2010, "Shadow banking and financial regulation," presentation at International Monetary Fund conference, Conference on Operationalizing Systemic Risk Monitoring, Washington, DC, May 27, available at: www.imf.org/external/np/seminars/eng/2010/mcm/pdf/Ricks.pdf.

Taylor, John B., 2009, "The financial crisis and the policy responses: An empirical analysis of what went wrong," National Bureau of Economic Research, working paper, No. 14631, January.

Tirole, Jean, 2010, "Lessons from the crisis," in *Balancing the Banks: Global Lessons from the Financial Crisis*, Mathias Dewatripont, Jean-Charles Rochet, and Jean Tirole (authors), Keith Tribe (trans.), Princeton, NJ: Princeton University Press, pp. 10–77.

Walter, John R. and John A. Weinberg, 2002, "How large is the federal financial safety net?" *Cato Journal*, Vol. 21, No. 3, Winter, pp. 369–393.

PART III

Financial Stability via Regulation

Part III of this volume includes discussions about regulatory reform resulting from Dodd–Frank as a means to improve financial market stability. A major theme in Dodd–Frank is that the more traditional microprudential regulatory tools, which address individual firms, may be inadequate to create a safe and stable financial system. There is a need for adding a more "macroprudential" approach aimed at affecting system-wide risks to complement the microprudential approaches (which also need to be improved). How will macroprudential regulation be implemented? If systemically important firms are to be treated differently, i.e., with more regulatory scrutiny, what criteria will be used in determining which firms are systemically important? How will the firm-specific level of scrutiny be calibrated? How will derivative markets be affected by movement away from bilateral, over-the-counter (OTC) market transactions? How is the implementation of new regulations proceeding? Here we present four unique perspectives on efforts to implement new regulations to generate a more stable financial system.

Daniel Tarullo, Governor at the Board of Governors of the Federal Reserve System, discusses how Dodd–Frank requires financial regulators to reemphasize financial stability. Although financial stability had historically driven most major financial market legislation (e.g., the Federal Reserve Act and the Banking Act of 1933), regulators and legislators tended to down-play it over the past 50 years. Instead, most regulatory efforts were aimed at the oversight of individual institutions. Dodd–Frank mandates that regulators refocus, and implement regulations aimed at containing systemic risk. He discusses a broad array of sources of systemic risk and means to develop a "financial stability regulatory system" aimed at containing that risk.

Mark Van Der Weide, senior associate director of supervision and regulation at the Board of Governors of the Federal Reserve System, discusses the Federal Reserve's on-going efforts to mitigate threats to financial stability. Much of his discussion addresses efforts directed at identifying and quantifying systemically important financial institutions (SIFIs), an issue that raised significant concerns when Dodd–Frank was originally passed. What criteria should be considered? What weights should be applied to the criteria? Once institutions have been identified, how should the regulatory agencies decide how to calibrate the regulatory apparatus to best address systemic concerns?

Scott O'Malia, commissioner of the Commodity Futures Trading Commission (CFTC), discusses how the CFTC has been implementing its responsibilities under the act. He raises concerns about whether the commission is keeping the market adequately informed about regulatory developments. Additionally, he expresses concern about the commission's ability to keep pace with industry developments and to leverage technology to support its enhanced regulatory role. He proposes a number of adjustments to the existing implementation processes.

Wayne Abernathy, executive vice president at the American Bankers Association, discusses the process by which the new regulations have been developed and implemented. As many of the act's original deadlines have been missed, Abernathy questions whether the process has gone as smoothly as suggested by financial regulators. However, he acknowledges the magnitude of the task and suggests that some modifications to the act may be necessary if its original intent is to be realized. He also raises concern about the competitive impact of the regulatory efforts across different classes of banks — for example, money center banks versus community banks.

Chapter 3

Financial Stability Regulation

Daniel K. Tarullo[1]

As one would expect of a piece of legislation that has 16 titles and runs 849 pages in the Statutes at Large, the Dodd–Frank Wall Street Reform and Consumer Protection Act ranges widely in addressing problems both directly and indirectly associated with the financial crisis. Taken as a whole, though, the primary aim of those 849 pages can fairly be read as a reorientation of financial regulation towards safeguarding "financial stability" through the containment of "systemic risk," phrases that both recur dozens of times throughout the statute. The law, explicitly in many provisions and implicitly in many others, directs the bank regulatory agencies to broaden their focus beyond the soundness of individual banking institutions, and the market regulatory agencies to move beyond their traditional focus on transaction-based investor protection.

This emphasis on financial stability and systemic risk is hardly surprising in light of the damage done by the financial crisis and the ensuing Great Recession, from which we continue to recover only slowly. Indeed, concern about financial stability and systemic risk has at times been a crucial impetus for financial reform in the United States. Much of the New Deal legislation that defined the financial regulatory structure for more than 40 years was in direct response to what we would today call systemic concerns, including banking panics and excessive leverage in equity markets. Twenty years before the New Deal, the creation of the Federal Reserve had been intended at least as much as a financial stability measure as an instrument of monetary policy.

---

[1]Daniel Tarullo is Governor, Board of Governors of the Federal Reserve System. This speech was presented on October 10, 2012 at the University of Pennsylvania Law School, Philadelphia, Pennsylvania.

But seen in the light of more recent history, Dodd–Frank represents something of an about-face for financial regulation, which had largely neglected systemic concerns in the decades preceding the crisis. Even the Sarbanes–Oxley Act of 2002, while far-reaching in many respects, was very much a traditional piece of securities legislation insofar as it focused on investor protection. Banking law reforms enacted after the 1980s savings and loan debacle had traces of concern with financial stability, but the emphasis was still on the regulation of individual depository institutions. Most other banking law changes of the 1980s and 1990s, culminating in the Gramm–Leach–Bliley Act in 1999, were essentially deregulatory.[2] These laws, along with the administrative actions that both preceded and implemented them, removed many restrictions on activities, affiliations, and the geographic reach of commercial banks without substituting new regulatory mechanisms to control the institution-specific risks that could arise from the growth of financial services conglomerates, much less the systemic risks created by the rapid integration of capital markets and traditional lending activities.[3] The major regulatory initiative of this period was the Basel II package of changes to capital requirements, an exercise whose shortcomings included an enhancement, rather than diminution, of regulatory incentive for procyclicality in bank lending, and thus could arguably *increase* systemic risk.

By the time financial stress began rising rapidly in the second half of 2007, systemic risk and financial instability had come to seem more theoretical than real to many regulators, academics, and financial market participants. There had been little in the way of Congressional discussion of systemic risk issues, and little in the way of well-developed recommendations. To be sure, some academics — mostly finance professors — and a few intrepid, heterodox voices among central bank research staffs identified risks that might be building and, in general terms, the need for macroprudential regulation to complement traditional microprudential oversight. But even they tended more to diagnosis and warning than to prescription. Thus, although major regulatory legislation is often preceded by long periods during which key ideas and proposals are circulated and discussed, Congress was writing on a mostly blank slate in crafting an immediate legislative response to the financial crisis.

---

[2]For example, the Garn–St. Germain Act of 1982, P.L. 97-320; 96 Stat. 1469, authorized banks to offer a deposit account with deregulated interest rates, and the Riegle–Neal Interstate Banking & Branching Efficiency Act of 1994, P.L. 103-328; 108 Stat. 2338, substantially liberalized restrictions on interstate banking.

[3]Section 108 of Gramm–Leach–Bliley did mention financial stability, but in the context of requiring a study of potential subordinated debt requirements for large insured depository institutions and bank holding companies whose failure could adversely affect financial stability.

The necessarily somewhat extemporized character of Dodd–Frank has had several consequences for the development of financial stability regulation. First, many of the new authorities and requirements of Dodd–Frank require extensive elaboration through administrative rulemaking, often coordinated or agreed among three or more agencies. Second, as I will explain in a moment, the provisions of the law that use the concept of risk-to-financial-stability as a directly applicable legal standard provides only general guidance for regulators in applying that standard. This is not unusual for statutes in new areas of regulation, but it still poses a challenge for regulators, particularly in the early stages of implementation or enforcement. Third, broad as Dodd–Frank is in some respects, it does not grant direct regulatory authority in some areas that academic and agency analysis suggests may pose systemic risk. Finally, the law made important institutional changes, creating novel governmental entities specifically designed to address financial stability, and binding existing agencies more closely together in their rulemaking and supervisory activities. The relationships among existing agencies and the evolving practice of these new entities may in turn pose some novel practical and administrative law issues.

My remarks this afternoon address some aspects of the job of creating a financial stability regulatory system in light of these features of Dodd–Frank and of the fact that theories of financial stability that might inform the fashioning of this system are in many respects still undeveloped or, at the least, contested. I will begin with a brief survey of Dodd–Frank's financial stability provisions before turning to a few examples.

Dodd–Frank as a statutory framework for financial stability regulation

Dodd–Frank creates a legal and institutional framework within which financial stability regulation is to be developed but, with a couple of notable exceptions, it does not delineate the steps that should actually be taken to promote financial stability. A useful point of comparison is the Banking Act of 1933, which did not use the terms "financial stability" or "systemic risk," but which specified the Glass–Steagall rule separating commercial from investment banking, limited transactions of banks with their affiliates, and established the federal deposit insurance system to prevent banking runs and panics. While statutory modifications and considerable administrative implementation of course followed over the years, the key elements of the regulatory scheme for financial stability were contained within the original legislation itself.

In contrast, there are relatively few Dodd–Frank provisions that more or less directly affect the policy changes intended to reduce risks to financial stability. Even the so-called Volcker Rule, which prohibits proprietary trading by banks, bank holding companies, and their affiliates,[4] will require considerable regulatory build-out before its constraints will be clear. Provisions that require only modest administrative interpretation, such as the limit on acquisitions that would bring a financial firm's consolidated liabilities to more than 10% of the aggregate consolidated liabilities of all financial companies,[5] are not central elements of the legislation. At the risk of some oversimplification, one can classify most uses of the financial stability concept in Dodd–Frank into four categories: (1) as a goal for a new regulatory authority, (2) as an instruction for ongoing analysis and monitoring, (3) as a direct legal standard, and (4) as a factor for consideration in decisions on applications for various proposed actions subject to regulatory approval.

First, financial stability is used as a stated goal motivating a new regulatory or supervisory authority without itself being the standard used in the realization of that authority. For example, Dodd–Frank reverses the restrictions that Gramm–Leach–Bliley placed on the powers of the Federal Reserve Board to examine subsidiaries of bank holding companies regulated by other agencies by referring explicitly to the Board's need to be informed of risks within the subsidiaries that may "pose a threat to … the stability of the financial system of the United States."[6] Another example is Section 165, which requires that the Federal Reserve establish a special set of prudential requirements for bank holding companies with more than $50 billion in assets in order to "prevent or mitigate risks to the financial stability of the United States that could arise from the material financial distress or failure, or ongoing activities of large, international financial institutions." Similarly, the far-reaching requirement in Title VII that five federal financial regulators establish margin requirements for uncleared swaps written by swap dealers and other major market participants is intended to "offset the greater risk to the [dealers] and the financial system arising from the use of [uncleared] swaps."[7]

Second, Dodd–Frank takes a number of steps to enhance the capacity of the government to monitor and analyze threats to financial stability. Most prominent among these are the creation of the Financial Stability Oversight Council (FSOC)

---

[4]DFA §619.

[5]DFA §622, adding Section 14 to the Bank Holding Company Act of 1956 (12 U.S.C. 1841 *et seq.*).

[6]DFA §604(b), amending §5(c)(2) of the Banking Holding Company Act.

[7]Section 731, amending Commodities Exchange Act by adding new Section 4s — this is §4s(e)(3)(A).

and the Office of Financial Research (OFR).[8] The FSOC is composed of ten voting and five nonvoting members — the heads of relevant federal offices and regulatory agencies, and three representatives of state financial regulators.[9] As I will discuss in a moment, the FSOC as a collective entity has a limited, though important, direct regulatory role. Much of its time, however, will be spent fulfilling its mandate from Congress to assess risks to financial stability, including — where appropriate — making recommendations for action to agencies under existing regulatory authority or to Congress to fill gaps in existing authority in response to identified systemic risks.[10] The stated purpose of OFR is to support the FSOC and its member agencies through research, the collection and standardization of data, the development of tools for measuring and monitoring risk, and related activities.[11] FSOC and OFR are each also required to make an annual report to Congress on financial stability.[12]

The third use of financial stability in Dodd–Frank is as a direct legal standard for the exercise of a regulatory authority, as opposed to my first category of Dodd–Frank provisions, which simply cite financial stability concerns as a motivation for a regulatory or supervisory program. To date, the most conspicuous of this type of provision have been the authorities granted the FSOC to designate nonbank financial companies and financial market utilities as "systemically important." The first of these authorities is directed at financial firms that are not

[8]Others include the authority granted the SEC to require reporting of certain information by hedge funds (§404) and the creation of a new Federal Insurance Office, which is charged with "identifying issues or gaps in the regulation of insurance that could contribute to a systemic crisis in the insurance industry or the United States financial system." 31 U.S.C. 313(c)(1)(A), as added by DFA §502.

[9]There are 10 voting members and 5 non-voting members. The voting members are the Secretary of the Treasury, who serves as the Chairperson of the FSOC; the Chairman of the Board of Governors of the Federal Reserve System; the Comptroller of the Currency; the Director of the Consumer Financial Protection Bureau; the Chairman of the Securities and Exchange Commission; the Chairperson of the Federal Deposit Insurance Corporation; the Chairperson of the Commodity Futures Trading Commission; the Director of the Federal Housing Finance Agency; the Chairman of the National Credit Union Administration Board; and an independent member with insurance expertise. The non-voting members are the Director of the OFR, the Director of the Federal Insurance Office, a state insurance commissioner selected by the state insurance commissioners, a state banking supervisor chosen by the state banking supervisors, and a state securities commissioner designated by the state securities supervisors.

[10]DFA §120. The FSOC is also required to issue an annual report to Congress assessing the impact of market and regulatory developments on, and threats to, the financial stability of the United States. DFA §112(a)(2)(N).

[11]DFA §153(a).

[12]DFA §111(2)(N) and §153(d).

bank holding companies, and thus not subject to capital requirements and other parts of the holding company regulatory regime. This authority is a direct response to experience in the financial crisis. During 2008, serious problems at AIG and the five so-called "free-standing" investment banks — that is, firms not part of a bank holding company — contributed substantially to the severe stress in the financial system, with the failure of Lehman Brothers in September igniting the most acute phase of the crisis.

The standard to be applied by the FSOC is whether "material financial distress at the U.S. nonbank financial company, or the nature, scope, size, scale, concentration, interconnectedness, or mix of the activities of the U.S. nonbank financial company, could pose a threat to the financial stability of the United States."[13] There follows a lengthy list of "considerations" to be taken into account by the FSOC. However, particularly insofar as the last of these is "any other risk-related factors that the Council deems appropriate,"[14] the list does not provide extensive guidance for the FSOC in applying the basic standard. Any companies so designated by the FSOC will be subject to supervision by the Federal Reserve, as well as to the special Section 165 prudential standards I mentioned earlier. To date, no firms have been designated, though the FSOC is actively considering possible designees. Of course, the five previously free-standing investment banks have either been dismantled (Lehman), converted into bank holding companies (Goldman Sachs and Morgan Stanley), or absorbed into a bank holding company (Bear Stearns and Merrill Lynch).

The other designation authority granted the FSOC is for financial market utilities, defined as multilateral transfer, clearing, or settlement systems for payments, securities, or other financial transactions among financial institutions.[15] Once designated as systemically important,[16] financial market utilities are subject to prudential standards established by the Federal Reserve, the Securities and Exchange Commission, and the Commodities Futures Trading Commission for the purpose of reducing systemic risk and supporting financial stability.[17] Here, in addition to providing considerations for the FSOC in making its determination, the statute elaborates the standard of "systemically important" a bit, defining that term to mean a situation "where the failure of or a disruption to the functioning of a financial market utility or the conduct of a payment, clearing or settlement

[13]DFA §113(C)(1).

[14]DFA §113(a)(2)(K).

[15]DFA §803(6).

[16]DFA §805.

[17]DFA §805.

activity could create, or increase, the risk of significant liquidity or credit problems spreading among financial institutions or markets and thereby threaten the stability of the financial system of the United States."[18] In July, the FSOC designated eight financial market utilities as systemically important and they are now subject to special risk-management standards.[19]

In addition to these designation authorities, Dodd–Frank grants the FSOC very broad scope for dealing with a large bank holding company or designated nonbank financial company that "poses a grave threat to the financial stability of the United States."[20] Upon the recommendation of the Board of Governors, the FSOC may limit mergers, products, or activities of the firm. If these actions are inadequate to mitigate the grave risk, the FSOC may require the firm to divest assets or off-balance sheet items.

The fourth use of financial stability in Dodd–Frank is as a factor to be taken into account in various regulatory determinations. So, for example, the list of considerations in the International Banking Act for the Federal Reserve in determining whether to permit the establishment of a foreign bank office, or to terminate an existing such office, was augmented with a financial stability factor — specifically, whether the home country of a bank that presents a risk to the stability of the U.S. financial system has taken, or is taking, appropriate regulatory steps to mitigate that risk.[21]

Similarly, Dodd–Frank added "risk to the stability of the U.S. banking or financial system" to the non-exhaustive lists of factors set forth in the Bank Merger Act and the Bank Holding Company Act for consideration by banking regulators in evaluating a proposed merger or acquisition by a bank or bank holding company. There are actually three statutory provisions governing these transactions — Section 3(c) of the Bank Holding Company Act for bank acquisitions by holding companies, Section 4(j) of the Bank Holding Company Act for nonbank acquisitions by holding companies, and the Bank Merger Act for mergers by banks. The statutory standards, and thus the import of the factors, are somewhat different.[22] In all three instances, however, the financial stability factor is not

---

[18]DFA §803(9).

[19]U.S. Department of the Treasury (2012). "Financial Stability Oversight Council Makes First Designations in Effort to Protect Against Future Financial Crises," press release, July 18.

[20]DFA §121(a).

[21]DFA §173.

[22]The two dealing with the acquisition of merger of banks simply require that each factor be "taken into consideration," whereas the provision for acquisition of nonbanks requires consideration of the factors in the context of a determination of whether the proposed transaction "can reasonably be expected to produce benefits to the public that outweigh possible adverse effects." 12 U.S.C. 1843(j)(2)(A).

in itself dispositive, in contrast to the statutory provisions covering designation of systemically important institutions or special actions to address grave threats to financial stability.

This brief review shows how ubiquitous the concepts of financial stability and systemic risk are in Dodd–Frank. The law creates or strengthens numerous forms of regulatory authority that can be used to control numerous practices or circumstances associated with financial instability. Yet the statute itself provides only limited guidance to regulators on how to implement financial stability where it is established as a standard, or how to weigh it against economic growth and other considerations where it is used as an informing concept for a regulatory exercise or a factor to be considered in regulatory approvals. Moreover, one does not really find in the statute or in its legislative history an implicit theory of financial stability from which to infer answers to the regulatory questions just noted. Instead, Dodd–Frank directs regulation at a number of perceived vulnerabilities created by large financial firms in particular, and to some degree in the financial system as a whole. To the extent one can fairly induce an underlying principle; it is that the moral hazard associated with too-big-to-fail institutions should be counteracted in a variety of ways.

The emphasis on too-big-to-fail institutions is both understandable and appropriate in light of the experiences of 2008, including the major injections of government capital to stabilize some of the nation's largest firms. And the absence of an informing, grand unified theory of financial stability is hardly surprising in light of the history to which I alluded earlier. Indeed, two years after passage of Dodd–Frank, there is not really an officially embraced consensus theory of how financial stability is undermined. The first report of the new OFR — one of the more useful analyses of financial stability issued by the official sector — does not attempt a theory of financial stability. It defines financial stability descriptively rather than analytically, "that the financial system is operating sufficiently to provide its basic functions for the economy even under stress,"[23] and pragmatically tries to identify risks and vulnerabilities.

Somewhat confusingly, and a bit unaccountably, the wording of the financial stability factor also differs. In the Bank Holding Company §4(j)(2)(A) and Bank Merger Act lists, the new factor is simply "risk to the stability of the United States banking or financial system." In the Bank Holding Company Act §3(c) list, the factor is "greater or more concentrated risks to the stability of the United States banking or financial system." While the import of this different wording does not seem great, it is unclear why it was chosen in this provision and not in the Bank Merger Act, which also covers bank acquisitions.

[23]Office of Financial Research, U.S. Department of the Treasury, *2012 Annual Report (PDF)* (Washington: Office of Financial Research), p. 1.

Yet much of the theoretical work on financial stability of the last several years has suggested that financial instability is, in important ways, endogenous to the financial system, or at least the kind of financial system that has developed in recent decades. The OFR Report just cited went on to note that the financial crisis had "served as a painful reminder that the financial system is prone to internal instability."[24] Contributions to the literature by academics such as Markus Brunnermeier, Gary Gorton, Perry Mehrling, Andrew Metrick, Hyun Song Shin, Andrei Shleifer, and Jean Tirole,[25] although differing in some important specifics, all paint a picture of a financial system prone to instability for reasons in addition to, and quite independent of, classic too-big-to-fail concerns. Their various analyses suggest the possibility of destabilization even in a financial world with no dominant firms, but many medium-sized entities.

This perspective focuses on one of the most important effects of the progressive integration of capital markets and conventional lending activities, something now popularly known as "shadow banking" — that is, credit intermediation involving maturity transformation, and often significant leverage, that is wholly or partly outside the traditional banking system. This intermediation depends critically on the creation of instruments that are thought to be safe and liquid, and as such, "cash equivalents" similar in function to insured deposits in the commercial banking system. These instruments, much desired by certain kinds of investors, are short-term liabilities of the shadow banking intermediary, which backs them with a portfolio of longer-term assets that, because of some combination of high diversification and low-default risk, are expected to perform very well under nearly all circumstances, but carry significant tail risks that are not fully appreciated ex ante.

A now notorious example of a shadow banking intermediary was a special investment vehicle (SIV) sponsored by a financial firm. A SIV bought tranches of securitized mortgages with AAA credit ratings, which it financed through the

---

[24]Office of Financial Research, *2012 Annual Report*, p. 16.

[25]Some representative examples include: Markus Brunnermeir, Andrew Crocket, Charles Goodhart, Avinash D. Persaud, and Hyun Shin (2009), "The Fundamental Principles of Financial Regulation," Geneva Reports on the World Economy 11 (Geneva, Switzerland: International Center for Monetary and Banking Studies, June); Gary Gorton and Andrew Metrick (2010), "Regulating the Shadow Banking System," Brookings Papers on Economic Activity (Washington, DC: Brookings Institution, Fall), pp. 261–297; Nicola Gennaioli, Andrei Shleifer, and Robert W. Vishny (2012), "Neglected Risks, Financial Innovation, and Financial Fragility," *Journal of Financial Economics*, Vol. 104(3), pp. 452–468; Perry Mehrling (2011), *The New Lombard Street* (Princeton, NJ: Princeton University Press); Jean Tirole (2011), "Illiquidity and All Its Friends," *Journal of Economic Literature*, Vol. 49(2), pp. 287–325.

issuance of short-term instruments that were regarded by investors as essentially a cash equivalent. But during the crisis, when tail risk materialized, investors came to understand that even the upper tranches of subprime and other mortgage securitizations might not be spared significant losses because of the dramatic fall in housing prices and the equally dramatic rise in defaults. At the same time, questions arose about the continued willingness and ability of sponsors to provide support to the SIVs, despite a history of their having done so on both contractual and discretionary bases. A kind of run ensued, as investors realized that their instruments were not truly "equivalent" to cash and refused to roll over their short-term funding of the shadow banking intermediary. Such SIVs are gone, but other forms of shadow banking continue in such well-established forms as money market funds and repo markets.

The vulnerability of shadow banking to runs, as investors rapidly withdraw funding, can lead to systemic problems as consequential as those associated with classic runs on traditional banks. If shadow banking intermediaries must rapidly liquidate longer-term assets that they can no longer fund, the impact extends across the financial system. The resulting declines in asset prices trigger margin calls on other investors, who may then need to deliver by selling their own holdings, accelerating the fire sale of these, and potentially other, assets. In the worst case, the result can be the kind of generalized asset price decline and liquidity freeze observed at the height of the financial crisis.

Dodd–Frank does include some significant provisions that, when implemented, could mitigate some of the risks associated with the shadow banking system and the potential for fire sales more generally. Among these are the requirements for margining of over-the-counter derivatives, increased use of central clearing facilities for derivatives, and higher prudential standards for systemically important financial market utilities. But Dodd–Frank does not fashion a far-reaching system of regulatory authority for the shadow banking system to parallel the one it creates for systemically important institutions, or even to address fully the significant connections — through implicit support and other channels — between the shadow banking system and systemically important institutions. This is particularly noteworthy, as there is clearly some potential for enhanced capital, liquidity, and other prudential requirements for bank holding companies to cause more activity to migrate to the shadow banking system.

With this background, I turn now to a closer look at a few instances of the challenges both in elaborating the financial stability standards of Dodd–Frank with respect to systemically important institutions and in addressing the shadow banking system.

Evaluating financial stability concerns associated with large institutions

As a prelude to this discussion, let me acknowledge that this is hardly the first time Congress has enacted intentionally protean statutory standards in response to a serious economic problem, and then relied on some combination of administrative regulation, law enforcement, and the courts to develop and adapt those standards as learning and experience grow. The antitrust laws provide a good example. The clause "contract, combination, or conspiracy in restraint of trade"[26] that is so familiar to us today posed its own major challenge of interpretation immediately after passage of the Sherman Act in 1890. Indeed, in the first cases brought under Section 1, both the Justice Department and the Supreme Court came close to reasoning that a very broad range of contracts by definition restrained some trade and thus might be illegal.[27] These interpretations were soon abandoned, but they stand as an admonition that early decisions under a new law can, in retrospect, look to have been somewhat makeshift.

Systemic risk capital surcharges

My first example is drawn from the Federal Reserve Board's experience in developing enhanced capital standards for bank holding companies with more than $50 billion in assets, as required by Section 165 of Dodd–Frank. As I noted a few moments ago, this is one of the Dodd–Frank provisions that establishes financial stability as its aim, but not as a direct statutory standard. Section 165 requires that the standards intended to prevent risks to financial stability increase in stringency, based on the same non-exhaustive list of factors used for the designation of non-bank systemically important financial firms,[28] but provides no further guidance.

In undertaking this task, we began with the premise that a financial stability motivation for capital requirements is necessarily somewhat different from the institution-centered approach of traditional capital standards, as embodied in the various Basel capital frameworks. Firm-centered requirements are informed by asking what level of capital would be necessary to allow the firm to remain a viable financial intermediary even after absorbing losses that, within a fairly high level of confidence, might be encountered over some relevant timeframe. The financial stability approach begins from the fact that there would be very large

[26] 15 U.S.C. §1.

[27] See, e.g., United States v. Trans-Missouri Freight Assn., 166 U.S. 290 (1897).

[28] Section 165(b)(3) adds two additional considerations: (1) whether the firm owns an insured depository institution and (2) the nonfinancial activities and affiliations of the firm.

negative externalities associated with the disorderly failure of any systemically important financial institution, distinct from the costs incurred by the firm and its stakeholders.

The failure of such a firm, especially in a period of stress, significantly increases the chances that other financial firms will themselves experience great stress, for two reasons. First, direct counterparty impacts can lead to a classic domino effect. Second, because losses in a tail event are much more likely to be correlated for firms deeply engaged in trading, structured products, and other capital market instruments, all such firms are vulnerable to accelerating losses as troubled firms sell their assets into a declining market. Enhanced capital requirements should take into account these costs that a systemically important firm's failure will inflict on the rest of the financial system, not the amount of loss its shareholders and creditors will incur. Thus, the aim of financial stability capital standards is to reduce further the probability that the firm might fail under stress through holding additional capital. These additional capital requirements can also help offset any funding advantage derived from the perceived status of such institutions as too-big-to-fail.

In acting on this rationale for capital standards to mitigate risks to financial stability, we first sought to ensure that there would be an international initiative to develop financial stability capital standards for global systemically important financial institutions, since the severe distress or failure of a foreign banking institution of broad scope and global reach could have effects on the U.S. financial system comparable to those caused by failure of a similar domestic firm. The Basel Committee agreed to take up this agenda and is well on its way to completing a framework covering more than two dozen large financial firms from around the world. Our intention has been to make our enhanced capital standards under Section 165 congruent with the Basel Committee's framework.

The task of determining how much additional capital is needed to reduce the probability of a systemically important firm's failure to more acceptable levels is not a straightforward one. Conceptually, there is a good starting point, in what has been termed the "expected impact" approach, which calls for additional capital to reduce the probability of the firm's failure sufficiently to equalize the expected impact on the financial system of the failure of a systemically important firm and the failure of a banking firm just outside systemic status.[29]

[29]For example, if the loss to the financial system from the failure of a systemically important firm would be five times that resulting from failure of the non-systemic firm, then the firm would have to hold additional capital sufficient to make the expected probability of failure one-fifth that of the non-systemic institution.

But implementing this concept is complicated by the fact that, despite some very useful metrics that have been developed in the last few years for measuring the systemic risk associated with a particular firm, there is certainly no generally accepted approach.[30] Each has its shortcomings as well as its strengths. Thus it is not realistic to think that, at least in the foreseeable future, the concept of a capital surcharge precisely offsetting the systemic risk actually created by that firm can be achieved in practice. Indeed, differences among reasonable assumptions in applying the expected impact approach led to a fairly broad range of potential surcharges. The 1–2.5% amounts negotiated within the Basel Committee are at the low end of that range, reflecting a good deal of caution — frankly, a bit more caution than I think would have been desirable, even given the uncertainties. Moreover, the Basel Committee decided to use "buckets," grouping banks presenting roughly similar risks, rather than a customized calibration based on a single score. Even though the Basel Committee does have an algorithm that produces such a score, it recognized that there is inevitably imprecision involved, and thus will look for obvious breaks in these scores in order to assign the banks to a limited number of buckets carrying differing capital surcharges.[31]

---

[30] Among the useful efforts along these lines are a measure of Conditional Value-at-Risk (CoVaR) (See Tobias Adrian and Markus Brunnermeier (2011), *CoVaR (PDF)*, Federal Reserve Bank of New York Staff Reports 348 (New York: Federal Reserve Bank of New York, September) and a measure of systemic risk based on each firm's contribution to the expected capital shortfall of the entire financial system in a crisis (See Christian T. Brownlees and Robert F. Engle (2011), "Volatility, Correlation and Tails for Systemic Risk Measurement," New York University Working Paper (New York: New York University, June). The concept behind the latter measure is also described in Viral V. Acharya, Christian Brownlees, Farhang Farazmand, and Matthew Richardson, "Measuring Systemic Risk," in *Regulating Wall Street: The Dodd–Frank Act and the New Architecture of Global Finance* (Wiley Publishers, 2011), pp. 87–119. Updated systemic risk rankings are maintained by the authors at http://vlab.stern.ny.edu. A helpful review of the efforts to measure systemic risk is Monica Billio, Mila Getmansky, Andrew W. Lo, and Loriana Pelizzon (2010), "Measuring Systemic Risk in the Finance and Insurance Sectors," MIT Sloan School Working Paper 4774-10 (Cambridge, MA: MIT Sloan School of Management, March).

[31] It is worth noting, in this regard, that in developing systemic risk capital requirements one early idea was to construct a continuously varying function for calculating a systemic risk surcharge. That is, a formula for calculating a firm's "systemic footprint" based on relevant characteristics such as size of assets, liabilities, counterparty exposures, and the like would yield a specific capital surcharge for each firm with more than $50 billion in assets. While the difficulties with this approach went beyond the false precision that it would have given the surcharge that was certainly one consideration in declining to adopt this approach.

Financial stability analysis in merger applications

The second interpretive challenge, which I will address in more detail, arises from the addition of a financial stability factor to the review conducted by the Federal Reserve Board of proposed mergers and acquisitions involving banks and bank holding companies.[32] In some respects, this process resembles the pre-merger reviews conducted by the antitrust agencies under the Hart–Scott–Rodino Act. But the differences are also instructive. One is that under the Bank Holding Company Act, the impact of a transaction on financial stability is not itself dispositive. The Board could approve an acquisition even if it determined that there was some adverse effect on financial stability if it also determined that the transaction would produce benefits outweighing the financial stability concerns by, for example, increasing competition or efficiencies or public convenience. This balancing requirement contrasts with an antitrust pre-merger review, in which the focus is solely on whether the transaction would substantially lessen competition.[33] The statutory formulation appears to reflect a Congressional supposition that, like many social desiderata, the pursuit of financial stability may at times

[32]Another important provision requiring interpretation of financial stability as a legal standard is the designation of systemically important nonbank institutions by the FSOC. As noted earlier, this is an instance in which an evaluation of financial stability effects is the direct test for action. In implementing this authority the FSOC took a methodical, comparative approach. Details can be found in Financial Stability Oversight Council (2012), "Authority to Require Supervision and Regulation of Certain Nonbank Financial Companies," Federal Register, Vol. 77 (April 11), pp. 21637. In the first stage of the process it has established, the FSOC applies a purely quantitative screen in order to identify nonbank financial companies that merit further consideration. In Stage 2, the Council conducts an in-depth analysis of each firm that has been identified through the Stage 1 screens, based on information that is either publicly available or already in the possession of financial regulators. After this analysis is complete, firms that the Council believes merit further consideration will be moved into Stage 3, during which information will also be collected directly from the firms. On the basis of this review, the Council may vote by the necessary two-thirds majority to designate the firm as systemically important. The Council has also elaborated, in general terms, the conditions under which it would determine that a "threat to financial stability" may exist and the transmission channels through which distress at a firm could affect the broader economy. What is noteworthy for my purposes today — beyond the elaborate nature of this exercise — is that ultimately the FSOC will make each determination on a very company-specific basis, with attention to the particular risks posed by each individual company. Indeed, recognizing that the assessment of different kinds of financial firms may require varying analytic frameworks, the FSOC has segmented its work. So, for example, it will consider asset managers and hedge funds separately from other forms of financial intermediaries.

[33]In fact, of course, the antitrust agencies and the courts have over the years given greater or lesser weight to possible efficiencies resulting from a merger, thereby introducing a consideration other than competition as such.

require trade-offs with other desirable aims. This conclusion is reinforced by other parts of Dodd–Frank, such as the earlier-mentioned provision permitting extraordinary measures to be imposed on a firm, but only if it is found to pose a *grave* threat to financial stability.

Another salient point of difference is that Hart–Scott–Rodino was not enacted until 1976, following more than 60 years of merger analysis by the antitrust agencies and merger jurisprudence by the courts. Indeed, the agencies had already published a set of merger guidelines in 1968. While the Antitrust Division or the Federal Trade Commission could, and did, begin pre-merger reviews with a well-developed analytic framework, there is no legacy of administrative or judicial analysis of the financial stability effects of mergers. We literally have had to start from scratch. Let me describe just a few of the conceptual and practical issues that have already arisen in discussions at the Board on some hypothetical situations that might arise in implementing the required consideration of financial stability.[34]

One important issue is raised by the possibility that an acquisition may decrease the chances of material distress at a financial firm while simultaneously increasing the potential negative externality on the financial system as a whole should the firm nonetheless become seriously compromised. To borrow credit risk terminology, the probability of default (PD) may be reduced, but the loss given default (LGD) may increase. You can imagine this circumstance where, for example, an acquisition would demonstrably reduce a firm's dependence on short-term wholesale funding by providing more deposits or other reliable funding sources, but where the firm's increased size and market connections would compound the damage to counterparties, intermediation, and asset markets in the event of unmanageable stress. In such a case, are risks to financial stability increased, unaffected on balance, or actually decreased?

In theory, as is done in credit risk modeling to calculate capital needs, one could multiply PD by LGD to yield a single "systemic financial risk" number for both the status quo and the post-acquisition firm, in order to determine — or at least create a presumption of — which outcome is preferable from a financial stability perspective. This would be the financial stability equivalent of the Herfindahl–Hirschman Index (HHI) in antitrust.[35] But we are still in the relatively

[34]As noted earlier, the two governing provisions in the Bank Holding Company Act differ somewhat. For the present purpose of discussing financial stability analysis, however, we need not dwell on these differences.

[35]The HHI is calculated by squaring the market share of each firm in a particular market and then adding those squared market shares. The antitrust agencies have specified the relative level of scrutiny

early stages of exploring the utility of different approaches to measuring both these variables, and we do not have a single well-established metric for either variable today. As already noted in my discussion of systemic risk surcharges, the quantification of a "systemic LGD" seems particularly challenging.

A second issue is time contingency. Consider an acquisition that, in calm times, seems pretty clearly to increase the systemic footprint of an already large, interconnected acquiring institution without having a material positive effect on the resilience of that firm during a stress period. That starkly stated circumstance would seem a prototypical case in which a conclusion of an adverse effect on financial stability would be reached. But now suppose that the target firm is already under substantial pressure in an increasingly stressed financial environment and that the potential acquirer appears relatively strong. A case could be made that allowing the acquisition in that circumstance would *support* financial stability by relieving funding and other counterparty pressures, and forestalling distressed asset sales and other problematic developments. Continuing my comparison to antitrust law, this outcome would be an analogue to a failing firm defense.

Of course, this was precisely the rationale in 2008 for the government not only permitting, but encouraging, JP Morgan's acquisition of Bear Stearns and Washington Mutual, Bank of America's acquisition of Merrill Lynch and, to some degree, Wells Fargo's acquisition of Wachovia.[36] The result is that the concentration at the top of the U.S. financial services industry is even greater than before the crisis. Allowing the acquisition I have hypothesized here could buy some immediate stabilization, but at the cost of arguably greater moral hazard and risks to financial stability over the medium term. The orderly liquidation authority for systemically important institutions created by Dodd–Frank may provide a third alternative, but even if implemented successfully and as intended, the new Title II would be most effective in containing moral hazard by ensuring that shareholders and management of the failed firm bear heavy costs. It would not necessarily prevent all the damage to the financial system and the broader economy that would attend failure of a large financial firm.

A third kind of issue arises specifically because of the transaction-driven nature of the Bank Holding Company Act merger review provisions. Some of these issues are procedural or practical in nature. For example, in evaluating the

---

that can be expected from particular combinations of changes in, and post-merger HHIs, although they are careful to point out that HHI is not a "rigid screen." U.S. Department of Justice, Horizontal Merger Guidelines §5.3 (August 19, 2009).

[36]In the Wells-Wachovia and JPMorgan-Washington Mutual cases, concerns about the impact of Wachovia's failure on the Deposit Insurance Fund may also have played a role.

impact of a proposed acquisition on financial stability, should a firm get "credit" for recent or planned actions to reduce its systemic footprint through sales of subsidiaries or other assets? This would be an analogue to the divestitures that are often required as a condition of merger approvals by the antitrust agencies. If a similar idea were implemented in the financial stability context, should the package of asset acquisitions and reductions be negotiated beforehand with supervisors and, if so, would that package itself have to be subject to Board approval?

Other issues presented by the focus on specific transactions go deeper. Suppose a large regional bank and a broker–dealer proposed to merge. Standing alone, that transaction might well look to increase risks to financial stability, not only because of the initial combined size of the firms, but because the broker–dealer operation would presumably grow when affiliated with a larger commercial bank, since the merged firm could offer a greater range of services to clients. But would prohibiting that transaction mean that the current small group of very large, integrated financial firms would have their market positions essentially protected by the financial stability considerations? Such an outcome would be ironic indeed. The Federal Reserve could, if it so chose, avail itself of the discretion to balance different effects by allowing the merger on pro-competition grounds. Such a decision would place the Fed in the position of effectively deciding broader questions of industry structure in the context of a single case. But, then again, a prohibition of the merger would do the same, the only difference being the substantive structure being chosen.

Yet even before this kind of balancing of positive and adverse effects was reached, there would surely be an argument that ensconcing the existing large integrated firms would itself increase risks to financial stability, since these firms that are each the product of prior mergers might be the only ones capable of growing more in key parts of the financial services market. Here again, the absence of a theory of financial stability that informs the law complicates the problem, though it is not altogether clear that convergence around such a theory would solve it.

The foregoing questions underscore the difficulties entailed in anticipating the range of financial issues that may be presented in merger cases and in trying to resolve the issues that have been anticipated solely through consideration of hypotheticals. This conclusion is one of the reasons the Federal Reserve decided not to develop and issue a rule or detailed guidance on the financial stability factor. There simply isn't the accumulation of experience and of thoughtful evaluation of these issues by people both in and out of government to inform something akin to the merger guidelines published by the antitrust agencies.

Accordingly, the Federal Reserve is very much taking a case-by-case approach to these reviews. As described in a recent order, "the Board expects that it will generally find a significant adverse effect if the failure of the resulting firm, or its inability to conduct regular-course-of-business transactions, would likely impair financial intermediation or financial market functioning so as to inflict damage on the broader economy."[37] The Board will consider a variety of factors that could indicate the potential for damage, including the size of the resulting firm, the availability of substitute providers for any critical products or services, the interconnectedness of the firm with the banking and financial system, the contribution of the firm to the complexity of the financial system, and the extent of cross-border activities of the firm.[38] I would expect that, over time, our discussion of these factors in the context of specific transactions will provide firms, their attorneys, and other members of the public with more guidance as to how a specific case is likely to be analyzed. At some point, we and others in the official sector may become comfortable enough with a particular measure of systemic risk that it will be a starting point for analysis in these cases. But I suspect it will be much longer, if ever, before such a measure could provide the extent of presumptive sorting that HHI does in antitrust analysis today.

While the absence of experience and a comprehensive informing theory make detailed guidance infeasible in the foreseeable future, I do think we should be able to elaborate certain categories of presumptive approvals and denials more quickly. Before I suggest how, let me emphasize that here I am speaking for myself only, since the full Board will address these issues only in future orders. We have already suggested a limited presumptive safe harbor where an acquisition involves less than $2 billion in assets or results in a firm with less than $25 billion in total assets.[39] Personally, I would set the size of the resulting firm higher than $25 billion, but somewhat lower than the $50 billion Dodd–Frank threshold over which a firm is subject to special prudential standards.

At the other end of the spectrum, I would urge a strong, though not irrebuttable, presumption of denial for any acquisition by any firm that falls in the higher end of the list of global systemically important banks developed by the Basel Committee for purposes of assessing capital surcharges.[40] Firms at the lower end

[37]Board of Governors of the Federal Reserve, Capital One Financial Corporation, McLean, Virginia, Order Approving the Acquisition of a Savings Association and Nonbanking Subsidiaries (PDF), FRB Order No. 2012-2 (February 14, 2012) at p. 28.

[38]Board of Governors of the Federal Reserve, Order Approving Acquisition, pp. 28–29.

[39]Board of Governors of the Federal Reserve, Order Approving Acquisition, p. 30.

[40]There are eight U.S. banks on this list, as well as many foreign-based firms with significant U.S. operations. However, the buckets to which they will be assigned will not be finalized under more up-to-date data is available and analyzed next year. Once final agreement has been reached by the Basel Committee, ordering the systemically important banks into categories with progressively increasing

of the Basel Committee list, or that U.S. authorities may later designate as domestic systemically important banks under a parallel Basel Committee exercise,[41] might have a slightly less robust, but still significant presumption against acquisitions. I would not apply the presumption in the case of certain *de minimis* acquisitions or in cases where asset dispositions were judged to offset any increase in systemic risk from the proposed new acquisition.

It is reasonable to ask why these negative presumptions are appropriate, given my general view that the absence of both experience and consensus theory make a case-by-case approach necessary. One answer is that, notwithstanding the fact that analytic tools for assessing a firm's systemic footprint are in a relatively early stage of development, everything we *do* know suggests that the firms on the Basel Committee list strongly implicate the kinds of systemic considerations mentioned by Congress. Second, it does seem incumbent on us to provide at least *some* guidance to firms where we can, particularly to inform smaller, less connected firms of the kinds of mergers that are unlikely to raise financial stability concerns and, conversely, to give firms that are already of systemic importance a sense of which mergers will face very close scrutiny.

A third answer is that, once an acquisition is consummated, Dodd–Frank provides only narrow authority to order divestiture on financial stability grounds. Though the Board can recommend action by the FSOC, I have already noted that the test for such action is "grave threat to financial stability," presumably a significantly higher standard than the "risk to financial stability" that can constitute an adverse effect for purposes of Sections 3 and 4 of the Bank Holding Company Act. Unlike Section 7 of the Clayton Act, which permits the antitrust authorities either to restrain a merger beforehand or undo it thereafter, the Federal Reserve's authority under the Bank Holding Company Act to disallow the merger on

---

surcharges, the Federal Reserve Board intends to propose matching provisions for covered U.S. banks under its Section 165 authority. In conducting our annual reviews of the capital levels and planning processes of major U.S. bank holding companies, we have already instructed the eight firms on the Basel Committee list to include their estimated required surcharge in their plan for reaching their ultimate capital requirement.

[41] The Basel Committee has not yet completed its work on this initiative. Its proposal has been published in Basel Committee on Banking Supervision, Consultative Document on a Framework for Dealing with Domestic Systemically Important Banks (June 2012). The proposal is that national authorities would designate these institutions (as compared to the global systemically important banks, which are to be designated by the Basel Committee itself), and that the nature of the enhanced loss absorbency for any such institutions also be left to national discretion (as compared to the global systemically important banks, for which capital surcharges are to be required and their amounts specified by the Basel Committee).

financial stability grounds appears to lapse after the merger is completed, but for the narrow authority vested in the FSOC. Of course, one motivation for the passage of Hart–Scott–Rodino in 1976 was the perceived reluctance of courts to order potentially disruptive divestitures once companies had completed the merger. In any case, the legal and practical impediments to such action counsel an additional measure of caution by the Federal Reserve in considering acquisitions by firms that can reasonably be expected to raise significant financial stability concerns.

For all the attention paid to financial stability analysis in the last few years, it is still — relatively speaking — a fledgling enterprise. Even if we hypothesize a viable working theory of financial stability that commands a rough consensus, translating that theory into administrable standards and processes is a task that will take years.[42] But while the absence of well-established systemic risk measures may counsel caution in approaching merger analysis, and while it has surely already affected the formulation of capital surcharges in the Basel Committee, it may well be leaving a gap in financial stability regulation. One of the difficulties in building out a financial stability analysis is the absence of an upper bound point of reference. There is no statutory basis for identifying a certain systemic footprint above which the risks to financial stability are not worth bearing compared to whatever possible benefits may be associated with the operation of the largest, most interconnected firms.

Similarly, the absence in the financial stability area of the equivalent of the monopolization provision in Sherman Act Section 2 to complement the merger provisions in Clayton Act Section 7 creates an anomalous regulatory feature. It means that the current structure for financial stability regulation permits substantial increases in systemic risk by an institution, so long as it is generated from internal growth. To the extent that a growing systemic footprint increases perceptions of at least some residual too-big-to-fail quality in such a firm, notwithstanding the panoply of measures in Dodd–Frank and our regulations, there may be funding advantages for the firm, which reinforces the impulse to grow. There is, then, a case to be made for specifying an upper bound.

In these circumstances, however, with the potentially important consequences of such an upper bound and of the need to balance different interests and social goals, it would be most appropriate for Congress to legislate on the subject. If it

[42] A paper by Katharina Pistor explains how the regulatory implications of three different theories of financial stability would differ. Katharina Pistor (2012), "On the Theoretical Foundations for Regulating Financial Markets," Columbia Law School Public Law & Legal Theory Working Paper 12-304, June.

chooses to do so, there would be merit in its adopting a simpler policy instrument, rather than relying on indirect, incomplete policy measures such as administrative calculation of potentially complex financial stability footprints. The idea along these lines that seems to have the most promise would limit the non-deposit liabilities of financial firms to a specified percentage of U.S. gross domestic products, as calculated on a lagged, averaged basis. In addition to the virtue of simplicity, this approach has the advantage of tying the limitation on growth of financial firms to the growth of the national economy and its capacity to absorb losses, as well as to the extent of a firm's dependence on funding from sources other than the stable base of deposits. While Section 622 of Dodd–Frank contains a financial sector concentration limit, it is based on a somewhat awkward and potentially shifting metric of the aggregated consolidated liabilities of all "financial companies."

Of course, the difficult question would be the applicable percentage of GDP. The answer would depend on a judgment as to how much of an impact the economy could absorb. It would also entail a judgment as to how large and complex a firm needs to be in order to achieve significant economies of scale and scope that carry social benefit. Depending on the answers to these questions, there may be a need to balance the relevant costs and benefits. There would also be important secondary questions such as whether to exclude from a firm's calculated liabilities only insured deposits and which asset base to use in calculating non-deposit liabilities. And depending on how Congress answered all these questions, there could well be need for defining transition periods and compliance margins. Even good answers to all these questions would produce a policy instrument that could seem excessively blunt to some. But this is a debate well worth having.

Financial stability and the shadow banking system

Having just a few months ago devoted an entire speech to the shadow banking system,[43] I wanted to spend more time today on the interpretive issues just discussed. However, to give a sense of the complementary regulatory challenges in dealing with the shadow banking system, let me describe one specific, current issue and just briefly mention a much broader concern.

---

[43]Daniel K. Tarullo (2012), "Shadow Banking After the Financial Crisis," remarks delivered at the Federal Reserve Bank of San Francisco Conference on Challenges in Global Finance, San Francisco, California, June 12.

The specific issue is that of money market funds. As many of us in the government have pointed out, money market funds remain a major part of the shadow banking system and a key potential systemic risk even in the post-crisis financial environment. In fact, the industry's survival in its present form is likely due in no small part to the unprecedented interventions by the Treasury and the Federal Reserve in providing insurance and liquidity support, respectively, to the industry in response to the run prompted by the failure of the Reserve Primary Fund in 2008.

The interesting point here is that a regulatory agency, the Securities Exchange Commission (SEC), has ample regulatory authority to address the systemic risk problem. Indeed, the legality of money market funds continuing to publish a fixed net asset value (NAV) of $1 per share, even as the actual value of the underlying assets varies within a modest range, is itself the consequence of the SEC's Rule 2a-7, which exempts money market mutual funds from the requirement of a floating NAV generally applicable to open-end mutual funds. In amending its rules in 2010, the SEC took some good first steps to improve the resilience of money market funds, but many — including Chairman Schapiro — do not believe these are sufficient to mitigate the run potential in money market funds.

Unfortunately, a majority of the current SEC commissioners has to this point been opposed to moving forward with the reform measures Chairman Schapiro has proposed. The FSOC, meanwhile, has endorsed further reform along these general lines. The question, then, is how the FSOC and its other member agencies should proceed given that the SEC has declined to act. I should note here that, during the debates preceding Dodd–Frank, some versions of proposals for what eventually became the FSOC would have empowered the FSOC to override agency action or inaction within its sphere of authority. Others, including many who favored strong reforms, opposed this power, which would have created a kind of super-agency with veto authority over all the regulators. Instead, the FSOC has the more limited authority to present an agency with recommendations for action and the right to receive an explanation should the agency not accept those recommendations.

As you may have seen, two weeks ago Treasury Secretary Geithner sent a letter to the members of the FSOC in his capacity as its chair, in which he urged the Council to use its authority under Section 120 of Dodd–Frank, and to consider alternative actions to reduce the structural vulnerabilities associate with money market funds "in the event the SEC is unwilling to act in a timely manner."[44]

[44]Treasury Secretary Timothy F. Geithner (2012), letter to members of the Financial Stability Oversight Council, September 27.

These alternatives could include FSOC designation of money market funds as systemically important and thus subject to the prudential requirements promulgated under Dodd–Frank. They could also include action by FSOC member agencies, such as the bank regulatory agencies imposing restrictions on regulated financial institutions' ability to sponsor, borrow from, invest in, or provide credit to money market funds that do not have structural protections. From my perspective, at least, each of the options open to the FSOC and the rest of its constituent agencies is decidedly a second-best alternative as compared to a change in SEC rules to remove the fixed NAV exception, to require a capital buffer that would staunch or buffer runs, or measures of similar effect. And, when I say second-best here, I mean to include the funds themselves. The protective tools available to the rest of us do not fit the problem precisely and thus will not regulate at the least cost to the funds while still mitigating financial risk. But that is the legal situation we all confront. My hope, of course, is that recent indications that other SEC commissioners are now willing to move forward with reforms will lead to the SEC adopting first-best measures in the near-term.

The money market fund example is a noteworthy case study in substantial part because of the interesting institutional issues it raises. More generally, though, the capacity of private financial market actors to create what are, at least in normal times, considered cash equivalents raises broader financial stability questions. Specifically, there may be a need for new macroprudential instruments, such as comprehensive authority to impose margins on all cash-like instruments, regardless of whether a firm creating those instruments is a regulated entity such as a bank holding company. Such possibilities obviously carry significant consequences, not just for the liquidity available to the financial system, but also for values such as the concentration of governmental authority. This is a topic on which much further thought is needed.

Conclusion

It may not always be the case that the most interesting time to be involved in a regulatory area is at its early stages, but I am reasonably certain it applies to the formation of a system for the regulation of systemic risk. From the standpoint of a regulator, the key challenge in these early stages is to be neither excessively self-confident about what we know about financial stability so as to produce unfortunate unintended consequences, nor excessively tentative so as to fail to take steps to counter the very real risks that do exist, in keeping with the aims stated by Congress. As I hope was apparent, that effort at balance informed my suggestions as to how we should apply the financial stability factor in our pre-merger reviews under the Bank Holding Company Act.

Before concluding, I want to make one final reference to antitrust law. As you know, the evolution of antitrust in recent decades was heavily influenced by the work of academics — specifically, law professors and industrial organization economists. That was due in part, I think to the practice of the Antitrust Division of the Justice Department and the Competition Bureau of the Federal Trade Commission recruiting so many present and future academics to work in those agencies for a few years. Indeed, quite a few heads of the Antitrust Division and the FTC were themselves academics, often law professors. The result was a cross-pollination of theoretical advances and institutionally grounded knowledge that is unusual, if not unique in regulatory areas. While it may be difficult to replicate this pattern in the nascent field of financial stability regulation, there is ample room — and need — for some version of this cross-pollination. Issues such as those I have discussed today can only profit from an academic perspective, informed by practical and institutional considerations. Obviously, I am standing this afternoon in front of an almost ideal audience to provide that perspective, and I look forward to hearing your lectures in the future.

Chapter 4

Implementing Dodd–Frank: Identifying and Mitigating Systemic Risk

Mark Van Der Weide[1]

The 2008 financial crisis revealed some basic flaws in our financial system and in our financial regulatory framework. Specifically, the crisis demonstrated that the failure or the material financial distress of some of our largest, most complex firms could pose a threat to the financial stability of the United States.

The crisis also made manifest that the existing framework for government oversight of our major financial firms and our authority for resolving those firms when they get into trouble were suboptimal. Bankruptcy proceedings, which could be quite panic-inducing, and federal government assistance were the only available options for addressing the failures of some of these large, nonbank financial firms.

As a result of these infirmities in our regulatory framework and the imprudent risk-taking of many financial firms, unprecedented government assistance was necessary to support these firms and the broader financial system to prevent an economic catastrophe. Market participants before the crisis assumed there was a nonzero probability that our most colossal firms would receive government assistance if they became troubled. But the actions taken by the federal government during the crisis, although necessary, I think, to prevent the implosion of our financial system and significant damage to the real economy, have certainly solidified this market perception.

---

[1]Mark Van Der Weide is Senior Associate Director in the Division of Banking Supervision and Regulation at the Board of Governors of the Federal Reserve System. The material in this article was originally published in the Federal Reserve Bank of Chicago's *Economic Perspectives,* Volume 36, 3rd quarter, 2012. The views expressed are those of the author and may not be those of the Board of Governors of the Federal Reserve System or other members of its staff.

So taking on this moral hazard problem, this "too-big-to-fail" (TBTF) problem, and the threats to financial stability that are imposed by our most systemic financial firms are the central goals of the Dodd–Frank Wall Street Reform and Consumer Protection Act and of the Fed's implementation of the act. That will be the focus of my remarks today.

Addressing problems with "systemically important financial institutions" (SIFIs) is a necessary condition to protecting financial stability. However, it is not a sufficient condition. Systemic risk can certainly be generated and propagated outside of our largest financial firms. It can arise in systemic herds, that is, collections of firms that individually may not be systemic but collectively are systemic. Money market mutual funds would be a great example of that. It can arise in common funding patterns across broad financial sectors, and it can arise in collective underestimations of risk by the financial sector broadly during an irrationally exuberant credit boom. So efforts to tamp down on systemic risk need to address the SIFI problem at a minimum, but they also need to pitch themselves quite a bit more broadly.

In this article, I will outline some of the core efforts that the Federal Reserve has been taking to implement the Dodd–Frank Act (DFA) and some related reforms to improve supervision and regulation of the most systemic firms and also to promote financial stability. I will also discuss some of the key challenges the Fed faces in implementing the act. I'll start by describing some of the work we have been doing as part of the Financial Stability Oversight Council (FSOC) and then rotate pretty quickly to talk about things that we are doing independently.

Work of the Financial Stability Oversight Council

The DFA created the FSOC principally to help identify and mitigate threats to the financial stability of the United States. We have made some meaningful progress as we have established the organizational structure of the FSOC, and its committee structure was designed to help us get our duties done.

We have also completed a number of studies that were required by the act on some of the important provisions in Dodd–Frank, including the Volcker Rule, financial sector concentration limits, risk retention, and the macroeconomic effects of systemic risk regulation. And we are working on additional studies, including one on contingent capital instruments and secured creditor haircuts.

A key task of the FSOC in the coming months will be to finalize its conceptual framework for identifying and designating nonbank financial firms that could pose a threat to financial stability. The council has issued for public comment several advance notices of proposed rulemaking and several proposed rulemaking documents on how to get that job done. What should the substantive framework be and what should the process be for designating such firms?

Consistent with SIFI identification principles that the Financial Stability Board (FSB) has articulated, the council has indicated that the core factors that we intend to look at when deciding whether a particular firm is systemic are size, interconnectedness, and availability of substitutes for the services provided by the firm. A set of secondary factors has also been identified that includes the extent of leverage, maturity transformation, and the extent of existing regulation that applies to those firms. Now, those six factors are obviously concepts — they are not formulas. It is going to take a lot of work to figure out within each of those categories how to quantify systemic importance and how to weigh the categories against each other.

Many comments on the FSOC's proposals in this area have urged us to be as transparent as possible about the standards by which firms will be designated. And we are looking for ways to increase the predictability of council decision-making in this area. It is important that we be consistent, though, with our prevailing need, I think, for an adaptive SIFI designation framework that is robust to financial innovation and to the intense heterogeneity in the U.S. financial sector. In any event, we are committed to providing very high levels of due process to any firm that the FSOC considers a potential candidate for designation and consequent oversight by the Fed.

Macroprudential regulatory policy

In addition to its role as a member of the FSOC, the Federal Reserve has other important responsibilities under the DFA to help promote financial stability. As Chairman Bernanke has noted, a key element of the DFA is its injunction to the Fed and other financial regulators to employ macroprudential approaches to supervision and regulation.[2] We are to oversee financial firms and to review their mergers and acquisitions activity with a view toward protecting the financial stability of the broader financial system, not just protecting the solvency of individual firms. We have a lot to do in fleshing out how precisely to implement that mandate.

[2] Ben S. Bernanke (2011), "Implementing a macroprudential approach to supervision and regulation," speech delivered at, and included in the *Proceedings* of the Federal Reserve Bank of Chicago's 47th Annual Conference on Bank Structure and Competition, pp. 1–8.

I want to highlight a few points on macroprudential regulatory policy before moving on to address some of the more concrete provisions of the DFA. I think the Chairman made a crucial distinction between what I consider the two major strands of macroprudential regulation. The first is the structural or spatial components of it and the second is the temporal, time-related components.

On the spatial/structural side, it is very important that we endeavor to mitigate threats to financial stability that can come from structural problems in our financial system — for example, from excessive entanglements among firms, from excessive herding behavior by financial firms, and from the high risk of contagion effects in the financial markets. But at the same time, we have to look at the time-varying element. We have to work to mitigate threats from the buildup of excessive risk during credit booms or other types of financial booms. So we have to watch for problems on the upside. At the same time, we have to pay attention to what the right tools are on the downside. You try to mitigate threats that might build up from the deleveraging or de-maturity transforming activities of financial firms that are rushing to crouch defensively as they see an economic thunderstorm approaching.

A final macroprudential comment I want to make deals with the occasional tension between microprudential and macroprudential goals. Typically, micro- and macroprudential goals reinforce each other. Strengthening capital requirements across the financial system, for example, will make individual banks safer and that will help make the broader financial system more resilient. However, they do not always reinforce each other. For example, actions by a particular firm to improve its capital adequacy, such as by selling assets or cutting back on lending, might very well serve microprudential goals and make the bank safer and sounder. But if we are in a recession, or a period of financial instability, that kind of behavior can be quite inconsistent with macroprudential goals for maintaining liquidity in the system and moving forward.

In addition to managing the potential conflicts between micro- and macroprudential goals, we also need to carefully measure the costs of macroprudential policies. These can be measured in terms of higher credit costs, lower credit availability, and slower economic growth. Those costs need to be contrasted with any systemic risk mitigation benefits we can achieve from the macroprudential policies.

Prudential standards for large bank holding companies and nonbanks

The second element of the DFA that I want to discuss is the obligation of the Fed to develop more stringent prudential standards for large bank holding companies

(BHCs) and nonbank financial firms that the council designates as SIFIs. This is one of the Fed's most important Dodd–Frank implementation duties and it is consuming a great deal of the blood, sweat, and tears of Fed lawyers, economists, and supervisors. Fortunately, the act gives the Fed a great deal of flexibility in how we design this framework, although it does hardwire a few parameters.

The act tells us that we have to apply the framework to BHCs above $50 billion in assets. We are also required to have the framework increase in proportion to what I like to call the "systemic footprint" of firms, that is, the size, interconnectedness, and complexity of firms in that set of BHCs above $50 billion.

Third, the act specifies the types of regulatory standards we need to apply in an enhanced way to the big firms. We need to calculate additional capital requirements, additional leverage requirements, and additional liquidity requirements. We have to develop single counterparty credit limits. We have to conduct stress tests, to develop living wills, and to design an early remediation framework.

The act required that we implement these enhanced standards by January 2012, although they did not have to go into effect then. Our goal with this package of standards will be to produce a well-integrated set of rules that meaningfully reduces the probability of default of our largest financial firms and at the same time minimizes the losses to the financial system and the economy if such a firm should fail.

The enhanced standards should force these firms to internalize any cost that they would pose to the financial system if they were to fail or become distressed. It should help offset the implicit subsidy that some of them enjoy due to the "TBTF" phenomenon and it should give the firms incentives to shrink their systemic footprint.

I am not in a position to give you a sneak peek as to how the Fed plans to come out on this set of enhanced standards for SIFIs. However, I can say that the included firms will not all be treated equally. They are not equally systemically important. This generates some challenges for the Fed.

I want to highlight some of the challenges in designing this new framework. The first issue deals with the proportionality of the regulatory process. I think the DFA was spot-on in requiring the Fed to make sure that we do not apply a one-size-fits-all approach to every BHC above $50 billion. However, designing exactly how to do that gradation — how to make the regulatory framework proportional to the systemic footprint of the firms above $50 billion — is not an easy task.

We have been spending a lot of energy trying to figure out what the differences are in the systemic footprint between a Huntington Bank Shares or a Zions Bancorp sitting just north of $50 billion and the colossuses that we deal with such as Citi, JPMorgan, and Goldman Sachs. We need some way to measure how much more systemically important the largest of the firms are relative to the firms just above the threshold.

Once we develop a means to measure the proportional size, complexity, and interconnectedness of these firms, how do we adapt the regulatory apparatus to those differentials? Do we have some kind of continuous function of the systemic footprint of the firm for some or all the standards? Do we have a multi-bucket, a many-bucket approach, or do we just have a small number of buckets? We need to answer these questions realizing that there are costs and benefits to each of those approaches and they vary somewhat between capital rules, liquidity rules, single counterparty credit limits, and stress-testing. We are currently evaluating approaches to deal with that gradation/proportionality question.

A second core issue we have is calibration. This is difficult. It is one thing to say that you want SIFIs to internalize their externalities or to absorb any implicit subsidy they receive from market perceptions that they are "TBTF." It is quite another thing to actually calibrate a regulatory regime to achieve those goals with any precision. As we designed the enhanced standards framework, we have been attentive and will continue to be attentive to the cumulative, quantitative, and qualitative costs of these rules. We will do our best to consider the costs of the aggregate package that constitutes the higher regulatory standards for SIFIs.

A third challenge for the Fed is the integration issue. Importantly, we are not designing each of these standards in isolation. We have different people thinking about how to develop a capital surcharge, liquidity requirements, single counterparty credit limits, stress tests, and living wills for large, systemically important firms. At the same time, we have an overarching team of people making sure that these separate work streams link well together to produce a well-integrated set of rules that will apply to banks where the whole is more than the sum of the parts.

A fourth issue that is consuming much of our time deals with foreign banks. In the DFA, Congress set the $50 billion threshold and said we had to apply that to any U.S. BHC, but also to any foreign bank that is treated as a BHC under federal law. There are a lot of foreign banks that satisfy these criteria. In fact, there are more such foreign banks than domestic banks. Here again, Congress, I think quite wisely, gave the Fed substantial discretion in how we implement our U.S. SIFI framework for foreign banks.

In determining that framework, Congress told us that we could consider national treatment, equality of competitive opportunity, and the quality of home country regulation for these firms. However, deciding on the appropriate factors and appropriate weights of those factors is a complicated process. Foreign banks operate in the United States in a complex and diverse set of ways. They have branches. They have agencies. They have subsidiary banks. They have subsidiary

BHCs. They have subsidiary broker–dealers. We are spending a lot of time trying to determine the extent to which we should apply these standards to the parent foreign bank, or to just the U.S. operations of the firm, and how to best incorporate the adequacy of the home country regulatory framework into that calculus. I consider addressing this foreign bank adaptation issue to be one of the most difficult tasks we have in getting the SIFI framework figured out.

Resolvability of financial firms

The last issue I want to talk about on the SIFI regulatory front is how to improve the resolvability of financial firms. Under the DFA, the Fed and other regulators are required to work to reduce the expected adverse impact of a SIFI failure on the financial system. There are two ways to do that. One is to reduce the probability of the firm's failure. The second is to reduce the impact on the system if the firm does fail. In Basel II-speak, there are probability-of-default (PD)-related tools and there are loss-given-default (LGD) tools.

As Pat Parkinson explained at the 2010 Conference on Bank Structure and Competition, financial regulators historically have focused almost exclusively on the PD-related tools, that is, reducing the probability of a firm's failure.[3] They have given very short shrift to any kind of tools that would reduce the impact of that failure on the financial system. For example, we have given financial firms great flexibility in how they organize their internal structures, even if those internal structures might make them difficult to resolve if they fail. This is going to have to change in the post-apocalyptic Dodd–Frank world. As macroprudential supervisors, I think we can no longer rely solely on the traditional ex ante going concern, prudential tools like capital and liquidity that are designed to reduce the probability of a firm's failure. We are going to have to incorporate ex post, resolvability-enhancing tools to reduce the loss to the financial system when these firms fail. This is a complicated endeavor and we have a lot of work to do to figure out how to get this right.

I want to touch on a few challenges concerning this resolvability issue. The first challenge is to determine the most socially efficient means to improve the resolvability of SIFIs. This could include requirements that the firms simplify

---

[3]Patrick M. Parkinson (2010), "Restoring market discipline on large financial institutions," in *The Future of the Financial Services Industry — Structure, Regulation & Performance*, proceedings of the 46th Annual Conference on Bank Structure and Competition, Federal Reserve Bank of Chicago, pp. 38–43.

their internal organizational structures by reducing the number of legal entities (and in doing so reducing the intrafirm guarantees, funding relationships, and derivative transactions). There could also be a movement toward requiring firms to operate their system-critical businesses in financially and operationally autonomous packets. I think we have a lot of work to do to try to figure out which of these tools might make sense.

A second sub-issue under this resolvability framing is to determine how aggressive we want to be on the resolution front. We need to be able to answer the question of how much going-concern costs we are willing to impose on the firms to achieve resolvability benefits. On this point, the comments made by Wayne Abernathy are certainly correct. There will be going-concern costs for firms to simplify their organizational structures. So we need to be able to strike the right balance between the benefits on the resolvability front and the costs on the going-concern front.

The final sub-issue under resolvability deals with choosing the right mix of policy tools. We have these two types of tools: the PD tools and the LGD tools. We need to strike the right balance between the two. Should the emphasis mostly be on the PD tools? On the LGD tools? What is the appropriate balance? Again, we have started to think about these issues, but I think a lot of work remains to be done.

Financial stability efforts here and abroad

I am obviously giving very short shrift to other sub-issues concerning Dodd–Frank issues that we are working on. Let me simply list some of these efforts. We are working with our U.S. regulatory colleagues at other agencies to implement financial stability-related reforms. Those include risk-retention requirements for securitization sponsors; margin requirements for non-cleared over-the-counter derivatives; incentive compensation rules; limits on the proprietary trading and private fund investment activities of banking firms; and risk-management standards for central counterparties and other financial market utilities. We are also working in close coordination with the Office of Thrift Supervision, the Office of the Comptroller of the Currency, and the Federal Deposit Insurance Corporation as we prepare to take over supervisory authority for thrift holding companies.

Finally, in addition to the massive amount of energy being spent by regulators to implement the DFA, there have also been a lot of discussions concerning how to make the international financial system safer. The Basel Committee, FSB, and the G20 leaders have been doing a lot of work on issues such as improving capital requirements and the overall prudential framework for globally active banking firms. The Fed has played an important role in those discussions and I think there have been some pretty significant achievements in the Basel III Accord.

There is still a lot of work that will be done internationally in parallel with Dodd–Frank implementation in the United States. The key issues that remain for the international community include determining how to increase the loss-absorbency of systemic firms beyond those of other banks, the so-called SIFI capital surcharge issue. There is also the issue of assessing the potential role of contingent capital and bail-in mechanisms for addressing systemic banking firms. And there is the issue of how best to strengthen resolution regimes around the world to enable governments to minimize the costs resulting from the failure of a large, complex international bank.

Let me close by just saying the DFA gives the Fed and other financial regulators new powers and new responsibilities to protect U.S. financial stability. With a few exceptions, Congress wisely chose not to micromanage the ways and means by which we get to the financial stability goals. I think that was a wise decision. We have a lot of degrees of freedom. I think that increases our obligation to get the job done correctly. We are determined to accomplish that, but I think we have a long way to go before we get to the end of the journey.

Chapter 5

Implementing the Dodd–Frank Act: Progress to Date and Recommendations for the Future

Scott D. O'Malia[1]

I know that I don't have to tell you that the Commodity Futures Trading Commission has been extraordinarily busy in its efforts to fulfill the regulatory mandates of the Dodd–Frank Wall Street Reform and Consumer Protection Act. As of May 2011, the CFTC has put forth 66 proposed and final rules under the Dodd–Frank Act (DFA). Not even counting the last four rule proposals the CFTC voted on, we're at over 1,046 dense *Federal Register* pages filled with legal jargon and regulatory requirements. If you were to run the comment periods on all of those proposals consecutively, it would take 2,964 days, or a little over 8 years. I doubt I have to give those numbers much context; they speak for themselves. But just for fun, if you were to lay each of those *Federal Register* pages end to end, they'd stretch two-thirds of the way up the newly renamed Willis Tower in Chicago. And we're not done yet, so I am sure we'll reach the top of the tower before this is all over.

Sequencing and implementation

When you're putting out that much paper, I think you should have a plan for how to get through it. We are nearly halfway through the rulemaking process and we

[1]Scott D. O'Malia is commissioner of the Commodity Futures Trading Commission (CFTC). The material in this article was originally published in the Federal Reserve Bank of Chicago's *Economic Perspectives*, Volume 36, 3rd quarter, 2012. The views expressed are the author's and do not necessarily reflect the views of the CFTC.

are just about to start consideration of the final rules. As Winston Churchill once advised, "If you are going through hell, keep going." I'm going to accept that advice, but I have made two recommendations for the chairman of the CFTC to make our trip a little better.

First, I have asked the chairman to put forward a provisional sequencing of the final rules to allow the market to comment on where you think we got it right and, of course, where we can do better. Second, and even more importantly, the CFTC should set an implementation schedule for all of the Dodd–Frank rules and publish it in the *Federal Register* for comment. This will allow the market to suggest changes to the schedule before the CFTC misses the mark. Market participants need to know when they will be expected to implement the rules so that appropriate investment, staffing, and reorganization decisions can be made. Until a final schedule is published, market participants will continue to play a very high-stakes game of pin-the-tail-on-the-donkey. Providing an additional level of transparency is entirely appropriate. We have already conceded we can't meet the deadline set by Congress in the first place, so providing a plan will not keep the CFTC from meeting that date.

CFTC–SEC roundtables

The CFTC and Securities and Exchange Commission (SEC) conducted a roundtable discussion on Dodd–Frank implementation in May 2011. From this discussion, I took away three very clear messages that the public was sending the CFTC.

First, market participants would like an implementation schedule so they can make investments to comply with the rules. Second, there is nothing the market can't build, integrate, and execute, but the CFTC must provide clear rules and enough time to implement the rules. The panelists made it clear they needed months, not years, to implement these rules. Third, phased implementation of the rules is essential to ensure that all the pieces work together.

What was not clear from this discussion, however, was the appropriate phasing. There was not consensus about whether we should start with participants, products, or both, nor about how the CFTC would handle the challenges presented by the clearing mandate for standardized over-the-counter (OTC) derivatives. So, we have more work to do on this front. The ball is now in our court. The market has been frank about the challenges and has only asked for schedules, regulatory certainty, and patience.

Regulating the swaps markets

Still, we are making a good deal of progress in our rulemaking process. In fact, we are exceeding expectations. At the last CFTC open meeting, we finally released the much-anticipated joint proposal with the SEC on definitions of products, including swaps.[2] As you know, the CFTC had previously released proposals addressing the definition of swap execution facilities (SEFs), as well as the definitions of swap dealers and major swap participants. While we all share as common ground the goal of reducing systemic risk, we do have some differences of opinion as to the best way to meet that goal.

Swap dealer and end-user definitions

For example, I believe our proposed definition of swap dealer is too broad and will likely capture commercial entities that use swaps primarily to hedge their risks. As a result, these entities, which do not pose systemic risk, will see their costs go up. In contrast, the proposed definition of end-user was too narrow. That proposal even missed an uncontroversial opportunity to clearly exempt certain Farm Credit System (FCS) financial entities — or FCS banks — from clearing requirements. Congress made it clear that regulators were permitted to exempt these banks. The CFTC failed to make it clear that FCS banks' swap transactions would qualify for the bona fide hedging exemption.

Capital and margin

My concerns with the proposed definitions of swap dealer and end-user also have implications for the recently proposed capital and margin rules. For example, if the definition of swap dealer captures commercial end-users, then they will be required to take a direct capital charge for the credit and market risks associated with each swap they enter into with other commercial end-users. Also, there is no language in the margin proposal that makes it clear that end-users won't be assessed margin. Instead, the proposal states that each swap dealer may accept margin in a manner agreed to by the parties in a credit support arrangement. In stark contrast, the prudential regulators have put forward draft rules that prohibit

---

[2]Working definitions of these products and related terms are available at ww.cftc.gov/Consumer Protection/EducationCenter/CFTCGlossary/glossary_s.

bank swap dealers from posting margin to their counterparties and provide no capital threshold exemptions for end-users.

What does all of this mean? I believe costs for commercial end-users will increase. Congress did not want us to impose increased costs on commercial firms that are not systemically relevant and force those firms to decide between hedging risk and investing in their business. Unfortunately, I believe the draft rules ignored congressional direction.

Swap execution facilities

One element of the new market structure, which seems to have captured everyone's imagination, is the SEF. This new exchange offers the best opportunity to improve swaps market transparency and improve our ability to manage risk with real-time pricing, contract standardization, and better liquidity. I am often reminded that the swaps market developed in parallel with the futures market because of the important differences in liquidity between those markets. A one-size-fits-all approach — namely, a central limit order book — will not work in the swaps market because it is less liquid. The CFTC's SEF proposal allows for both limit-order-book and request-for-quote approaches in order to provide flexibility and to encourage liquidity formation.

I believe the number and variety of SEF platforms in existence and under development highlight the innovative capabilities of this market and confirm that no technological challenge is too big for it. To highlight what the market is capable of when it is given clear direction, I hosted an SEF showcase back at the end of March 2011 at the CFTC headquarters in Washington, DC. I invited any organization that developed an SEF platform to participate and show off its technology. No one was turned away, and the exchange of ideas among the participants promoting 16 different SEF platforms, representing all asset classes, lasted all day.

I was impressed with how quickly and creatively potential SEFs met the proposed requirements outlined in the CFTC's rulemaking, but I think we need to continue to provide flexibility in our rules to allow SEFs to innovate and compete for business. Also, I want to make sure that without penalty this market can execute transactions of sufficient size to meet participants' needs. We've received feedback from the public that the requirement that bids for less liquid swaps are shown to at least five dealers and the requirement that any order be visible to the market for at least 15 seconds (as with SEC rules for other securities) would harm the market.

Technology

We have massive new responsibilities under the DFA that will require a heightened focus on technology investments, data management, and analysis. We cannot continue to use yesterday's solutions for today's problems. We can't continue to ignore the fact that the markets we regulate are no longer dominated by traders who take orders over landline telephones and stand in crowded pits yelling out bids and offers that only the initiated can understand. I don't need to tell anyone from Chicago that those scenes are more part of our past than our present. Today, the futures and swaps markets are by and large electronic markets, heavily dependent upon advanced technologies. It's time that the CFTC adapts to that reality.

If we are to establish a credible surveillance and oversight program of both the futures and swaps markets, the CFTC needs to move past its antiquated ways of doing business. I am repeatedly struck by the lack of technological capacity at the agency. Our forms and filings are not required to be filed electronically, and those that are filed electronically do not automatically populate our trade surveillance databases. We have only a few automated surveillance alerts. None of those monitor real-time trading. While we rely on each designated contract market (DCM) to police its own trading to a certain degree, we have long recognized the interconnectedness of the market as a whole but have done little to address that reality.

Anniversary of the Flash Crash

May 6, 2011, was the first anniversary of the Flash Crash, an event that "highlighted the interconnectedness of the equities and derivatives markets."[3] In minutes the markets dropped an unprecedented $1 trillion. Thankfully, the market recovered, but not before it gave us a terrible example of how badly things can go when we don't have the right safeguards in place.

On February 18, 2011, over 9 months after the Flash Crash, a joint CFTC–SEC advisory committee released a report that contained 14 recommendations. Both commissions will seek to integrate most of the recommendations into the Dodd–Frank rulemaking. They included putting circuit breakers or pauses in place; requiring DCMs to have strict supervisory requirements for firms

[3] Joint CFTC–SEC Advisory Committee on Emerging Regulatory Issues, 2011, "Recommendations regarding regulatory responses to the market events of May 6, 2010," Report, Washington, DC, February 18, available at: www.cftc.gov/ucm/groups/public/@aboutcftc/documents/file/jacreport_021811.pdf.

implementing algorithmic trading; reporting measures; and establishing pre-trade risk safeguards. The Technology Advisory Committee (TAC), which I chair at the CFTC, formed a subcommittee to also look at safeguards and pre-trade practices for firms that engage in direct market access. The subcommittee came up with several pre-trade risk-management measures — which included pre-trade quantity limits on individual orders and price collars; execution and message throttles; a kill button on existing orders; clear error trade and order cancellation policies at the exchange level; and trading functionalities that operate within parameters set by clearing firms.

But the joint CFTC–SEC advisory committee noted that since May 6, 2010, there have been at least three other "crashes" related to algorithmic trading, which I believe have shaken market confidence and will undermine the important role both the equities and futures markets play. The CFTC can't possibly review each and every algorithm and certify its performance — that would be impossible. Instead, we are hoping to establish rigorous standards by which all firms must comply if they are going to utilize algorithms in their trading strategies.

CFTC's own technological divide

As market participants make investments in their technological capabilities to keep up with the ever-improving speed of business, the CFTC must also make critical investments in our own capabilities. For the past year, I have requested the CFTC be reorganized to create an Office of Data Collection and Analysis. This office should focus on securing and managing all of the CFTC's trade and surveillance data, working with all other divisions to monitor the futures and swaps markets and performing broad risk analysis for the CFTC. This office can drive the automation of cross-market surveillance programs, including the development of our own algorithms, enabling the CFTC to keep pace with new computer-generated trading styles as well as nefarious activities. Using the additional resources provided by Congress, we should attack our highest-priority technological challenges, such as automating our surveillance and integrating the swaps market data with futures market data.

Technology Advisory Committee

Finally, if we are going to keep pace with the market's appetite for new technological capabilities, we have got to keep a dialogue going with market participants about where the market is headed. I mentioned the work of the TAC to help identify possible safeguards in response to the Flash Crash of May 6, 2010. I recently established another TAC subcommittee to focus on developing standardized reference data for the universe of legal and financial terms used to describe, define, and value various derivatives and other financial instruments. The creation of standardized reference points and data terms will aid in the development of universal entity, product, and/or instrument identifiers and provide greater consistency in the collection, reporting, and management of individual transactions.

Sound and fury signifying nothing?

It's easy to focus on how much is changing because of the DFA. The CFTC and the other federal financial regulators are writing rules at a frenetic pace, and the market is already positioning itself to deal with the changes to come. There's no doubt that much is changing and that a lot of good will come of this. Earlier I quoted Winston Churchill, so let me close with some more of his good advice: "However beautiful the strategy, you should occasionally look at the results."

As such, I find myself asking if we are really going to change the fundamentals of the market. If we take the flexibility out of the swaps market by trying to make those unique instruments trade as though they're futures and if we ignore the characteristics that make swaps useful tools to hedge risk, aren't we sacrificing market innovation for the lazy comfort of sticking to what is more familiar?

From the way the draft rules seem to be shaping up, I would argue that the dealers will remain in a key market-making role, though it will be a more expensive responsibility. Do we want a market that leaves dealers as the prime market-makers in the swaps arena, which would result in less competition, not more? Much of this will depend on whether or not we can move to more-standard products and reduce the customization of these products.

While I didn't mention it before, I am interested to know what others think the impacts of establishing two different margining regimes for futures and swaps will be. Will there be any opportunities to better manage risk in the futures and swaps markets? Or might capital flee into fewer but more-esoteric, bespoken products traded in dark OTC markets that can't be cleared?

And finally, a question for all of us to consider: If we have perpetuated concentrations of risk and harmed competition, have we really fixed the nemesis that is "too-big-to-fail"? If we haven't, I'm afraid that at the end of the day, we may have created a good deal of sound and fury that for the American people will signify nothing.

I'm looking forward to the ongoing discussions on these issues and to doing some of that listening that I have been counseled I should do. I know that if we are going to find answers to any of these questions, it will be because we were thoughtful and took into consideration the views of the entire market.

Chapter 6

Dodd–Frank Act Implementation: Well Into It and No Further Ahead

Wayne A. Abernathy[1]

A parlor game that we have inflicted on our family and friends involves one person reading the first line of a book while the others try to guess the title and author. For example, here is one that some of you would get right away, although it might cause others of you to struggle: "It is a truth universally acknowledged that a single man in possession of a good fortune must be in want of a wife." Of course, that is from Jane Austen's *Pride and Prejudice*. Those of you who guessed that one right away may be feeling very smug.

Here is another, a first line that my children would get every time, but one that may not be as familiar to adults: "Mr. and Mrs. Dursley, of number four, Privet Drive, were proud to say that they were perfectly normal, thank you very much." And of course, that is from J. K. Rowling's *Harry Potter and the Sorcerer's Stone*.[2]

One of my own favorites, which I am sure just about everyone would quickly identify because of the boost to the book's sales from the Obama administration, is this opening line: "Who is John Galt?" This line of dialogue is uttered at the beginning of Ayn Rand's *Atlas Shrugged*.[3]

---

[1]Wayne A. Abernathy is the executive vice president for financial institutions policy and regulatory affairs at the American Bankers Association. The material in this article was originally published in the Federal Reserve Bank of Chicago's *Economic Perspectives,* Volume 36, 3rd quarter, 2012. The views expressed are the author's and do not necessarily reflect those of the American Bankers Association or any of its member institutions.

[2]J. K. Rowling (1998). *Harry Potter and the Sorcerer's Stone*, New York: Scholastic/Arthur A. Levine Books.

[3]Ayn Rand (1957). *Atlas Shrugged*, New York: Random House.

No doubt most of you have found these first lines to be relatively easy chestnuts. Consider the game from another direction. What if you had to come up with the first line yourself? What would be the appropriate first line for the Dodd–Frank Act (DFA)? Of course, technically it is as follows: "This Act may be cited as the "Dodd–Frank Wall Street Reform and Consumer Protection Act." Unlike the other first lines, however, that is far too prosaic and tells us really nothing, providing us no legitimate clue as to the real contents awaiting the reader. It does little to prepare you adequately for what follows. Maybe this first line would be better for the act: "Marley was dead: to begin with." That line actually opens Charles Dickens's *A Christmas Carol.* And it is certainly better and more informative than what opens the act now, but in view of the act's impact on the banking industry, I feel some partiality for yet another first line: "One January day, thirty years ago, the little town of Hanover, anchored on a windy Nebraska tableland, was trying not to be blown away." That is the opening line to *O Pioneers!* by Willa Cather. Although this book is less well known than Dickens's holiday classic, Cather's novel provides us with a first line that is more appropriate for describing the act's effects.

Secretary Geithner's six principles

Just how is implementation of the DFA faring? How might we measure its progress? Within two weeks of enactment, Treasury Secretary Timothy F. Geithner did the nation an important service by outlining the Obama administration's vision for the implementation of this unprecedented legislation. In an address delivered on August 2, 2010, at New York University's Stern School of Business, Secretary Geithner outlined six principles that would not only guide but govern how the administration would proceed with the act's implementation.[4] This was an important and necessary speech because the legislation's 2,319 pages are surprisingly short on details, delegating the duty of writing them to the executive branch.

As a measure of the value that the Obama administration had given to the principles laid out in the speech, Secretary Geithner made the bold but appropriate declaration to the world that "you should hold us accountable for honoring them."[5] No one should complain, then, if 18 months following enactment we do

---

[4]Timothy F. Geithner (2010). "Rebuilding the American financial system," speech at New York University, Stern School of Business, August 2, available at: www.treasury.gov/press-center/press-releases/Pages/tg808.aspx.

[5]*Ibid.*

just that. How is the Obama administration, by its own chosen yardstick, doing at implementing the DFA?

First principle: Speed

Secretary Geithner described his first principle in these words: "First, we have an obligation of speed." He elaborated on that principle by stating the following:

> We will move as quickly as possible to bring clarity to the new rules of finance. The rule writing process traditionally has moved at a frustrating, glacial pace. We must change that.[6]

This was a bold promise, given the unprecedented rulemaking challenge. At least in the financial regulatory history of the United States, there has never been anything like it. I have seen no definitive count of the number of regulations that the DFA calls forth. The numbers seem to range between 250 and 400 — numbers so large that they are numbing. It all defies hyperbole. The Fair and Accurate Credit Transactions Act, adopted in 2003, astonished the financial industry with more than a dozen significant new regulations to be written. Looking at the Dodd–Frank challenge, I note that the following words of the Lord Chancellor in Gilbert and Sullivan's comic opera *Iolanthe* are appropriate: "I conceive you may use any language you choose to indulge in, without impropriety." In short, it is an impossible task — one on which the regulators are surely working as best they can. From early on, they all fell behind and have no hope of catching up. The law firm Davis Polk & Wardwell LLP keeps a monthly "progress report" on the rulemaking. The report found that by January 2012 some 200 statutory deadlines for new regulations had come and gone, and 75% of them had been missed.[7] One proposed rule — the so-called Volcker rule[8] — alone contains an astonishing 1,400 questions from regulators back to the public for input. This is hard stuff if you want to get it right.

Secretary Geithner's first principle sounds much like Glendower's boast to Hotspur in William Shakespeare's *Henry IV* that he "can call spirits from the

---

[6] *Ibid.*

[7] Davis Polk & Wardwell LLP, 2012, *Dodd–Frank Progress Report*, January, p. 2, available at: www.davispolk.com/publications/list.aspx.

[8] See http://lexicon.ft.com/Term?term=volcker-rule.

vasty deep." To which we may be forgiven for rejoining with Hotspur, "But will they come when you do call for them?"

To Secretary Geithner's credit, he also said in his speech, probably drawing upon his vast government experience, "Now, this process is very broad in scope and very complicated. It will take time."[9] In view of all that, it is perplexing that there have been other voices from the Treasury Department calling for what some might characterize as "pedal to the metal" implementation, despite the impossibility of meeting the DFA deadlines.

Second principle: Transparency and consultation

Consider Secretary Geithner's next principle: "Second, we will provide full transparency and disclosure." The Treasury Secretary explained this principle this way:

> The regulatory agencies will consult broadly as they write new rules. Draft rules will be published. The public will have a chance to comment. And those comments will be available for everyone to see.[10]

The latter parts of this pledge are unsurprising. They are the law. With regard to consulting broadly, that is certainly intended by the law on federal rulemaking, too. If Secretary Geithner meant anything beyond doing what the Administrative Procedure Act and other relevant statutes require, then the record to date has been spotty. Again, this is not meant as a pointed criticism of the rule writers. It is tough for regulatory staff to write so many complex rules in such a short amount of time as the DFA allows and, at the same time, meet with the people who will have to live with the consequences. Yet meeting with those people is exactly what is needed if we want to have rules that do not do much more harm than good.

Especially at the beginning of the process, proposed rules were published with unusually short comment periods. Many were offered as interim final rules, which mean that they went into effect immediately upon publication, even while they were open for comment as drafts. Consultation with industry members, affected parties, and the public while the rules were still being thought over and before their formal presentation has been the exception rather than the norm. In more recent weeks, regulators have slowed down the process and increased their consultation with others when necessary, possibly ignoring the statutory deadlines.

---

[9]Geithner (2010).

[10]*Ibid.*

That is all to the good and will make for better rulemaking and fewer mistakes needing correction later.

Third principle: Avoiding layering of new rules on top of old ones

Here is the third principle, in Secretary Geithner's words: "Third, we will not simply layer new rules on top of old, outdated ones." This very welcome idea was explained like this:

> Everyone that is part of the financial system — the regulated and regulators — knows that we have accumulated layers of rules that can be overwhelming, and these failures of regulation were in some ways as appalling as the failures produced where regulation was absent.
>
> So alongside our efforts to strengthen and improve protections for the economy, we will eliminate rules that did not work. Wherever possible, we will streamline and simplify.[11]

President Obama reinforced this message of reducing the regulatory burden in an initiative that he announced on January 24, 2011. The premise and the promise were both right on target. All banks and their customers feel the weight of excess regulation (ask anyone who has been through a mortgage closing, for just one example). Sadly, the promise remains unfulfilled. In a news article in May 2011 examining this very issue, *American Banker* editor at large, Barbara A. Rehm, observed, "None of the numerous people interviewed could name a single rule that has been repealed or simplified."[12] The situation has not improved since May 2011.

Fourth principle: Innovation

The fourth principle addresses an issue of progress that is important to banks and bank customers. Secretary Geithner said, "Fourth, we will not risk killing the freedom for innovation that is necessary for economic growth." The description provided for this principle is as follows:

> Our system allowed too much freedom for predation, abuse and excess risk, but as we put in place rules to correct for those mistakes, we have to strive

---

[11] *Ibid.*

[12] Barbara A. Rehm (2011). "The principal issues with the Geithner principles," *American Banker*, May 2, available at: www.americanbanker.com/issues/176_84/geithner-dodd-frank-1036842-1.html.

> to achieve a careful balance and safeguard the freedom, competition and innovation that are essential for growth.[13]

Given how relatively few of the DFA rules have been finalized and how even fewer of them have gone into effect, it may now be too early to test this principle. It is clear, however, that there has been no innovation in financial services since the enactment of the DFA, unless we should count the degradation in customer services developing in response to the Durbin Amendment's price controls on debit card interchange fees.[14]

Rather than a realization of the promises of Secretary Geithner, what we have been seeing is more of a fulfillment of the predictions of investigative journalist John Stossel (commenting on the behavioral costs of regulation):

> The bigger harm is the indirect cost, all the money businesses spend trying to wade through the red tape (lobbying, filling out forms, hiring lawyers), plus the damage the regulation does to the American spirit. So much creativity now goes not into inventing things, but into gaming the system, manipulating the regulatory leviathan.[15]

Fifth principle: Level playing field

Secretary Geithner combined the fifth principle with its explanation in this way:

> Fifth, we will make sure we have a more level playing field — not just between banks and non-banks here in the United States — but also between our financial institutions and those in Europe, Japan, China, and emerging markets who are all competing to finance global growth and development. We will do this by setting high global standards and blocking a "race to the bottom" from taking place outside the United States.[16]

Again, these promises are good and reassuring, likely to raise no objections other than those from nonbanks and foreigners. Advocates for the new federal

[13] Geithner (2010).

[14] Interchange fees are per debit (or credit) transaction fees paid by merchants' financial institutions to the card issuer. For details on the Durbin Amendment, see http://thomas.loc.gov/cgi-bin/bdquery/z?d111:SP03989.

[15] John Stossel (2004). *Give Me a Break: How I Exposed Hucksters, Cheats, and Scam Artists and Became the Scourge of the Liberal Media ...*, New York: HarperCollins, p. 49.

[16] Geithner (2010).

Consumer Financial Protection Bureau (CFPB) have repeatedly pledged to go after nonbanks. Additionally, those making pronouncements regarding the new Financial Stability Oversight Council (FSOC) have pledged to extend the FSOC's monitoring for systemic risk to nonbanks. Finally, defenders of the new, elevated capital standards for banks and the Volcker rule have assured us that these regulations will be embraced internationally.

As of this writing, all of these pledges have yet to be fulfilled, and the assurances remain largely unrealized. CFPB leaders continue their rhetorical offensive, but six months after receiving responsibility for 17 consumer laws and following the appointment of a bureau director, no action has been taken against any nonbanks; in addition, a rigorous nonbank examination program has not emerged from the planning stages. FSOC continues to promulgate rules about how it will go about designating certain nonbanks as systemically important financial institutions (SIFIs), as well as guidelines for what it will do to nonbank SIFIs. However, at the time of this writing, not a single nonbank firm has been declared to be a SIFI, despite the fact that it was the collapse of the "shadow" banking system[17] that inaugurated the recent financial crisis. The cloud of burdensome uniform international capital rules has spread across the globe, but the Europeans are already trying to figure out how to fudge them as they recognize the contractionary effect of excessively high capital requirements. No nation outside of the United States has embraced the Volcker rule. Indeed, the word is that European financial authorities are preparing to lodge protests against it with the U.S. Treasury Department.

Sixth principle: Coordination and cost–benefit analysis

Perhaps the Treasury Secretary did not want seven principles, so he combined two for his sixth and last:

> Finally, we will bring more order and coordination to the regulatory process, so that the agencies responsible for building these reforms are working together, not against each other. This requires us to look carefully at the overall interaction of regulations designed by different regulators and assess the overall burden they present relative to the benefits they offer.[18]

---

[17]The shadow banking system represents the network of financial firms (for example, hedge funds and insurance companies) that are outside the traditional banking system.

[18]Geithner (2010).

Again, these are worthy desiderata that all can embrace. The DFA significantly increased the number of federal regulators and expanded their scope, so coordination — hard to come by leading up to and during the financial crisis — is essential to a cohesive regulatory program. Rigorous cost–benefit analysis is essential for the justification of any federal regulatory program if it is not to become detrimental to the public good.

Sadly, these remain unfulfilled goals rather than operative administration mandates. One of the most common criticisms of Dodd–Frank implementation has been a lack of order and coordination in the regulatory process. Instead, the DFA has succeeded in replacing the financial crisis with a regulatory crisis. No agency has been able to reach equanimity about its primary job, in large part because each agency has been so preoccupied with implementation issues; in addition, cooperation with other agencies appears to have been achieved only when driven by necessity or convenience. As agencies are grappling with impossible rulemaking tasks, most of them are also engaged in major structural reorganizations and shifts in the areas of responsibility.

A good example is consumer protection regulation. A whole new federal agency, the CFPB, was created to centralize consumer protection in one agency. Not to be left out of this area of regulation, the Federal Deposit Insurance Corporation (FDIC) has established its own division of consumer protection, and the Office of the Comptroller of the Currency has found consumer protection to be part of its remaining safety and soundness responsibilities. Additionally, the DFA encourages state attorneys general to get more actively involved in enforcing federal consumer protection standards. There are and will continue to be more independent regulatory and enforcement players wearing consumer protection sashes than there were in 2007.

It is worth noting with some comfort that the DFA reinforces the importance of regulators conducting cost–benefit analyses in the promulgation of the new rules, and the courts are showing some appetite for enforcing those statutory requirements. It cannot be said that the regulatory analyses are anywhere near adequate yet, but regulators are paying more attention, as are the entities being regulated.

Failing to follow the Geithner principles

By the standard of the six principles set out by Secretary Geithner, the implementation of the DFA — as measured a year and a half after its enactment — is not going well. Not only is it failing to follow the Geithner principles, it is violating them in many cases.

Acknowledging that this is actually the case is not the same as placing fault with those charged with the act's implementation. Nothing like this has ever been tried before in the history of the United States. Writing 400 financial regulations of the highest significance and the greatest complexity in a couple of years has clearly been too much to expect. Policymakers in Congress and in the executive branch can easily discern from the experience thus far that a reform of the DFA is in order, as others have recognized in the past for many far less ambitious legislative projects.

Getting on with the work to end our self-inflicted regulatory crisis should be among the highest priorities. It is hard for regulators to do their jobs while enmeshed in impossible implementation tasks — and even harder for financial institutions and their customers to get on with life while all this regulatory reshuffling and reconstruction take place. The Gramm–Leach–Bliley Act (also known as the Financial Services Modernization Act of 1999) was built upon the foundation of functional regulation. The DFA has produced dysfunctional regulation.

Unless the failings of the DFA are addressed, the closing line of that legislation will not be: "And they lived happily ever after." A more appropriate final line might be one borrowed from *The Guns of August* by historian Barbara W. Tuchman:

> After the first thirty days of war in 1914, there was a premonition that little glory lay ahead.[19]

[19] Barbara W. Tuchman (1962). *The Guns of August*, New York: Macmillan, Chapter 22.

PART IV

Financial Stability via Efficient Failure Resolution

This part discusses the failure resolution process introduced by Dodd–Frank for large, complex financial institutions. For years, there has been a general outcry against the use of large bank "bailouts" that have regulators (and, therefore, taxpayers) come to the rescue of large troubled firms. These bailouts have been justified because they prevent adverse spillover effects from a failed firm toward other firms, and to the economy more broadly. Such bailout policies create a group of large financial firms that are considered "too-big-to-fail" (TBTF). In addition to imposing costs on the public, the general argument against such bailout policies is that they reduce market discipline and allow the TBTF firms to take on excessive risk. This excessive risk, somewhat paradoxically, increases the probability of future failures.

Dodd–Frank explicitly addresses the TBTF problem and calls for a new failure resolution process that is only to be used for systemically important firms whose failure through the traditional resolution processes would result in significant adverse systemic consequences. Dodd–Frank's goal is to explicitly end TBTF in the United States by requiring that losses from the failure be incurred by shareholders and creditors (and possibly other firms in the industry) and that no cost is borne by taxpayers.

Dodd–Frank spells out the role of the Federal Deposit Insurance Corporation (FDIC), in certain limited cases, as the orderly liquidation authority for institutions deemed to be systemically important. Chapters in this part provide insights into the FDIC's evolution of thought about how best to implement this resolution authority. Sheila Bair, past Chairman of the FDIC, sets the stage by describing why there is a need to end TBTF bailout policies and introduce an alternative, more efficient, resolution process. She describes the distortions created by a TBTF policy and explains how attempting to rescue these firms can actually result in additional costs to the industry. Next, a FDIC staff study analyzes the advantages of the new resolution tools and procedures introduced in Dodd–Frank. This is done by showing how the Lehman Brothers failure, which occurred before the act was passed, could have been better handled with use of the new tools. That is followed by a chapter by the current Chairman of the FDIC, Martin Gruenberg, discussing how resolution policy had evolved with an emphasis on what is termed the *single point of entry* methodology. Finally, a study by the FDIC and the Bank of England discusses resolution strategies for the failure of globally active, systemically important, financial institutions. Again, reading through the chapters chronologically shows the evolution of policies and strategies as the Dodd–Frank procedures were implemented.

Chapter 7

We Must Resolve to End Too-Big-To-Fail

Sheila C. Bair[1]

I am very pleased to have the opportunity to address this conference once again as FDIC Chairman. For nearly 50 years, the Bank Structure Conference has been a vitally important forum for addressing the challenges facing the financial services industry. It all began in the early 1960s as a series of symposia on competition and market structure in what was then, in many respects, a much more heavily regulated banking industry. In those days, branching restrictions, product and service limitations, and interest-rate ceilings were the norm. But by the 1970s, the focus shifted somewhat to the need for banking deregulation in a fast-changing financial landscape.

With the crises of the 1980s, the issues of moral hazard — resulting from the federal safety net and the resulting need for better market discipline — came to the fore. And more recently, the emphasis has shifted again to financial innovation and nonbank financial providers, followed, of course, by debate as to the causes of the recent crisis and the reforms needed to prevent such a disaster from recurring.

Besides its uncanny knack for identifying emerging policy issues, this conference series is also remarkable for the way it brings together three groups of people — academics, bankers, and regulators — who sometimes speak different languages, but who must work together to resolve those difficult issues. And what keeps you coming back to this conference year after year, I suspect, is a shared commitment to some common goals.

---

[1]This speech was presented before the Federal Reserve Bank of Chicago's 47th Annual Conference on Bank Structure and Competition and published in *Proceedings of a Conference on Bank Structure and Competition*, Federal Reserve Bank of Chicago, May 2011, Chicago. At the time, Sheila Bair was chairman of the Federal Deposit Insurance Corporation (FDIC).

All of us have a vital stake in financial stability. And we all want to see a financial system that consistently supports the real economy by efficiently allocating capital and credit to its highest and best use.

Balancing the government's role

Because banking and finance are so critical to our economy, and because they are prone to bouts of instability, we have long recognized a vital — but limited — role for government in our financial system. Public confidence, market liquidity, and financial stability are all inherently public goods. Only government has the capacity to carry out prudential supervision, serve as lender of last resort, provide iron-clad guarantees that can forestall runs, and promptly and efficiently resolve banking institutions when they fail.

Under the guidance of statute, the FDIC, the Federal Reserve, and the other banking authorities have long sought to achieve a delicate balance in the role that government plays in the banking industry. One important task is to promote confidence and stability through the deposit insurance guarantee and the lender-of-last-resort function. But it is equally important that we uphold regulatory discipline through prudential supervision and promote market discipline by clearly limiting the extent of the government backstop.

In the wake of the recent crisis, we are working to implement an updated statutory mandate under the Dodd–Frank Act. As we do so, there is once again much debate over the lessons of the crisis and the proper role of government in the financial sector.

On one hand, there is concern that new regulations could impose onerous costs on banks and our economy, stifling financial innovation and economic growth. On the other, there is genuine alarm about the immense scale and seemingly indiscriminate nature of the government assistance provided to large banks and nonbank financial companies during the crisis, and what effects these actions will have on the competitive landscape in banking.

These bailouts were necessary because these institutions had been permitted to become so large, complex, and interconnected that the prospect of their failure was a threat to overall financial stability. They were Too-Big-To-Fail (TBTF). Richmond Federal Reserve Bank President Jeffrey Lacker recently reminded us of the drawbacks of a federal safety net policy of constructive ambiguity that allows regulators to talk tough during good times, but keep their options open during a crisis. But if there ever was a constructive ambiguity about the scope of the federal safety net and the existence of TBTF, it was surely made obsolete by the events of late 2008 and early 2009.

In the wake of that experience, all of us in this room have a vital interest and a collective responsibility to do what it takes to restore the balance between a safety net that assures stability and public confidence, and the need to place clear and credible limits on that safety net. In short, we must restore market discipline in the financial sector. That will be the focus of my remarks today.

The roots of the problem

The financial crisis of 2008 centered on the so-called shadow banking system — a network of large-bank affiliates, special-purpose vehicles, and nonbank financial companies that existed largely outside of the prudential supervision and capital requirements that apply to federally insured depository institutions in the U.S. In addition, the shadow banking system also fell largely outside of the FDIC's process for resolving failed insured financial institutions through receivership.

Several large, complex U.S. financial companies at the center of the 2008 crisis could not be wound down in an orderly manner when they became nonviable. Major segments of their operations were subject to the commercial bankruptcy code, as opposed to bank receivership laws, or they were located abroad and therefore outside of U.S. jurisdiction. The size and complexity of these institutions, and the inadequacy of the bankruptcy process as a means to preserve value after their failure, rendered these companies TBTF.

In the heat of the crisis, policymakers frequently resorted to bailouts instead of letting these firms collapse into bankruptcy. The fear was that the losses generated in a failure would cascade through the financial system, freezing financial markets and stopping the economy in its tracks. The worst fears of policymakers were realized when Lehman Brothers — a large, complex nonbank financial company — filed for bankruptcy on September 15, 2008.

The long-term outcome for Lehman creditors clearly demonstrates the shortcomings of bankruptcy as a means to resolve failed financial companies. The firm managing the Lehman bankruptcy reports that more than $75 billion in value was destroyed by the bankruptcy process itself, including tens of billions of dollars from the inability to roll over valuable derivatives contracts. More than two-and-a-half years after Lehman's failure, the process has cost over $1.2 billion in legal and other professional fees, and many creditors still don't know what their claims will be worth.

Anticipating the complications of this process, counterparties across the financial system reacted to the Lehman failure by running for the safety of cash and other government obligations. Subsequent days and weeks saw the collapse of interbank lending and commercial paper issuance, and a near complete disintermediation of the shadow banking system. The only remedy was massive intervention on the part of governments around the world, which pumped equity capital into banks and other financial companies, guaranteed certain non-deposit liabilities, and extended credit backed by a wide range of illiquid assets to banks and nonbank firms alike. Even with these emergency measures, the economic consequences of the crisis have been enormous.

Competitive implications of TBTF

The dilemma policymakers faced in the failure of large, complex financial institutions resembles a classic hostage drama, where the imperative of saving lives in the short run comes at the expense of encouraging more hostage-taking in the future. And so it is with the largest U.S. banks and other financial companies, which have every incentive to render themselves so large, so complex, and so opaque that no policymaker would dare risk letting them fail in a crisis. With the benefit of this implicit safety net, these institutions are insulated from the normal discipline of the marketplace that applies to smaller banks and practically every other private company.

Understanding the game, and having recently seen the nation's largest financial institutions receive hundreds of billions of dollars in taxpayer assistance, the market appears to expect more of the same going forward. In February, Moody's reported that its ratings on the senior unsecured debt of eight large U.S. banking organizations received an average "uplift" of 2.2 ratings notches because of the expectation of future government support. Meanwhile, the largest banks continue to enjoy a large competitive advantage over community banks in funding markets. In the fourth quarter of last year, the average interest cost of funding earning assets for banks with more than $100 billion in assets was about half the average for community banks with less than $1 billion in assets. Indeed, I would also argue that well-managed large banks are disadvantaged. TBTF narrows the funding advantage they would otherwise enjoy over weaker competitors.

This situation can only be regarded as a new and dangerous form of state capitalism, where the market assumes large, complex, and powerful financial companies are in line to receive generous government subsidies in times of financial distress. Unless reversed, we can expect to see more concentration of market power in the hands of the largest institutions, more complexity in financial structures and relationships, more risk-taking at the expense of the public, and, in due time, another financial crisis.

The new SIFI resolution framework

At the core of the reform legislation passed last summer are measures that create a new resolution framework that will apply to the so-called systemically important financial institutions, or SIFIs, that are associated with the problem of TBTF.

This new SIFI resolution framework has three basic elements. First, the new Financial Stability Oversight Council (FSOC), chaired by Treasury and made up of the other financial regulatory agencies, is responsible for designating SIFIs based on criteria that are now being established by regulation. Once designated, the SIFIs will be subject to heightened supervision by the Federal Reserve and required to maintain detailed resolution plans that demonstrate that they are resolvable under bankruptcy — not bailout — if they should run into severe financial distress.

Not only will these plans provide valuable advance information that will assist in implementing an orderly resolution, but the law also authorizes the FDIC and the Federal Reserve to require, if necessary, changes in the structure or activities of these institutions to ensure that they meet the standard of being "resolvable" in a crisis.

Finally, the law provides for a third alternative to bankruptcy or bailout — an Orderly Liquidation Authority, or OLA, that gives the FDIC many of the same trustee powers over SIFIs that we have long used to manage failed-bank receiverships. While this authority strictly prohibits bailouts, the FDIC could use it to conduct advance planning, to temporarily operate and fund the institution under government control to preserve its value as a going concern, and to quickly pay partial recoveries to creditors through advance dividends, as we have long done in failed-bank receiverships. The result would be a faster resolution of claims against the failed institution, smaller losses for creditors, reduced impact on the wider financial system, and an end to the cycle of bailouts.

The history of the recent crisis is replete with examples of missed opportunities to sell or recapitalize troubled institutions before they failed. But with bailout off the table, management will have a greater incentive to bring in an acquirer or new investors before failure, and shareholders and creditors will have more incentive to go along with such a plan in order to salvage the value of their claims. These new incentives to be more proactive in dealing with problem SIFIs will reduce their incidence of outright failure and also lessen the risk of systemic effects arising from such failures.

Doubts and misconceptions about the new resolution framework

The problem is that, even as we put this game plan into action, some still don't believe that policymakers have the means or the will to take the difficult steps needed to close down the SIFIs in a crisis, and will ultimately back down and just bail them out again. Part of the problem is a misunderstanding of the process. And part of it is a low opinion of the political will in Washington to make hard and unpopular decisions.

For example, we have heard some say that being designated as a SIFI will confer a competitive advantage by anointing an institution as TBTF. But the reality is that SIFIs will be subject to heightened supervision and higher capital requirements. They will also be required to maintain resolution plans and could be required to restructure their operations if they cannot demonstrate that they are resolvable.

Needless to say, nobody is signing up in advance to be a SIFI. In fact, it is just the opposite. It might be far better to fall just short of SIFI status in terms of size, complexity, and interconnectedness. In that case, your institution would be spared all of the additional regulatory burdens, but policymakers could still face significant challenges in effecting an orderly resolution in a crisis. That's why it is important that the FSOC move forward and develop some hard metrics to guide the SIFI designation process. We need to be able to gather information on a broad range of potential SIFIs in order to develop a sense of the difficulties that might arise in resolving them.

Ultimately, the "resolvability" of an institution should determine if it is designated as a SIFI. Upholding this standard will be essential if we are to avoid the "deathbed designation" of SIFIs that would put the resolution authority in the worst possible position in a crisis.

Misunderstandings also abound as to the nature of the OLA. Some have called it a bailout mechanism, while others see it as a fire sale that will destroy the value of receivership assets. Neither is true.

While it is positioned as a backup plan in cases where bankruptcy would threaten to result in wider financial disorder, the OLA is actually a better-suited framework for resolving claims against failed financial institutions. It is a transparent process that operates under fixed rules that prohibit any bailout of shareholders and creditors or any other type of political favoritism, which is a legitimate concern in the case of an ad-hoc emergency rescue program. Not only would the OLA work faster and preserve value better than bankruptcy, but the regulatory authorities who will administer the OLA are in a far better position to coordinate with foreign regulators in the failure of an institution with significant international operations.

The FDIC has made considerable progress in forging bilateral agreements with other countries that will facilitate orderly cross-border resolutions. And we currently co-chair the Cross Border Resolutions Group of the Basel Committee. It is worth noting that not a single other advanced country plans to rely on bankruptcy to resolve large, international financial companies. Most are implementing special resolution regimes similar to the OLA. Under the OLA, we can buy time, if necessary, and preserve franchise value by running the institution as a bridge bank, and then eventually sell it in parts or as a whole. It is a game-changer in terms of the ability to provide continuity and minimize losses in financial institution failures.

Resolution plans must be credible and actionable

A major improvement in the SIFI resolution process is also one that, in my opinion, has been somewhat underestimated by the skeptics. And that is the requirement for SIFI resolution plans.

When a large, complex financial institution gets into trouble, time is the enemy. The larger, more complex, and more interconnected a financial company is, the longer it takes to assemble a full and accurate picture of its operations and develop a resolution strategy. By requiring detailed resolution plans in advance, and authorizing an on-site FDIC team to conduct pre-resolution planning, the SIFI resolution framework regains the informational advantage that was lacking in the crisis of 2008.

The FDIC recently released a paper detailing how the filing of resolution plans, the ability to conduct advance planning, and other elements of the framework could have dramatically changed the outcome if they had been available in the case of Lehman. Under the new SIFI resolution framework, the FDIC should have a continuous presence at all designated SIFIs, working with the firms and reviewing their resolution plans as part of their normal course of business. So our presence will in no way be seen as a signal of distress. Instead, it is much more likely to provide a stabilizing influence that encourages management to more fully consider the downside consequences of its actions, to the benefit of the institution and the stability of the system as a whole.

As far-reaching as these changes are, their ultimate effectiveness will still depend on the willingness of the FDIC and the Federal Reserve to actively use their authority to require organizational changes that promote the ability to resolve SIFIs. As currently structured, many large banks and nonbank SIFIs maintain thousands of subsidiaries and manage their activities within business lines that cross many different organizational structures and regulatory jurisdictions. This can make it very difficult to implement an orderly resolution of one part of the company without triggering a costly collapse of the entire company.

To solve this problem, the FDIC and the Fed must be willing to insist on organizational changes that better align business lines and legal entities well before a crisis occurs. Unless these structures are rationalized and simplified in advance, there is a real danger that their complexity could make a SIFI resolution far more costly and more difficult than it needs to be.

Such changes are also likely to have collateral benefits for the firm's management in the short run. A simplified organizational structure will put management in a better position to understand and monitor risks and the inter-relationships among business lines, addressing what many see as a major challenge that contributed to the crisis. That is why — well before the test of another major crisis — we must define high informational standards for resolution plans and be willing to insist on organizational changes where necessary in order to ensure that SIFIs meet the standard of resolvability.

What you can do to shape the outcome

In the wake of a crisis, there is a natural tendency for memories to fade. The economic pain caused by the financial crisis will subside in time, and even the Bank Structure Conference will eventually move on to consider other topics and other challenges. In an ever-changing financial landscape, it can be difficult to maintain a long-term focus on the lessons of the last crisis and the imperatives of preparing to deal with the next one. Most of all, it is extremely difficult to overcome the political resistance that comes from large, powerful financial organizations when they are asked to make potentially costly changes at a time when the danger of a financial crisis appears remote.

As I mentioned at the outset, everyone in this room has a vital stake in the outcome of these reforms. And, because this is such a knowledgeable and influential group, all of you have a role to play in their failure or their success. Given the challenges before us, one response that many seem to have is a certain cynicism and detachment about the process. It's easy to be a doubter and simply resign yourself to the idea that it is just too difficult, and that we will never be able to really put an end to TBTF.

If enough of us do that, then the ratings agencies will end up being right in terms of their expectation of future government support. Open-ended state subsidies to large financial companies in times of crisis could become a permanent part of the landscape, with all of the attendant implications that has for risk-taking and the competitive structure in banking.

But, knowing this group as I do now, after almost five years as FDIC Chairman, I think you have a far more productive role to play in shaping the outcome of this critical policy debate. I urge you to actively use your influence to ensure that the new SIFI resolution framework will be equal to the great task that is before us. Conduct your own analysis of the regulations as they are proposed, and engage the process in comment letters, op-eds, blog posts, and research papers. Ask the hard questions that need asking:

- Are regulators carrying out the intent of the reforms?
- Does all the right firms designated as SIFIs?
- Are they developing credible resolution plans?
- Are the largest financial companies structured in a way that renders them resolvable in a crisis?
- Is progress being made in coordinating resolution plans on the international front?
- And, most importantly, are we meeting the market test of credibility? (The answer to this question will be evident in credit spreads, funding costs, and other market indicators.)

Conclusion

While it is important that you critique the actions of all parties to this debate — including regulators, financial companies, and other market participants — it is equally important that you use your knowledge and your influence to help explain the parameters of this debate and the stakes involved to the American people. These issues are complex and are generally not well-understood by the public. But the people in this room are among the world's leading experts on these issues. With your active engagement, I am confident that we can build the broad-based political support that will be needed to change the status quo and build the foundation for a stronger and more competitive financial sector in the years ahead.

Chapter 8

The Orderly Liquidation of Lehman Brothers Holdings Inc. Under the Dodd–Frank Act

Federal Deposit Insurance Corporation[1]

Introduction

The bankruptcy filing of Lehman Brothers Holdings Inc. (Lehman or LBHI) on September 15, 2008, was one of the signal events of the financial crisis. The disorderly and costly nature of the LBHI bankruptcy — the largest, and still ongoing, financial bankruptcy in U.S. history — contributed to the massive financial disruption of late 2008. This paper examines how the government could have structured a resolution of Lehman under the orderly liquidation authority (OLA) of Title II of the Dodd–Frank Wall Street Reform and Consumer Protection Act

[1]This article originally appeared in the *FDIC Quarterly*, Vol. 5(2), pp. 31–49. It was written not long after Dodd–Frank became law and was meant to describe how the resulting new resolution authorities could have been used to produce a better result surrounding the failure of Lehman Brothers. Since that time, the FDIC has developed an alternative resolution strategy (the *Single Point of Entry* methodology) that is described in Gruenberg, Martin J., 2012, "Implementing Dodd–Frank: Orderly resolution," *Economic Perspectives*, Federal Reserve Bank of Chicago, Volume 36, Third Quarter, pp. 98–102; and in a joint paper by the FDIC and Bank of England, "Resolving Globally Active, Systemically Important, Financial Institutions," December 2012. Both articles are reprinted in this volume. While the current article shows the advantages of the new resolution powers provided by Dodd–Frank, it does not precisely describe how the FDIC would implement a SIFI resolution today.

(Dodd–Frank Act) and how the outcome could have differed from the outcome under bankruptcy.

The Dodd–Frank Act grants the Federal Deposit Insurance Corporation (FDIC) the powers and authorities necessary to effect an orderly liquidation of systemically important financial institutions (SIFIs). These authorities are analogous to those the FDIC uses to resolve failed insured depository institutions under the Federal Deposit Insurance Act (FDI Act).[2] The keys to an orderly resolution of a systemically important financial company that preserves financial stability are the ability to plan for the resolution and liquidation, provide liquidity to maintain key assets and operations, and conduct an open bidding process to sell the company and its assets and operations to the private sector as quickly as practicable. The FDIC has developed procedures that have allowed it to efficiently use its powers and authorities to resolve failed insured institutions for over 75 years. The FDIC expects to adapt many of these procedures, modified as necessary, to the liquidation of failed SIFIs.

The events leading to the Lehman bankruptcy

Background

The events leading up to Lehman's bankruptcy are documented in a number of books and articles; but perhaps most extensively in two documents: the Report of Anton R. Valukas, Examiner, Bankruptcy of LBHI, and the Trustee's Preliminary Investigation Report of the Attorneys for James W. Giddens, Trustee for the Securities Investors Protection Act (SIPA) Liquidation of Lehman Brothers, Inc. The analysis in this paper assumes that the events leading up to Lehman's bankruptcy filing took place roughly as described in these two reports.

Prior to 2006, Lehman had been described as being in the "moving business," primarily originating or purchasing loans and then selling them through securitizations.[3] Beginning in 2006, the firm shifted to an aggressive growth business strategy, making "principal" investments in long-term, high-risk areas such as commercial real estate, leveraged lending and private equity. Even as the subprime crisis grew, the firm continued its rapid growth strategy throughout 2007.

---

[2]12 U.S.C. §1811 *et seq.*

[3]Anton R. Valukas, *Examiner's Report: Bankruptcy of Lehman Brothers Holdings Inc.*, Vol. 2, 43, (March 11, 2010) (hereinafter, Examiner's Report).

At the beginning of 2008, with no end of the sub-prime crisis in sight, Lehman again revised its business strategy and began the process of deleveraging. However, by the end of the first quarter of 2008, the firm had made no substantial progress in either selling assets or in raising large amounts of equity. Richard S. Fuld, Jr., Lehman's CEO, told the Examiner that he had decided that Lehman would not raise equity unless it was at a premium above book value.[4]

After Bear Stearns failed and was purchased by JPMorgan Chase on March 15, 2008, Lehman was seen by many as the next most vulnerable investment bank.[5] At this time, Lehman began raising equity and seeking investment partners. In late March, Lehman contacted Warren E. Buffett, unsuccessfully seeking an investment from either Mr. Buffett or one of Berkshire Hathaway's subsidiaries. At the beginning of April, Lehman completed a $4 billion convertible preferred stock issuance. In late May, Lehman began talks with a consortium of Korean banks, but no deal was reached. On June 7, Lehman announced a $2.8 billion loss for the second quarter and on June 12, it raised $6 billion in preferred and common stock, resulting in $10 billion in the aggregate of new capital for the second quarter of 2008.

By mid-June, Lehman recognized that its commercial real estate portfolio was a major problem and began to develop a "good bank-bad bank" plan to spin off the portfolio. It identified $31.6 billion in assets that would be placed in a so-called bad bank to be named SpinCo, which would reduce Lehman's balance sheet and shed risky assets. For a number of reasons, the plan never came to fruition.[6]

Although the consortium of Korean banks withdrew from negotiations, one of the consortium's banks, the government-owned Korean Development Bank (KDB), continued to express an interest in buying or making a substantial investment in Lehman. The talks between Lehman and KDB went through a number of iterations, with KDB becoming increasingly concerned about Lehman's risky assets. In August, KDB proposed an investment in a "Clean Lehman," where all risk of future losses (risky assets) would be spun off from Lehman. By late August, KDB decided that the deteriorating global financial situation and the declining value of Korea's currency made that transaction too problematic and withdrew from further negotiations.[7]

---

[4] *Id.* at 150–152. Lehman did raise capital at a later date. Presumably more could have been raised at this time if Lehman had been willing to consider less favorable terms to the then-current shareholders.

[5] *Id.* at 612–613.

[6] *Id.* at 640–662.

[7] *Id.* at 668–681.

In July 2008, Lehman contacted Bank of America with a proposal whereby Bank of America would buy a 30% interest in LBHI, but the discussions never culminated in a transaction. In late August, Lehman again contacted Bank of America, this time about helping finance SpinCo. Lehman subsequently asked Bank of America to consider buying the entire firm, but Bank of America did not pursue a transaction.

MetLife had also been in contact with Lehman about a possible purchase. MetLife began due diligence in early August, but decided within a few days that Lehman's commercial real estate and residential real estate assets were too risky. Also in August, the Investment Corporation of Dubai explored a potential investment principally in Lehman's Neuberger Berman wealth and asset management business. Discussions ceased in early September.[8]

By the late summer of 2008, Lehman's liquidity problems were becoming acute. Lehman's urgent need to find a buyer was precipitated in part by panic in the financial markets following the two largest players in the U.S. mortgage market, Fannie Mae and Freddie Mac, being placed into conservatorship on September 7, 2008, and the ensuing devaluation of those institutions' common and preferred stock. On September 9, Treasury Secretary Henry M. Paulson, Jr. contacted Bank of America and asked it to look into purchasing Lehman.[9] During that conversation on September 9, Secretary Paulson informed Bank of America that the government would not provide any assistance.[10] Bank of America began due diligence, and on September 11 told Secretary Paulson that there were so many problems with the assets on Lehman's balance sheet that Bank of America was unwilling to pursue a privately negotiated acquisition. Secretary Paulson then told Bank of America that, although the government would not provide any assistance, he believed a consortium of banks could be encouraged by the government to assist Bank of America in an acquisition of Lehman by taking the bad assets in a transaction similar in certain respects to the 1998 rescue of Long-Term Capital Management.[11] Bank of America then agreed to continue to consider the purchase of Lehman. At various times in the following two days, Bank of America discussed its analysis of Lehman with the Treasury Department and concluded that Lehman had approximately $65–67 billion in commercial real estate and residential mortgage-related assets and private equity investments that it was unwilling to purchase

[8] *Id.* at 687–694.

[9] Henry M. Paulson, Jr., *On the Brink: Inside the Race to Stop the Collapse of the Global Financial System*, 177 (2010) (hereinafter, *On the Brink*).

[10] *Id.* at 177, 184–185.

[11] *Id.* at 199–206.

in any acquisition without the government providing loss protection. Independently, on September 13, Merrill Lynch approached Bank of America and shortly thereafter Bank of America agreed to acquire Merrill Lynch.[12]

Lehman reported further losses on September 10, and announced plans to restructure the firm.[13] The panic also affected Lehman's trading counterparties, which began to lose confidence in the firm. Many of these counterparties withdrew short-term funding, demanded increasingly greater overcollateralization on borrowings or clearing exposures, demanded more collateral to cover their derivatives positions and subsequently began to move their business away from Lehman. Lehman's clearing banks also began to demand billions of dollars of additional collateral.

A final attempt at a sale of Lehman occurred on September 11, 2008, when Lehman was contacted by Barclays, a large U.K. commercial and investment bank.[14] Barclays commenced due diligence of Lehman on September 12 and soon identified $52 billion in assets that it believed Lehman had overvalued and that Barclays would not purchase as part of the transaction. As in the case of Bank of America, these assets were concentrated in commercial real estate, residential real estate, and private equity investments. For a variety of reasons, Barclays could not get immediate regulatory approval from the U.K. authorities and the transaction was abandoned on September 14.[15]

LBHI started work on a plan for an "orderly" wind-down. The plan estimated it would take six months to unwind Lehman's positions and made the assumption that the Federal Reserve Bank of New York would assist Lehman during the wind-down process.[16] On September 14, 2008, the Federal Reserve Bank of New York told LBHI that, without the Barclay's transaction, it would not fund Lehman.

Chapter 11 filing

With no firm willing to acquire LBHI and without funding from the central bank, LBHI filed for Chapter 11 bankruptcy on September 15, 2008.[17] On that date, a

---

[12]Examiner's Report at 696–703.

[13]Lehman Brothers Holdings Inc., Periodic Report on Form 8-K, September 10, 2008.

[14]Similar to the case of Bank of America, Barclays contacted Lehman at Treasury's encouragement. Barclays and Bank of America were proceeding under similar expectations that there would not be any government assistance.

[15]Examiner's Report at 703–11 and *On the Brink* at 203–11.

[16]Examiner's Report at 720–21.

[17]LBHI filed for bankruptcy protection on Monday, September 15, 2008, at 1:30 am EDT. *Id.* at 726.

number of LBHI affiliates also filed for bankruptcy protection and Lehman's U.K. broker–dealer, Lehman Brothers International (Europe) (LBIE), filed for administration in the United Kingdom. These events adversely affected the ability of Lehman's U.S. broker–dealer, Lehman Brothers Inc. (LBI), to obtain adequate funding and settle trades. LBI remained in operation until September 19, when it was placed into a SIPA liquidation.[18]

The Lehman bankruptcy had an immediate and negative effect on U.S. financial stability and has proven to be a disorderly, time-consuming, and expensive process.[19] Of Lehman's creditors, the one that experienced the most disruption was the Reserve Primary Fund, a $62 billion money market fund. On the day of the filing, the fund held $785 million of Lehman's commercial paper, representing 13.8% of the amount outstanding as of May 31, 2008.[20] The fund immediately suffered a run, facing redemptions of approximately $40 billion over the following two days. With depleted cash reserves, the fund was forced to sell securities in order to meet redemption requests, which further depressed valuations. The fund's parent company announced it would "break the buck" when it repriced its shares at $0.97 on September 16, 2008. During the remainder of the week, U.S. domestic money market funds experienced approximately $310 billion in withdrawals, representing 15% of their total assets and eventually prompting the U.S. Treasury to announce a temporary guarantee of money market funds.[21]

LBHI's default also caused disruptions in the swaps and derivatives markets and a rapid, market-wide unwinding of trading positions for those financial markets contracts not subject to the automatic stay in bankruptcy. For example, LBHI's bankruptcy filing affected LBI's exposure in the commodities markets via its positions that settled on markets operated by CME Group. LBI's assets on CME Group markets were largely contracts to hedge risk for the energy business

---

[18]LBHI's demise left LBI unable to obtain adequate financing on an unsecured or secured basis. LBI lost customers and experienced both an increase in failed transactions and additional demands for collateral by clearing banks and others. See *Trustee's Preliminary Investigation Report of the Attorneys for James W. Giddens, Trustee for the SIPA Liquidation of Lehman Brothers, Inc.*, 10, 25, 26, 56.

[19]After more than two years in bankruptcy proceedings, total fees paid to advisers involved in the Lehman bankruptcy have exceeded $1 billion. *See* Liz Moyer, *Lehman Fees Hit $1 Billion and Counting*, *Wall Street Journal*, November 23, 2010, available at: http://online.wsj.com/article/.SB200 01424052748704243904575630653803513816.html.

[20]Lehman used November 30 as its year end for financial reporting purposes. Accordingly, May 31, 2008, was the date of the close of its second quarter financial period.

[21]*President's Working Group on Financial Markets: Money Market Fund Reform Options* (October 2010), available at: http://www.treasury.gov/press-enter/press-releases/Documents/10.21%20 PWG%20Report%20Final.pdf.

conducted in its other entities. LBHI typically was guarantor of the swap contracts of its subsidiaries and affiliates. For those derivative financial instruments for which LBHI acted as guarantor, the Chapter 11 filing of LBHI constituted a default under the International Swaps and Derivatives Association agreements governing the swaps, which had the effect of allowing termination of those trades. This left naked hedges and exposed LBI to considerable pricing risk since it was not able to offer both sides of the hedge when liquidating the portfolio.[22] Similarly, the Options Clearing Corporation (OCC) threatened to invoke its emergency clearing house rules which would allow it to liquidate all of LBI's positions unless a performing third party agreed to assume the positions. The Depository Trust & Clearing Corporation (DTCC) shared the same concerns as the CME Group and the OCC, and was unwilling to perform settlement and transfer functions for LBI unless a performing third party assumed all potential liability. When Barclays refused to assume the potential liability, the DTCC began liquidating LBI's positions as a broker–dealer whose membership had been terminated on September 22, 2008. Consequently, account transfer requests from customers that were already in process were canceled. The DTCC also reversed all account transfers that had taken place on September 19, 2008, a Friday. As a result, $468 million of customer assets that otherwise would have been immune from seizure were seized.[23] It was not until February 11, 2009, that a court order restored the reversed transactions.

Other unsecured creditors of LBHI are projected to incur substantial losses. Immediately prior to its bankruptcy filing, LBHI reported equity of approximately $20 billion; short-term and long-term indebtedness of approximately $100 billion, of which approximately $15 billion represented junior and subordinated indebtedness; and other liabilities in the amount of approximately $90 billion, of which approximately $88 billion were amounts due to affiliates. The modified Chapter 11 plan of reorganization filed by the debtors on January 25, 2011, estimates a 21.4% recovery for senior unsecured creditors. Subordinated debt holders and shareholders will receive nothing under the plan of reorganization, and other unsecured creditors will recover between 11.2% and 16.6%, depending on their status.[24]

Just prior to Lehman's bankruptcy filing, the firm had identified $31.6 billion in commercial real estate assets of questionable value. Potential acquirers of Lehman had identified additional problematic assets — for a total value between

---

[22] SIPA Trustee Report Section V.B., p. 66.

[23] *Id.* at 73.

[24] Joseph Checkler, *Lehman's New Creditor Plan Doesn't Factor in Key Group*, *Wall Street Journal*, January 27, 2011. The plan of reorganization is subject to approval by creditors.

$50 billion and $70 billion. Even if there had been a total loss on these assets, which would have eliminated any shareholder and subordinated debt holder potential for recovery, a quick resolution of LBHI that maintained the operational integrity of the company including its systems and personnel could have left general unsecured creditors with substantially more value than projected from the bankruptcy. By preserving the going-concern value of the firm, creditors could have been provided with an immediate payment on a portion of their claims through either an advance dividend or the prompt distribution of proceeds from the sale of assets. The panic selling that ensued — further precipitating a decline in asset values and a decline in the value of collateral underlying the firm's derivatives portfolio — could have been avoided and markets would likely have remained more stable.

The resolution and receivership process for failed banks

Resolution process

The FDIC has been successful in using its authority under the FDI Act to maintain stability and confidence in the nation's banking system, including in the resolution of large, complex insured depository institutions. The FDIC, as receiver for an insured depository institution, is given broad powers and flexibility under the FDI Act to resolve an insured depository institution in a manner that minimizes disruption to the banking system and maximizes value. The FDIC is given similar tools to those under the Dodd–Frank Act to accomplish these goals, including the ability to create one or more bridge banks, enforce cross-guarantees among sister banks, sell and liquidate assets, and settle claims. When an insured bank fails, the FDIC is required by statute to resolve the failed bank in the least costly way, to minimize any loss to the deposit insurance fund, and, as receiver, to maximize the return on the assets of the failed bank.[25] Banks and thrifts are typically closed by their chartering authority when they become critically undercapitalized and have not been successful in their plan to restore capital to the required levels.[26] The

[25]The FDIC is required, pursuant to 12 U.S.C. §1823(c)(4), to resolve failed insured depository institutions in the manner that is least costly to the deposit insurance fund. The Dodd–Frank Act does not require that a least cost determination be made in respect of a covered financial company, though the FDIC is required, to the greatest extent practicable, to maximize returns and minimize losses in the disposition of assets. *See* Section 210(a)(9)(E) of the Dodd–Frank Act, 12 U.S.C. §5390(a)(9)(E).

[26]Some banks, particularly large banks, may also be closed due to a liquidity failure (an inability to pay debts as they become due).

FDIC is then appointed receiver.[27] When structuring a bank resolution, the FDIC can pay off insured depositors and liquidate the bank's assets, sell the bank in whole or in part (a purchase and assumption transaction, or P&A), or establish a bridge institution — a temporary national bank or federal thrift — to maintain the functions of the failed bank during the process of marketing the bank's franchise. Senior management and boards of directors are not retained, and no severance pay or "golden parachutes" are permitted.

Final planning and marketing for a bank resolution normally begins 90–100 days prior to the institution being placed into receivership, though the process may be accelerated in the event of a liquidity failure. It begins when a bank's problems appear to be severe enough to potentially cause it to fail. During this period, the FDIC coordinates its actions — including the scheduling of the failure — with other regulators. When a bank becomes critically undercapitalized, the primary federal regulator (PFR) has up to 90 days to close the institution and appoint the FDIC as receiver. The FDIC and the PFR require that the bank seek an acquirer or merger partner, and insist that top management responsible for the bank's failing condition leave in order to improve the prospects for such, before the FDIC has to exercise its powers as receiver. The FDIC's authority to take over a failed or failing institution, thus wiping out stockholders and imposing losses on unsecured and uninsured creditors, not only provides an incentive for management to actively seek an acquirer, but also encourages the institution's board of directors to approve (or recommend for approval to shareholders) such transactions to avoid the risk of an FDIC receivership.

During this planning phase, the FDIC collects as much information as possible about the bank and structures the resolution transaction. This information assists the FDIC in determining the best transaction structures to offer potential acquirers. The FDIC also values bank assets and determines which assets may be particularly problematic for an acquiring institution and may need to be retained in the receivership for disposition after resolution or covered by some level of risk protection. Qualified bidders are contacted to perform due diligence, subject to a

---

[27]As a receiver, the FDIC succeeds to the rights, powers, and privileges of the failed bank and its stockholders, officers, and directors. It may collect all obligations and money due to the institution, preserve and liquidate the institution's assets and property, and perform any other function of the institution consistent with its appointment as receiver. It has the power to sell a failed bank to another insured bank, and to transfer the failed bank's assets and liabilities without the consent or approval of any other agency, court, or party with contractual rights. The FDIC may also, as permitted by statute, repudiate contracts such as leases that are burdensome to the receivership and may rid the receivership of burdensome obligations. The FDIC operates its receiverships independently of the court or bankruptcy system, although certain of the FDIC's actions are subject to judicial review.

confidentiality agreement. Due diligence is offered both on-site and off-site through the use of secure internet data rooms. Bidders are then asked to submit bids on the basis of the transaction structures offered by the FDIC. The FDIC analyzes the bids received and accepts the bid that resolves the failed bank in the least costly manner to the deposit insurance fund. The least-cost requirement ensures that the deposit insurance fund will not be used to protect creditors other than insured depositors and prevents differentiation between creditors except where necessary to achieve the least costly resolution of the failed bank. Then, at the point of failure, the institution is placed into receivership and immediately sold — with the sale resulting in a transfer of deposits and assets that renders the process seamless to insured depositors. The FDIC is also able to make an immediate payment, or advance dividend, to uninsured creditors not assumed by the assuming institution based upon estimated recoveries from the liquidation.

The orderly liquidation of covered financial companies

Introduction

Title II of the Dodd–Frank Act defines the framework for orderly resolution proceedings and establishes the powers and duties of the FDIC when acting as receiver for a covered financial company.[28] The policy goal of the Dodd–Frank Act is succinctly summarized in Section 204(a) as the liquidation of "failing financial companies that pose a significant risk to the financial stability of the United States in a manner that mitigates such risk and minimizes moral hazard." Creditors and shareholders are to "bear the losses of the financial company" and the FDIC is instructed to liquidate the covered financial company in a manner that maximizes the value of the company's assets, minimizes losses, mitigates risk, and minimizes moral hazard.[29]

This section discusses the key provisions of Title II and highlights the differences between the resolution of a SIFI under Title II of the Dodd–Frank Act and a proceeding under the Bankruptcy Code.[30] What follows is a brief summary of the appointment process and five of the most important elements of the authority

[28] A failed SIFI is deemed a covered financial company for purposes of Title II of the Dodd–Frank Act once a systemic determination has been made by the Secretary of the Treasury pursuant to Section 203(b) thereof, 12 U.S.C. §5383(b). *See* " — Appointment," *infra.*

[29] *See* Sections 204(a)(1) and 210(a)(9)(E) of the Dodd–Frank Act, 12 U.S.C. §§5384(a)(1) and 5390(a)(9)(E).

[30] 11 U.S.C. §101 *et seq.*

available to the FDIC as receiver of a covered financial company. Those five elements are: (i) the ability to conduct advance resolution planning for SIFIs through a variety of mechanisms similar to those used for problem banks (these mechanisms will be enhanced by the supervisory authority and the resolution plans, or living wills, required under Section 165(d) of Title I of the Dodd–Frank Act); (ii) an immediate source of liquidity for an orderly liquidation, which allows continuation of essential functions and maintains asset values; (iii) the ability to make advance dividends and prompt distributions to creditors based upon expected recoveries; (iv) the ability to continue key, systemically important operations, including through the formation of one or more bridge financial companies; and (v) the ability to transfer all qualified financial contracts[31] with a given counterparty to another entity (such as a bridge financial company) and avoid their immediate termination and liquidation to preserve value and promote stability.[32]

Appointment

Under Section 203 of the Dodd–Frank Act, at the Secretary of the Treasury's (Secretary) request, or of their own initiative, the Board of Governors of the Federal Reserve System (Federal Reserve) and the FDIC are to make a written recommendation requesting that the Secretary appoint the FDIC as receiver for a SIFI that is in default or danger of default.[33] The recommendation to place a broker or dealer, or a financial company in which the largest domestic subsidiary is a broker or dealer, into receivership is made by the Federal Reserve and the Securities and Exchange Commission (SEC), in consultation with the FDIC. Similarly, the recommendation to place an insurance company or a financial company in which the largest domestic subsidiary is an insurance company, is

[31] Generally, qualified financial contracts are financial instruments such as securities contracts, commodities contracts, forwards contracts, swaps, repurchase agreements, and any similar agreements. *See* Section 210(c)(8)(D)(i) of the Dodd–Frank Act, 12 U.S.C. §5390(c)(8)(D)(i).

[32] *See generally* Section 165 of Title I of the Dodd–Frank Act, 12 U.S.C. §5365 and "The Orderly Resolution of Covered Financial Companies — Special Powers under Title II — Oversight and Advanced Planning," *infra*.

[33] Upon a 2/3 vote by the boards of both the FDIC and the Federal Reserve, a written recommendation is delivered to the Secretary. The recommendation includes: an evaluation of whether the financial company is in default or is in danger of default; a description of the effect the failure of the financial company would have on U.S. financial stability; an evaluation of why a case under the Bankruptcy Code is not appropriate; an evaluation of the effect on creditors, counterparties, and shareholders of the financial company and other market participants, and certain other evaluations required by statute. *See* Section 203(a)(2) of the Dodd–Frank Act, 12 U.S.C. §5383(a)(2).

made by the Federal Reserve and Director of the newly established Federal Insurance Office, in consultation with the FDIC.

The Secretary is responsible for making a determination as to whether the financial company should be placed into receivership, and that determination is based on, among other things, the Secretary's finding that the financial company is in default or in danger of default; that the failure of the company and its resolution under otherwise applicable State or Federal law would have serious adverse consequences on the financial stability of the United States; and that no viable private sector alternative is available to prevent the default of the financial company.[34]

The Dodd–Frank Act provides an expedited judicial review process of the Secretary's determination. Should the board of directors of the covered financial company object to the appointment of the FDIC as receiver, a hearing is held in federal district court, and the court must make a decision on the matter within 24 hours. Upon a successful petition (or should the court fail to act within the time provided), the Secretary is to appoint the FDIC receiver of the covered financial company.[35]

Special powers under Title II

Ability to preserve systemic operations of the covered financial company

The Dodd–Frank Act provides an efficient mechanism — the bridge financial company — to quickly preserve the going-concern value of the firm's assets and business lines. There are no specific parallel provisions in the Bankruptcy Code,[36] and therefore it is more difficult for a debtor company operating under Chapter 11 of the Bankruptcy Code to achieve the same result as expeditiously, particularly where circumstances compel the debtor company to seek bankruptcy protection before a wind-down plan can be negotiated and implemented. Where maximizing or preserving value depends upon a quick separation of good assets from bad assets, implementation delays could adversely impact a reorganization or liquidation proceeding.

The Dodd–Frank Act authorizes the FDIC, as receiver of a covered financial company, to establish a bridge financial company to which assets and liabilities of the covered financial company may be transferred.[37] Fundamental to an orderly

[34] *See* Section 203(b) of the Dodd–Frank Act, 12 U.S.C. §5383(b).

[35] *See* Section 202(a)(1)(A) of the Dodd–Frank Act, 12 U.S.C. §5382(a)(1)(A).

[36] Similar to the FDIC's repudiation powers provided by Section 210(c)(1) of the Dodd–Frank Act, 12 U.S.C. §5390(c)(1), a bankruptcy trustee is authorized to reject certain contracts (which may be related to certain problem assets) of the debtor.

[37] *See* Section 210(h) of the Dodd–Frank Act, 12 U.S.C. §5390(h). There are statutorily imposed limitations upon the transfer of assets and liabilities from the receiver to the bridge financial company,

liquidation of a covered financial company is the ability to continue key operations, services, and transactions that will maximize the value of the firm's assets and operations and avoid a disorderly collapse in the marketplace. To facilitate this continuity of operations, the receivership can utilize one or more bridge financial companies. The bridge financial company is a newly established, federally chartered entity that is owned by the FDIC and includes those assets, liabilities, and operations of the covered financial company as necessary to achieve the maximum value of the firm. Shareholders, debt holders, and other creditors whose claims were not transferred to the bridge financial company will remain in the receivership and will receive payments on their claims based upon the priority of payments set forth in Section 210(b) of the Dodd–Frank Act. Like the bridge banks used in the resolution of large insured depository institutions,[38] the bridge financial company authority permits the FDIC to stabilize the key operations of the covered financial company by continuing valuable, systemically important operations.

While the covered financial company's board of directors and the most senior management responsible for its failure will be replaced, as required by Section 204(a)(2) of the Dodd–Frank Act,[39] operations may be continued by the covered financial company's employees under the strategic direction of the FDIC, as receiver, and contractors employed by the FDIC to help oversee those operations. These contractors would typically include firms with expertise in the sector of the covered financial company. In addition, former executives, managers and other individuals with experience and expertise in running companies similar to the covered financial company would be retained to oversee those operations.

A bridge financial company also provides the receiver with flexibility in preserving the value of the assets of the covered financial company and in effecting an orderly liquidation. The receiver can retain certain assets and liabilities of the covered financial company in the receivership and transfer other assets and liabilities, as well as the viable operations of the covered financial company, to the bridge financial company. The receiver may also transfer certain qualified financial contracts to the bridge financial company, as discussed below. The bridge financial company can operate until the receiver is able to stabilize the systemic

including a prohibition against a bridge financial company assuming any liability that is regulatory capital of the covered financial company. *See* Section 210(h)(1)(B)(i) of the Dodd–Frank Act, 12 U.S.C. §5390(h)(1)(B)(i). Additionally, the liabilities transferred from a covered financial company to a bridge financial company are not permitted to exceed the assets so transferred. *See* Section 210(h)5)(F) of the Dodd–Frank Act, 12 U.S.C. §5390(h)(5)(F).

[38]*See* 12 U.S.C. §1821(n).

[39]This may be contrasted with a typical Chapter 11 resolution, in which the management of the pre-insolvency institution will continue to manage the operations of the debtor institution.

functions of the covered financial company, conduct marketing for its assets and find one or more appropriate buyers.[40]

Transfer of qualified financial contracts

Under the Bankruptcy Code, counterparties to qualified financial contracts with the debtor company are permitted to terminate the contract and liquidate and net out their position. The debtor company or trustee has no authority to continue these contracts or to transfer the contracts to a third party, absent the consent of the counterparty, after the debtor company's insolvency. A complex, systemic financial company can hold very large positions in qualified financial contracts, often involving numerous counterparties and back-to-back trades, some of which may be opaque and incompletely documented. A disorderly unwinding of such contracts triggered by an event of insolvency, as each counterparty races to unwind and cover unhedged positions, can cause a tremendous loss of value, especially if lightly traded collateral covering a trade is sold into an artificially depressed, unstable market. Such disorderly unwinding can have severe negative consequences for the financial company, its creditors, its counterparties, and the financial stability of the United States.

In contrast, the Dodd–Frank Act expressly permits the FDIC to transfer qualified financial contracts to a solvent financial institution (an acquiring investor) or to a bridge financial company.[41] In such a case, counterparties are prohibited from terminating their contracts and liquidating and netting out their positions on the grounds of an event of insolvency.[42] The receiver's ability to transfer qualified financial contracts to a third party in order for the contracts to continue according

---

[40] In 2008, the FDIC implemented a successful resolution of IndyMac Bank through a transaction involving a "pass-through conservatorship," which is similar to the utilization of a bridge financial company. The transfer of assets to a *de novo* institution, named IndyMac Federal Bank, and its subsequent sale to a private investor in 2009 enabled the FDIC to sell the core business intact. This was more efficient and less costly than a liquidation and retained the value of the institution's assets. As of January 31, 2009, IndyMac Federal Bank had total assets of $23.5 billion and total deposits of $6.4 billion. The assuming institution agreed to purchase all deposits and approximately $20.7 billion in assets at a discount of $4.7 billion. The FDIC retained the remaining assets for future disposition. *See* Press Release, FDIC, *FDIC Closes Sale of IndyMac Federal Bank*, Pasadena, California (March 20, 2009), available at: http://www.fdic.gov/news/news/press/2009/pr09042.html.

[41] *See* Section 210(c)(9) of the Dodd–Frank Act, 12 U.S.C. §5390(c)(9).

[42] The exemption from the automatic stay under the Bankruptcy Code in the case of qualified financial contracts generally works well in most cases. However, for SIFIs, in which the sudden termination and netting of a derivatives portfolio could have an adverse impact on U.S. financial stability, the nullification of the *ipso facto* clause is needed. By removing a right of termination based solely upon the failure of the counterparty, the bridge financial company structure provides the flexibility to

to their terms — notwithstanding the debtor company's insolvency — provides market certainty and stability and preserves the value represented by the contracts.[43]

By the time of the failure of the troubled financial company, most if not all of its qualified financial contracts would be fully collateralized as counterparties sought to protect themselves from its growing credit risk. As a result, it is likely that a transfer of qualified financial contracts to a third party would involve the transfer of fully collateralized transactions and not expose the receiver to risk of loss.[44] To the extent the derivatives portfolio included qualified financial contracts which were under-collateralized or unsecured, the FDIC, as receiver of the covered financial company, would determine whether to repudiate or to transfer those qualified financial contracts to a third party based upon the FDIC's obligation to maximize value and minimize losses in the disposition of assets of the entire receivership.

Funding

A vital element in preserving continuity of systemically important operations is the availability of funding for those operations. A Chapter 11 debtor operating under the Bankruptcy Code will typically require funds in order to operate its business — referred to as debtor-in-possession financing (DIP financing). Although the Bankruptcy Code provides for a debtor company to obtain DIP financing with court approval, there are no assurances that the court will approve the DIP financing or that a debtor company will be able to obtain sufficient — or any — funding or obtain funding on acceptable terms, or what the timing of such funding might be. For a SIFI, the market may be destabilized by any delay associated with negotiating DIP financing or uncertainty as to whether the bankruptcy court will approve DIP financing. Further, the terms of the DIP financing may limit the debtor's options for reorganizing or liquidating and may diminish the

---

incentivize qualified financial contract counterparties to either maintain their positions in such contracts, or exit their positions in a manner which does not jeopardize U.S. financial stability.

[43]There are implications under the Dodd–Frank Act to transferring all of a covered financial company's qualified financial contracts to a bridge financial company in order to avoid such contracts' termination by their counterparties. As such contracts continue, following such transfer, to be valid and binding obligations of the bridge financial company (before being eventually wound down), the bridge financial company is required to perform the obligations thereunder, including in respect of meeting collateral requirements, hedging, and being liable for gains and losses on the contracts.

[44]Title VII of the Dodd–Frank Act, 15 U.S.C. §8301 *et seq.*, contemplates requirements for increased initial and variation margin.

franchise value of the company, particularly when the DIP financing is secured with previously unencumbered assets or when the terms of the DIP financing grant the lender oversight approval over the use of the DIP financing.

The Dodd–Frank Act provides that the FDIC may borrow funds from the Department of the Treasury, among other things, to make loans to, or guarantee obligations of, a covered financial company or a bridge financial company to provide liquidity for the operations of the receivership and the bridge financial company. Section 204(d) of the Dodd–Frank Act provides that the FDIC may make available to the receivership funds for the orderly liquidation of the covered financial company.[45] Funds provided by the FDIC under Section 204(d) of the Dodd–Frank Act are to be given a priority as administrative expenses of the receiver or as amounts owed to the United States when used for the orderly resolution of the covered financial company, including, *inter alia*, to: (i) make loans to or purchase debt of the covered financial company or a covered subsidiary; (ii) purchase (or guarantee) the assets of the covered financial company or a covered subsidiary; (iii) assume or guarantee the obligations of a covered financial company or a covered subsidiary; and (iv) make additional payments or pay additional amounts to certain creditors. In the unlikely event that recoveries from the disposition of assets are insufficient to repay amounts owed to the United States, there will be a subsequent assessment on the industry to repay those amounts. By law, no taxpayer losses from the liquidation process are allowed.

Once the new bridge financial company's operations have stabilized as the market recognizes that it has adequate funding and will continue key operations, the FDIC would move as expeditiously as possible to sell operations and assets back into the private sector. Under certain circumstances the establishment of a bridge financial company may not be necessary, particularly when the FDIC has

[45]The FDIC may issue or incur obligations pursuant to an approved orderly liquidation plan (up to 10 percent of the total consolidated assets of the covered financial company) and pursuant to an approved mandatory repayment plan (up to 90% of the fair value of the total consolidated assets of the covered financial company that are available for repayment). *See* Sections 210(n)(6) and (9) of the Dodd–Frank Act, 12 U.S.C. §5390(n)(6) and (9). To the extent that the assets in the receivership are insufficient to repay Treasury for any borrowed funds, any creditor who received an additional payment in excess of what other similarly situated creditors received, which additional payment was not essential to the implementation of the receivership or the bridge financial company, may have the additional payment clawed back. See Section 210(o)(1)(D)(i) of the Dodd–Frank Act, 12 U.S.C. §5390(o)(1)(D)(i). This provision is consistent with Title II's directive to minimize moral hazard. To the extent that the clawbacks of additional payments are insufficient to repay Treasury for any borrowed funds, the FDIC is required to assess the industry. *See* Section 210(o)(1)(B) of the Dodd–Frank Act, 12 U.S.C. §5390(o)(1)(B).

the ability to pre-plan for the sale of a substantial portion of the firm's assets and liabilities to a third party purchaser at the time of failure.

The rapid response, preservation of systemically important operations and immediate funding availability under the Dodd–Frank Act may be expected to provide certainty to the market, employees, and potential buyers. This promotes both financial stability and maximization of value in the sale of the assets of the covered financial company.

Advance dividends and prompt distributions

The FDIC, as receiver for a covered financial company, satisfies unsecured creditor claims in accordance with the relevant order of priorities set forth in Section 210(b) of the Dodd–Frank Act. To provide creditors with partial satisfaction of their claims as expediently as practicable, the FDIC, as receiver, is able — though not required — to make advance dividends to unsecured general creditors based upon expected recoveries. The FDIC may use funds available to the receivership, including amounts borrowed as discussed above under " — *Funding*," to make these advance dividends in partial satisfaction of unsecured creditor claims.[46] These advance dividends would be made at an amount less than the estimated value of the receivership assets so as not to leave the receivership with a deficit in the event the realized value is less than the expected value of the liquidation.

The FDIC, as receiver, also makes periodic distributions to unsecured creditors from the sale of assets. Accordingly, an unsecured creditor will not be required to wait until all claims are valued, or until all assets are disposed of, before receiving one or more substantial payments on his claim. The ability promptly to provide creditors with partial satisfaction of claims following the failure of a covered financial company serves the Title II mandate of mitigating systemic impact, particularly in the case of key counterparties. The FDIC has successfully provided advance dividends to unsecured creditors (including uninsured depositors) and distributions from the sale of assets to unsecured creditors in the resolution of insured depository institutions under the FDI Act to quickly move funds to claimants and to help to stabilize local markets.

In large, complex bankruptcy cases such as Lehman, a creditor may not receive any payment on his claim for a considerable period of time following the commencement of the bankruptcy case. One reason for this is that it often takes a great deal of time to establish both the size of the pool of assets available for general

---

[46]Amounts which may be borrowed from the Department of the Treasury are based upon the assets, or assets available for repayment, of the covered financial company. *See* footnote 44, *supra*.

unsecured creditors and the legitimate amounts of the claims held by such creditors. Litigation is typically needed to establish both of these numbers, which can require years of discovery followed by trial, then more years of appeals and remands.

If sufficient certainty can be attained regarding a portion of the claims, the Chapter 7 trustee will petition the court for permission to make an interim distribution, or the Chapter 11 trustee or DIP will provide in the plan of reorganization or plan of liquidation for interim distributions as various stages of the restructuring are reached.[47] However, except in the case of "prepackaged" plans of reorganization, even an interim distribution can take months or years to materialize. In the case of LBHI, there has been no distribution to general unsecured creditors more than two years after LBHI's initial bankruptcy filing.

Oversight and advanced planning

An essential prerequisite for any effective resolution is advance planning, a well-developed resolution plan, and access to the supporting information needed to undertake such planning.

Bankruptcy proceedings are typically challenging in the case of SIFIs in part because the participants have little notice or opportunity for advance preparation

---

[47] In recent years a common practice has developed in bankruptcy cases of allowing payments shortly after the filing of a Chapter 11 petition to certain priority creditors (wage claimants (up to $11,725), employee benefits claimants (up to $11,725), taxing authorities and several less frequently used groups) if sufficient assets are at hand, on the theory that such creditors will be paid first anyway at the time final distributions are made (thus, no creditor's rights will be impaired so long as the equity in available assets clearly exceeds the total priority claims). Permission to make such payments is generally sought as part of the DIP's "first day motions," and such creditors generally receive payment within three to five days of the date of filing of the petition. A secondary consideration for paying prepetition wages is the desire on the part of management to retain an experienced work force at a time of turmoil. A second practice has developed in large Chapter 11 bankruptcy cases of paying "critical vendors" after obtaining a "first day order" shortly after the petition is filed. While such vendors have the status of general unsecured creditors, an argument is typically made to the Bankruptcy Court that certain trade creditors are considered key suppliers to the DIP, and may refuse to do business with the Chapter 11 debtor unless they receive immediate payment on their prepetition claim, thus causing the entire reorganization effort to fail through loss of the going concern. This practice is more controversial than that of paying priority claimants, since (except in "prepackaged" bankruptcy cases) it is often very difficult to predict at the outset of the case what the percentage payout to general unsecured creditors will be at the end of the case. The practice has also come under criticism in recent years and has been cut back. One reason for the cutback is that there is little formal support in the Bankruptcy Code for the practice. *See In re Kmart Corp.*, 359 F. 3d 866 (7th Cir. 2004) and discussion in Turner, Travis N., "Kmart and Beyond: A 'Critical' Look at Critical Vendor Orders and the Doctrine of Necessity," 63 Wash. & Lee L. Rev. 431 (2006).

or coordination. The bankruptcy court, which must approve actions by the debtor outside of the ordinary course of business, may have little or no knowledge about the SIFI, and would have to rely upon the management of such institution for requisite information.

Title I of the Dodd–Frank Act significantly enhances regulators' ability to conduct advance resolution planning in respect of SIFIs through a variety of mechanisms, including heightened supervisory authority and the resolution plans, or living wills, required under Section 165(d) of Title I of the Dodd–Frank Act.[48] The examination authority provided by Title I of the Dodd–Frank Act will provide the FDIC with on-site access to SIFIs, including the ability to access real-time data.[49] This will enable the FDIC, working in tandem with the Federal Reserve and other regulators, to collect and analyze information for resolution planning purposes in advance of the impending failure of the institution.

An essential part of such plans will be to describe how this process can be accomplished without posing systemic risk to the public and the financial system. If the company does not submit a credible resolution plan, the statute permits increasingly stringent requirements to be imposed that, ultimately, can lead to divestiture of assets or operations identified by the FDIC and the Federal Reserve to facilitate an orderly resolution. The Dodd–Frank Act requires each designated financial company to produce a resolution plan, or living will, that maps its business lines to legal entities and provides integrated analyses of its corporate structure; credit and other exposures; funding, capital, and cash flows; domestic and foreign jurisdictions in which it operates; its supporting information systems and other essential services; and other key components of its business operations, all as part of the plan for its rapid and orderly resolution. The credit exposure reports required by the statute will also provide important information critical to the FDIC's planning processes by identifying the company's significant credit exposures, its component exposures, and other key information across the entity and its affiliates. The elements contained in a resolution plan will not only help the FDIC and other domestic regulators to better understand a firm's business and how that entity may be resolved, but the plans will also enhance the FDIC's ability to coordinate with foreign regulators in an effort to develop a comprehensive and coordinated resolution strategy for a cross-border firm.[50]

---

[48]*See generally* Section 165 of Title I of the Dodd–Frank Act, 12 U.S.C. §5365.

[49]*See* "Orderly Resolution of Lehman under the Dodd-Frank Act — March–July, Due Diligence and Structuring the Resolution — Planning in the Crisis Environment," *infra*.

[50]Domestic and foreign regulators are currently actively involved through the Financial Stability Board's Cross-Border Crisis Management Group to develop essential elements of recovery

Structure and bidding

Once the structure is developed, the FDIC would seek bids from qualified, interested bidders for the business lines or units that have going-concern value. The FDIC would analyze the bids received and choose the bid or bids that would provide the highest recovery to the receivership. The winning bidder would be informed and would take control of the business lines or units concurrent with the closing of the institution. Losses would be borne by equity holders, unsecured debt holders and other unsecured creditors that remain in the receivership. These creditors would receive payment on their claims in accordance with the priority of payment rules set forth in the Dodd–Frank Act.[51] The FDIC could make advance dividend payments to creditors based upon an upfront conservative valuation of total recoveries. As recoveries are realized, the FDIC could also pay out distributions to creditors as it has done successfully with failed insured banks. See " — *Special Powers under Title II — Advance Dividends and Prompt Distributions*," above.

Orderly resolution of Lehman under the Dodd–Frank Act

March–July, due diligence and structuring the resolution

Planning in the crisis environment

As the financial crisis enveloped Bear Stearns, the FDIC would have worked closely with the Federal Reserve and other appropriate regulators to gather information about the systemically important firms that may fall under the FDIC's resolution authority. At a minimum, the firms' resolution plans would have been reviewed jointly by the FDIC and the Federal Reserve to make sure that the plans were credible and up-to-date. The information supporting these plans and any additional information that the FDIC and Federal Reserve would have received

and resolution plans that will aid authorities in understanding subject firms' global operations and planning for the orderly resolution of a firm across borders. A number of jurisdictions are currently working to develop legislative and regulatory requirements for recovery and resolution plans, and domestic U.S. authorities are working to align regulatory initiatives in order to have a comprehensive and coordinated approach to resolution planning. For example, in January 2010, the FDIC and the Bank of England entered into a Memorandum of Understanding concerning the consultation, cooperation, and exchange of information related to the resolution of insured depository institutions with cross-border operations in the United States and the United Kingdom.

[51] *See* Section 210(b)(1) of the Dodd–Frank Act, 12 U.S.C. §5390(b)(1).

through on-site discussions with the firms during their review of the resolution plans would have provided the FDIC with valuable information necessary for effective resolution planning, information not available to the FDIC prior to the passage of the Dodd–Frank Act. In this regard the FDIC's presence would not be indicative that a resolution is imminent, but rather that in a crisis the FDIC seeks to assure that all firms' resolution plans are sufficiently robust to allow an orderly liquidation of any particular firm that might fail.

For Lehman, if senior management had not found an early private sector solution, the FDIC would have needed to establish an on-site presence to begin due diligence and to plan for a potential Title II resolution. Lehman was not the only firm in possible trouble and the FDIC would likely have had a heightened presence in other subject firms at the time. Thus, the market would not necessarily have taken the FDIC's heightened presence as a signal that a failure was imminent as the market already was aware of Lehman's problems. While it is possible in this situation or in other situations that the FDIC's on site presence could create signaling concerns, this argues for the FDIC having a continuous on-site presence for resolution planning during good times.

Discussions with Lehman

In the various accounts of the failure of Lehman it is noteworthy that senior management discounted the possibility of failure until the very last moment.[52] There was apparently a belief, following the government's actions in respect of Bear Stearns, that the government, despite statements to the contrary, would step in and provide financial assistance and Lehman would be rescued. If Title II of the Dodd–Frank Act had been in effect, the outcome would have been considerably different. Lehman's senior management would have understood clearly that the government would not and could not extend financial assistance outside of a resolution because of the clear requirements in the Dodd–Frank Act that losses are to be borne by equity holders and unsecured creditors, and management and directors responsible for the condition of the failed financial company are not to be retained.

To convey this point to Lehman and its Board of Directors, the FDIC could have participated in a meeting in the spring of 2008, together with Lehman's Board of Directors, the Federal Reserve, and the SEC, to outline the

[52]According to the Examiner's Report, following the near collapse of Bear Stearns in March 2008, "Lehman knew that its survival was in question." Lehman's management believed, however, that government assistance would be forthcoming to prevent a failure. *See* Examiner's Report at 609, 618.

circumstances that would lead to the appointment of the FDIC as receiver for one or more Lehman entities, and what that resolution would entail. The regulators would have emphasized that any open-company assistance or "too-big-to-fail" transaction would be unavailable,[53] and that the alternative to a sale of the company or a substantial capital raising would be a bankruptcy under the Bankruptcy Code or a resolution under Title II with no expectation of any return to shareholders.

The regulators could have set a deadline of July to sell the company or raise capital. This would have clearly focused Lehman's Board of Directors on the urgency of the matter and encouraged the Board to accept the best non-government offer it received notwithstanding its dilutive nature; virtually any private sale would yield a better return for shareholders than the likely negligible proceeds shareholders would receive in an FDIC receivership, as equity holders have the lowest priority claims in a receivership.

Lehman's senior management and Board of Directors may have been more willing to recommend offers that were below the then-current market price if they knew with certainty that there would be no extraordinary government assistance made available to the company and that Lehman would be put into receivership. Such avenues may have been available. For instance, KDB is reported to have suggested paying $6.40 per share when Lehman's stock was trading at $17.50 on August 31 — just 15 days prior to Lehman's bankruptcy filing.

Forcing Lehman to more earnestly market itself to a potential acquirer or strategic investor well in advance of Lehman's failure would serve several other goals, even if such private sector transaction were unsuccessful. The FDIC would be able to use this marketing information to identify appropriate bidders who would be invited to join in the FDIC-led due diligence and bidding process as described in " — *Due Diligence*" and " — *Structuring the Transaction*," below.

The preferred outcome under the Dodd–Frank Act is for a troubled financial company to find a strategic investor or to recapitalize without direct government involvement or the FDIC being appointed receiver. To that end, the recommendation and determination prescribed by Sections 203(a)(2)(E) and (b)(3) of the Dodd–Frank Act, respectively, concern the availability of a viable private sector alternative. Requiring a troubled financial company to aggressively market itself, pre-failure, helps to ensure that exercise of the orderly resolution authority in Title II is a last resort. In this matter, the FDIC's experience with troubled banks is instructive. The commencement of the FDIC's due diligence process has

[53]The Preamble to the Dodd–Frank Act notes that it was enacted, *inter alia*, "to end 'too-big-to-fail' [and] to protect the American taxpayer by ending bailouts."

frequently provided the motivation senior management has needed to pursue sale or recapitalization more aggressively. Between 1995 and the end of 2007, the FDIC prepared to resolve 150 institutions. Of this number, only 56 — that is, 37% — eventually failed. Of course, many fewer problem banks have been able to find merger partners or recapitalize since the crisis began. However, from 2008 to 2010, of the 432 banks where the FDIC began the resolution process, 110 — 25% — avoided failure, either by finding an acquirer or recapitalizing.

Due diligence

Just as when an insured depository institution is a likely candidate for an FDI Act receivership, the FDIC will need to gather as much information as possible about a SIFI in advance of any Title II resolution. In the case of LBHI, the SEC and the Federal Reserve Bank of New York began on-site daily monitoring in March 2008, following the collapse and sale of Bear Stearns, at which point the FDIC would already have been on-site at Lehman to facilitate the FDIC's Title I resolution planning and monitoring activities.[54] The FDIC would have determined, jointly with other supervisors, the condition of the company for the purposes of ordering corrective actions to avoid failure, and it otherwise would have prepared for a Title II orderly resolution.

The FDIC would continue assembling information about the condition and value of Lehman's assets and various lines of business. In preparing for a Title II resolution of a company subject to heightened prudential standards under Title I, the FDIC will have access to the information included in such company's resolution plan, or living will.[55] Though that resolution plan is designed to provide for the resolution of the SIFI under the Bankruptcy Code, it would provide regulators with invaluable information about the institution's structure, organization, and key operations that could form the basis for an orderly liquidation under Title II. It is the FDIC's experience that management of a troubled institution often has an overly optimistic view of the value of its franchise and the firm's prospect for recovery. Thus, while the resolution plan would provide key financial and other

[54] *See "Orderly Resolution of Lehman under the Dodd–Frank Act — March–July, Due Diligence and Structuring the Resolution — Planning in the Crisis Environment," supra.*

[55] Had the Dodd–Frank Act been enacted sufficiently far in advance of Lehman's failure, undoubtedly much more supervisory information would have been available in March 2008. The Federal Reserve and the FDIC would have had the detailed information presented in Lehman's statutorily required resolution plan under Title I of the Dodd–Frank Act. *See* Section 165(d) of Title I of the Dodd–Frank Act, 12 U.S.C. §5365(d).

data about the consolidated entity, an independent examination of the troubled firm may have been necessary. The FDIC will also have access to real-time data from on-site monitoring conducted by the FDIC and other prudential regulators.

The FDIC's participation in gathering information and in exercising its examination authority would be done in coordination with the on-site monitoring activities of the SEC and the Federal Reserve Bank of New York. The development of additional information to facilitate a potential resolution would be done in a manner that would not disrupt the business operations or indicate an imminent failure of the financial company. As regulated entities under the Dodd–Frank Act, heightened supervision by the FDIC, the Federal Reserve, and other prudential regulators will be normal. As a result, these information-gathering activities should neither signal increased distress nor precipitate market reaction.

While conducting due diligence, the FDIC would have begun developing the transaction and bid framework by analyzing the legal structure of the firm, its operations, and its financial data. In this case, LBHI was a large holding company with major overseas operations.[56] As with any large, complex financial company, there were many interrelations among the major affiliates of the group. LBHI was the guarantor of all obligations of LBI and the source of funding for a number of other Lehman entities. LBI was the employer of record for much of the company, including various foreign subsidiaries.

LBI was also the owner and operator of key IT systems used throughout the company and provided custody and trade execution services for clients of foreign Lehman entities, primarily for trades conducted by LBIE in the United States. Likewise, LBIE provided custody and trade execution services for clients of LBI conducting trades outside of the United States. The interconnected nature of Lehman's operations would have argued for maintaining maximum franchise value by developing a deal structure that would have maintained the continuing uninterrupted operation of the major business lines of the firm by transferring those assets and operations to an acquirer immediately upon the failure of the parent holding company.[57]

---

[56]The principal operating entities in the holding company were LBI, the U.S. broker–dealer, and LBIE, the U.K.-based broker–dealer. Lehman also had a smaller Asian trading operation headquartered in Japan, and various smaller subsidiaries in other countries.

[57]By completing a sale at the time of failure of the parent holding company, the acquirer would have been able to "step into the shoes" of LBHI and provide liquidity, guarantees, or other credit support to the newly acquired subsidiaries. Were the FDIC unable to promptly complete such a transaction, it could provide any necessary liquidity to certain key subsidiaries, such as LBIE, pending a sale of those assets. *See* footnote 58, *infra*.

During the FDIC's investigation of the Lehman group, it would have identified subsidiaries which would be likely to fail in the event of a failure of LBHI but would likely not be systemic and would provide little or no value to the consolidated franchise. The FDIC would not have recommended a resolution under Title II for those subsidiaries, and they would likely have been resolved under the Bankruptcy Code or other applicable insolvency regime.[58] The assets of these subsidiaries would not have been part of a Title II receivership, other than the receiver's equity claim; the FDIC would have had no expected return on the equity for any such non-systemic subsidiary placed into bankruptcy. The FDIC also would have identified any subsidiary that would be likely to fail in the event of a failure of LBHI, and whose failure likely would be systemic. The FDIC would have made an evaluation as to whether the resolution of any such subsidiary under Title II would have aided in the orderly resolution of the parent company.[59]

As is the case with insured depository institutions that have foreign operations, the FDIC would have begun contacting key foreign financial authorities on a discrete basis to discuss what legal or financial issues might arise out of an FDIC receivership, or out of foreign resolution regimes in the case of Lehman entities operating outside of the United States, and how those resolutions could be coordinated. In addition, foreign financial authorities would have been consulted when foreign financial companies and investors expressed interest in investing in or purchasing Lehman. These discussions would have addressed, at a minimum, the financial strength of the acquirer, types of approvals that would be required to consummate a transaction, and any identified impediments to the transaction. Regular, ongoing contact would be particularly important after the transaction structure was determined and qualified bidders had been contacted and had expressed interest.

---

[58]*See* Section 202(c)(1) of the Dodd–Frank Act, 12 U.S.C. §5382(c)(1).

[59]Upon a parent entering a Title II receivership, the FDIC may appoint itself receiver over one or more domestic covered subsidiaries of a covered financial company in receivership in accordance with the self-appointment process set forth in Section 210(a)(1)(E) of the Dodd–Frank Act, 12 U.S.C. §5390(a)(1)(E). This appointment process requires a joint determination by the FDIC and the Secretary of the Treasury that the covered subsidiary is in default or danger of default, that putting it into receivership would avoid or mitigate serious adverse effects on U.S. financial stability, and that such action would facilitate the orderly liquidation of the covered financial company parent. Once in receivership, the covered subsidiary would be treated in a similar manner to any other covered financial company: its shareholders and unsecured creditors would bear the losses of the company, and management and directors responsible for the company's failure would not be retained. The receiver, to aid in the orderly liquidation of the company, could extend liquidity to it in accordance with Section 204(d) of the Dodd–Frank Act, 12 U.S.C. §5384(d).

Valuation and identification of problem assets

On a consolidated basis, LBHI and its subsidiaries had total assets of $639 billion, with $26.3 billion in book equity and total unsecured long-term and short-term borrowings of $162.8 billion as of May 31, 2008. The parent company, LBHI, had $231 billion in assets, with $26.3 billion in book equity and $114.6 billion in unsecured long-term and short-term borrowings. On September 14 (just prior to bankruptcy), LBHI (unconsolidated) was slightly smaller with $209 billion in assets, $20.3 billion in book equity, and $99.5 billion in long-term and short-term unsecured debt, including $15 billion in subordinated debt. In addition, LBHI's short-term unsecured debt included $2.3 billion in commercial paper — almost 40% of the approximately $5.7 billion in commercial paper outstanding enterprise wide.

By March 2008, Lehman had recognized that its commercial real estate related holdings were a major impediment to finding a merger partner. Its SpinCo proposal identified $31.7 billion in significantly underperforming commercial real estate related assets. During the week leading up to Lehman's bankruptcy filing, Bank of America identified an additional $38.3 billion in suspect residential real estate related assets and private equity assets that it would not purchase in an acquisition. Barclay's identified $20.3 billion of similar potentially additional problem assets in its due diligence. In the FDIC's resolution process, the FDIC's structuring team as well as prospective bidders would have had sufficient time to perform due diligence and identify problem asset pools. While Lehman was seeking an investor pre-failure, the FDIC would have identified and valued these problem asset pools in order to set a defined bid structure for Lehman. The bid structure would have allowed prospective acquirers to bid upon options to purchase all of Lehman's assets in a whole financial company P&A with loss sharing on defined pools of problem assets, or a purchase which excludes those problem asset pools. In the latter bid option, the receivership estate would have purchased the problem assets out of Lehman's subsidiaries at their fair market value prior to consummating the purchase agreement with the acquirer. These problem assets, in addition to those directly owned by the holding company, could have been retained in the receivership or placed into a bridge financial company prior to future disposition. Either bid would have allowed a further option for the prospective acquirer to pay to assume the commercial paper and other critical short-term securities of Lehman. The bidding structure is discussed more fully in *August, Begin Marketing Lehman*, below.

Both bid structures are intended to provide comfort to not only the potential acquirer, but also to its regulators, concerning the potential down-side exposure to problem assets. In excluding pools of identified problem assets from a bid, an acquirer is protected directly by effectively capping its exposure to such assets — which are left with the receivership — at zero. This risk minimization comes at the cost of lost potential upside from returns on servicing the troubled assets, higher administrative costs of the receiver, and a less attractive bid. In the loss-sharing structure, a potential acquirer receives tail-risk protection: the acquirer is able to cap its exposure to an identified pool of problem assets at set levels. This comfort is particularly important where a potential acquirer is unable to undertake in-depth due diligence on such assets, or must do so on an abbreviated time table. This down-side protection will also be important to regulators, as it mitigates the risk of an acquirer experiencing financial distress due to the problem assets of an acquiree.[60]

Structuring the resolution

During due diligence, the FDIC would have identified certain pools of assets of Lehman — including certain commercial real estate, residential real estate, and private equity assets — that would make a whole financial company P&A transaction difficult. See " — *Valuation and Identification of Problem Assets*," above. These troubled assets were estimated to be between $50 and $70 billion in book value.

The FDIC would have set up a data room to enable potential acquirers to conduct due diligence, and would have begun developing a marketing structure for Lehman and its assets. The FDIC would have identified potential acquirers of Lehman. Criteria would have included maximization of value on the sale, the stability of the potential acquirer, and the ability of the acquirer expediently to consummate an acquisition.[61] Having identified the potential acquirers, the FDIC would have explained the bid structure, and invited the firms to conduct (or continue) due diligence of Lehman.

During this time, the FDIC would have continued to monitor Lehman's progress in marketing itself. This would have encouraged Lehman to consummate a nongovernment transaction, which remained the best outcome for all parties. It would also have provided the FDIC with key information concerning interested acquirers and potential issues and concerns of such acquirers in completing a transaction.

---

[60] Both Barclays and its U.K. regulators were concerned with exposure to problem assets of Lehman following a potential acquisition by Barclays. *See* footnote 68, *infra*.

[61] We also note the impact of Section 622 of the Dodd–Frank Act, 12 U.S.C. §1852, which could prohibit a large financial company from entering into a transaction to acquire another financial company if the *pro forma* liabilities would exceed certain statutory levels.

Also during this time, as is the case with insured depository institutions that have foreign operations, the FDIC would have continued a dialogue with key foreign financial authorities to discuss what legal or financial issues might arise out of an FDIC receivership, or out of foreign resolution regimes in the case of Lehman entities operating outside of the United States, and how those resolutions could be coordinated.[62] Specifically, the FDIC would address issues of ring-fencing of assets, particularly of Lehman's U.K.-based broker–dealer. See " — *Due Diligence*," above.

August, begin marketing Lehman

Assuming Lehman were unable to sell itself, the FDIC would have commenced with marketing Lehman.[63] The FDIC would have set a defined bidding structure. Prospective acquirers previously identified (as discussed in " — March–July, Due Diligence and Structuring the Resolution — *Structuring the Transaction*," above) would have been invited to bid based on the following options:

Option A: Whole financial company purchase and assumption with partial loss share (loss-sharing P&A). Under this option, the assets and operations of Lehman are transferred to the acquirer with no government control and no ongoing servicing of Lehman assets by the government. Due to the problem assets discussed above, however, it may be necessary for the receivership estate to offer a potential acquirer protection from loss in respect of that identified pool of problem assets. In this type of transaction, the acquirer purchases the assets at their gross book value, and assumes, at a minimum, the secured liabilities. Depending on the bid, other liability classes may be assumed as well. Since the book value of assets must always exceed the amount of liabilities assumed in this structure, the acquirer, after factoring its discount bid for the assets, must also provide a

---

[62]For example, in the case of East West Bank's acquisition of United Commercial Bank, San Francisco, California, the FDIC engaged with the China Banking Regulatory Commission and the Hong Kong Monetary Authority in advance of the resolution to discuss potential acquirers, regulatory approvals and options for resolving or selling the assets and liabilities of United Commercial Bank's wholly owned subsidiary in China and its foreign branch in Hong Kong.

[63]Any agreement reached in respect of Lehman would be contingent upon its failure, a systemic determination under Section 203(b) or 210(a)(1)(E) of the Dodd–Frank Act, 12 U.S.C. §§5383(b) or 5390(a)(1)(E), as applicable, and the appointment of the FDIC as receiver under Section 202 of the Dodd–Frank Act, 12 U.S.C. §5382. In the case of Lehman, and for purposes of our analysis, had there been a viable acquirer or strategic investor pre-failure, no Title II resolution would be required. As discussed in "The Events Leading to the Lehman Bankruptcy," *supra,* and in footnote 68, *infra*, no such private sector alternative was available.

combination of cash and a note payable to the receivership estate to balance out the transaction.[64] The receivership estate's share of loss payments are made through reductions in the outstanding balance of the note payable as loss claims occur over time.

Transactions offering an option for a sharing of potential future losses between the acquirer and the FDIC have been frequently used to resolve failed banks. Loss-share transactions allow the FDIC to obtain better bids from potential assuming institutions by sharing a portion of the risk on a pool of assets. This has been particularly important during periods of uncertainty about the value of assets. The FDIC's experience has been that these transactions result in both better bid prices and improved recoveries for the receivership and receivership creditors.

Another benefit of loss sharing is that the FDIC is able to transfer administration of the failed financial company's problem assets to the assuming institution and receive a premium for the failed company's franchise value, thereby maximizing value. By having the assuming company absorb a portion of the loss, the FDIC induces rational and responsible credit management behavior from the assuming institution to minimize credit losses. Compared to the alternative of retaining problem assets in receivership, the loss-share structure tends to be more efficient, as it limits losses and administrative costs of the receivership.

The FDIC would therefore permit bidders to bid on a structure based on a sale of the whole financial company, with partial but substantial coverage of losses on those identified problem assets.[65] The loss-share structure encourages bidders to maximize their bids by offering downside credit risk protection from loss on an identified pool of problem assets. This can produce a more efficient outcome as it incentivizes the acquirer to maximize recoveries while reducing administrative costs of the receivership. See " — *The Resolution and Receivership Process for Failed Banks — Loss Share*," above.

Option B: Modified purchase and assumption without loss share, which excludes certain identified problem assets (modified P&A, similar to a good bank–bad bank resolution strategy). Under this option, the majority of the assets and operations of Lehman are transferred to the acquirer. Identified pools of problem

---

[64] A simple formula to reflect the amount of the acquirer's note payable is: Book value of assets purchased less the sum of (book value of liabilities assumed plus discount bid plus cash payment) is equal to note payable.

[65] To the extent problem assets were held directly by LBHI, or LBHI experienced significant intercompany exposures to losses in subsidiaries and affiliates, loss sharing would be more likely to be a preferred bid structure.

assets would not be included in the transaction, but retained for disposition at a later date.[66]

Liabilities: While the FDIC would transfer the assets of Lehman to the acquirer in accordance with Option A or Option B described above, most unsecured creditor claims would remain with the receivership, including shareholder claims and claims of holders of unsecured, long-term indebtedness. Fully secured claims would be transferred, along with the collateral, to the acquirer. The bid participants would have the opportunity to bid on acquiring certain short-term indebtedness of Lehman, particularly Lehman's outstanding commercial paper. In order for this bid structure to be successful, bidders would need to bid an amount sufficient to cover the loss that the commercial paper and other short-term creditors would have otherwise incurred had the creditors remained in the receivership.

In comparing bids under Option A and Option B, the receivership estate's cost of managing and disposing of the identified problem assets would be taken into consideration. Depending on the bid, the acquirer would purchase the acquired assets through a combination of one or more of cash, notes, and assumed liabilities.

It should be noted that the proposed bid structure represented by Option A and Option B represents one set of options for disposing of the assets and operations of a covered financial company in an efficient manner. The FDIC would have the flexibility to restructure these bids as the facts and circumstances of a particular covered financial company warrant in order to satisfy the FDIC's statutory mandates of promoting financial stability, maximizing recoveries, and minimizing losses.

Early September, closing

Following due diligence, interested parties would have submitted closed, or sealed, bids. The FDIC would have evaluated the bids based upon the requirement under the Dodd–Frank Act to maximize value upon any disposition of assets.[67] Bids would have been evaluated on a present-value basis. The FDIC would have selected the winning bid, and the acquirer and the FDIC, as the receiver for LBHI, would enter into a conditional P&A agreement based upon the agreed upon bid structure.[68]

---

[66]As discussed under " — March–July, Due Diligence and Structuring the Resolution — Due Diligence," *supra*, subsidiaries holding such assets would generally be resolved under the Bankruptcy Code. To the extent any subsidiary was deemed systemic, it could be put into a separate receivership under Title II, its assets liquidated and its claims resolved in accordance with the Dodd–Frank Act.

[67]*See* Section 210(a)(9)(E) of the Dodd–Frank Act, 12 U.S.C. §5390(a)(9)(E).

[68]*See* footnote 62, *supra*.

We have assumed, for the limited purpose of this discussion, that Barclays would have provided a winning bid to complete an acquisition of Lehman.[69]

We have further assumed that, as LBHI reached a point at which it was in default or in danger of default, a systemic determination would have been made by the Secretary of the Treasury and the FDIC would have been appointed receiver of LBHI.[70]

At the time a determination was made that Lehman should be put into receivership and the FDIC named receiver, the assets and select liabilities of Lehman would have been transferred to Barclays as the acquiring institution based upon the structure of the winning bid.[71] Barclays would have maintained the key operations of Lehman in a seamless manner, integrating those operations over time. Disruptions to the market likely would have been minimal. Barclays would have continued to make scheduled payments on liabilities transferred to it, including secured indebtedness and, to the extent assumed by Barclays, commercial paper.[72] To the extent Barclays' winning bid had been based upon a whole financial company with loss share, it would have been responsible for servicing problem assets in accordance with the terms of the loss-sharing P&A agreement.

---

[69]We note that this analysis is purely hypothetical in nature, and a bid conducted by the FDIC could have produced strong bids by a number of potential acquirers. Barclays, however, was close to completing a transaction with Lehman in September 2008. It was unable to proceed based upon the risk of financial loss due to problem assets it identified in its due diligence and the inability to gain an exemption from U.K. regulators from the requirement to hold a shareholder vote prior to approving a transaction with Lehman based upon the proposed structure. The FDIC believes it would have been able to alleviate Barclays' concerns — and facilitate requisite regulatory approvals — by structuring the transaction as a loss-sharing P&A or as a modified P&A. For the purpose of this discussion, therefore, a winning bid from Barclays would be one reasonable outcome from the bidding process outlined in "*— August, Begin Marketing Lehman*," *supra*.

[70]For a detailed discussion of the recommendation, determination, and appointment process under Sections 203 and 202 of the Dodd–Frank Act, 12 U.S.C. §§5383 and 5382, see "*The Orderly Liquidation of Covered Financial Companies — Appointment*," *supra*.

[71]There is a danger of value dissipation — in proportion to the size and complexity of the covered financial company — the longer such covered financial company stays in receivership prior to a sale being consummated. Accordingly, the FDIC would generally prefer, where possible, to time a sale of the assets and operations of the covered financial company at or near the date of failure. The FDIC may also transfer key operations to a bridge financial company, as described *under "The Orderly Resolution of Covered Financial Companies — Special Powers under Title II — Ability to Preserve Systemic Operations of the Covered Financial Company," supra.* These same challenges are faced in the resolution of larger insured depository institutions under the FDI Act.

[72]Despite paying a premium to assume the commercial paper obligations, an acquirer may have been incentivized to bid on such business due to the incremental franchise value of the business line and to preserve customer goodwill.

Lehman's derivatives trading was conducted almost exclusively in its broker–dealer, LBI, and in LBI's subsidiaries.[73] As a result, Barclays' acquisition of the broker–dealer group would have transferred the derivatives operations, together with the related collateral, to Barclays in its entirety as an ongoing operation. At the moment of failure, Barclays would have assumed any parent guarantee by Lehman outstanding in respect of the subsidiaries' qualified financial contracts. This action should have substantially eliminated any commercial basis for the subsidiaries' counterparties to engage in termination and close-out netting of qualified financial contracts based upon the insolvency of the parent guarantor. This would have removed any financial incentive to do so as well, as a financially secure acquirer would have assumed the obligations and provided guarantees to the same extent as its predecessor, in part to preserve the significant franchise value of the derivatives portfolio (including the underlying collateral).[74] The more limited derivatives operations conducted by LBHI would have been subjected to haircuts to the extent that any net amount due to a counterparty was not collateralized or hedged. Particularly in the future, it is expected that the vast majority of the derivatives transactions of a covered financial company will be fully collateralized.

Barclays would have purchased the acquired assets through a combination of one or more of the following: cash, notes, and the assumption of liabilities. The FDIC, as receiver for Lehman, would have disposed of any problem assets left behind in the receivership or managed the loss-share agreement with Barclays in respect of those assets, and would have settled creditor claims in accordance with the priority for repayment set forth in the Dodd–Frank Act.[75]

The likely treatment of creditors

As mentioned earlier, by September 2008, LBHI's book equity was down to $20 billion and it had $15 billion of subordinated debt, $85 billion in other outstanding short- and long-term debt, and $90 billion of other liabilities, most of which represented intracompany funding. The equity and subordinated debt represented a

[73] LBHI conducted its derivatives activities primarily in subsidiaries of LBI (the broker–dealer), including Lehman Brothers Special Financing Inc., Lehman Brothers Derivatives Products, Inc., and Lehman Brothers Financial Products, Inc.

[74] Under the International Swaps and Derivatives Association master agreements (and trades placed thereunder), parties may choose whether to be governed by New York or English law. To the extent that parties to a particular qualified financial contract are validly governed by English law (and a court recognizes and applies such choice of law), such contract may not be subject to the Dodd–Frank Act in terms of nullification of its *ipso facto* clause.

[75] *See* Section 210(b)(1) of the Dodd–Frank Act, 12 U.S.C. §5390(b)(1).

buffer of $35 billion to absorb losses before other creditors took losses. Of the $210 billion in assets, potential acquirers had identified $50 to $70 billion as impaired or of questionable value. If losses on those assets had been $40 billion (which would represent a loss rate in the range of 60 to 80%), then the entire $35 billion buffer of equity and subordinated debt would have been eliminated and losses of $5 billion would have remained. The distribution of these losses would depend on the extent of collateralization and other features of the debt instruments.

If losses had been distributed equally among all of Lehman's remaining general unsecured creditors, the $5 billion in losses would have resulted in a recovery rate of approximately $0.97 for every claim of $1.00, assuming that no affiliate guarantee claims would be triggered. This is significantly more than what these creditors are expected to receive under the Lehman bankruptcy. This benefit to creditors derives primarily from the ability to plan, arrange due diligence, and conduct a well-structured competitive bidding process.

The Dodd–Frank Act provides a further potential benefit to creditors: earlier access to liquidity. As described above, the acquirer would have provided a combination of cash and a note to the receiver. Under the Dodd–Frank Act, the FDIC could have promptly distributed the cash proceeds from the sale of assets to claimants in partial satisfaction of unsecured creditor claims.[76] The FDIC would also have been able to borrow up to 90% of the fair value of the note available for repayment — together with the fair value of any assets left in the receivership available for repayment — from the orderly liquidation fund and advance those funds to the receivership.[77] These borrowed funds could have been made available to creditors immediately in the form of advance dividends to satisfy a portion of creditor claims based upon the total expected recovery in the resolution. This is in contrast to the actual circumstances of the LBHI bankruptcy, in which there has been no confirmed plan of reorganization or cash distribution to unsecured creditors of LBHI more than two years after the failure of Lehman.

Conclusion

Title II of the Dodd–Frank Act provides "the necessary authority to liquidate failing financial companies that pose a systemic risk to the financial stability of the

[76] *See "The Orderly Resolution of Covered Financial Companies — Special Powers under Title II — Advance Dividends and Prompt Distributions," supra*, for a discussion of the ability to make both prompt distributions and advance dividends in a Title II receivership.

[77] *See* footnote 44 and accompanying discussion, *supra*.

United States in a manner that mitigates such risk and minimizes moral hazard."[78] These powers and authorities are analogous to those the FDIC uses to resolve failed insured depository institutions under the FDI Act. In the case of Lehman, following appointment by the Secretary of the Treasury, the FDIC could have used its power as receiver and the ability to facilitate a sale under Title II of the Dodd–Frank Act to preserve the institution's franchise value and transfer Lehman's assets and operations to an acquirer. The FDIC would have imposed losses on equity holders and unsecured creditors, terminated senior management responsible for the failure of the covered financial company, maintained Lehman's liquidity, and, most importantly, attempted to mitigate and prevent disruption to the U.S. financial system, including the commercial paper and derivatives markets. The very availability of a comprehensive resolution system that sets forth in advance the rules under which the government will act following the appointment of a receiver could have helped to prevent a "run on the bank" and the resulting financial instability. By maintaining franchise value and mitigating severe disruption in the financial markets, it is more likely that debt holders and other general creditors will receive greater recoveries on their claims under the Dodd–Frank Act than they would have otherwise received in Chapter 7 liquidation or in Chapter 11 reorganization.

The key to an orderly resolution and liquidation of a SIFI is the ability to plan for its resolution and liquidation, provide liquidity to maintain key assets and operations, and preserve financial stability. During the planning phase, the FDIC, working in tandem with the Federal Reserve and the SEC, would have been able to identify problem assets; require management to raise capital or find an acquirer; gather information about the institution's structure, organization, and key operations; prepare the resolution transaction structure and bids; and seek potential acquirers. During this phase, the FDIC would have contacted the relevant foreign and domestic regulatory authorities and governments to coordinate the resolution. Through this process, the FDIC would have minimized losses and maximized recoveries in the event the SIFI failed and was put into receivership.

Perhaps most importantly, the Dodd–Frank Act provides the means to preserve systemically important operations and reduce systemic consequences while limiting moral hazard by imposing losses on the stockholders and unsecured creditors of the failed SIFI rather than on the U.S. taxpayer. In so doing, the FDIC is able to fulfill its statutory mandate to preserve financial stability and serve the public interest.

---

[78] Section 204(a) of the Dodd–Frank Act, 12 U.S.C. §5384(a).

Afterword

This paper has focused on how the government could have structured a resolution of Lehman under Title II of the Dodd–Frank Act following the failure of such firm.

In so doing, we have made a number of assumptions and caveats to provide a framework for the analysis and to maintain consistency with the historical record. That is, while we have assumed that the Dodd–Frank Act had been enacted pre-failure, and that the FDIC would have been able to avail itself of the pre-planning powers available under Title I, including having access to key data of subject institutions through resolution plans and on-site monitoring, we have not assumed away the failure of Lehman.

The OLA of Title II would be a remedy of last resort, to be used only after the remedies available under Title I — including the increased informational and supervisory powers — are unable to stave off a failure. In particular, it is expected that the mere knowledge of the consequences of a Title II resolution, including the understanding that financial assistance is no longer an option, would encourage a troubled institution to find an acquirer or strategic partner on its own well in advance of failure. Likewise, on-site monitoring and access to real-time data, provided under Title I, is expected to provide an early-warning system to the FDIC and other regulators well in advance of a subject institution's imminent failure.

We have also stuck closely to the facts in identifying the most likely acquirer of Lehman as Barclays, while also discussing the potential role played by Bank of America and KDB. Lehman, while a complex firm, had value primarily as an investment bank. Thus, its resolution was focused on keeping the investment bank's operations intact in order to preserve its going-concern value. In other cases, a large financial firm with many pieces such as a large commercial bank, an insurance company, and a broker-dealer, might represent a financial firm that is no longer too big to fail, but may be too big to continue to exist as one entity.[79] Over the longer term, the development of resolution plans will enable the FDIC

---

[79] *See*, e.g., Simon Johnson & James Kwak, 13 Bankers: *The Wall Street Takeover and the Next Financial Meltdown* (2010); Michael McKee and Scott Lanman, "Greenspan Says U.S. Should Consider Breaking Up Large Banks," Bloomberg, October 15, 2009, available at: http://www.bloomberg.com/apps/news?pid=newsarchive&sid=aJ8HPmNUfchg; Lita Epstein, "Breaking up 'too big to fail' banks: Britain leads, will U.S. follow," DailyFinance, November 2, 2009, available at http://www.dailyfinance.com/story/investing/breaking-up-banks-too-big-to-fail-britian-leads-but-will-u-s/19220380/. The Dodd–Frank Act includes provisions intended to prevent the creation of ever-larger financial companies, including Section 622 thereof, 12 U.S.C. §1852. *See* footnote 60, *supra*.

to prepare to split up such a firm in order to facilitate a Title II liquidation. The FDIC could pursue a number of alternatives instead of a whole financial company purchase-and-assumption transaction, including a spin-off of assets, an initial public offering, a debt-to-equity conversion, or some other transaction that would satisfy regulatory concerns about concentration while minimizing losses to the failed company's creditors.

Chapter 9

Implementing Dodd–Frank: Orderly Resolution

Martin J. Gruenberg[1]

I would like to take the opportunity to discuss one of those challenging issues — the orderly resolution of systemically important financial institutions (SIFIs). The Dodd–Frank Wall Street Reform and Consumer Protection Act provided important new authority to the FDIC to resolve SIFIs. Prior to the recent crisis, the FDIC's receivership authority was limited to federally insured banks and thrift institutions. There was no authority to place the holding company or affiliates of an insured institution or any other nonbank financial company into an FDIC receivership to avoid systemic consequences. The lack of this authority severely constrained the ability of the government to resolve a SIFI. This authority has now been provided to the FDIC under the Dodd–Frank Act (DFA).

The question is whether the FDIC can develop the operational capability to utilize this authority effectively and a credible strategy under which an orderly resolution of a SIFI can be carried out without putting the financial system itself at risk. These key challenges have been the focus of the FDIC's efforts since the enactment of Dodd–Frank in July 2010. I would like to focus my comments on the progress we have made in meeting these important challenges.

---

[1]Martin J. Gruenberg is Chairman of the Federal Deposit Insurance Corporation (FDIC). The material in this article was originally published in the Federal Reserve Bank of Chicago's *Economic Perspectives,* Volume 36, 3rd quarter, 2012. The views expressed are the author's and do not necessarily reflect the views of the FDIC.

Orderly liquidation authority, resolution planning, and the Office of Complex Financial Institutions

The FDIC has taken a number of steps since Dodd–Frank was passed to carry out its new systemic resolution responsibilities. First, the FDIC established a new Office of Complex Financial Institutions to carry out three core functions:

- Monitor risk within and across these large, complex financial firms from the standpoint of resolution;
- Conduct resolution planning and develop strategies to respond to potential crisis situations; and
- Coordinate with regulators overseas regarding the significant challenges associated with cross-border resolution.

For the past year, this office has been developing its own resolution plans in order to be ready to resolve a failing systemic financial company. These internal FDIC resolution plans, developed pursuant to the orderly liquidation authority (OLA) provided under Title II of Dodd–Frank, apply to a SIFI many of the same powers that the FDIC has long used to manage failed-bank receiverships. This internal resolution planning work is the foundation of the FDIC's implementation of its new responsibilities under Dodd–Frank.

Second, the FDIC has largely completed the basic rulemaking necessary to carry out its responsibilities under Dodd–Frank. In July 2011, the FDIC Board approved a final rule implementing Title II — OLA. This rule addressed, among other things, the priority of claims and the treatment of similarly situated creditors.

Last September, the FDIC Board adopted two rules regarding resolution plans that SIFIs themselves will be required to prepare — the so-called living wills.

The first resolution plan rule, jointly issued with the Federal Reserve, requires bank holding companies with total consolidated assets of $50 billion or more, and certain nonbank financial companies that the Financial Stability Oversight Council designates as systemic, to develop, maintain, and periodically submit resolution plans to regulators.

Complementing this joint rulemaking, the FDIC issued another rule requiring any FDIC-insured depository institution with assets over $50 billion to develop, maintain, and periodically submit plans outlining how the FDIC would resolve it through the FDIC's traditional resolution powers under the Federal Deposit Insurance Act.

These two resolution plan rules are designed to work in tandem and complement each other by covering the full range of business lines, legal entities, and capital-structure combinations within a large financial firm. Both of these resolution plan requirements will improve efficiencies, risk management, and contingency planning at the institutions themselves. Importantly, they will supplement the FDIC's own resolution planning work with information that would help facilitate an orderly resolution in the event of failure.

With the joint rule final, the FDIC and the Federal Reserve have started the process of engaging with individual companies on the preparation of their resolution plans. The first plans, for companies with assets over $250 billion, were due in 2012.

Resolution strategy

What I would like to do now is describe the current thinking on our strategy for resolving a large systemically important financial firm.

The FDIC's resolution strategy has three key goals. The first is financial stability, ensuring that the failure of the firm does not place the financial system itself at risk. The second is accountability, ensuring that the investors in the failed firm bear the firm's losses. The third is viability, converting the failed firm through the public receivership process into a new, well-capitalized, and viable private sector entity. As I describe the strategy, I will try to identify how each of these goals is being addressed.

We can start by considering the type of firm that we may be presented with. It is likely to be a firm with several business lines — perhaps commercial banking, capital markets, global asset management, and transaction services — and which operates across national borders. The corporate structure is likely to be a holding company with a parent at the top and multiple layers of subsidiaries. The number of subsidiaries will be in the hundreds, if not thousands. It is also likely that the structure of the legal entities within the company will not be aligned with the business lines. Additionally, intracompany risk transfers and financial relationships will not be transparent.

While there are numerous differences between a typical bank resolution and what the FDIC would face in resolving a SIFI, I want to focus on a few key differences.

The first is whether the proximate cause of failure is capital depletion or liquidity pressures. The typical path toward failure for an insured bank starts with bad loans. As the bank sets aside reserves for and charges off credit losses, capital ratios fall, triggering the requirements of prompt corrective action. The bank is required to either raise capital or find a buyer. In the meantime, the bank normally continues to operate in large measure because its major source of liquidity is insured deposits, which are not likely to run. Eventually, if it is unable to raise capital or find a buyer, the chartering agency closes the bank. Essentially, the bank has failed a market test of viability.

In the case of a large financial firm, it is likely that its problems will also arise from the losses it has suffered in one or more of its business lines. However, it is also likely that this firm relies to a greater extent on market sources of funding and thus would face liquidity pressures not typically present in the case of an insured bank. There are several implications to this. The FDIC and other regulators will have less time to craft a resolution. There may not be time for the firm to undergo a market test of viability. Finally, there may be a significant need to shore up liquidity in the course of the resolution.

In addition, the resolution of a large U.S. financial firm involves a more complex corporate structure than the resolution of a single insured bank. Large financial companies conduct business through multiple subsidiary legal entities with many interconnections, owned by a parent holding company. A resolution of the individual subsidiaries of the financial company would increase the likelihood of disruption and loss of franchise value by disrupting the interrelationships among the subsidiary companies. A much more promising approach from the FDIC's point of view is to place into receivership only the parent holding company while maintaining the subsidiary interconnections.

Another difference arises from sheer size alone. In the typical bank failure, there are a number of banks capable of quickly handling the financial, managerial, and operational requirements of an acquisition. This is unlikely to be the case when a large financial firm fails. Even if it were the case, it may not be desirable to pursue a resolution that would result in an even larger, more complex institution. This suggests the need to create both a bridge financial institution and the means of returning control and ownership to private hands.

Finally, in the case of a failure of an insured bank, the FDIC acts as both a resolution authority and a deposit insurer. In resolving a firm that is not an insured bank, the FDIC will be acting only as a resolution authority and not in any capacity that is analogous to deposit insurer. The new resolution authority does not provide insurance or credit protection for creditors and counterparties, and creditors will always be subject to potential losses. This is a central feature of the new resolution authority and is designed to ensure that there is market accountability.

Taking these factors into account, let me now describe how we envision the resolution of a large, SIFI. Assume for this exercise that credit or market losses have weakened the capital position of the firm, causing funding sources to withdraw and creating severe liquidity pressure. Despite the losses sustained, the firm has several business lines that have considerable value if the operations are preserved.

As I suggested earlier, the most promising resolution strategy from the FDIC's point of view will be to place the parent company into receivership and to pass its assets, principally investments in its subsidiaries, to a newly created bridge holding company. This will allow subsidiaries that are equity solvent and contribute to the franchise value of the firm to remain open and avoid the disruption that would likely accompany their closing. Because these subsidiaries will remain open and operating as going-concern counterparties, we expect that qualified financial contracts will continue to function normally as the termination, netting, and liquidation will be minimal. In short, we believe that this resolution strategy will preserve the franchise value of the firm and mitigate systemic consequences. This responds to the goal of financial stability.

Equity claims of the firm's shareholders and the claims of the subordinated and unsecured debtholders will be left behind in the receivership. In exchange, the receivership will have the equity in the bridge holding company as an asset. Therefore, initially, the bridge holding company will be owned by the receivership. The next stage in the resolution is to transfer ownership and control of the surviving franchise to private hands. But before this happens, we must ensure that the bridge has a strong capital base and address whatever liquidity concerns remain.

To create the capital base of the bridge, some of the debt of the former parent company, which has been left in the receivership, will be converted to equity in the new bridge holding company. To do this, the FDIC will estimate the extent of losses in the receivership and apportion these losses to the firm's equity and subordinated and unsecured debtholders, according to their order of priority. In all likelihood, the firm's equity holders will be wiped out and their claims will likely have little or no value.

To capitalize the new company, therefore, the FDIC expects that it will have to look to subordinated debt or even senior unsecured debt claims as the immediate source of capital. These debtholders can thus expect that their claims will be written down to reflect any losses in the receivership that the shareholders cannot cover and that, like those of the shareholders, these claims will be left in the receivership.

At this point, the remaining claims of the debtholders will be converted, in part, into equity claims that will serve to capitalize the new company. The debtholders will also receive convertible subordinated debt in the new company. This debt will provide a cushion against further losses in the firm, as it can be converted into equity if needed. Finally, any remaining claims of the failed firm's debtholders will be transferred to the new firm in the form of new unsecured debt. These measures go to the goals of accountability for investors in the failed company and the viability of the new, well-capitalized private entity.

The transfer of the business lines from a weakened holding company to a newly capitalized bridge entity should do much to alleviate the liquidity pressures by allowing the bridge entity to fund itself directly from the market. Nevertheless, it may be the case that more liquidity support is needed, either for immediate cash needs or to allow parts of the organization to roll over its debt. The new resolution authority comes with access to a new source of liquidity support provided by the DFA: the Orderly Liquidation Fund, or OLF, located in the Treasury Department. The OLF must either be repaid from recoveries on the assets of the failed firm or from assessments against the largest, most complex financial companies. Taxpayers cannot bear any loss from the resolution of a financial company under the DFA. The OLF does address a critical issue to prevent a systemwide collapse (such as we saw with the 2008 Lehman bankruptcy), because it provides an emergency source of liquidity to allow the bridge financial company to complete transactions that provide real value and prevent contagion effects.

While the OLF can be a source of direct funding for the resolution, it can also be used to provide guarantees, within limits, on the debt of the new company. The guarantees could be quite similar to the debt guarantee that was provided through the Debt Guarantee Program, or DGP, which was part of the FDIC's Temporary Liquidity Guarantee Program. Even though there were limits on firms' use of the DGP, the program was quite effective in allowing firms to access liquidity and in opening up credit markets. We expect that our resolution strategy will rely more on the use of guarantees than on direct funding from Treasury, while adhering to the statutory mandate confining its use to liquidity support.

In addition to capital and liquidity, effective governance will be an important issue to address for both the transitional bridge holding company and the newly recapitalized private sector company into which the bridge company will be converted. Initially, the FDIC, as receiver, will own the bridge company and will immediately appoint a temporary new board of directors and chief executive officer (CEO) from the private sector to run the bridge under the FDIC's oversight during the first step of the process.

The second step will be the conversion of the debtholders' claims to equity. The old debtholders of the failed parent will become the owners of the new company and, thus, be responsible for electing a new board of directors. The new board will in turn appoint a CEO of the fully privatized new company. For a variety of reasons, we would like this to be a rapid transition.

In summary, what we envision is a resolution strategy under which the FDIC takes control of the failed firm at the parent holding company level and establishes a bridge holding company as an interim step in the conversion of the failed firm into a new, well-capitalized private sector entity. We believe this strategy holds the best possibility of achieving our key goals of maintaining financial stability, holding investors in the failed firm accountable for the losses of the company, and producing a new, viable private sector company out of the process.

Cross-border issues

I would like to say a few words about the crucial international and cross-border issues. As I mentioned earlier, the type of firm we would need to resolve will likely have significant international operations. This creates a number of challenges, as the International Conference co-sponsored each Fall by the Federal Reserve Bank of Chicago has explored over the years.[2] We take these challenges very seriously, and we have been actively working on them with our foreign colleagues.

The FDIC has participated in the work of the Financial Stability Board through its membership on the Resolution Steering Group, which produced the *Key Attributes of Effective Resolution Regimes for Financial Institutions*.[3] We have also participated in the Cross-Border Crisis Management Group and a number of technical working groups, and have co-chaired the Basel Committee's Cross-border Bank Resolution Group since its inception in 2007.

In addition, the FDIC is actively reaching out on a bilateral basis to the foreign supervisors and resolution authorities with jurisdiction over the foreign operations of key U.S. SIFIs. Our goal is to forge a more collaborative process and lay the foundation for more reliable cooperation based on mutual interests in national and global financial stability. The focus of our bilateral discussions has been to identify and mitigate impediments to orderly resolution that are unique to specific jurisdictions and to examine possible resolution strategies and practical issues related to their implementation.

We conducted a heat-map exercise that determined that the operations of U.S. SIFIs are concentrated in a relatively small number of jurisdictions, particularly

[2]More information about this conference series is available at www.chicagofed.org/webpages/events/international_series.cfm.

[3]For further information see Financial Stability Board, 2011, *Key Attributes of Effective Resolution Regimes for Financial Institutions*, report, October, available at: www.financialstabilityboard.org/publications/r_111104cc.pdf.

the United Kingdom (U.K.). Working with the authorities in the U.K., we have made substantial progress in understanding how possible U.S. resolution structures might be treated under existing U.K. legal and policy frameworks. We have examined potential impediments to efficient resolutions in depth, and we are working on a cooperative basis to explore methods of resolving them.

The FDIC is also negotiating the terms of memoranda of understanding pertaining to resolutions with regulators in various countries that will provide a formal basis for information sharing and cooperation, relating to our resolution planning and implementation functions under the legal framework of the DFA.

While a full discussion of this topic is beyond the scope of this article, I will offer one point. The resolution strategy we have outlined, which calls for the continued operations of key subsidiaries both here and abroad, offers the promise of overcoming many of the cross-border issues that have been identified in both theory and practice.

Conclusion

In conclusion, I have tried to sketch out the progress the FDIC has made since the enactment of the DFA to develop the operational capability to carry out its new systemic resolution authorities, as well as a resolution strategy that can credibly envision how a SIFI can be closed without putting the financial system itself at risk. As we carry forward this work, we believe it is important to be as transparent as possible so as to gain the benefit of the wisdom of others, as well as to establish an understanding by financial markets and the public of what we are doing. For this reason, we have been actively reaching out to the financial industry, academia, and the public interest community.

I would like to conclude by noting that developing a credible capacity to place a SIFI into an orderly resolution process is essential to subjecting these companies to meaningful market discipline. Without this capability, these institutions — which by definition pose a risk to the financial system — create an expectation of public support to avert failure. That distorts the financial marketplace, giving these institutions a competitive advantage that allows them to take on even greater risk, and creating an unlevel playing field for other financial institutions that are not perceived as benefiting from potential public support. Therefore, there is a very strong public interest in the FDIC developing the capability to carry out its new systemic resolution responsibilities in a credible and effective way.

Chapter 10

Resolving Globally Active, Systemically Important Financial Institutions

Federal Deposit Insurance Corporation and the Bank of England[1]

Executive summary

The financial crisis that began in 2007 has driven home the importance of an orderly resolution process for globally active, systemically important, financial institutions (G-SIFIs). Given that challenge, the authorities in the United States (U.S.) and the United Kingdom (U.K.) have been working together to develop resolution strategies that could be applied to their largest financial institutions. These strategies have been designed to enable large and complex cross-border firms to be resolved without threatening financial stability and without putting public funds at risk. This work has taken place in connection with the implementation of the G20 Financial Stability Board's (FSB's) *Key Attributes of Effective Resolution Regimes for Financial Institutions*. The joint planning has been productive and effective. It has enhanced the resolution planning process in both jurisdictions, tackled key issues in relation to cross-border coordination, and identified potential challenges that will be addressed through further work.

This paper focuses on the application of "top-down" resolution strategies that involve a single resolution authority applying its powers to the top of a financial group, that is, at the parent company level. The paper discusses how such a top-down strategy could be implemented for a U.S. or a U.K. financial group in a cross-border context.

[1]This paper was written jointly by the Federal Deposit Insurance Corporation (FDIC) and the Bank of England and was made public on December 10, 2012.

In the U.S., the strategy has been developed in the context of the powers provided by the Dodd–Frank Wall Street Reform and Consumer Protection Act of 2010. Such a strategy would apply a single receivership at the top-tier holding company, assign losses to shareholders and unsecured creditors of the holding company, and transfer sound operating subsidiaries to a new solvent entity or entities.

In the U.K., the strategy has been developed on the basis of the powers provided by the U.K. Banking Act 2009 and in anticipation of the further powers that will be provided by the European Union Recovery and Resolution Directive (RRD) and the domestic reforms that implement the recommendations of the U.K. Independent Commission on Banking (ICB). Such a strategy would involve the bail-in (write-down or conversion) of creditors at the top of the group in order to restore the whole group to solvency.

Both the U.S. and U.K. approaches ensure continuity of all critical services performed by the operating firm(s), thereby reducing risks to financial stability. Both approaches ensure activities of the firm in the foreign jurisdictions in which it operates are unaffected, thereby minimizing risks to cross-border implementation. The unsecured debt holders can expect that their claims would be written down to reflect any losses that shareholders cannot cover, with some converted partly into equity in order to provide sufficient capital to return the sound businesses of the G-SIFI to private sector operation. Sound subsidiaries (domestic and foreign) would be kept open and operating, thereby limiting contagion effects and cross-border complications. In both countries, whether during execution of the resolution or thereafter, restructuring measures may be taken, especially in the parts of the business causing the distress, including shrinking those businesses, breaking them into smaller entities, and/or liquidating or closing certain operations. Both approaches would be accompanied by the replacement of culpable senior management.

This paper outlines several common considerations that affect these particular approaches to resolution in the U.S. and the U.K., including the need to ensure sufficient loss absorbency at the top of the group. The FDIC and the Bank of England will continue to work together on these resolution strategies.

Introduction

The FDIC and the Bank of England — together with the Board of Governors of the Federal Reserve System, the Federal Reserve Bank of New York, and the Financial Services Authority — have been working to develop resolution strategies for the failure of globally active SIFIs or G-SIFIs with significant operations on both sides of the Atlantic. This work has taken place in connection with the implementation of the FSB's *Key Attributes of Effective Resolution Regimes for Financial Institutions* (Key Attributes), as well as in connection with the reforms to the legal arrangements for handling the failure of financial institutions that were instituted in the U.S. and the U.K. in response to the recent financial crisis.

The goal is to produce resolution strategies that could be implemented for the failure of one or more of the largest financial institutions with extensive activities in our respective jurisdictions. These resolution strategies should maintain systemically important operations and contain threats to financial stability. They should also assign losses to shareholders and unsecured creditors in the group, thereby avoiding the need for a bailout by taxpayers. These strategies should be sufficiently robust to manage the challenges of cross-border implementation and to the operational challenges of execution.

As highlighted in the FSB's recently published draft Guidance on Recovery and Resolution Planning,[2] strategies for resolution may broadly be categorized as either applying resolution powers to the top of a group by a single national resolution authority (single point of entry), or applying resolution tools to different parts of the group by two or more resolution authorities acting in a coordinated way (multiple points of entry). Which strategy is most suitable to resolving the group will depend upon a range of factors. For example, a single point of entry strategy may offer the simplest and most effective choice if the debt issued at the top of the group is sufficient to absorb the group's losses. Where this is not the case, a multiple points of entry strategy will be more suitable, particularly if different parts of the group can continue on a standalone basis.

The focus of this chapter is on a single point of entry resolution approach. It is hoped that the detail it provides on the single point of entry approach, when combined with the published FSB Guidance on Recovery and Resolution Planning, will give greater predictability for market participants about how resolution authorities may approach a resolution. This predictability cannot, however, be absolute, as the resolution authorities must not be constrained in exercising discretion in pursuit of their statutory objectives in how best to resolve a firm.

Post-crisis resolution strategy

The financial crisis that began in late 2007 highlighted the shortcomings of the arrangements for handling the failure of large financial institutions that were in

[2]See FSB Consultative Document "Recovery and Resolution Planning: Making the Key Attributes Requirements Operational," www.financialstabilityboard.org/publications/r_121102.pdf.

place on either side of the Atlantic. Large banking organizations in both the U.S. and the U.K. had become highly leveraged and complex, with numerous and dispersed financial operations, extensive off-balance-sheet activities, and opaque financial statements. These institutions were managed as single entities, despite their subsidiaries being structured as separate and distinct legal entities. They were highly interconnected through their capital markets activities, interbank lending, payments, and off-balance-sheet arrangements.

The legislative frameworks and resolution regimes at the time were ill-suited to dealing with financial institution failures of this scale and interconnectedness. In the U.S., the FDIC only had the power to place an insured depository institution into receivership; it could not resolve failed or failing bank holding companies or other nonbank financial companies that posed a systemic risk. In the U.K., until 2009 there was no special resolution regime available for banks or other financial companies, whatever their size or complexity, and as a result the U.K. was reliant on standard insolvency procedures such as administration.

As demonstrated by the Title I requirement of the Dodd–Frank Wall Street Reform and Consumer Protection Act of 2010 (Dodd–Frank Act), the U.S. would prefer that large financial organizations be resolvable through ordinary bankruptcy. However, the U.S. bankruptcy process may not be able to handle the failure of a systemic financial institution without significant disruption to the financial system.

Similarly, the U.K. administration process often takes time and involves significant uncertainty regarding the outcome. Forcing large financial organizations through administration can create significant and systemic risks for the real economy by interrupting critical services, disrupting key financial relationships, and freezing financial markets. In addition, it can destroy value, harming the real economy.

Given these problems with the bankruptcy process, the U.S. and the U.K. authorities resorted to providing large scale public support to failing financial companies during the 2007–2009 crisis to prevent further systemic disruption. This public support has exposed taxpayers to loss and resulted in the bailout of multiple financial institutions and their creditors.

Following the crisis, an overhaul of the framework for dealing with large and complex financial institution failures was required. While it may be useful to strengthen the current bankruptcy code or administration rules to improve the handling of financial failures, systemic considerations warrant having an alternative resolution strategy.

A resolution strategy for a failed or failing G-SIFI should assign losses to shareholders and unsecured creditors, and hold management responsible for the failure of the firm. The strategy should provide continuity of the critical services that the institution provides within the financial system and to the real economy, thereby minimizing systemic risk. The strategy should also enable a prompt transition of the firm's ongoing operations to full private ownership and control without taxpayer support. Given the cross-border nature of G-SIFIs, the resolution strategy should ensure financial stability concerns are addressed across all jurisdictions in which the firm operates. To be successful, such an approach will require close cooperation between home and foreign authorities.

Under the strategies currently being developed by the U.S. and the U.K., the resolution authority could intervene at the top of the group. Culpable senior management of the parent and operating businesses would be removed, and losses would be apportioned to shareholders and unsecured creditors. In all likelihood, shareholders would lose all value and unsecured creditors should thus expect that their claims would be written down to reflect any losses that shareholders did not cover. Under both the U.S. and U.K. approaches, legal safeguards ensure that creditors recover no less than they would under insolvency.

An efficient path for returning the sound operations of the G-SIFI to the private sector would be provided by exchanging or converting a sufficient amount of the unsecured debt from the original creditors of the failed company into equity. In the U.S., the new equity would become capital in one or more newly formed operating entities. In the U.K., the same approach could be used, or the equity could be used to recapitalize the failing financial company itself — thus, the highest layer of surviving bailed-in creditors would become the owners of the resolved firm. In either country, the new equity holders would take on the corresponding risk of being shareholders in a financial institution. Throughout, subsidiaries (domestic and foreign) carrying out critical activities would be kept open and operating, thereby limiting contagion effects. Such a resolution strategy would ensure market discipline and maintain financial stability without cost to taxpayers.

Legislative frameworks for implementing the strategy

It should be stressed that the application of such a strategy can be achieved only within a legislative framework that provides authorities with key resolution powers. The FSB Key Attributes have established a crucial framework for the implementation of an effective set of resolution powers and practices into national regimes. In the U.S., these powers had already become available under the Dodd–Frank Act (DFA). In the U.K., the additional powers needed to enhance the existing resolution framework established under the Banking Act 2009 (the Banking Act) are expected to be fully provided by the European Commission's proposals for a European Union RRD and through the domestic reforms that implement the recommendations of the U.K. ICB, enhancing the existing resolution framework established under the Banking Act. The development of effective resolution strategies is being carried out in anticipation of such legislation.

U.S. regime

The framework provided by the DFA in the U.S. greatly enhances the ability of regulators to address the problems of large, complex financial institutions in any future crisis. Title I of the DFA requires each G-SIFI to periodically submit to the FDIC and the Federal Reserve a resolution plan that must address the company's plans for its rapid and orderly resolution under the U.S. Bankruptcy Code. The FDIC and the Federal Reserve are required to review the plans to determine jointly whether a company's plan is credible. If a plan is found to be deficient and adequate revisions are not made, the FDIC and the Federal Reserve may jointly impose more stringent capital, leverage, or liquidity requirements, or restrictions on growth, activities, or operations of the company, including its subsidiaries. Ultimately, the company could be ordered to divest assets or operations to facilitate an orderly resolution under bankruptcy in the event of failure. Once submitted and accepted, the SIFIs' plans for resolution under bankruptcy will support the FDIC's planning for the exercise of its resolution powers by providing the FDIC with an understanding of each SIFI's structure, complexity, and processes.

Title II of the DFA provides the FDIC with new powers to resolve SIFIs by establishing the orderly liquidation authority (OLA). Under the OLA, the FDIC may be appointed receiver for any U.S. financial company that meets specified criteria, including being in default or in danger of default, and whose resolution under the U.S. Bankruptcy Code (or other relevant insolvency process) would likely create systemic instability.[3] Title II requires that the losses of any financial company placed into receivership will not be borne by taxpayers, but by common and preferred stockholders, debt holders, and other unsecured creditors, and that management responsible for the condition of the financial company will be replaced. Once appointed receiver for a failed financial company, the FDIC would be required to carry out a resolution of the company in a manner that mitigates

[3]The process for such appointment is set forth in Sections 202 and 203 of the Dodd–Frank Act, 12 U.S.C. §§5382 and 3.

risk to financial stability and minimizes moral hazard.[4] Any costs borne by the U.S. authorities in resolving the institution not paid from proceeds of the resolution will be recovered from the industry.

U.K. regime

In the U.K., the Banking Act provides the Bank of England with tools for resolving failing deposit-taking banks and building societies.[5] Powers similar to those of the FDIC are available, including powers to transfer all or part of a failed bank's business to a private sector purchaser or to a bridge bank until a private purchaser can be found. The Banking Act also provides the U.K. authorities with a bespoke bank insolvency procedure that fully protects insured depositors while liquidating a failed bank's assets. These powers have proved valuable; for example, during the crisis they allowed the authorities to transfer the retail and wholesale deposits, branches, and a significant proportion of the residential mortgage portfolio of a failed building society to another building society.

The Banking Act powers do not, however, provide a wholly effective solution to the failure of a large, complex, and international financial firm. The critical economic functions of a G-SIFI are currently intertwined legally, operationally, and financially across jurisdictions and legal entities. For U.K. firms, these functions frequently reside in the same entities as the firms' core unsecured liabilities. Using the existing statutory transfer powers would involve separating and transferring large and complex businesses from within operating entities to a purchaser or bridge bank, while leaving behind the remaining liabilities and bad assets in the failed firm to be wound up through insolvency. These operating companies may have several thousand counterparties, customers, and contracts. Such a transfer would be almost impossible to achieve over a resolution weekend without destroying value and causing financial stability concerns in multiple jurisdictions.

The introduction of a statutory bail-in resolution tool (the power to write down or convert into equity the liabilities of a failing firm) under the RRD is critical to implementing a whole group resolution of U.K. firms in a way that reduces the risks to financial stability. A bail-in tool would enable the U.K. authorities to recapitalize an institution by allocating losses to its shareholders and unsecured creditors, thereby avoiding the need to split or transfer operating entities. The

[4]See Section 204(a) of the Dodd–Frank Act, 12 U.S.C. §5384.

[5]In addition, the U.K. Treasury is empowered to take a bank into Temporary Public Ownership where the power is necessary to resolve or reduce a serious threat to U.K. financial stability. The powers are set out in Articles 9 and 13 of the Banking Act.

provisions in the RRD that enable the resolution authority to impose a temporary stay on the exercise of termination rights by counterparties in the event of a firm's entry into resolution (in other words, preventing counterparties from terminating their contractual arrangements with a firm solely as a result of the firm's entry into resolution) will be needed to ensure the bail-in is executed in an orderly manner.

The existing Banking Act does not cover nondeposit-taking financial firms, notably investment banks and financial market infrastructures (clearing houses in particular), the failure of which, in many cases, would also have significant financial stability consequences. The Banking Act also has limitations with regard to the application of resolution tools to financial holding companies. The U.K. is in the process of expanding the scope of the Banking Act to include these firms. This is expected to be achieved through the introduction of the U.K. Financial Services Bill,[6] which is due to complete its passage through Parliament by the end of this year.

In addition to expanding the U.K. resolution regime, the Financial Services Bill will significantly enhance the U.K.'s approach to banking supervision. Going forward, the framework for prudential supervision in the U.K. will emphasize supervisory judgment, rather than supervision based solely on rules. Under this framework, considerations of resolvability or ease of resolution would become a core part of the supervisory process.

In conjunction with the Financial Services Bill, the adoption of the recommendations of the ICB will also significantly improve the resolvability of the U.K. domestic retail bank by ring-fencing it from the rest of the group. This will help to preserve core domestic intermediation services if a group-wide resolution is not feasible for some reason.

To ensure that banks are resolvable, the Financial Services Authority (and in the future, the Prudential Regulation Authority[7] (PRA)) will require firms under the Financial Services Act 2010 to produce Recovery and Resolution Plans (RRPs). Firms will submit the information that the authorities will need to prepare resolution plans and to assess resolvability. Where barriers to resolution are identified,

---

[6]See http://www.hm-treasury.gov.uk/consult_financial_sector_resolution_broadening_regime.htm.

[7]Once the Financial Services Bill comes into force in 2013, the Financial Services Authority will be replaced by two new regulatory bodies, the PRA and the Financial Conduct Authority. The PRA, a subsidiary of the Bank of England, will become the prudential regulator of deposit-takers, insurers, and the largest investment firms. It will have the objective of promoting the safety and soundness of these firms, in part through minimizing the adverse effect of their failure on the U.K. financial system.

firms will be required to remove them through changes to their structure and operations. The proposed RRD provides authorities with the necessary powers to achieve this, including the ability to require changes to the legal or operational structures of institutions, and to require firms to cease specific activities.[8]

Description of the resolution strategies

U.S. approach to single point of entry resolution strategy

Under the U.S. approach, the FDIC will be appointed receiver of the top-tier parent holding company of the financial group following the company's failure and the completion of the appointment process set forth under the DFA. Immediately after the parent holding company is placed into receivership, the FDIC will transfer assets (primarily the equity and investments in subsidiaries) from the receivership estate to a bridge financial holding company. By taking control of the SIFI at the top of the group, subsidiaries (domestic and foreign) carrying out critical services can remain open and operating, limiting the need for destabilizing insolvency proceedings at the subsidiary level. Equity claims of the shareholders and the claims of the subordinated and unsecured debt holders will likely remain in the receivership.

Initially, the bridge holding company will be controlled by the FDIC as receiver. The next stage in the resolution is to transfer ownership and control of the surviving operations to private hands. Before this happens, the FDIC must ensure that the bridge has a strong capital base and must address whatever liquidity concerns remain. The FDIC would also likely require the restructuring of the firm — potentially into one or more smaller, non-systemic firms that could be resolved under bankruptcy.

By leaving behind substantial unsecured liabilities and stockholder equity in the receivership, assets transferred to the bridge holding company will significantly exceed its liabilities, resulting in a well-capitalized holding company. After the creation of the bridge financial company, but before any transition to the private sector, a valuation process would be undertaken to estimate the extent of losses in the receivership and apportion these losses to the equity holders and subordinated and unsecured creditors according to their order of priority. In all likelihood, the equity holders would be wiped out and their claims would have little or no value.

[8] See Article 14(4) of the proposed RRD, including 14(4)(e) "requiring the institution to limit or cease specific existing or proposed activities," and 14(4)(g) "requiring changes to legal or operational structures of the institution so as to reduce complexity in order to ensure that critical functions may be legally and economically separated from other functions through the application of the resolution tools."

To capitalize the new operations — one or more new private entities — the FDIC expects that it will have to look to subordinated debt or even senior unsecured debt claims as the immediate source of capital. The original debt holders can thus expect that their claims will be written down to reflect any losses in the receivership of the parent that the shareholders cannot cover and that, like those of the shareholders, these claims will be left in the receivership.

At this point, the remaining claims of the debt holders will be converted, in part, into equity claims that will serve to capitalize the new operations. The debt holders may also receive convertible subordinated debt in the new operations. This debt would provide a cushion against further losses in the firm, as it can be converted into equity if needed. Any remaining claims of the debt holders could be transferred to the new operations in the form of new unsecured debt.

The transfer of equity and investments in operating subsidiaries to the bridge holding company should do much to alleviate liquidity pressures. Ongoing operations and their attendant liabilities also will be supported by assurances from the FDIC, as receiver. As demonstrated by past bridge-bank operations, the assurance of performance should encourage market funding and stabilize the bridge financial company. However, in the case where credit markets are impaired and market funding is not available in the short term, the DFA provides for FDIC access to the Orderly Liquidation Fund (OLF), a fund within the U.S. Treasury. In addition to providing a back-up source of funding, the OLF may also be used to provide guarantees, within limits, on the debt of the new operations. An expected goal of the strategy is to minimize or avoid use of the OLF. To the extent that the OLF is used, it must either be repaid from recoveries on the assets of the failed financial company or from assessments against the largest, most complex financial companies.[9] The DFA prohibits the loss of any taxpayer money in the orderly liquidation process.

U.K. approach to single point of entry resolution strategy

The U.K.'s planned approach to single point of entry also involves a top-down resolution. On the basis that the RRD will introduce a broad bail-in power, the U.K. authorities would seek to recapitalize the financial group through the imposition of losses on shareholders and, as appropriate, creditors of the firm via the exercise of a statutory bail-in power. This U.K. group resolution approach need

[9]The FDIC is also allowed to claw back any advance payments to claimants of the receivership if losses exceed original estimates. The set of companies that may be subject to an assessment, and the extent to which their assessment is subject to adjustment for certain risk factors, is set out in Section 210(o) of the Dodd–Frank Act.

not employ a bridge bank and administration, although such powers are available in the U.K. and may be appropriate under certain circumstances.

Current proposals for implementing such a strategy incorporate a period in which equity and debt securities would be transferred from the shareholders and debt holders to an appointed trustee. The trustee would hold the securities during a valuation period in which the extent of the losses expected to be incurred by the firm would be established and, in turn, the recapitalization requirement determined. During this period, listing of the company's equity securities (and potentially debt securities) would be suspended. Once the recapitalization requirement has been determined, an announcement of the final terms of the bail-in would be made to the previous security holders. This announcement would include full details of the write-down and/or conversion.

Debt securities would be cancelled or written down in order to return the firm to solvency by reducing the level of outstanding liabilities. The losses would be applied up the firm's capital structure in a process that respects the existing creditor hierarchy under insolvency law. The value of any loans from the parent to its operating subsidiaries would be written down in a manner that ensures that the subsidiaries remain solvent and viable.

Completion of the exchange would see the trustee transfer the equity (and potentially some of the existing debt securities written down accordingly) back to the original creditors of the firm. Those creditors unable to hold equity securities (for example, for reasons of investment mandate restrictions) would be able to request that the trustee sell the equity securities on their behalf. The trust would then be dissolved and the equity securities (and potentially debt securities) of the firm would resume trading. The firm would now be recapitalized and primarily owned by the (appropriate layer of) original creditors of the institution. As described later, the process would be accompanied by restructuring measures to address the causes of the firm's failure and to restore the business to viability.

The U.K. has also given consideration to the recapitalization process in a scenario in which a G-SIFI's liabilities do not include much debt issuance at the holding company or parent bank level but instead comprise insured retail deposits held in the operating subsidiaries. Under such a scenario, deposit guarantee schemes may be required to contribute to the recapitalization of the firm, as they may do under the Banking Act in the use of other resolution tools. The proposed RRD also permits such an approach because it allows deposit guarantee scheme funds to be used to support the use of resolution tools, including bail-in, provided that the amount contributed does not exceed what the deposit guarantee scheme would have as a claimant in liquidation if it had made a payout to the insured depositors. That is consistent with the contribution requirement that is already imposed on the Financial Services Compensation Scheme in the U.K. in the exercise of resolution powers[10] and simulates the losses that would have been incurred by those deposit guarantee schemes during bank insolvency. But insofar as a bail-in provides for continuity in operations and preserves value, losses to a deposit guarantee scheme in a bail-in should be much lower than in liquidation. Insured depositors themselves would remain unaffected. Uninsured deposits would be treated in line with other similarly ranked liabilities in the resolution process, with the expectation that they might be written down.

Following the recapitalization process, the firm would be restructured to address the causes of its failure. It should then be solvent and viable, and as a result in a position to access market funding. In recognition of the fact that it will take time for losses to be assessed for purposes of recapitalization, and that it will take time to execute the restructuring plan that will underpin the firm's viability, immediate access may prove difficult. In certain circumstances, to reduce the immediate funding need and so facilitate market access, illiquid assets might be removed from the balance sheet of the firm and transferred into an asset management company to be worked out over a longer period.

If market funding were not immediately available, temporary funding may need to be provided by the authorities to meet the firms' liquidity needs. The funding would only be provided on a fully collateralized basis with appropriate haircuts applied to the collateral to reduce further the risk of loss. In the unlikely event that losses were associated with the provision of temporary public sector support, such losses would be recovered from the financial sector.

It is important to note that the strategy described above would not necessarily be appropriate for all U.K. G-SIFIs in all circumstances. Other strategies may be more appropriate depending on the structure of a group, the nature of its business, and the size and location of the group's losses. For example, in cases where the losses on assets in a particular operating subsidiary were potentially so great that they could not be absorbed by bailing in at group level or where the business had incurred such significant losses and was so weighed down by toxic assets that the capital needs in resolution were too difficult to estimate credibly, resolution at the level of one or more operating subsidiaries may be more appropriate. In this situation, the application of resolution tools to operating subsidiaries would be easier if the subsidiaries providing critical economic services were operationally and financially ring-fenced from the rest of the group.

---

[10]The provisions for the Financial Services Compensation Scheme to contribute to the costs of a resolution are set out in Article 171ff of the Banking Act 2009.

This is one of the advantages of the ring-fence which is being introduced in the U.K. It will provide flexibility in the event of fatal problems elsewhere in the group to transfer the ring-fenced entity to a bridge bank or purchaser in its entirety. If losses were concentrated in the ring-fenced entity and capital in the ring-fenced entity was insufficient to absorb them, then losses could be borne by creditors of the ring-fenced bank (including debt holders where the ring-fenced bank had issued debt into the market). This could be achieved either by bail-in or by transferring the operations of the ring-fenced bank to a bridge bank, leaving uninsured creditors behind in administration. Draft legislation to establish this ring-fence of the largest retail deposit-takers is due to be introduced into Parliament early in 2013 and if passed will provide valuable additional flexibility in implementing resolution strategies to preserve the provision of core services in the U.K. business of U.K. G-SIFIs.

Key common considerations for U.S. and U.K. approaches

As outlined above, high-level transaction structures have been developed for each jurisdiction. As discussed in the FSB Guidance on Recovery and Resolution Planning, for any resolution to be effective, consideration needs to be given in advance to various preconditions and operational requirements. Several of these considerations in relation to a top-down resolution strategy are discussed in more detail below.

Resolution and restructuring measures

A top-down resolution by definition focuses on assigning losses and establishing new capital structures at the top of the group. This approach keeps the rest of the group, potentially comprised of hundreds or thousands of legal entities, intact. However, a top-down resolution would need to be accompanied, or shortly followed, by significant restructuring measures to address the causes of the firm's failure and to underpin the firm's viability. Such a restructuring may include shrinking the G-SIFI's balance sheet, breaking the company up into smaller entities, and/or selling or closing certain operations. The newly restructured companies will all need to have strong corporate governance and management oversight, which would likely necessitate significant changes to management and board personnel and processes. In both countries, it is likely that supervisory actions will continue after the return to private ownership to ensure that the firm is on a stable and sustainable footing and the problems that caused the firm to fail in the first place have been properly dealt with.

In the U.S., effective governance will be an important issue for both the transitional bridge financial company and the newly capitalized entity or entities into which the bridge will transition. The FDIC, as receiver, will control the bridge financial company and would immediately appoint a temporary board of directors and Chief Executive Officer (CEO) to run the bridge. The claims of the failed G-SIFI's unsecured creditors will be converted into equity and, as a result, the former creditors will become owners of the new private sector operations. They will thereafter be responsible for electing a new board of directors, which will in turn appoint a new CEO.

During the period in which the FDIC controls the bridge financial company, decisions will be made on how to on simplify and shrink the institution. It also would likely require restructuring of the firm — perhaps into one or more smaller, non-systemic firms. Consideration will also be given to how to create a more stable, less systemically important institution. Required changes, including divestiture, may be influenced by the failed firm's Title I resolution plan. Once determined, the required actions and relevant time frames for their execution will be specified in formal supervisory agreements with the new owners of the private sector operations.

The required actions would be executed in private markets by the new owners. For example, the new owners might be required to sell a portion of their branch structure to reduce their footprint, divest their foreign operations, or separate their commercial and investment banking operations. The resulting new private sector operations would be smaller, more manageable — and perhaps more profitable. They would also be easier to examine and supervise. Importantly, all new operations must be resolvable under bankruptcy without public support.

In the U.K., similar considerations would enter into decisions on the restructuring process. Depending on the specific timeline for resolution, the restructuring may occur primarily either during the trustee stage (before the delivery of equity securities to the creditors) or during the stage following the dissolution of the trust. The extent of the restructuring measures required would depend on the cause of failure, and the extent to which losses were contained within a particular pool of assets or legal entity. If losses at the firm were localized, the restructuring measures required may be limited. These would likely require a sale or wind-down of relevant business lines and withdrawal from loss-making activities. The senior management that were responsible for bringing the firm into distress would also be replaced. On the other hand, if losses at the firm were pervasive and spread across multiple business lines, a more fundamental restructuring of the firm's business would be required. This would likely include a complete governance overhaul and a thorough reorganization of the activities of the institution. In the extreme case, much of the institution may enter managed wind-down over a prolonged period of time. In such a scenario, it is likely that a legal and operational ring-fencing of a banking group's retail banking activities from the group's investment banking activities would prove particularly valuable in facilitating such a restructuring.

Maintaining financial stability

Both the U.S. and U.K. resolution proposals are designed to maintain financial stability by ensuring that critical business functions continue to be performed. Critical business functions are generally performed at the level of the operating subsidiaries — assets of the holding companies of U.S. and U.K. G-SIFIs tend to comprise little more than the equity stakes in the operating subsidiaries. The newly resolved group would be solvent and viable, and should be in a position therefore to access market funding or, if necessary, funding from the authorities as discussed above. Liquidity will be downstreamed in a "business as usual" manner to the operating subsidiaries immediately following the resolution weekend. As described above, the balance sheets of the operating subsidiaries should be broadly unaffected by the resolution action at the top of the group. To recapitalize the operating subsidiaries that had incurred losses, the equity or debt held by the parent in those subsidiaries would need to be written down. The parent and, indirectly, the subsidiary operating companies may also be subject to change of control procedures arising from a switch of ownership from the existing shareholders to creditors.[11] Provision of critical shared services across the group should be unaffected.

Given minimal disruption to the balance sheet of the operating companies, and given that the group should be recapitalized following the assignment of losses to shareholders and creditors, counterparties should not have strong incentives to cease trading with the operating companies during and following the resolution. The contingency plans are designed to minimize the triggering of cross-defaults or closeout of netting arrangements at the operating companies. In certain cases, a stay on termination rights may be applied to ensure that termination of counterparty relationships cannot be triggered solely as a result of entry into resolution. A stay may assist in promoting the continuity of a variety of critical economic functions that are dependent on maintaining counterparty relationships (for example, those functions relating to wholesale market activities) and also avoiding the rapid, disorderly, and potentially value-destructive closeout of financial contracts

[11] Subject to appropriate regulatory approvals.

and liquidation of securities. The stay could also minimize the closeout risk that may result from cross-default clauses within financial contracts. In the scenario in which the holding company is placed into receivership, the stay would extend to certain subsidiary counterparties subject to financial contracts that reference the holding company. Given cross-border considerations, it is important that stays on termination apply to both domestic and foreign operations of G-SIFIs. In certain cases, authorities cannot currently extend stays on termination to foreign operations. Supporting actions by host authorities may be required (as included in the Key Attributes), or it may be necessary to introduce clauses that recognize foreign resolution actions, including stays on termination, into counterparty documentation.

Similarly, because the group remains solvent, retail or corporate depositors should not have an incentive to "run" from the firm under resolution insofar as their banking arrangements, transacted at the operating company level, remain unaffected. In order to achieve this, the authorities recognize the need for effective communication to depositors, making it clear that their deposits will be protected.

If continuity of critical functions is to be achieved, the firm will need continuing access to core services provided by the financial market infrastructures (for example, payment systems and central counterparties) during and following resolution. To achieve this, authorities in both the U.S. and U.K. have begun a process of engaging with such infrastructures to develop effective procedures relating to the treatment of members who have entered resolution.

Minimization of cross-border coordination risk

It should be stressed that a key advantage of a whole group, single point of entry approach is that it avoids the need to commence separate territorial and entity-focused insolvency proceedings, which could be disruptive, difficult to coordinate, and would depend on the satisfaction of a large number of pre-conditions in terms of structure and operations of the group for successful execution. Because the whole group resolution strategies maintain continuity of business at the subsidiary level, foreign subsidiaries and branches should be broadly unaffected by the resolution action taken at the home holding company level. The strategies remove the need to commence foreign insolvency proceedings or enforce legal powers over foreign assets (although, as discussed later, it may be necessary to write down or convert debt at the top of the group that are subject to foreign law). Liquidity should continue to be downstreamed from the holding company to foreign subsidiaries and branches. Given minimal disruption to operating entities, resolution authorities, directors, and creditors of foreign subsidiaries and branches should have little incentive to take action other than to cooperate with the implementation of the group resolution. In particular, host stakeholders should not have an incentive to ring-fence assets or petition for a preemptive insolvency — preemptive actions that would otherwise destroy value and may disrupt markets at home and abroad.

A key part of the work undertaken by the U.S. and the U.K. has been to identify the regulatory obligations of foreign authorities in response to a resolution originated by a home authority. Where any impediments to effective whole group resolution have been identified, authorities are in the process of exploring methods to overcome them.

The Key Attributes stress the importance of a globally coordinated approach to resolution, and emphasize that resolution authorities should consider the potential impact of their resolution actions on the financial stability of foreign jurisdictions. The Key Attributes propose a framework that would facilitate cross-border cooperation between resolution authorities. This framework would help to ensure that local resolution authorities support a resolution carried out by a foreign authority.

A central element of the cross-border cooperation process set out in the Key Attributes is the establishment of Crisis Management Groups (CMGs) — groups composed of supervisors, central banks, and resolution authorities of the key jurisdictions in which a G-SIFI operates. Members of these groups are expected to enter into firm-specific cross-border cooperation agreements that detail the proposed means by which a particular resolution should be coordinated between authorities. To provide a platform for such cooperation agreements, authorities in the home jurisdiction are required to submit firm-specific resolution strategies to members of the CMG for consultation by the end of 2012.[12]

These resolution strategies set out at a high level the key elements of the approach to resolution and outline the use of key resolution powers. The strategies will be translated into detailed resolution plans for each firm during the first half of 2013.[13] These resolution plans will provide specific detail on implementing the proposed resolution strategy, including consideration of entities to which resolution powers may be applied and the possible roles of relevant national resolution authorities. Subsequently, firm-specific resolvability assessments will be developed by the end of 2013. The resolvability assessments will identify barriers to implementation of the resolution plans, and will be key to demonstrating the

[12]See FSB Progress Report on the Resolution of SIFIs: http://www.financialstabilityboard.org/publications/r_121031aa.pdf.

[13]See aforementioned FSB Guidance for Recovery and Resolution Planning.

extent to which the resolution plan for each G-SIFI is feasible and credible without severe systemic disruption and without exposing taxpayers to loss. In addition, certain U.S. and U.K. G-SIFIs have been required to make their first full RRP submissions in 2012 to support the development of viable resolution plans by the authorities. These submissions will help to expose, among other things, actions that firms will need to take to improve their resolvability.

Write-down of liabilities and conversion of debt into equity

Under a top-down resolution, shareholders and certain creditors at the top of the group absorb losses and recapitalize the group as whole. For a top-down approach to work, there must be sufficient loss-absorbing capacity available at the top of the group to absorb losses sustained within operational subsidiaries.

In the U.S., the capital structures of large financial holding companies are characterized by equity and large amounts of unsecured debt of various maturities. This debt is structurally subordinated within the group, and limited external unsecured debt tends to be raised at entities below the financial holding company. Regulation may be adopted to ensure that sufficient debt is held at the top-tier holding company level.

In the U.K., on the other hand, financial holding companies at the top of the group often do not account for a significant proportion of the group's unsecured debt raised by groups externally. Looking ahead, either the groups could restructure so that more debt is issued out of the holding company or the U.K. authorities could look to bail-in the liabilities of the top operating companies within each group. The latter course would require careful planning given that senior unsecured bonds typically rank alongside other unsecured liabilities that are unlikely to be bailed-in. Detailed consideration of this part of the resolution strategy for individual banking groups will need to take account of the precise provisions of the RRD as eventually passed into law. Also, both the draft RRD and the U.K. government's plans for implementing the ICB report include requirements aimed at ensuring that banks have sufficient capital and debt in issue to make them resolvable using bail-in or other resolution tools. The U.K. authorities will in due course consider how the final versions of those requirements should be applied to U.K. G-SIFIs given their group structures and resolvability.

Consideration also needs to be given to ensuring that debt issued at the top of the group that is subject to foreign law can be written down or converted alongside liabilities subject to the law of the home jurisdiction. This may be crucial to ensuring that the firm's recapitalization needs can be met and that creditors are treated fairly. Ensuring that foreign law securities can be written down or converted into equity alongside securities issued under the law of the home jurisdiction may require the inclusion of contractual recognition of foreign resolution proceedings within debt contracts.

Valuation

During resolution, a valuation process will need to be undertaken to assess the losses on assets that the firm has incurred and the capital needed under stress assumptions to restore confidence in the firm, which will determine the extent to which creditor claims should be written down and converted. The valuation will determine how far up the capital structure the write down or conversion of debt may need to apply (that is, whether shareholders and subordinated debt holders can fully absorb losses in order to recapitalize the firm, or whether senior unsecured creditors would also need to be included). The valuation process will in turn determine what financial instruments if any — for example, common equity in the new firm or warrants — the different classes of original creditors of the firm should receive.

Given the differences in the U.S. and U.K. resolution processes, the precise valuation requirements and timelines are unlikely to be the same for the two jurisdictions. Consideration is being given in both jurisdictions as to how much of the valuation process can be prepared in advance of resolution (for example, as part of enhanced preparation under the U.K. Proactive Intervention Framework[14]). Consideration is also being given as to whether new financial statements would be required, and whether the firm's external auditors would need to be replaced for the valuation process to provide sufficient comfort to the market that the ongoing operations were fully (re)capitalized and solvent. An effective valuation process should facilitate the issuance of new securities and other financial instruments, and would likely be required by rating agencies in order to make a judgment on the creditworthiness of the resolved institution. The U.S. and U.K. authorities are considering how a credible valuation could be carried out quickly and effectively, and with flexibility to respond to the characteristics of particular institutions and the nature of their failures.

Listing requirements post-resolution

To return the firm to the market effectively, the public listing of its equity and debt securities would need to resume. Insofar as new debt or equity instruments are

[14]The PRA's Proactive Intervention Framework will provide a systematic approach for the assessment of a firm's proximity to failure to enable supervisors to identify and respond to emerging risks at an early stage. See "The PRA's approach to banking supervision," October 2012.

issued, listing rules may require that a prospectus or other offering documentation be provided to investors. This would likely include audited financial statements for the firm, and may therefore take a significant amount of time to achieve.

Under the U.S. approach, a new parent entity is established during resolution. Therefore, new securities would need to be issued in satisfaction of creditor claims. Such securities would either need to be issued pursuant to effective registration statements, or may, in certain instances, be listed pursuant to an exemption from registration.

In the case of a U.K. resolution, new equity and debt securities would not necessarily need to be issued following resolution. Under certain circumstances, it is possible, subject to a number of conditions, that existing equity and debt securities could resume trading without the need for a prospectus.

In both jurisdictions, engagement with securities regulators well in advance of, and also during, resolution will be key to ensuring that public listing can be achieved in a timely manner following resolution.

Conclusion

In both the U.S. and the U.K., legislative reforms already made or planned in response to the financial crisis provide new powers for resolving failed or failing G-SIFIs. The FDIC and the Bank of England have developed resolution strategies that take control of the failed company at the top of the group, impose losses on shareholders and unsecured creditors — not on taxpayers — and remove top management and hold them accountable for their actions. These strategies provide an efficient path for returning the systemically important parts of the G-SIFI to the private sector by exchanging or converting a sufficient amount of creditor claims from the failed company into capital in the newly resolved entities. Because the resolution action is taken at the top of the group and by the home authorities, continuity of all critical services would be maintained and subsidiaries (foreign and domestic) would remain open and operating with access to sufficient liquidity. As a result, the strategy achieves the important goals of imposing market accountability and maintaining financial stability in all jurisdictions in which the firm operates.

The FDIC and the Bank of England continue to work to ensure that their respective resolution strategies will be fully operational. Importantly, the process of cross-border dialogue that has facilitated the above strategies reflects a shared public interest in developing the capacity to resolve a G-SIFI in a credible and effective manner, and offers a model for multilateral resolution planning more broadly.

PART V

An Alternative View: Financial Stability via Bank Breakups

In Part V, critics who question the efficacy of the new resolution process discuss alternative means to avoid financial instability surrounding the failure of a large, complex financial firm. Instead of relying on the new failure resolution processes for systemically important firms, distortions resulting from too-big-to-fail (TBTF) policies should be eliminated by imposing changes and limitations to industry structure. That is, if TBTF creates problems (and there is general agreement that it does create the problems covered by Sheila Bair in Chapter 7), we should simply not allow banks to become TBTF. For those already in this category, 'break them up'.

Two chapters discuss the advantages of such a policy. The first chapter is by Thomas Hoenig, past president of the Federal Reserve Bank of Kansas City, current Vice Chairman of the FDIC, and one of the first to argue for breaking up the large financial firms. In his analysis, he discusses the basic costs and benefits of such a policy. He questions whether the social benefits from bank size and complexity out-weigh the costs from the distortions associated with TBTF firms. The second chapter is by Richard Fisher and Harvey Rosenblum, President and Executive Vice President, respectively, at the Federal Reserve Bank of Dallas. They discuss how the TBTF problem evolved, particularly during the recent financial crisis, and how Dodd–Frank attempts to address it. They offer what they believe to be a preferred solution — the Dallas Fed Proposal — and discuss the various dimensions in which they believe it to be superior.

A third chapter by William Dudley, President of the Federal Reserve Bank of New York, raises questions about the practicality of some of the proposed changes to financial industry structure. Recognizing the problems associated with TBTF, he argues for a multi-front approach. Policymakers should address the issue at the firm level by making firm failure less likely (perhaps by increasing capital and liquidity requirements) and possibly limiting additional firm growth via mergers by the largest, most complex financial institutions. However, concentrating exclusively at the firm level may be suboptimal. The issue should also be addressed at the market level by inducing changes in market practices to limit systemic risk and enable markets to better withstand failures when they do occur. That said, Dudley notes that a blunter approach may yet prove necessary.

Chapter 11

Do SIFIs Have a Future?

Thomas M. Hoenig[1]

Introduction

We are approaching the one-year anniversary of the Dodd–Frank Act. With so much of the Act's implementation work unfinished, it is not an anniversary that we can celebrate; rather it is an opportunity to take stock. In that vein, I congratulate the organizers of this conference for bringing together such an excellent group of individuals to do just that. In particular, I want to recognize the New York University Stern School of Business and economics faculty for the outstanding research they have done on critical financial reform issues. Their collaborative efforts have produced a series of must-read books that have a combination of rigorous economic analysis and practical policy prescriptions that is rarely seen these days.

Much of the Dodd–Frank discussion revolves around the economic distortions and disruptions caused by the largest and most complex financial companies, the so-called systemically important financial institutions, or SIFIs.

As we consider the topic of SIFIs, let me ask the following questions: How can one firm of relatively small global significance merit a government bailout? How

---

[1] At the time of this speech, Thomas M. Hoenig was President and Chief Executive Officer of the Federal Reserve Bank of Kansas City. The speech was presented at a conference on "Dodd–Frank, One Year On" sponsored by the Pew Financial Reform Project and New York University Stern School of Business, June 27, 2011 in Washington, D.C. He has recently intensified his call for considering the need to break up large systemically important financial institutions (SIFIs): see Thomas S. Hoenig and Charles S. Morris (2013), "Restructuring the banking system to improve safety and soundness," in *The Social Value of the Financial Sector: Too Big to Fail or Just too Big?* Viral Acharya, Thorsten Beck, Douglas Evanoff, George Kaufman and Richard Portes (eds.), World Scientific Publishing Co. Pte. Ltd, New Jersey.

can a single investment bank on Wall Street bring the world to the brink of financial collapse? How can a single insurance company require billions of dollars of public funds to stay solvent and yet continue to operate as a private institution? How can a relatively small country such as Greece hold Europe financially hostage? These are the questions for which I have found no satisfactory answers. That's because there are none. It is not acceptable to say that these events occurred because they involved SIFIs.

Because there are no satisfactory answers to these questions, I suggest that the problem with SIFIs is they are fundamentally inconsistent with capitalism. They are inherently destabilizing to global markets and detrimental to world growth. So long as the concept of a SIFI exists, and there are institutions so powerful and considered so important that they require special support and different rules, the future of capitalism is at risk and our market economy is in peril.

To more fundamentally address this issue, we must go beyond today's Dodd–Frank. We must confine the use of the safety net to its original intent. We must reduce the artificial complexity of existing financial structures. The rewards of success must be balanced against the credible consequences of failure. In achieving such goals, we will enhance the stability of the fundamental mechanism through which monetary policy is conducted and the economy depends.

The decline in competition and accountability in banking

The U.S. economy is the most successful in the history of the world. It achieved this success because it is based on the rules of capitalism, in which private ownership dominates markets and individuals reap the rewards of their success. However, for capitalism to work, businesses, including financial firms, must be allowed, or compelled, to compete freely and openly and must be held accountable for their failures. Only under these conditions do markets objectively allocate credit to those businesses that provide the highest value.

For most of our history, the United States held fast to these rules of capitalism. It maintained a relatively open banking and financial system with thousands of banks from small community banks to large global players that allocated credit under this system. As late as 1980, the U.S. banking industry was relatively unconcentrated, with 14,000 commercial banks and the assets of the five largest amounting to 29% of total banking organization assets and 14% of GDP.

Today, we have a far more concentrated and less competitive banking system. There are fewer banks operating across the country, and the five largest institutions control more than half of the industry's assets, which is equal to almost 60%

of GDP. The largest 20 institutions control 80% of the industry's assets, which amounts to about 86% of GDP.

Here's the irony: This marked increase in concentrated power, and therefore, more concentrated risk, reflects past efforts to assure greater economic stability. This might best be described as "good intentions/bad outcomes" syndrome. For example, the Federal Reserve was founded following the 1907 Banking Panic and was charged with providing liquidity support to solvent banks that were experiencing funding problems. After the Great Depression, the Federal Deposit Insurance Corp. was created to provide limited deposit insurance to protect small depositors and to further increase the resiliency of the financial system.

Then, over the past 30 years, this safety net has expanded far beyond its original intent. More recently, Glass–Steagall was repealed, giving high-risk firms almost unlimited access to funds generated through their new access to the safety net. Finally, following a series of crises during the late 1980s and 1990s, the government confirmed that because of systemic impact, some institutions were just too big to fail — the largest institutions could put money in nearly any asset regardless of risk, and their creditors would not be held accountable for the risk taken. Predictably, the industry's risk profile increased dramatically. The SIFI was born.

Is it any wonder then that in the fall of 2008 we experienced the greatest financial crisis since the Great Depression? Financial institutions had again become irresponsible in their lending practices. They had increased their leverage ratios to unprecedented levels. They became "dry kindle" for a financial fire and, with the end of the housing boom, the match was struck.

Now, with their bailout costs amounting to billions of taxpayer dollars, SIFIs are larger than ever. Strikingly, they are arguing that they should not be held to stronger capital standards if the United States hopes to remain globally competitive. That assertion is nonsense. The remainder of my remarks today will describe how the United States can achieve a stronger, more stable financial system in order to secure its future as a global economic leader.

Proposal to reduce costs and risks to the safety net and financial system

Following this financial crisis, Congress and the administration turned to the work of repair and reform. Once again, the American public got the standard remedies — more and increasingly complex regulation and supervision. The Dodd–Frank reforms have all been introduced before, but financial markets skirted them. Supervisory authority existed, but it was used lightly because of political pressure and the misperceptions that free markets, with generous public support, could self-regulate.

Dodd–Frank adds new layers of these same tools, but it fails to employ one remedy used in the past to assure a more stable financial system — simplification of our financial structure through Glass–Steagall-type boundaries. To this end, there are two principles that should guide our efforts to restore such boundaries. First, institutions that have access to the safety net should be restricted to certain core activities that the safety net was intended to protect — making loans and taking deposits — and related activities consistent with the presence of the safety net.

Second, the shadow banking system should be reformed in its use of money market funds and short-term repurchase agreements — the repo market. This step will better assure that the safety net is not ultimately called upon to bail them out in crisis.

Restricting activities of banking organizations

Consistent with the first principle, banking organizations with access to the safety net should be generally confined to the following activities: commercial banking, underwriting securities and advisory services, and asset and wealth management services. Underwriting, advisory, and asset and wealth management services are mostly fee-based services that do not put much of a firm's capital at risk. In addition, asset and wealth management services are similar to the trust services that have always been allowable for banks.

In contrast, banking organizations should be expressly prohibited from activities that include dealing and market-making, brokerage, and proprietary trading, which expose the safety net but have little in common with core banking services.[2] Within the protection of the safety net, they create expansive risks that are difficult to assess, monitor or control.

Thus, banking organizations would not be allowed to do trading, either proprietary or for customers, or make markets because such activity requires the ability to do trading. In addition, allowing customer but not proprietary trading would make it easy to game the system by "concealing" proprietary trading as part of the inventory necessary to conduct customer trading. Also, prime brokerage services not only require the ability to conduct trading activities but also essentially allow companies to finance their activities with highly unstable uninsured

[2]This categorization of financial activities is from Matthew Richardson, Roy Smith and Ingo Walter in Chapter 7 of *Regulating Wall Street: The Dodd–Frank Act and the New Architecture of Global Finance*, Viral V. Acharya, Thomas F. Cooley, Matthew Richardson, Ingo Walter (eds.), New York University Stern School of Business, John Wiley & Sons Inc., 2010.

"deposits." This combination of factors, as we have recently witnessed, leads to unstable markets and government bailouts.

Critics of this proposal contend that institutions grow to be large and complex because of economies of scale and scope and they need the size and related complexities to be profitable and to compete globally. They believe firms must have broad, mostly unrestricted access to all financial activities to provide one-stop shopping and compete on a global basis. Arguments also are given that large banks and securities firms are necessary to make efficient markets for securities trading essential for carrying out monetary policy.

These arguments are unconvincing and, in fact, mislead. First, yes, it would be unfortunate if restricting activities were to drive U.S. banks and jobs to other countries. However, we have 200 years of banking success in this country to refute that assertion. More recently, under Glass–Steagall, U.S. banks and investment banks were highly competitive and successful as each specialized in lending to or underwriting businesses all over the world. There is considerable evidence that under Glass–Steagall the United States was at no competitive disadvantage to Europe, with its mingled merchant banking system. The United States led the world — because it had strong, prudently run institutions that knew how to manage money in the best interests of the client.

Second, there is no strong evidence of unlimited economies of scale and even less for wide economies of scope. Although both exist, they are captured at an asset size far less than that of SIFIs today.

Third, large corporations would have ample convenient access to commercial and traditional investment banking services inside commercial banking. They would have to go to securities dealers to purchase swaps and other derivatives for hedging purposes, something that has been done in the past without difficulty.

Finally, it also seems improbable to me that any country should be willing or able to expand its safety net or to expose its taxpayers to the undefined risks of protecting ever-larger and more complex banking organizations. Instead, what countries should be focused on now is getting back to fundamentals aimed at simplifying highly complex and unstable SIFIs. The focus should be on financial stability.

Reforming the shadow banking system

A legitimate concern of limiting the safety net is that this could worsen the risk of financial instability by pushing activities to the unregulated shadow banking system. Clearly, focusing solely on the regulated banking industry and ignoring the unregulated shadow banking system would not solve the problem and, in fact, might expand the shadow banking sector that was an integral part of the financial crisis.

Much of the instability in the shadow banking system stems from its use of short-term funding for longer-term investment. The solution to this instability problem is not to provide a safety net for the shadow banks and regulate them more but, instead, to remove exceptions in which money market instruments are treated essentially as deposits. The current exceptions encourage significant short-term funding of longer-term assets.

First, investors in money market mutual and other investment funds that are allowed to maintain a fixed net asset value of $1 have an incentive to run if they think their fund will "break the buck." Thus, if the fixed $1 net asset value is eliminated and the share values of such funds are required to float with their market values, shadow bank reliance on this source of short-term funding and the associated threat of disruptive runs would be greatly reduced.

Second, the potential disruptions to funding stemming from the repo financing of shadow banks should be ended. One of the sources of instability during the crisis was repo runs, particularly on repo borrowers using subprime mortgage-related assets as collateral. Essentially, these borrowers funded long-term assets of relatively low quality with very short-term liabilities.

These practices would be greatly reduced by rolling back the bankruptcy law for repo collateral to the pre-2005 rules. Prior to then, if a repo borrower defaulted, mortgage-related collateral could not be immediately taken and sold by the creditors. Returning to these rules would discourage the use of mortgage-related assets as repo collateral and reduce the potential for repo runs. Term lending through securitization would continue, probably at a smaller scale, with more closely matched term wholesale funding provided by institutional investors such as mutual funds, pension funds and life insurance companies.

These changes to the rules for money market funds and repo instruments would increase the stability of the shadow banking system because term lending outside the safety net would be less dependent on "demandable" funding and more reliant on term funding, and the pricing of risk would better reflect the actual risk incurred.

A final note: Implications for monetary policy

Finally, as a member of the Federal Open Market Committee, I realize that we must consider the potential effects of these proposals on the conduct of monetary policy. The impact could be significant because, as currently practiced, monetary policy operations are channeled through a limited number of counterparties called primary dealers. These dealers are required to participate in all auctions of U.S. government debt and represent a key element in the implementation of policy.

Currently, there are only 20 primary dealers. They are the largest financial firms operating in the United States, and most are affiliated with commercial banks. It is with this relationship that the changes I propose could affect the conduct of monetary policy. Specifically, given that primary dealers could no longer be affiliated with commercial banks, would this inhibit market-making in securities, including Treasuries, and therefore interfere with the conduct of monetary policy?

The answer is "no." It is not necessary that primary dealers be affiliated with banks. It is only necessary that they be institutions that deal in U.S. Treasuries and participate in auctions of U.S. government debt. Prior to the 1990s merger boom among investment banks and the Gramm–Leach–Bliley Act, it was typical that half or more of the primary dealers were not affiliated with commercial banks. Therefore, the fact that primary dealers are not commercial banks would have little effect on the Federal Reserve's ability to conduct monetary policy.

I would add that although commercial banks could not be primary dealers, they could remain a key part of the monetary policy mechanism. Recently, the Federal Reserve gained experience in using the Term Auction Facility (TAF). The TAF might very successfully be used in conjunction with primary dealer operations to conduct policy well into the future.

As you may recall, during the financial crisis, the TAF was an important component of monetary policy. For example, the TAF was introduced in December 2007 with an initial auction of $20 billion. The facility was then ramped up to almost $500 billion by March 2009 — about one-fourth of the assets on the Federal Reserve's balance sheet. The maturity of TAF loans was generally 28 days or 84 days.

By broadening the Federal Reserve's monetary tools to include the TAF to provide term funds through the banking system in parallel with the primary dealers, we could greatly expand the number of counterparties used in the conduct of monetary policy. Thus, the TAF and primary dealers would provide deep markets for the term portion of policy; primary dealers and traditional open-market operations would continue as the means for managing day-to-day operations and for maintaining the federal funds rate close to the target. With more counterparties, we enhance competition and enable nearly all banks to play a role in the conduct of monetary policy. This would make the largest banks less "SI" and more "FI."

Conclusion

The financial system has become far less competitive and far more volatile with the onset of systemically important institutions. Though large firms remain a critical part of our economic system in the United States, they should not become so dominant that they become unaccountable to our capitalistic system. We can make the necessary reforms to end the unique status of the SIFI and, in doing so, restore much of our global competitive vigor. Only from a position of financial strength can the United States remain the global economic leader.

Chapter 12

Ending Taxpayer-Funded Bailouts: Dodd–Frank Promises More Than It Can Deliver

Richard W. Fisher and Harvey Rosenblum[1]

Following every financial crisis, legislators promise voters "Never Again." Yet financial crises seem to recur about every 15 years on average. Some crises are bigger than others, but they keep coming back in mutated forms, none exactly like their predecessors. In this sense, our political leaders have kept at least some of their promise to address the causes of "the last crisis." Then financial markets, institutions and firms innovate, evolve and morph in ways that get around the best-intentioned legislation and the resulting regulations.

In this chapter, we argue that the 2010 Dodd–Frank Wall Street Reform and Consumer Protection Act ("Dodd–Frank") will not accomplish its stated goals of ending "Too-Big-To-Fail" (TBTF) nor will it end taxpayer funded bailouts — it will not work, period. This conclusion holds, we believe, even if today's financial system were frozen in its current configuration, with no evolution. Supporting our view requires an examination of the financial industry's structure, incentives and competitive environment as they had evolved *prior to* Dodd–Frank. Because Dodd–Frank did nothing to significantly alter industry structure and incentives, it simply will not change the behaviors that produced the 2008–2009 financial crisis. In this sense, it is just a matter of time before taxpayer-funded bailouts of

[1]Richard Fisher is President and CEO and Harvey Rosenblum is executive vice president and director of Research at the Federal Reserve Bank of Dallas. The authors thank David Luttrell and Elizabeth Organ for excellent research assistance in writing this chapter. The views expressed are those of the Federal Reserve Bank of Dallas and not necessarily those of others in the Federal Reserve System.

the largest, most complex financial institutions recur, becoming the distinguishing feature of the U.S. economic and financial landscape.

The situation

The United States is burdened by a highly concentrated financial system where the 11 largest banking institutions control roughly two-thirds of banking industry assets (see Figure 1). This excessive concentration intensified during the 2008–2009 financial crisis when several, presumably healthy big banks absorbed some of their failing rivals. Another round of consolidation will likely accompany the next crisis, further reducing competition and resulting in a lopsided financial system that raises the potential damage of another financial meltdown.

Steps must be taken to eliminate implicit government support for the biggest firms, which often encourages excessive risk-taking and results in management being focused on short-term rewards instead of long-term performance. By

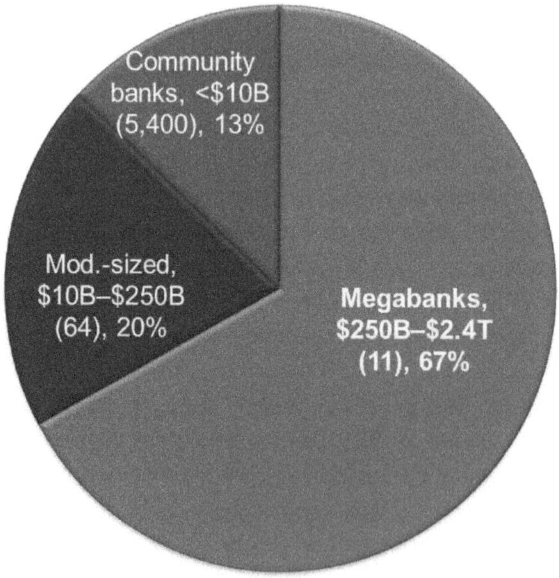

Figure 1. Composition of the U.S. Banking Industry.

Notes: Data for commercial banks and bank holding companies as of year-end 2012. Asset size is based on the total assets of a U.S. banking organization (holding company, when applicable).

Data Sources: Call Report, Federal Financial Institutions Examination Council; Consolidated Financial Statements for Bank Holding Companies (FR Y-9C), National Information Center data, Federal Reserve System.

limiting the government backstop, financial institutions will be subject to market discipline and the very real possibility of failure if they make poor decisions. No individual financial institution should be capable of holding the government, and by extension, taxpayers, hostage to cover its losses. The Dallas Fed has proposed a three-step plan that strictly limits the federal safety net to traditional commercial bank depository institutions and advocates institutional restructuring, both of which would level the playing field and correct misaligned incentives.

The problem: More than concentration

The mere 0.2% of banks deemed TBTF are treated differently from the other 99.8%, and differently from other businesses. Small and midsized institutions — that each have an asset size of less than $250 billion and, as a whole, account for about one-third of industry assets — face the credible and palpable threat of closure from their regulators, as well as market discipline from owners and/or creditors. The largest institutions, however, are not subject to a sufficient amount of regulatory or market discipline, rendering them seemingly exempt from the normal processes of bankruptcy and creative destruction.

Implicit government policy has allowed the banking giants and their counterparties to take excessive risks without fear of failure if their bets go bad. The banks' creditors believe the government will backstop their investments, simultaneously undermining the profitability and viability of smaller institutions that enjoy no such implicit guarantee. Economics 101 tells us that if you want more of something, you should subsidize it. The irony is that government policy subsidizes excessive risk taking, the very thing we want to reduce.

Although TBTF financial institutions were not the sole cause of the financial crisis, they were a primary mechanism through which shocks were transmitted throughout the financial and economic systems. Many TBTF banks and their subsidiaries were major players in shadow banking activities dependent on short-term, non-deposit wholesale funding — using financial instruments such as commercial paper and money market funds — that spread systemic risk pervasively at the height of the crisis.

The TBTF mindset also emboldens a sense of immunity from the law. As Attorney General Eric Holder acknowledged in testimony to the U.S. Senate on March 6, 2013, when banks are considered TBTF it is "difficult to prosecute them … if we do bring a criminal charge, it will have a negative impact on the national economy."[2]

---

[2]Alan Zibel and Brent Kendall, "Holder: Banks May Be Too Large to Prosecute," *Wall Street Journal,* March 6, 2013.

Megabanks fund themselves more cheaply than do smaller banks. Studies, including those published by the Bank for International Settlements and the International Monetary Fund, estimate this cost-of-funds advantage to be as much as 1% point, or some $50 billion to $100 billion annually, in the period surrounding the financial crisis.[3] In a popular post by editors at Bloomberg, the 10 largest U.S. banks are estimated to enjoy an aggregate longer-term subsidy of $83 billion per year.[4] Andrew Haldane, executive director for financial stability at the Bank of England, estimates the current implicit TBTF subsidy to be roughly $300 billion per year for the 29 global institutions identified as "systemically important."[5]

Whatever the precise subsidy number is, it is significant, it has not disappeared,[6] and it enables the biggest banking organizations, along with their many nonbank subsidiaries (investment firms, securities lenders, finance companies, etc.), to grow larger and riskier. It makes for an uneven playing field, tilted to the advantage of the giant banking organizations, and it places the financial system and the economy in perpetual jeopardy.

The Dodd–Frank Act's purported solution

Dodd–Frank is long on process and complexity but likely will be short on results. Its 849 pages of legislation and more than 9,000 pages of proposed regulations all but guarantee that the regulatory agencies responsible for implementing and enforcing Dodd–Frank remain two or three steps behind the industry. Even the seemingly straightforward "Volcker Rule" — restricting banks' proprietary trading for their own accounts — gave rise to a nearly 130-page proposed rule with 383 questions for comment. Rules that are not easily understood simply cannot be enforced; excessively complicated regulation only adds to the uncertainty that bedevils investors and businesses. Additionally, Dodd–Frank puts smaller institutions, which have fewer resources to devote to complying with the new law, at a disadvantage relative to their largest competitors.

---

[3]See Bank for International Settlements, *BIS Annual Report 2011/12*, pp. 75–76; and Kenichi Ueda and Beatrice Weder di Mauro, "Quantifying Structural Subsidy Values for Systemically Important Financial Institutions," International Monetary Fund, Working Paper No. 12/128, May 1, 2012.

[4]See Bloomberg View, 2013, "Why Should Taxpayers Give Big Banks $83 Billion a Year?" *Bloomberg*, February 20.

[5]See Andrew Haldane, 2012, "On Being the Right Size," Speech at the 2012 Beesley Lectures, Institute of Economic Affairs, Bank of England, October 25.

[6]Moody's estimates the credit uplift to be one or two notches as of March 27, 2013; see Financial Stability Oversight Council, *2013 Annual Report*, Chart 7.b.1, p. 146.

Regulators cannot enforce rules that are not easily understood. Nor can they enforce these rules without creating armies of new supervisors. The U.S. House of Representatives Committee on Financial Services aggregates information from the Federal Register that estimates the cumulative hours needed for the affected agencies, like the Federal Reserve (the "Fed"), to fulfill new requirements called for by Dodd–Frank. This Committee estimated that, as of July 2012, it would take 24,180,856 hours each year to comply with new rules already finalized for implementation of the Act.[7] And the rulemaking process is unlikely to be completed before 2017, possible considerably later.

Dodd–Frank was well-intentioned, but its stated promise — to end "too-big-to-fail" — rings hollow. Rather than resolve TBTF, Dodd–Frank essentially codified these mega-institutions' existence by designating some as "systemically important," thereby separating them from other banks and reinforcing their special status as being failure-proof.

Dodd–Frank's fundamental shortcomings

Dodd–Frank is likely the longest and most complex piece of financial legislation in U.S. history to date. A partially accurate description of Dodd–Frank can be found printed on T-shirts available for purchase on the Internet. The printed maxim says: "I can explain it to you, but I can't understand it for you." To describe Dodd–Frank appropriately would require the following revision: "I can neither explain it to you, let alone understand it myself." A hallmark of good legislation — and good writing in general — is that it (1) can be easily understood and (2) is unlikely to be misunderstood. Dodd–Frank fails both these tests; it is simply incomprehensible, even by the experts who have devoted hundreds, even thousands, of hours trying.

Just as important as its overabundance of pages and conflicting mandates, Dodd–Frank's glaring omission is any sense of urgency for getting the statutes implemented into workable regulations in a timely way. Those who continue to support Dodd–Frank seem to be acting on the belief that the next financial crisis is at least a decade away. Just as worrying, Dodd–Frank's supporters believe firmly that the tools created by Dodd–Frank to be used in the next financial crisis will actually be used as intended, in spite of the discretion granted to the first responders to act differently.

The Orderly Liquidation Authority — When a financial institution is designated "Systemically Important" as required under Title I of Dodd–Frank (and

---

[7]See House Committee on Financial Services, *Dodd–Frank Burden Tracker*, updated July 9, 2012.

becomes known by the acronym "SIFI"), it will be viewed by the market as being the first to be saved by the first responders in a financial crisis. In other words, these SIFIs occupy a privileged space in the financial system (one pundit referred to the acronym as meaning "save if failure impending"). As a corollary, a banking customer has a disincentive to do business with smaller competitors, because a non-SIFI does not have an implied government funding lifeline. Even if a SIFI ends up holding more capital than a smaller competitor, the choice remains for where you would like to hold important financial relationships: with an institution with a government backstop or one without? Thus, the playing field remains uneven; the advantages of size and perceived subsidy accrue to the behemoth banks. Dodd–Frank does not eliminate this perception.

Adding insult to injury, Title II of Dodd–Frank describes and designates the Orderly Liquidation Authority (OLA) as the resolution mechanism to handle the disposal of a giant, systemically disruptive financial enterprise. The three letters themselves evoke the deceptive doublespeak of an Orwellian nightmare. The "L," which stands for liquidation, will in practice become a simulated restructuring, as would occur in a Chapter 11 bankruptcy.[8] In reality, rather than fulfill Dodd–Frank's promise of "no more taxpayer funded bailouts," the U.S. Treasury will likely provide, through the Federal Deposit Insurance Company (FDIC), debtor-in-possession (DIP) financing to the failed companies' artificially kept alive operating subsidiaries for up to 5 years, but perhaps longer. Call it whatever you wish, but this is taxpayer funding at far-below-market rates.

We would call this form of "liquidation" a nationalized financial institution. During the 5-year resolution period, this nationalized institution does not have to pay any taxes of any kind to any government entity.[9] This looks, sounds, and tastes like a taxpayer bailout, just hidden behind different language. If it waddles like a duck and quacks like a duck, it must be a duck.

Moreover, if the reorganized company cannot repay the Treasury for its DIP financing, Title II suggests that the repayment should be clawed back via an assessment on the company's SIFI competitors. Thus, the Treasury will be made whole, but the other SIFIs that bear the special assessment would write-off the fee as a tax-deductible business expense, reducing the tax revenue of the Treasury, thereby

---

[8]See Joshua Rosner, 2013, Statement to the U.S. House Committee on Financial Services, Subcommittee on Oversight and Investigations, *Who is Too Big to Fail: Does Title II of the Dodd–Frank Act Enshrine Taxpayer Funded Bailouts?* Hearing, May 14.

[9]See David A. Skeel, Jr., 2013, Statement to the U.S. House Committee on Financial Services, Subcommittee on Oversight and Investigations, *Who is Too Big to Fail: Does Title II of the Dodd–Frank Act Enshrine Taxpayer Funded Bailouts?* Hearing, May 14.

indirectly imposing additional tax burdens on the nonbank public to pay the costs of running our government. This does not sound like a "no taxpayer-funded bailouts" solution. One form of explicit intervention appears to have been replaced by Title II of Dodd–Frank, a disguised form of taxpayer bailout. In addition, the OLA procedures are based on the tenuous assumption that only one giant firm will require assistance and that the remainder of the SIFIs will be financially healthy and will be able to absorb the Treasury's assessments to pay for the errors of their failed SIFI-sibling.

Title II promotes and sustains an unnatural longevity for zombie financial institutions. It does so at taxpayer expense and imposes a competitive disadvantage onto small- and medium-size financial institutions. It is these smaller financial institutions that are the primary providers of credit to the small- and medium-size businesses that, in turn, provide the bulk of innovation and job creation in the United States.[10]

Living wills — Some have held out hope that a key provision of Title I requiring banking organizations to submit detailed plans for their orderly resolution in bankruptcy, without government assistance, will provide for a roadmap to avoid bailouts. However, these "living wills" may prove futile in helping navigate a real-time "systemic" failure. Given the complexity and opacity of the TBTF institutions and the ability to move assets and liabilities across subsidiaries and affiliates (as well as off-balance-sheet), a "living will" would likely be ineffective, and likely obsolete, when it really mattered.

Higher capital requirements — Arguments to "give Dodd–Frank a chance" or to simply raise capital requirements fall short of what is needed to address TBTF. Living wills and higher capital requirements are potentially very helpful tools, but are not sufficient to ensure the survival of a company and will not eliminate the massive losses that can disrupt financial markets and the economy.

Banks are levered institutions and are vulnerable, given that they are usually levered with short-term debt like deposits and repo-like funding vehicles. Thus, capital helps to maintain confidence that the institution can sustain some losses and still remain open for business tomorrow.[11] But once investors and creditors begin to fear that losses have been understated or could be increasing at that institution or others, confidence begins to rapidly diminish, and almost no amount of capital is sufficient to forestall a collapse of confidence and a liquidity crisis.

---

[10] See Nathan Sheets and Robert A. Sockin, 2012, "Does Size Really Matter? The Evolving Role of Small Firms in the U.S. Economy," Citi Research, *Empirical & Thematic Perspectives*, December 10.

[11] See Anat Admati and Martin Hellwig, 2013, *The Bankers' New Clothes: What's Wrong with Banking and What to Do about It*, Princeton: Princeton UP.

When confidence begins to wane, liquidity dries up quickly. And the plunge in confidence is contagious, often having little to do with the underlying situation of each individual company. That's where the lender of last resort function of the Fed comes into play — the central bank lends to solvent companies, those with positive capital and good collateral. But such capital is only a small element in saving a company from extinction. Confidence matters even more.

Within the category of capital, it is loss-absorbing capital that buttresses confidence the most. Equity capital is the first to absorb losses; hence, it is the most expensive capital to raise. Debt doesn't absorb losses except in bankruptcy, at which point the company is dead. Risk-weighted capital is somewhat meaningless in the context of loss absorbency; any asset that incurs losses must be written off against equity capital, whether the loss was in business loans, mortgage loans, municipal bonds or agency debt. If losses thin out the capital cushion to the point of undermining confidence, the future viability of the company slips. Nobody knows the "magic" capital ratio that will prevent a loss of confidence, and we do not believe regulators will suddenly become better equipped to set higher magical ratios in the future for the largest, most politically connected banking institutions. Capital is necessary for viability (non-failure), but it is not sufficient.

As Dodd–Frank is being implemented, U.S. bank regulators are attempting to harmonize capital requirements for U.S. financial institutions with those being promulgated by the Basel Committee on Banking Supervision under the Third Basel Accord (Basel III). The problem is that Basel III is being designed and negotiated to replace Basel I and Basel II, neither of which set capital adequacy standards that were sufficiently high or robust enough to improve the stability of the banking and financial systems. In her book, *Bull by the Horns*, former FDIC chair Sheila Bair (2012) described in great detail the ways in which the Basel Committee was institutionally incapable of setting capital requirements that had the capability to foster stability and resilience in the banking system. By relying on mechanisms like Basel III whose predecessors have been so discredited by repeated failures, Dodd–Frank does not inspire much confidence that it will rely upon mechanisms likely to succeed in the future.

That being said, recently proposed rules indicate that the Fed is ready and willing to lead on capital requirements. Basel III called for a minimum 3% leverage ratio, or the ratio of capital to total (non-risk-weighted) assets. The Fed's proposal effectively requires a minimum ratio of 5% at the holding company level and 6% at any depository subsidiaries. With this step forward, the U.S. is primed to take the lead on requiring higher levels of capital at its largest financial institutions; other countries, like the U.K. and Switzerland, have made or are in the process of making similar moves to set higher ratios than those called for by Basel III.[12]

Frustration with the complexity of Dodd–Frank and Basel III and the time required to implement them has also resulted in legislative proposals, including the "21st Century Glass–Steagall Act" and the Brown–Vitter plan for higher capital requirements.[13] Senators Elizabeth Warren (D-MA) and John McCain (R-AZ) have put forward an attempt to reinstate the Glass–Steagall restrictions against conducting commercial and investment banking activities within a single institution. Senators Sherrod Brown (D-OH) and David Vitter (R-LA) have proposed a bill that relies heavily on simple, non-risk-weighted capital ratios. It raises the capital-requirement floor for any institution above $50 billion in assets to at least 8% equity capital over total consolidated assets. The largest institutions will face similar requirements of at least 15%, with surcharges to be determined by the FDIC. The bill would also halt the implementation of Basel III, restrict intercompany transfers and accounting sleight of hand, and prohibit many types of federal assistance for financial institutions and their subsidiaries.

If passed, the Brown–Vitter proposal may induce the largest institutions to downsize: At a conference in Chicago on May 10, 2013, Fed Chairman Bernanke himself suggested that higher capital requirements could be "an incentive to reduce or simplify [those] firms."[14] The straightforward capital ratios called for in the bill would likely reduce the regulatory burden on all firms, compared to the more complicated rulemakings required by Dodd–Frank and Basel III. However, in severely restricting the assistance available to any financial institution, Brown–Vitter may overly limit the Federal Reserve's options to mitigate a potential crisis or protect systemic stability in tumultuous times.

The discussion around capital is ultimately in a state of flux, with frequent new developments and differing views on what should be done. Capital requirements will certainly remain an important tool to stabilize the financial system from unnecessary shocks, and continued debate should strengthen the effectiveness of regulation.

Other problems with Dodd–Frank — Over the last few years, the banking system has cleaned up its balance sheet and boosted its capital cushion. The

---

[12] See Donna Borak, 2013, "Tougher than Basel? U.S. May Have Company, Fed's Tarullo Says," *American Banker*, July 15.

[13] See Terminating Bailouts for Taxpayer Fairness Act of 2013, S. 798, 113th Cong. (2013); and Michael R. Crittenden, 2013, "Lawmakers Move to Rebuild Wall Between Commercial and Investment Banking," *Wall Street Journal*, July 11.

[14] See Michael R. Crittenden, 2013, "Bernanke Signals Banks May Face Higher Capital Requirements," *Wall Street Journal*, May 11, p. A2.

improved health of the financial system gives the misleading impression of being a stable equilibrium.

Those who say "just give Dodd–Frank a chance" should note that partial repeal of Dodd–Frank has already occurred through the back door. Megabanks, in the United States and abroad, have pushed back to significantly weaken capital and liquidity standards, the statute's purported structural pillars.[15] Additionally, the section of the Act intended to increase transparency in derivatives markets (Title VII) is being undermined by legislative efforts to grant more entities "end-user exemptions" from the new rules. Complicated derivative transactions can conceal losses at troubled firms, making the orderly liquidation of large firms, an authority granted to the FDIC by Dodd–Frank, substantially more difficult.[16]

Moreover, the penance and legal penalties paid to date for egregious errors in mortgage finance, manipulation of the London interbank offered rate (LIBOR), and other legally and ethically questionable activities have been financially immaterial to the large banks (or at least appear insufficient to deter such practices). Under Dodd–Frank, taxpayers remain exposed to similar, possibly larger, losses among giant financial institutions during the next crisis.

Dodd–Frank perpetuates destructive ambiguity

In the midst of the 2008–2009 financial crisis, *seemingly* inconsistent policies were used by the Fed to deal with the collapse of major financial institutions. In March 2008, the Fed provided $29 billion of assistance to enable JP Morgan Chase to acquire Bear Stearns. In mid-September 2008, Lehman was allowed to fail by declaring Chapter 11 bankruptcy after the Fed did not provide any financial assistance. Only two days later, the Fed provided an initial loan of $85 billion to AIG, secured by 79.9% ownership of AIG, thereby quasi-nationalizing the

[15]Banks have also already found ways to sidestep many of the law's provisions; for example, foreign banks are restructuring operations in the United States to avoid capital requirements (see David Enrich, February 17, 2011, "Banks Find Loophole on Capital Rule," *Wall Street Journal*), and some institutions are making use of "capital relief trades," specialized credit default swaps that shift the risk associated with certain assets to another entity, fulfilling capital requirements while allowing the bank to keep those assets on its books (see Susanne Craig, April 10, 2013, "Seeking Relief, Banks Shift Risk to Murkier Corners," *New York Times*). The use of lobbyists and funding of academic research by the industry's trade associations, especially those that include the largest banking institutions, is on the rise; see Deborah Solomon, Robin Sidel and Aaron Lucchetti, May 9, 2013, "Big Banks Push Back Against Tighter Rules," *Wall Street Journal*, p. A1.

[16]See Mike Konczal, March 23, 2013, "Is it already time to weaken Dodd–Frank?" *The Washington Post*.

company. In reality, all three companies "failed" in the general economic sense of the term, but the prevailing view among the general populace and sophisticated investors alike is that Bear Stearns and AIG were "bailed out" by the Fed.

Fed Chairman Ben Bernanke tried to elaborate on the Fed's rationale and procedures for handling the failure of giant financial institutions,[17] but the distinctions and details fell on deaf ears in spite of Bernanke's efforts to explain that the Fed had not, nor would it ever in the future, bail out a private sector company in distress. Within weeks, the Fed's full-blown decision tree was published and posted on the Dallas Fed's website,[18] but the public was inundated with headlines and talking heads screaming, "Bailout!"

There are two distinctly different lessons from the 2008–2009 financial crisis. Lesson one is that, in an emerging financial crisis, the Fed will do what is necessary to protect the economic and financial *system*, but not protect the shareholders and managers of a company that is the target of intervention actions. Lesson two is very different: (1) giant financial firms are "bailed out," i.e., saved; and (2) the Fed has your back — as a very large (systemic) firm, you will be rescued from your big mistakes. From a public policy perspective, this dichotomy of views is totally unacceptable.

Financial crises are costly and disruptive events. But much unnecessary disruption can be mitigated by good communication from policy makers in the midst of the crisis and by providing clear, easily and widely understood rules of behavior and procedures to be followed in potential subsequent crises. In his iconic treatise on the recent financial crisis, David Wessel highlights remarks made by New York Fed President Tim Geithner:

> "… at times of crisis, Geithner said the government had to get both the *substance* and the *theater* right. Bernanke, Geithner, and even more so, Paulson muffed the theater. Because they didn't tell a convincing story … or offer a clear explanation … other accounts of varying plausibility filled the vacuum…"[19]

---

[17]See Benjamin Bernanke, 2008, "Current Economic and Financial Conditions," National Association for Business Economics 50th Annual Meeting, Washington, DC, October 7.

[18]See Harvey Rosenblum, Danielle DiMartino, Jessica J. Renier and Richard Alm, 2008, "Fed Intervention: Managing Moral Hazard in Financial Crises," Federal Reserve Bank of Dallas, *Economic Letter*, October.

[19]David Wessel, 2009, *In Fed We Trust: Ben Bernanke's War on the Great Panic*, New York: Crown Business 7–8.

In other words, what you say and how you say it are just as important as what you actually do, if not more so, especially during a crisis.[20] Good communication is paramount.

The Fed's communication problem pre-dated the 2008–2009 financial crisis. In 1998, the New York Fed organized a meeting during which more than a dozen private sector creditors of a hedge fund, Long-Term Capital Management ("LTCM"), were able to simulate a Chapter 11-type corporate reorganization of LTCM outside of Federal Bankruptcy Court. Thousands of articles were written about the "LTCM bailout"; the Federal Reserve defended its decision in congressional testimony, but the Fed never delineated the decision tree it used in averting that potential crisis, nor did the Fed provide any systematic explanation of how it would act in similar future situations. A widely, but not universally, held view within the Fed was that such silence — generally named *constructive ambiguity* — was necessary to minimize *moral hazard*. Moral hazard arises when economic agents believe they are protected, at least partially, from the consequences of their risky behaviors — that is, "someone has their back covered" with protection from downside risks. Moral hazard incentivizes excessive risk taking. By maintaining constructive ambiguity, the Fed mitigates moral hazard by encouraging the belief among businesses that (a) it is highly unlikely they will receive financial assistance from the Fed during a crisis and (b) even if the Fed were to provide some temporary assistance, it would not save the firm from failure. If this belief prevailed generally throughout the economy, firms would be unlikely to "game the system" and take excessive risk with the belief that they would get the upside from their bets, while the Fed and/or taxpayers would cushion the downside. On the other hand, moral hazard would run rampant and excessive risk taking would prevail if most firms operated with the belief that they were big and important enough that their failures could wreck the economy.

Constructive ambiguity can work to mitigate moral hazard provided that the vast majority of economic agents act on the belief that the probability of their company receiving financial assistance from the Fed is virtually zero. However, the current prevailing perception in the marketplace — and therefore the perception that drives the behaviors of most large enterprises, especially large financial

[20]As the FDIC's former General Counsel Michael Krimminger has pointed out in the case of Title II of Dodd–Frank, for a resolution regime to be effective, the responsible regulator (for Title II, the FDIC) needs to issue "a statement of policy" in advance of a crisis that is "sufficiently detailed to provide market participants with clear direction on the expected steps and parameters for action" (see Michael H. Krimminger, 2013, Statement to the U.S. House Committee on Financial Services, Subcommittee on Oversight and Investigations, *Who is Too Big to Fail: Does Title II of the Dodd–Frank Act Enshrine Taxpayer Funded Bailouts?* Hearing, May 14).

institutions — is that the next time trouble arises, the Fed (or some other governmental entity) will be there to provide assistance to you and many of your creditors, as well.

Under Dodd–Frank, the Fed's Section 13(3) power to provide financial assistance to an individual firm, even in "urgent and exigent" circumstances, has been rescinded.[21] Therefore, the perception of Fed protection, a "Bernanke Put" in the parlance of financial markets, is an *erroneous* perception. The term *destructive ambiguity* has been used to describe a situation in which people act on widespread erroneous beliefs, engaging in the same wrong behaviors over and over again.[22]

While Dodd–Frank is not the source of the prevailing situation of destructive ambiguity, it does perpetuate, and likely exacerbate, the ambiguities surrounding future crisis management. Again, much of this is not the fault of the legislation itself. Dodd–Frank was enacted to help deal with financial crises driven by the failure of giant, complex, systemically important financial institutions. Such crises occur infrequently, less than once a decade, and every financial crisis has its own unique characteristics. For policy decisions to provide clarity as to future actions, they must occur frequently and offer clear legal or administrative precedents that bind policymakers' future decisions and interpretations. Demonstrated and frequently observed policy consistency removes destructive ambiguity. The infrequent nature of financial crises is a constraint on eliminating destructive ambiguity.

Infrequency is not the only roadblock. Adding to the destructive ambiguity in crisis management policy is that, under Dodd–Frank, there is a new sheriff in town. The FDIC has been assigned the task of being the OLA, to preside over "orderly" behaviors and prevent chaotic ones. Experience gained from observing Fed actions and behaviors is now less useful. The FDIC has replaced the Fed, and the FDIC must follow the new rulebook, Dodd–Frank, even though 3 years after its adoption, less than half of its new rules have been completed. Additionally, the FDIC's behavioral record in its nearly 80 years of existence is only as the resolution authority for banks, and mostly small- to-medium-size banks at that. The FDIC has never intervened in cases like those of Bear-Stearns, Lehman, AIG, LTCM, or other mostly nonbank entities.

---

[21] With the revision of Section 13(3), the Fed lost its micro tools, but not its macro tools; i.e., the Fed retained its ability to offer protections to markets, but not specific troubled firms.

[22] For examples of destructive ambiguity both in a financial and in a non-financial setting, see Dmitri Vinogradov, 2012, "Destructive Effects of Constructive Ambiguity in Risky Times," *Journal of International Money and Finance* 31 : 1459–1481 and Michael Kagan, 2007, "Destructive Ambiguity: Enemy Nationals and the Legal Enabling of Ethnic Conflict in the Middle East," *Columbia Human Rights Law Review* 38.263, 264–319.

Moreover, in the midst of the 2008–2009 financial crisis, the FDIC's provision of extraordinary government assistance to Citibank and Bank of America was done in conjunction with the Fed and the U.S. Treasury, all prior to Dodd–Frank's rewriting of the rules of engagement. The bottom line is that destructive ambiguity, and the incorrect behaviors it encourages, has intensified since Dodd–Frank was signed by President Obama in July 2010.

Destructive ambiguity can be reduced by the FDIC through improved communication. This sounds easy, but is much easier said than done. First, the FDIC needs to make public its OLA decision tree for how a major failure would be handled. Second, it needs to conduct annual simulations of that process with public observers, including the media.[23] Third, the decision tree then needs to be updated and amended in light of experience gained from those training exercises. Fourth, and last, the FDIC — together with the Fed, the OCC, and the Treasury — needs to constantly issue, repeat, and reinforce the message of "no more bailouts" and what that really entails. Given that Dodd–Frank is a work in progress, new and untested in live financial markets, communication must rise to a new level. If Dodd–Frank is ever going to have a chance to accomplish its objective of ending TBTF, the regulatory agencies must put equal resources into getting the theater right, not just the policy substance. Otherwise, we will be back where we started: Bailout will be the default descriptor, and the insidious behaviors and pernicious impacts of TBTF will become a perpetual nightmare.

An effective solution: The Dallas Fed's reform proposal

The return of marketplace discipline and effective due diligence of giant banking institutions is long overdue. The Federal Reserve Bank of Dallas (the "Dallas Fed") has proposed a three-step process to level the playing field.[24]

First, we have proposed confining access to the federal safety net — the Federal Reserve's discount window and federal deposit insurance protection — to traditional commercial banks, and not to the nonbank affiliates of bank holding companies or the parent companies themselves, where the safety net was *never* intended to be.

---

[23]The Clearing House, in conjunction with a group of bankers, former regulators, lawyers and consultants, did conduct such a trial exercise; see The Clearing House, "Report on the Orderly Liquidation Authority Resolution Symposium and Simulation," January 2013.

[24]See Richard W. Fisher and Harvey Rosenblum, "Vanquishing Too Big to Fail," Federal Reserve Bank of Dallas, *2012 Annual Report*.

Second, we advocate that customers and creditors of companies affiliated with commercial banks sign a disclaimer acknowledging their understanding that there is no federal guarantee underpinning their relationship with these nonbank units or with the parent of any banking company. We believe these two steps would reduce the perverse incentives stemming from the implicit — but widely recognized — creditor protection offered to TBTF institutions. These two changes would help realign incentives to better resemble those faced by customers of smaller banks whose unsecured creditors and equity shareholders are exposed to losses. In short, our proposal would revive the forces of market discipline that fell dormant in recent years as creditors of the largest banking companies recognized the growing extent of the protection afforded by implicit government guarantees.

Third, we recommend that the largest financial holding companies be restructured so that every one of their corporate entities is subject to a speedy bankruptcy process, and in the case of banking entities themselves, that each be of a size that is "too small to save." The act of addressing institutional size is vital to underscoring that a clear regime shift has occurred and that the threat of failure is credible — thereby providing a convincing case that policy has truly changed. This step gets both the incentives and the structure right, neither of which is accomplished by relying on Dodd–Frank.

Regarding who should drive the financial reform process, we believe that the mandate, guiding principles, and deadlines for rightsizing are legislative matters for the Congress to determine. However, the design and details of each company's restructuring should be left to the management and board of directors representing the owner–shareholders. Strong management involvement is necessary to ensure that all spun-off banks and other subsidiaries are viable and profitable companies, able to attract and retain financial capital and management talent. Such restructuring of TBTF financial institutions should be accomplished with minimal statutory modifications and limited government intervention.

What the Dallas Fed Plan will do

The aim of our three-step proposal is simple: All banks would be subject to the same regulatory oversight — and most important, they would all be subject to the market discipline exercised by owners and creditors. Restructured, refocused, and unsubsidized financial conglomerates will still provide a full range of financial services. They will operate with a clarified understanding of the boundaries of FDIC protection and access to the Federal Reserve's discount window — only traditional commercial banking operations should benefit from the safety net. Additionally, in the long run, our efforts to level the playing field should decrease the regulatory burden for all banks, large and small, because rules will be clear, operations will be less complex, and market discipline can replace and reinforce supervisory discipline.

Our proposal would alter the structure of banking so that bailouts become unnecessary. It provides a clear, credible regime shift — a time-consistent policy, in economics parlance — that demonstrates that TBTF has ended. Under our proposed policy change, the largest banking institutions would pose far less systemic risk. The downsized, formerly TBTF banks would be just like the other 99.8%, failing with finality when necessary — closed on a Friday and reopened on Monday under new ownership and management in the customary process managed by the FDIC.

Our plan's effect on shadow banking activities, such as the use of special purpose vehicles and off-balance-sheet financing, is somewhat more nuanced. Those activities would occur in a separately funded, collateralized subsidiary that is clearly not covered by the federal safety net. With proper transparency for those organizations, equity and debt providers can consider appropriate risks, adjust funding costs accordingly, and provide market discipline that will help rein in excesses. Counterparty behaviors are likely to change significantly as the perception of government intervention fades following our plan's regime shift.

What the Dallas Fed Plan won't do

We concede our proposal doesn't have all the answers. It would not eliminate financial crises, but it should reduce their frequency and severity. Nor will it alter the human DNA of those who serve as "first responders" during the next crisis. However, our proposal should make the magnitude of the problems regulators face, and the tasks they need to perform, far more manageable. Under our plan, supervisory agencies would confront several thousand community banks, roughly a hundred moderate-size banks (by today's standards), but no megabanks. The nonbank and shadow bank companies would operate without a subsidized safety net and with long-overdue market discipline imposed by at-risk creditors.

There will always be some banks that are larger than the rest, and consequently, there will be temptation for regulators to label the "biggest few" as systemically important. The fluctuating nature of human resolve and political fortitude, as well as the problem of "regulatory capture," has been present in U.S. bank policy at least since the intervention/bailout of Continental Illinois and its creditors in 1984. Our proposal cannot and will not prohibit regulators from intervening to support the unsecured creditors of a failing banking institution. But our proposal reduces the dimensions of the problem — asset size and systemic footprint — by an order of magnitude and thereby should diminish the tendency to intervene out of fear of unknown systemic risks. In short, our plan would dramatically reduce the costs of non-intervention, that is, just saying "NO" to bailout requests.

The bigger picture

Had this plan been in place a decade ago, it would have altered many of the insidious behaviors that contributed to the crisis and likely would have avoided the bailouts and their aftermath, the cost of which will be borne by our nation's citizens for years to come. Estimates of the cost of the financial crisis, measured in lost output and jobs, range from $10–20 trillion.[25] In a roughly $15 trillion gross domestic product (GDP) economy, this represents one year of U.S. output down the drain.

The enduring repercussions of the crisis and the continuation of TBTF policies undermine citizens' faith in the rule of law and representative democracy. The rank of the United States in the Index of Economic Freedom, published by the Fraser Institute, has fallen from 2 to 18 since 2000.[26] Less secure property rights, bigger government, and increased regulation of business have all contributed to the growing perception that we have lost some of our economic and financial security.

Freedom is also undercut by the looming tax burden posed by megabank failures. Our proposal for financial reform addresses the growing inability of our financial system's insurer of last resort — the U.S. taxpayer — to backstop the financial system in future financial crises. In 1990, the four largest banking institutions had assets of $519 billion, about 9% of U.S. GDP. By 2011, the four largest banking organizations held assets exceeding $7.5 trillion, amounting to 50% of GDP (see Figure 2).[27]

---

[25] See U.S. Government Accountability Office, January 2013, *Financial Regulatory Reform: Financial Crisis Losses and Potential Impacts of the Dodd–Frank Act*, Publication No. GAO-13-180; Dennis Kelleher, Stephen Hall, and Katelynn Bradley, 15 September 2012, "The Cost of the Wall Street-Caused Financial Collapse and Ongoing Economic Crisis is More Than $12.8 Trillion," report by Better Markets, Inc.; and Tyler Atkinson, David Luttrell, and Harvey Rosenblum, "How Bad Was It? The Costs and Consequences of the 2007–2009 Financial Crisis," Federal Reserve Bank of Dallas, *Staff Papers* (forthcoming).

[26] See Fraser Institute, September 18, 2012, *Economic Freedom of the World: 2012 Annual Report.*

[27] The United States is not alone when it comes to large banking sectors. Many other nations have banking sectors that are even larger compared to their GDPs than that of the United States. For example, in 2010, the U.K. had total banking assets that were more than seven times its GDP, while Switzerland's banking sector was 6.6 times the size of its GDP (Financial Stability Board, January 25, 2012, "Peer Review of Switzerland," Figure 1, p. 9). Taxpayers in both the UK and Switzerland still

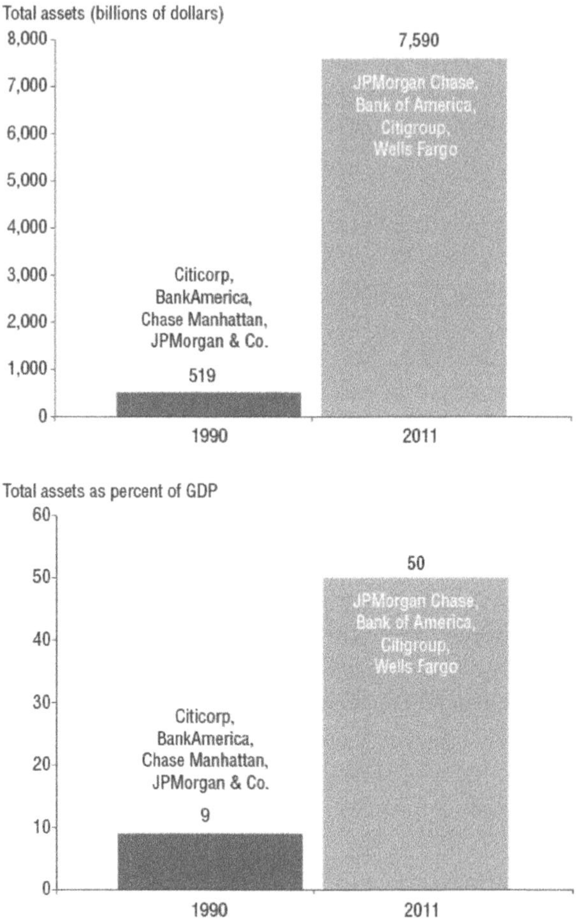

Figure 2. Growth of the Big Four Megabanks.

Notes: Asset size is based on the total assets of the U.S. banking organization (holding company, when applicable). Wells Fargo did not join the ranks of the Big Four until its 2008 acquisition of Wachovia.

Data Sources: Call Report, Federal Financial Institutions Examination Council; Consolidated Financial Statements for Bank Holding Companies (FR Y-9C), National Information Center data, Federal Reserve System.

That is just their on-balance-sheet assets; if U.S. bank balance sheets were adjusted to international standards (instead of U.S. Generally Accepted Accounting Principles), their asset sizes would reflect significantly more exposure to derivatives

bear the burdens of supporting a few giant banking institutions that remain quasi-nationalized since the crisis; see also Max Colchester and David Enrich, 14 May 2013, "Bank Bailout Blues Stall U.K. Recovery," *Wall Street Journal*, p. A1.

and mortgages currently excluded from U.S. regulatory filings. The biggest banks are even bigger than meets the eye. Part of their growth, both absolutely and relative to GDP, has been driven by the subsidized nature of TBTF banking.

Remember the corollary of the Economics 101 lesson: Subsidized activities will grow faster than unsubsidized activities. Taxpayers didn't approve their exposure to losses in the recent financial crisis or potentially in the next one. Massive taxpayer exposure resulted from the happenstance of TBTF banks responding to subsidies implicitly granted to the banking industry's giants. Such taxpayer exposure should not become embedded into the fabric of our financial system.

The final takeaways

We have argued from the outset of this chapter that Dodd–Frank promises to end the policy of TBTF, but likely does the opposite. Dodd–Frank reinforces the perverse incentives that have produced a highly concentrated banking industry where the giant banking institutions are subsidized by government policies that stifle competition from small–medium-size banks. To overcome this adverse feedback loop that is reinforced by Dodd–Frank, we have recommended that (1) the federal safety net be more clearly delineated and restricted; (2) customers acknowledge their understanding of their unprotected status in their dealing with all financial entities other than federally insured, traditional commercial banks; and (3) the banking industry be restructured so that TBTF banks become an anachronism — all banks that remain would be "too small to save."

On the surface, our proposal sounds like radical, sweeping reform. In reality, our proposal is modest in comparison with the quasi-nationalization of much of the banking industry that happened in 2008–2009. Additionally, our recommendation is actually in line with what the equity market has persistently suggested in recent years (see Figure 3). Even before the crisis, large, complex bank holding companies traded at a consistently lower price-to-tangible book value than their smaller, less complex counterparts. This gap persists today and reflects the difficulty of understanding what these companies do and estimating the risks embedded in their balance sheets. The message from the markets is clear: Simpler operations yield better market valuation relative to the firm's book value.

What our markets, and our nation, need is a simple, viable alternative to Dodd–Frank that realigns incentives and demonstrates conclusively that no institution remains TBTF as a result of implicit government backing. Our solution does just that, at a fraction of the bureaucratic costs of Dodd–Frank and in a manner that would likely be an order of magnitude more effective precisely because

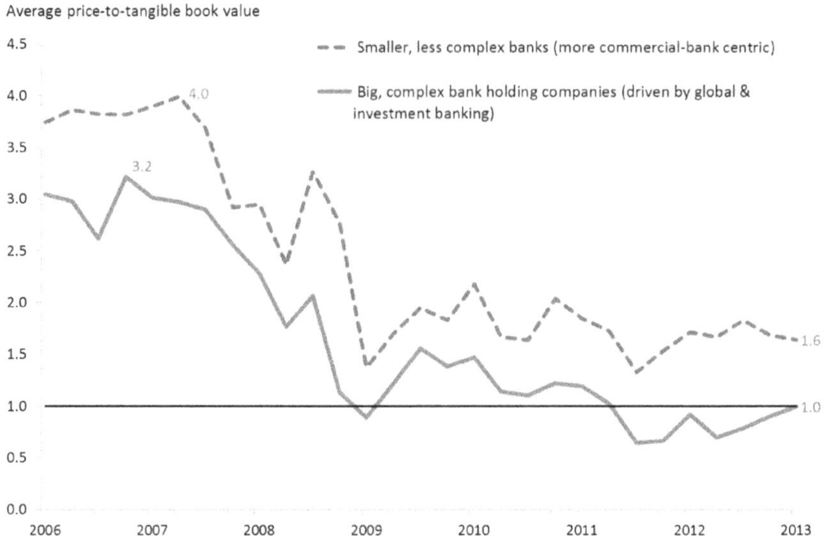

Figure 3. Persistent Gap between Price-to-Tangible Book Ratios.

Notes: The "big, complex" banks include JP Morgan, Citigroup, Bank of America, Goldman Sachs, and Morgan Stanley. The "smaller, less complex" banks include Wells Fargo, BB&T, SunTrust, Fifth Third, and M&T.

Data Sources: Bloomberg, author's calculations.

of its simplicity. Government support for TBTF firms cushions the largest financial institutions from real market discipline — simultaneously incentivizing excessive risk taxing, lax management practices, and creditor and shareholder complacency — and puts taxpayers at risk of a massive potential future tax burden should one of these companies run into trouble. The Dallas Fed plan changes the game by changing the playing field. An industry composed of small to mid-sized firms exposed to a credible threat of failure, with no expectation of government rescue, will truly be an industry free of TBTF players who have the ability to force taxpayers to fund their mistakes.

References

Admati, Anat and Martin Hellwig, 2013, *The Bankers' New Clothes: What's Wrong with Banking and What to Do about It*, Princeton: Princeton UP.

Atkinson, Tyler, David Luttrell, and Harvey Rosenblum, 2013, "How Bad Was It? The Costs and Consequences of the 2007–2009 Financial Crisis." Federal Reserve Bank of Dallas, *Staff Papers*.

Bair, Sheila, 2012, *Bull by the Horns: Fighting to Save Main Street from Wall Street and Wall Street from Itself.* New York: Free Press.

Bank for International Settlements, *BIS Annual Report 2011/12*. pp. 75–76.

Bernanke, Benjamin, 2008, "Current Economic and Financial Conditions." National Association for Business Economics 50th Annual Meeting, Washington, DC. October 7.

Bloomberg View, 2013, "Why Should Taxpayers Give Big Banks $83 Billion a Year?" *Bloomberg*, February 20.

Colchester, Max and David Enrich, 2013, "Bank Bailout Blues Stall U.K. Recovery." *Wall Street Journal*, May 14, p. A1.

Craig, Susanne, 2013, "Seeking Relief, Banks Shift Risk to Murkier Corners." *New York Times*. April 10.

Crittenden, Michael R., 2013, "Bernanke Signals Banks May Face Higher Capital Requirements." *Wall Street Journal*, May 11, p. A2.

Enrich, David, 2011, "Banks Find Loophole on Capital Rule." *Wall Street Journal*, February 17.

Financial Stability Board, 2012 "Peer Review of Switzerland." Figure 1, p. 9. January 25.

Financial Stability Oversight Council, 2013 *Annual Report*, Chart 7.b.1, p. 146.

Fisher, Richard W. and Harvey Rosenblum. "Vanquishing Too Big to Fail." Federal Reserve Bank of Dallas, 2012 *Annual Report*.

Fraser Institute, 2012, *Economic Freedom of the World: 2012 Annual Report*, September 18.

Haldane, Andrew, 2012, "On Being the Right Size." Speech at the 2012 Beesley Lectures, Institute of Economic Affairs, Bank of England, October 25.

House Committee on Financial Services, 2012, *Dodd–Frank Burden Tracker*, Online, Updated July 9.

Kagan, Michael, 2007, "Destructive Ambiguity: Enemy Nationals and the Legal Enabling of Ethnic Conflict in the Middle East." *Columbia Human Rights Law Review* 38.263, pp. 264–319.

Kelleher, Dennis, Stephen Hall, and Katelynn Bradley, 2012, "The Cost of the Wall Street-Caused Financial Collapse and Ongoing Economic Crisis is More Than $12.8 Trillion," Better Markets, Inc. September 15.

Konczal, Mike, 2013, "Is it already time to weaken Dodd–Frank?" *The Washington Post*, March 23.

Krimminger, Michael, 2013, Statement to the U.S. House Committee on Financial Services, Subcommittee on Oversight and Investigations. *Who is Too Big to Fail: Does Title II of the Dodd–Frank Act Enshrine Taxpayer Funded Bailouts?* Hearing, May 14.

Rosenblum, Harvey, Danielle DiMartino, Jessica J. Renier and Richard Alm, 2008, "Fed Intervention: Managing Moral Hazard in Financial Crises." Federal Reserve Bank of Dallas, *Economic Letter*, October.

Rosner, Joshua, 2013, Statement to the U.S. House Committee on Financial Services, Subcommittee on Oversight and Investigations. *Who is Too Big to Fail: Does Title II of the Dodd–Frank Act Enshrine Taxpayer Funded Bailouts?* Hearing. May 14.

Skeel, David A., Jr., 2013, Statement to the U.S. House, Committee on Financial Services, Subcommittee on Oversight and Investigations. *Who is Too Big to Fail: Does Title II of the Dodd–Frank Act Enshrine Taxpayer Funded Bailouts?* Hearing. May 14.

Solomon, Deborah, Robin Sidel and Aaron Lucchetti, 2013, "Big Banks Push Back Against Tighter Rules." *Wall Street Journal.* May 9, A1.

Terminating Bailouts for Taxpayer Fairness Act of 2013. S. 798. 113th Cong. (2013).

The Clearing House, 2013, "Report on the Orderly Liquidation Authority Resolution Symposium and Simulation." January.

U.S. Government Accountability Office, 2013, *Financial Regulatory Reform: Financial Crisis Losses and Potential Impacts of the Dodd–Frank Act.* Publication No. GAO-13-180. January.

Ueda, Kenichi and Beatrice Weder di Mauro, 2012, "Quantifying Structural Subsidy Values for Systemically Important Financial Institutions." International Monetary Fund, Working Paper No. 12/128. May 1.

Vinogradov, Dmitri, 2012, "Destructive Effects of Constructive Ambiguity in Risky Times." *Journal of International Money and Finance* 31, pp. 1459–1481.

Wessel, David, 2009, *In Fed We Trust: Ben Bernanke's War on the Great Panic*. New York: Crown Business.

Zibel, Alan and Brent Kendall, 2013, "Holder: Banks May Be Too Large to Prosecute." *Wall Street Journal.* March 6.

Chapter 13

Solving the Too-Big-To-Fail Problem

William C. Dudley[1]

It is a pleasure to have the opportunity to speak here today. I am glad to see the progress the city and region have made recovering from Sandy, but obviously significant challenges remain.

I am going to focus my remarks today on what is popularly known as the "too-big-to-fail" (TBTF) problem. In particular, should society tolerate a financial system in which certain financial institutions are deemed to be TBTF? And, if not, then what should we do about it?

The answer to the first question is clearly "no." We cannot tolerate a financial system in which some firms are TBTF — at least not ones that operate in any form other than that of a very tightly regulated utility.

The second question is the more interesting one. Is the current approach of the official sector to ending TBTF the right one? I'd characterize this approach as reducing the incentives for firms to operate with a large systemic footprint, reducing the likelihood of them failing, and lowering the cost to society when they do fail. Or would it be better to take the more direct, but less nuanced approach advocated by some and simply break up the most systemically important firms into smaller or simpler pieces in the hope that what emerges is no longer systemic and TBTF?[2]

As I will explain tonight, I believe we should continue to press forward on the first path. But, if we fail to reach our destination by this route, then a blunter approach may yet prove necessary. As always, my views may not necessarily reflect those of the Federal Reserve System.

---

[1]William C. Dudley is President and Chief Executive Officer at the Federal Reserve Bank of New York. The remarks were prepared for the Clearing House's Second Annual Business Meeting and Conference, New York City, November 15, 2012.

[2]This would presumably require legislation.

What is the too-big-to-fail problem?

The root cause of "too-big-to-fail" is the fact that in our financial system as it exists today, the failure of large complex financial firms generate large, undesirable externalities. These include disruption of the stability of the financial system and its ability to provide credit and other essential financial services to households and businesses. When this happens, not only is the financial sector disrupted, but its troubles cascade over into the real economy.

There are negative externalities associated with the failure of any financial firm, but these are disproportionately high in the case of large, complex and interconnected firms. Although the moniker is "TBTF," the magnitude of these externalities does not depend simply on size. The size of the externalities also depends on the particular mix of business activities and the degree of interconnectedness with the rest of the financial industry. One important element is the importance of the services the firm provides to the broader financial system and the economy and the ease with which customers can move their business to other providers. Another is the extent to which the firm's structure and activities create the potential for contagion — that is, direct losses for counterparties, fire sales of assets held by other leveraged financial institutions, or loss of confidence that might precipitate runs on other firms with similar business models.

The presence of large negative externalities creates a dilemma for policymakers when such firms are in danger of failing, particularly if the wider financial system is also under stress at the same moment. At that point in time, the expected costs to society of failure are very large compared to the short-run costs from providing the extraordinary liquidity support, capital or other emergency assistance necessary to prevent catastrophic failure.

The market's belief that a TBTF firm is more likely to be rescued in the event of distress than other firms weakens the degree of market discipline exerted by capital providers and counterparties. This reduces the firm's cost of funds and incents the firm to take more risk than would be the case if there were no prospect of rescue and funding costs were higher.

The fact that firms deemed by the market to be TBTF enjoy an artificial subsidy in the form of lower funding costs distorts competition to the detriment of smaller, less complex firms. This advantage, in turn, creates an unfortunate incentive for firms to get even larger and more complex. The funding benefit of being seen to be TBTF causes the financial system to become artificially skewed toward larger and more complex firms — in ways that are unrelated to true economies of scale and scope.

Now to be clear, I don't believe that firms necessarily deliberately set out to become TBTF. Nor do I think that TBTF was the main cause of the breakdown in market discipline that preceded the financial crisis. Many factors were at work, including the failure to grasp the riskiness of new types of credit products and business models, and principal–agent problems such as the "trader's put." But I do think TBTF contributed to the underpricing of risk in the system and did create a bad set of incentives, and if not addressed comprehensively, would likely be an even larger problem in the future.

So how did the problem become so serious?

The TBTF problem is not new. For example, the Federal Deposit Insurance Corporation (FDIC) and other federal regulatory agencies intervened to prevent the abrupt failure of Continental Illinois, then the seventh largest bank in the United States, in the 1980s. Had Continental Illinois been allowed to fail without any intervention, the comptroller of the currency later testified, "we could very well have seen a national, if not an international, financial crisis the dimensions of which were difficult to imagine."[3]

The comptroller went onto declare that the largest 11 national, commercial banks were TBTF.

But the problem has become more significant since that time for several reasons. First, the biggest financial institutions have become much larger, both in absolute terms and relative to the overall size of the banking system. This reflects many factors including the end of prohibitions on interstate banking, the repeal of the Glass–Steagall Act restrictions separating investment from commercial banking, the rapid growth of the capital markets, and the globalization of the economy — all of which created intense competitive pressures to expand in order to gain economies of scale and scope.

In commercial banking, consolidation occurred at a rapid pace. For example, Bank of America was the outgrowth of over 160 different mergers, which pushed up the size of the original acquirer from $23 billion of assets in 1980 to $2.2 trillion today. In the securities industry, some partnerships became public companies, in part, so that they could more easily obtain the capital needed to expand rapidly. For example, when Goldman Sachs went public in 1999, it had about 15,000 employees and $250 billion of assets. Just eight years later, the firm had expanded to 35,000 employees and $1.1 trillion of assets.

[3]C. T. Conover (1984), "Testimony: Inquiry Into the Continental Illinois Corp. and Continental Illinois National Bank." Hearings Before the Subcommittee on Financial Institutions Supervision, Regulation, and Insurance of the Committee on Banking, Finance and Urban Affairs, U.S. House of Representatives, 98th Cong., 2nd Session, September 18, 19 and October 4: 172–391, p. 288.

In the mid-1990s, the top five banks in the United States had total assets of $1 trillion or about 14% of gross domestic product (GDP). The top securities firms had total assets of $718 billion, or about 9% of GDP. By the end of 2007, the top five banks had assets of $6.8 trillion or 49% of GDP. Similarly, the top securities firms accounted for $3.8 trillion, or about 27% of GDP. In addition, the firms' off-balance-sheet exposures rose sharply.

Second, the complexity and interconnectedness of the largest financial firms increased markedly. Factors behind this include the adoption of a universal banking model by some commercial bank holding companies and the rapid growth of trading businesses, especially the over-the-counter (OTC) derivatives market. In the early 1980s, there were no true U.S. "universal banks" that combined traditional commercial banking with capital markets and underwriting activities. By 2007, there were several operating in the United States, including Citigroup, J.P. Morgan, UBS, Credit Suisse and Deutsche Bank. Also, the OTC derivatives business in foreign exchange, interest rate swaps and credit default swaps had exploded from its start in the early 1980s. The total notional value of the OTC derivatives outstanding for the five largest banks and securities firms currently totals about $200 trillion.

During this period, there was inadequate attention to the risks that were building up in the system. The regulatory and supervisory framework did not keep up with the changes in size, complexity, interconnectedness and globalization that created growing systemic risk externalities and widened the wedge between private and social costs in the event of failure.

Let me mention just a few of the issues:

- Capital regulation was lax both in terms of the amount of capital required and the quality of that capital. As a result, many banks did not have the capacity to absorb large shocks and retain access to wholesale funding.
- The oversight of the largest securities firms was particularly deficient in terms of ensuring that these firms had sufficient private resources to deal with shocks. The industry was also particularly exposed because in the United States, there was (and remains) no lender of last resort backstop for the securities industry except in extremis.[4]

[4]Under Section 13(3) of the Federal Reserve Act, the Federal Reserve is authorized to lend to individuals, corporations and partnerships. But this may occur only if a super majority of the Board of Governors of the Federal Reserve System has determined that circumstances are "unusual and exigent." Subsequently, the DFA further constrained this authority by prohibiting its use to rescue an individual company from bankruptcy.

- Although global integration brought with it a number of benefits, regulatory coordination did not keep pace with the globalization of financial firms and markets. This allowed the potential magnitude of the negative externalities associated with the failure of globally active firms to expand considerably.
- Policymakers allowed market structures, particularly in wholesale funding markets, to evolve in directions that were efficient from a private perspective in normal times, but amplified run dynamics and therefore externalities in times of stress. Examples include the growth in tri-party repo activities and the reliance of many large financial institutions on funding from money market mutual funds, as well as many other elements of the shadow banking system.

The TBTF problem was further aggravated by the financial crisis and the policy response. Faced with systemwide stress, the Federal Reserve, with the support of the U.S. Treasury, intervened to prevent the disorderly failure of Bear Stearns, a firm that would not have been high on the list of TBTF firms a few years earlier.

Meanwhile, the failure of Lehman Brothers demonstrated that the cost to society of the uncontrolled failure of a TBTF firm in a period of generalized stress was considerably greater than anticipated. Following the bankruptcy of Lehman, contagion spread by many channels, including prime brokerage, OTC derivatives positions, money market mutual funds, tri-party repo and wholesale funding markets. The loss in confidence disrupted the flow of credit throughout the global financial system, generating a global economic downturn and the worst contraction in the United States since the Great Depression.

Recognition of the costs generated by the Lehman failure led to extraordinary interventions to prevent further catastrophic failures. These included the rescue of AIG, the FDIC's Temporary Liquidity Guarantee Program (TLGP) program, the ring-fence of Citigroup's poorer quality assets, and the Treasury's Troubled Asset Relief Program (TARP) injection of capital into the largest U.S. financial institutions. Because this solidified in investors' minds that TBTF firms — after the Lehman debacle — would be protected, this worsened the TBTF problem.

The problem was exacerbated during the crisis by the acquisition of weakened firms by stronger firms, a development that was actively promoted by policymakers in a bid to avoid or temper the consequences of their failure. J.P. Morgan absorbed Bear Stearns and Washington Mutual and its assets grew from $1.5 trillion in 2007 to $2.3 trillion today; Wells Fargo purchased Wachovia and its assets increased from $575 billion in 2007 to $1.3 trillion today; and Bank of America purchased Countrywide and Merrill Lynch, increasing its assets from $1.7 trillion in 2007 to $2.2 trillion today. This, of course, made the surviving firms even bigger and more complex.

When the smoke had cleared, the situation was clearly untenable. The experience of the crisis increased the advantage from being perceived as TBTF, and, thus, strengthened the incentives to become bigger, more complex, and interconnected.

The Dodd–Frank Act (DFA) set out to end TBTF. One means was by eliminating the Federal Reserve's discretion to provide emergency financial support through a program open only to a single financial institution, and, in general, raising the bar for broader-based emergency interventions under Section 13.3 of the Federal Reserve Act.

But, as the DFA recognized, simply tying the Fed's hands on intervention is insufficient. It does not reduce the cost to society from the failure of a large and complex firm. In order for the non-intervention strategy to be both fully credible and consistent with the public interest, we need to tackle the underlying externalities and incentive problems that give rise to TBTF in the first place.

Tackling too-big-to-fail

As I see it, solving the TBTF problem requires working on a number of different margins. These include measures that are firm-specific and those that address the structure of the financial system more broadly.

One set of measures works to reduce the incentives for excessive risk-taking and to lower the probability that large financial firms fail or come close to failure. Another set lessens the disruption to the financial system and hence the cost their failure imposes on the broader economy and society as a whole. Along with measures that penalize characteristics associated with the negative externalities from failure, these changes work against the incentive to be TBTF.

Policy measures that alter incentives and reduce the probability of distress

A number of steps have already been taken that reduce the probability of failure. For example, there has already been considerable progress in forcing firms to bolster their capital and liquidity resources. On the capital side, consistent with the DFA, Basel III significantly raises the quantity and quality of capital required of internationally active bank holding companies. This ensures that the firm's shareholders will bear all the firm's losses across a much wider range of scenarios than before. This should strengthen market discipline. Meanwhile, to the extent that some of the specific activities that generate significant externalities are now subject to higher capital charges, this should cause banks to alter their business activities in ways that reduce both the likelihood and social cost of their failure.

Moreover, the new Basel regime explicitly adjusts capital requirements upward based on size, complexity, interconnectedness, global exposure and substitutability — attributes that are proxies for the negative externalities generated by failure. If a bank is deemed a global systemically important financial institution or G-SIFI, then it will have to hold a greater amount of capital relative to its risk-weighted assets compared to a less systemic institution.[5]

The notion behind the systemically important financial institution (SIFI) surcharge is a simple one. The cost to society from the failure of a large, complex firm is proportionally considerably higher than the cost to society of the failure of a non-systemic firm. As a result the capital buffer for the more systemic firm should be higher so that its expected probability of failure will be lower than for the less systemic firm.

The SIFI surcharge acts as a penalty for size and complexity, leaning against the funding cost advantage a firm may have because it is perceived to be TBTF. This helps level the playing field for smaller firms and reduces the incentive to seek to become TBTF in the first place.

Domestically, we have adopted a more forward-looking approach to capital through the use of stress tests, in particular the annual Comprehensive Capital Assessment Review (CCAR) program. By promoting transparency, CCAR also strengthens market discipline.

On the liquidity front, the largest, most systemically important bank holding companies will be required to hold a 30-day liquidity buffer — the so-called liquidity coverage ratio or LCR. The purpose of the LCR is to ensure that such a bank will have sufficient liquid resources so if it were to encounter business difficulties and temporarily lose access to market funding, it would still have some time to address its underlying problems. With a liquidity buffer, banks will not immediately be forced to sell illiquid assets during times of stress. This should enhance their stability, and provide some protection against the fire sale externalities we saw during the crisis: forced asset sales, falling asset prices, leading to rising capital losses at other firms that led, in turn, to further funding difficulties, asset sales and so on.

[5]Earlier this month, the Financial Stability Board published a list of 28 global systemically important banks or G-SIBs that will be subject to capital surcharges. The firms were arrayed in four buckets, with an increasing capital surcharge as a percent of risk-weighted assets imposed as one ascended upward to the higher buckets.

On the supervisory side, firms are now increasingly being evaluated on a cross-industry basis in order to identify best practices and to identify laggards that need to upgrade areas such as MIS, governance, model validation, and risk management practices.

Activity restrictions are another potential means to reduce the risk of failure. The biggest initiative in this area is the Volcker Rule. By limiting proprietary trading activities, the Volcker Rules seeks to reduce trading risk and the likelihood of failure.

In addition, the Financial Stability Oversight Council (FSOC) is in the process of identifying those non-bank financial firms that are systemically important. These firms will be subject to tougher prudential standards and supervisory oversight by the Federal Reserve.

Some argue that this designation process merely creates more TBTF firms. I see it differently. The system risk externalities do not depend on whether we label them systemic or not. If these risks are present, then we should face up to the issue with tougher standards and enhanced supervisory oversight rather than leave the issue unaddressed. This has to be a superior approach relative to pretending these firms could not be TBTF and the problem doesn't exist.

Policy measures to reduce the adverse systemic consequences from failure

Because no plausible level of capital and liquidity standards will be sufficient to reduce the probability of failure to zero, it also makes sense to work on the other major margin — to reduce the cost of the failure of a large, complex financial firm. We can do this by making changes so that such failures are less likely to impair the functioning of the broader financial system. In this area, although many initiatives are in train, I would conclude that we are still very far from where we need to be.

One simple but meaningful step that already has been enacted is to put a brake on the ability of the largest and most complex firms to become even larger and more complex. To this end, the DFA adds "the risk to stability of the U.S. banking or financial system" as an additional factor to be considered in evaluating a proposed merger or acquisition under the Bank Merger Act and the Bank Holding Company Act. As Governor Daniel Tarullo discussed in a recent speech, there is not a hard and fast rule to be applied here. But his view, which I share, is that there would be a "a strong, though not irrebuttable, presumption of denial [of a merger or acquisition] by any firm that falls in the higher end of the list of global systemically important banks ..."[6,7]

Another step for dealing with the firms that might be viewed by some as already TBTF is to understand better the interconnections and pathways through which the distress or failure of one firm impairs the larger system and causes harm to society. We have made progress through the supervisory process in mapping out critical activities performed by firms. Also, we have identified a number of areas, such as collateral management, where better practices could both improve the safety and soundness of the individual firm and reduce the negative externalities generated by a firm's failure.

Work is also underway to evaluate what changes would be required to make the future bankruptcy of large complex firms less disruptive, while also developing an alternative means for the orderly resolution of such firms outside the normal bankruptcy process.

The costs to society of large complex financial firms failing can be reduced at least to some degree by having firms, working in conjunction with their regulators, "pre-plan" their own failure through the so-called "living will" process. The largest and most systemically important banks submitted their "living wills" to the Federal Reserve and the FDIC this summer. We have reviewed the first iterations of their plans and are currently drafting feedback for the firms to incorporate in their next submissions. Through such "living wills," regulators are gaining a better understanding of the impediments to an orderly bankruptcy. This is the necessary first phase in the process of determining how to ameliorate these impediments over time and then doing so.

In my view, this initial exercise has confirmed that we are a long way from the desired situation in which large complex firms could be allowed to go bankrupt without major disruptions to the financial system and large costs to society.

---

[6]See Governor Daniel K. Tarullo, "Financial Stability Regulation," October 10, 2012. Mr. Tarullo added that "I would not apply the presumption in the case of certain *de minimis* acquisitions or in cases where asset dispositions were judged to offset any increase in systemic risk from the proposed new acquisition."

[7]Earlier this year, the Board of Governors issued an order approving Capital One Financial Corporation's acquisition of a federal savings bank, ING Bank. In that order, the Board set forth two principles that are relevant to this particular issue. First, the Board stated that it would generally find a significant adverse effect if the failure of the firm resulting from a merger or acquisition "would likely impair financial intermediation or financial market functioning so as to inflict material damage on the broader economy." Second, the Board observed that there are some small acquisitions or mergers that would not raise a financial stability concern, such as "a proposal that involves an acquisition of less than $2 billion in assets, [or] results in a firm with less than $25 billion in total assets ... ."

Significant changes in structure and organization will ultimately be required for this to be achieved. However, the "living will" exercise is an iterative process, and we have only taken the first step in a long journey.

The second way to potentially minimize the negative externalities from a firm's failure would be to avoid a bankruptcy proceeding altogether and instead resolve the firm under the Dodd–Frank Act's Title II orderly liquidation[8] authority.[9]

The "single point of entry" model has much promise, but much remains to be done before it could be implemented with confidence for a globally active firm. Title II authority is U.S. law. Subsidiaries and affiliates chartered in other countries could be wound down under the bankruptcy laws of those countries, if authorities there did not have full confidence that local interests would be protected. Certain Title II measures including the one-day stay provision with respect to OTC derivatives and other qualified financial contracts may not apply through the force of law outside the United States, making orderly resolution difficult.

The other essential dimension of solving TBTF is to make the financial system more robust — addressing structural vulnerabilities that tend to amplify shocks rather than absorb them. If the financial system can be made more resilient, it will be better positioned to withstand the failure of a large and complex firm and continue to provide essential financial services to the real economy.

I would highlight three areas of work that are critical to solving the TBTF problem. First, regulators and supervisors are pushing for changes in wholesale funding markets, a source of particular vulnerability during the crisis. This includes reforms to tri-party repo, which are underway, and necessary reforms to the money market mutual fund industry, which are being evaluated by the Securities and Exchange Commission (SEC) and the FSOC.

---

[8]The FDIC's "single point of entry" framework for implementing this authority envisages establishing a bridge company into which all the operating subsidiaries of the parent company would be transferred. The bridge company would be recapitalized by converting all or some of the parent company's subordinated and senior unsecured debt into fresh equity in the bridge company. The parent company would be allowed to fail. The transfer of the operating subsidiaries to the bridge company would allow critical operations to continue and provide time for the FDIC to move the systemically important operations back into private hands.

[9]The DFA orderly liquidation authority (OLA) is viewed as to be used only as a last resort under a very well-defined set of circumstances. To resolve a firm under the FDIC's OLA, a number of determinations must be satisfied. First, the troubled firm must be designated a covered financial company (CFC) and that it is in default or danger of default and a resolution under bankruptcy would result in adverse consequences. The determination to use OLA authority requires the assent of the Treasury Secretary after consultation with the President.

Second, the financial market infrastructures are being strengthened to make them more robust to the failure of individual firms. The Committee on Payments and Settlement Systems and the International Organization of Securities Commissions (IOSCO) has published a set of standards for financial market infrastructures called "Principles for Financial Market Infrastructures" that will serve as minimum standards globally.

Finally, the OTC derivatives market is being reformed with the aim of reducing bilateral exposures between firms and, thus, the systemic impact from any one firm failing. All standardized OTC derivatives in the interest rate, credit default, and equities markets will soon have to be centrally cleared through central counterparties (CCPs). The clearing of standardized derivatives trades through CCPs should reduce risk in the overall financial system by facilitating the netting down of OTC derivative exposures. Such trades will also have to be reported to trade repositories and information about the trades will be made available on a post-trade basis. This should make the OTC derivatives market more transparent and, thus, reduce the risk of contagion.

The way forward

We have made some progress on the TBTF problem, particularly in reducing the likelihood that a large complex firm will reach the point of distress at which society faces serious costs. But we have a considerable ways to go to finish the job and reduce to tolerable levels the social costs associated with such failures.

Further international coordination is almost certainly going to be necessary to ensure that bankruptcy regimes interact in ways that minimize negative externalities. At home we also need to ensure that different authorities and resolution regimes operate in a mutually consistent manner. In particular, we may need to revisit the SIPC regime that governs securities firms in bankruptcy. At present, the bankruptcy of a securities firm is very disruptive because the claims of all counterparties are typically frozen for a considerable period and the value of these claims is not easy to ascertain or monetize quickly.

As I have argued above, we shouldn't focus on solving TBTF exclusively at the level of the individual firm. We need significant changes in market structures and practices as well in order to have a financial system in which the key players can fail without big social costs.

We also must continue to ask ourselves the question of whether the steps in train go far enough. For example, one could make a good case that the capital surcharge for systemically important firms should be higher than that contemplated by the Basel Committee. Of course, such a judgment depends on how much other policies succeed in reducing the negative externalities their failure would generate.

Critics of our approach believe it would be better to just break up firms deemed TBTF now — perhaps through legislation requiring the separation of retail banking and capital markets activities or by imposing size restrictions that require firms to shrink dramatically from their current scale. My own view is that while this could yet prove necessary, it is premature to give up on the current approach: changing the incentives facing large and complex firms, forcing them to become more resilient, and making the financial system more robust to their failure.

In my opinion, there are shortcomings to reimposing Glass–Steagall-type activity restrictions or strict size limits. With respect to Glass–Steagall, it is not obvious to me that the pairing of securities and banking businesses was an important causal element behind the crisis. In fact, independent investment banks were much more vulnerable during 2008 than the universal banking firms which conducted both banking and securities activities. More important is to address the well-known sources of instability in wholesale funding markets and give careful consideration to whether there should be a more robust lender of last resort regime for securities activities.

With respect to size limitations, it is important to recognize that a new and much reduced size threshold could sacrifice socially useful economies of scale and scope benefits. And it could do this without actually solving the problem of system risk externalities that aren't related to balance sheet size.

Evaluating the socially optimal size, scope and organizational structure of financial firms is a complicated business, and so is establishing a viable transition path to a system of much smaller firms. It would be helpful in this regard if advocates of break-up solutions would put a bit more flesh on the bones and develop detailed proposals that address essential questions of how such downsizing or functional separation would be accomplished, and what benefits and costs could be expected.

Such an analysis should answer several questions: How would you force divestiture (in good times and bad)? Should firms be split up by activity or reduced pro-rata in size? How much would they have to be shrunk in order for the externalities of failure to no longer create TBTF problems? How would global trading and investment banking services and network-type activities be supported? Should some activities be retained in natural monopoly form, but subject to utility type regulation? How costly would it be to replicate support services or to manage liquidity and capital locally? Are there ways of designing size limits that cannot be arbitraged by banks via off-balance-sheet structures and other forms of financial innovation? So far, advocacy for the break-up path has been strong, but without the detail to assess whether this is indeed superior to the course we are currently following. But, I'm open-minded.

It is important to recognize that any credible approach to addressing the TBTF problem, including the one we are pursuing today, necessarily implies changes to the structure and business mix of financial firms and financial markets. Moreover, it is important to stress that not all of these adjustments will be in the private interests of these firms, and some will result in changes to the price and volume of certain financial services. These are intended consequences, not unintended consequences.

TBTF is an unacceptable regime. The good news is there are many efforts underway to address this problem. The bad news is that some of these efforts are just in their nascent stages. It is important that as the crisis recedes in memory, that these efforts not flag — this is a project that needs to be seen to a successful conclusion and then sustained on a permanent basis.

PART VI

Consumer Protection

Part VI consists of chapters describing and critiquing the goals/objectives and organizational structure of the consumer protection agency created by Dodd–Frank. The first two chapters are speeches presented by Richard Cordray, the first Director of the Consumer Financial Protection Bureau (CFPB). The first chapter sets the stage with the goals of the CFPB and the second discusses how the work of that agency is proceeding.

The third chapter in this part of the volume is written by Brenden Soucy of the Florida State University College of Law. Soucy critiques the new bureau, emphasizing structural and organizational problems that may prevent it from effectively achieving its stated goals. This is done by highlighting organizational deficiencies found with past U.S. regulatory agencies and contrasting them to the organizational structure of the CFPB. What has 'worked' and 'not worked' at regulatory agencies in the past? It is argued that the CFPB has many of the same organizational problems of past agencies that have either failed or have needed significant structural reform. A number of recommendations for reform are offered.

Chapter 14

Partnering: The Consumer Financial Protection Bureau and State Attorneys General

Richard Cordray[1]

Thank you, Attorney General Cooper, for that kind introduction, and thank you to NAAG for inviting me to speak with you about the new Consumer Financial Protection Bureau. I carry warm greetings to you from all of our growing team, and most especially from Professor Elizabeth Warren, who has been leading our efforts to stand up the Bureau.

I am honored to be here along with Len Kennedy, who is serving as our General Counsel, and Raj Date, who is our Associate Director of the Research, Markets and Regulations Division. Len comes to the consumer agency with a distinguished career as a lawyer for the FCC and as the General Counsel of Sprint/Nextel. Raj was one of the first people writing about the need for a consumer agency after he left his prior career in banking to start his own think tank. I feel extremely lucky to find myself now surrounded by such talented colleagues who are holding us to the highest standards as we focus on our role of protecting consumers.

I want to talk with you this morning about the purposes we understand ourselves to be serving at America's new Consumer Bureau. Like any other creature of federal law, our aims start with the authority vested in us by our enabling statute. In Title X of the Dodd–Frank Act (DFA) itself, the Congress identified

[1]At the time of this speech, Richard Cordray led the Consumer Financial Protection Bureau's (CFPBs) Enforcement Division. He was later appointed as the first director of the Bureau. These are public remarks presented at the March 2011 National Association of Attorneys General (NAAG) Spring meetings.

our principal objectives. Let me emphasize at the outset that we are committed to building a strong partnership with you to achieve each of these goals.

You can think of these five objectives as our mandate. They are broad and they are lofty, but with your help, we can continue the work of making them concrete and meaningful for American families. I am going to talk a little bit about each one of them in turn.

First, Congress told us we must ensure that consumers are provided with timely and clear information so they can make responsible decisions about financial transactions. Let me give you an example. Before the financial crisis hit this country, loose practices abounded in the mortgage origination market. Sellers were willing to arrange just about any kind of loan, no matter how poorly the borrower's capacity was documented, as indicated by terms like "SIVA" ("stated income/verified asset") and "NINJA" ("no income, no job, no assets"). In addition to this sort of sloppy or fictional underwriting, they offered teaser rates, masked the actual terms, and accepted yield spread premiums that rewarded them for driving people into more expensive loans than they actually qualified for. Taken together, these practices misled consumers into thinking that they could afford these loans, and that these loans were the best deals they could get.

When consumers sign a contract — for a home loan, a credit card, or any other type of financial product or service used in their personal and household affairs — they should be able to say, "I understand this agreement and all the important terms." And they should also be able to know that no unwelcome surprises are hidden from them. The Consumer Bureau is dedicated to eliminating the kinds of tricks and traps that were used to ensnare consumers in financial products they could not afford and that too often drove them into foreclosure or bankruptcy. You see the effects of these tricks and traps on your constituents firsthand, and I know that you are continuing to try to clean up the mess in each of your own states. We can learn from your experience about what information consumers really need to know in order to make not just better financial decisions, but wise financial decisions, and we look forward to tapping into your expertise in this area.

Second, Congress stated that we are to protect consumers from unfair, deceptive, or abusive acts and practices, and from discrimination. These are areas where you have preceded us. We will work directly with you, as well as with other Federal agencies like the Federal Trade Commission (FTC), to set enforcement priorities. We know that you have a lot of experience bringing these kinds of cases under your state laws, and we look forward to bringing our new authority to bear against bad actors in the marketplace. Rooting out these bad actors will be good not only for consumers, but also for community banks and other financial companies that are committed to honest dealing and quality customer service. These enforcement efforts will complement our other initiatives to promote fair, transparent, and competitive markets: it will help to ensure that those with a core business model built around treating people fairly — offering beneficial products in a transparent manner — will be the winners in the marketplace.

Third, Congress directed us to reduce unwarranted regulatory burdens by identifying and addressing outdated, unnecessary, or unduly burdensome regulations. Here is an outstanding example: Two distinct federal agencies are responsible for administering the Truth in Lending Act and the Real Estate Settlement Procedures Act. These two agencies have had discussions, going back for fifteen years, about harmonization and simplification of the mortgage disclosure forms mandated under each law — which you no doubt have noticed kills whole forests to provide the paper for ordinary real estate closings. Now, the Consumer Bureau is aiming to accomplish within one year what has been contemplated but not achieved for a decade and a half — and we think we have made real progress even before that one-year clock has started ticking. Success in this enterprise will mean clearer and more focused information for consumers, along with reduced costs for lenders — a true win–win for the American economy.

Fourth, Congress has emphasized that we are to enforce Federal consumer financial law consistently, without regard to the status of a financial services provider as a depository institution, in order to promote fair competition. What does this mean? To a large extent, this means doing the same sort of thing that law enforcement officials like you strive to do every day — enforce the law against unlawful practices in a way that levels the playing field for law-abiding individuals and businesses. As mandated by Congress, we will particularly seek to level the playing field so that bank and non-bank providers of consumer financial products and services can compete freely and fairly — which always redounds to the benefit of consumers. And we will be in a great position to do this because, for the first time, there will be one agency with supervisory authority over non-bank providers, as well as all of the nation's largest banks.

With new technology and fierce competition, financial institutions are developing new and fast-changing products and services that cut across existing regulatory frameworks. Payday lenders find themselves competing directly with newer financial products. We all have seen how debit cards and prepaid cards are now crowding into payment markets once ruled by checks and then by credit cards. These developments make it all the more crucial that we have a view of the whole playing field. Having that full picture — and leveling that playing field by treating the participants in the marketplace on par, regardless of their corporate structure or charter choice — is a new approach that will benefit consumers, financial institutions and other providers, and the broader economy. If we learned anything from the financial crisis, it is that gaps in Federal oversight can contribute to systemic failure by allowing unwarranted and unsustainable risks to be created in the economy.

Of course, attorneys general know as well as anyone that leveling the playing field between bank and non-bank providers of consumer financial products and services will require sustained resources in the form of consistent and reliable funding. The non-bank sector consists of tens of thousands of companies, and it has never before been supervised by a Federal agency. That is why it is so critical that the Consumer Bureau retains its independent funding model, a model that will allow it to respond rapidly and appropriately to legal violations and changes in the marketplace over time. Congress has depoliticized the funding of Federal banking supervisors consistently in the past, and the continuation of that precedent is critical for the Consumer Bureau to provide effective oversight over the non-bank sector and a level playing field on which banks and non-banks can compete equally. That is the way our regulatory world should look moving forward.

Fifth, and finally, it is our objective to make sure that markets for consumer financial products and services operate transparently and efficiently to facilitate access and innovation. To this end, I would note again that Raj Date is heading up our Research, Markets and Regulations Division. His part of the Bureau will track market practices, developments, successes, and failures, and make market data accessible and transparent to businesses and consumers — consistent, of course, with legitimate confidentiality concerns and privacy interests.

Already, we are working to understand the consequences of the recently enacted CARD Act by collecting information and data from credit card companies and other sources. The early returns indicate that in response to the CARD Act, issuers have eliminated some of the practices that can confuse customers and cost them money they did not reasonably expect to pay. Some issuers have gone further than what the law requires to curb re-pricing and over-limit fees. These are examples of how good data collection and analysis can help us understand how the market is responding to new laws and what new products and services may be emerging. At every opportunity, we will work to make our policy decisions based on hard data and rigorous analysis.

So these are the five main objectives that Congress set for us. I say “us” here because Congress authorized you to help the Consumer Bureau accomplish these purposes.

As you know, I was sitting on the other side of this podium less than a year ago. I know first-hand that you have been doing the important work of protecting consumers for a long time. You understand better than anyone the kinds of problems that consumers — your constituents — face from the ground up. We will be depending on your expertise and your experience as we work to achieve our mutual objectives. We will do this not just because the DFA generally provides for your authority to enforce the consumer bureau's governing statute and related regulations, but also because we can be more effective and efficient by working with you to police the financial marketplace. And I know that we will very much enjoy the opportunity that Congress has given us to do this important work together.

General Cooper's Presidential Initiative is extremely well-timed, and we look forward to showing financial companies and consumers across America that we can and will be forging a strong partnership that presents a united front in the fight for fairness in the marketplace.

Thank you for having us join you here today, and for all that you do on behalf of our country.

Chapter 15

Prepared Remarks Before the National Association of Attorneys General

Richard Cordray[1]

Thank you for having me here today. It is always a special occasion to speak with a group of people when you have walked in each other's shoes and you understand one another's concerns. When I was the Ohio Attorney General, I always enjoyed these NAAG meetings because I knew I was among colleagues who could appreciate the pressures exerted by the kinds of tough decisions we all had to make day in and day out. Many of those same intangibles remain relevant to me now in my new role as the first director of the Consumer Financial Protection Bureau.

A year ago, I came to speak to you. At that time, I was newly hired as the Chief of Enforcement at the Consumer Bureau. We had not yet opened our doors for business. We were just a tiny crew huddled into a few cramped offices. We spent our days trying to figure out how we were going to accomplish the many responsibilities Congress had set for us. But something special happened that day when my handful of staff and I came to visit you. Former Attorney General Jim Tierney said to me later, "I knew exactly who your people were. They had that look on their face." Puzzled, I asked him, "What look is that?" And he said, "They had that look like they just know they are going to change the world."

Time will tell if we actually will change the world for the better. But over the past year, we have had to think very hard about how we can begin to create a fairer, more transparent financial marketplace for American consumers. Making

[1] Richard Cordray serves as Director of the Consumer Financial Protection Bureau. These were public remarks presented at the Spring meeting of the National Association of Attorneys General (NAAG), Washington, DC, March 6, 2012.

prices and risks clear to protect people against fraud. And standing up for consumers to make sure they are treated fairly. That is our new job.

Back then, we joined General Cooper and the rest of you in NAAG's Presidential Initiative to develop a strong and lasting partnership between the State Attorneys General and the new Consumer Bureau. Today, I want to talk to you about the progress we have made and about how we have already begun to work closely with your staffs. Quite bluntly, we need your experience, your perspectives, and your coordination in a strategic effort to root out fraud and unfairness in the financial marketplace.

Already, we are excited to work with you on our new Repeat Offenders Against Military (ROAM) database, which will track completed enforcement actions against companies and individuals who repeatedly scam military personnel. By providing a national clearinghouse for such information, we will make it difficult — if not impossible — for predators against our military to roam from one base to another, shrouded in their relative anonymity as they cross state lines. Giving credit where it is due, I want to point out that this idea originated with General Schneiderman, and we were pleased to take him up on this suggestion.

We are also excited about several working groups we have underway with your staff. We are meeting regularly to discuss the challenges posed to our mutual constituents by payday loans, foreclosure scams, auto loans, and debt collection. These substantive groups allow us to keep each other updated and to launch joint initiatives in areas where we share jurisdiction. While we had been somewhat hamstrung for our first six months by not having a director, I am glad to say that problem has now been solved.

And so we are picking up momentum week by week, and we will be getting results for the people we serve. We are taking this same approach with the Federal Trade Commission (FTC), which has been a great and generous partner to our fledgling agency.

To advance these efforts, you will shortly be receiving a Memorandum of Understanding from us to establish a general framework to share information on consumer financial protection issues. A quick turnaround on this will help accelerate our partnership with each of you. We want to expand on what you already do so well — and we want you to take advantage of new resources we bring to the arena, including new analytical tools and insight into market trends.

In the Dodd–Frank Act, Congress gave us a broad range of tools to address the problems in the financial marketplace, and to fix them. Through our highly capable research team, we analyze what is happening with consumer financial products from mortgages to credit cards to payday loans. Through our supervision team, we are able to go on-site and examine those banks with more than $10 billion in assets, as well as their affiliates. We also are beginning to examine nonbank providers of consumer financial products and services, many of them for the first time at the federal level.

The enforcement team that I helped build can commence actions against market players who cheat consumers — and their competitors — by not following federal consumer financial laws. We also have the fair lending office, which works to ensure that individuals receive fair, equitable, and nondiscriminatory access to credit, as well as offices dedicated to protecting specific consumer groups with unique issues and challenges — notably service members, students, and older Americans — while also helping enable consumers to make sound financial decisions for themselves and their families.

With this array of tools, we can pick and choose those best suited to solve the problem at hand. Sometimes consumers simply need to Know Before You Owe, which is our signature initiative on mortgages, credit cards, and student loans. Sometimes writing a new rule makes the most sense. Sometimes our supervisory authority can identify and correct problems before they get out of hand. And sometimes holding a bad actor accountable through investigations and enforcement action is necessary. Our goal is straightforward but the responsibility looms large: We are determined to make consumer financial markets work better for all Americans, for the honest businesses that serve them, and for the economy as a whole.

The scope of our work together is brought into stark relief in the aftermath of the recent financial crisis, which has left a tremendous mess for us to clean up. Almost 4 million mortgages are more than 90 days delinquent. Perhaps as many as 10 million borrowers are at risk of default. So fixing the mortgage markets remains an urgent priority. We know you are all dealing with it in your respective states, and you will be for some time to come. We share your deep concern about the far-reaching effects on our communities.

The recent mortgage settlement was an important step forward. The five largest mortgage servicers, accounting for more than half of the market, will now be subject to improved servicing standards, backed by a strong and capable monitor to enforce the settlement terms. Servicers will have to properly document their authority to file a foreclosure action, as the law always required. The people who now benefit from these improvements should thank you, General Miller and General Suthers and all of you who worked so persistently to complete this process, which began when I was still the Ohio Attorney General and the robo-signing scandal first erupted.

Going forward, the Consumer Bureau now has an enormous role to play in ensuring that the great financial meltdown does not happen again. We now have the ability to examine participants in all segments of the mortgage market, and our authority over nonbanks will be especially helpful. Before the crisis hit, only part of this market was subject to federal oversight. How could that ever be expected to work? It most certainly did not. Bad practices drove out the good; our responsible community banks and credit unions were literally robbed of market share; and the whole stinking mess eventually collapsed, dragging down many innocent people along with it. I firmly believe that had the Consumer Bureau been in place 10 years ago, the crisis would have been headed off before it metastasized.

Over the next year, the Consumer Bureau will be putting in place new mortgage rules to protect consumers. We will be issuing a rule requiring mortgage servicers to provide consumers with better information in their billing statements. We will also be issuing rules on "force-placed insurance" to prevent servicers from charging for this product unless there is a reasonable basis to believe that borrowers have failed to maintain their own insurance. And we will issue new rules around hybrid, adjustable-rate mortgages. Consumers will be notified months ahead of their first interest rate adjustment and they will receive a disclosure of their new monthly payment, along with any available options to head off the higher rate, such as refinancing and renegotiation of loan terms.

We welcome your input on these tasks. But there are also other areas where we believe that we can forge an effective partnership with you. One that we wanted to discuss today is debt collection.

At a NAAG meeting last year in North Carolina, a speaker presciently warned that illegal debt collection activities would become a special and growing concern in the aftermath of the financial crisis. Just last week, we saw figures confirming his warning: Thirty million Americans are subject to third-party debt collectors. People have a lot of debt. And, let us face it: It is hard to collect debt in a tough economy.

I want to emphasize that many debt collectors play by the rules, work diligently to do the right thing, and comply with the law. But all too often they have insufficient or inaccurate information about the debts they are supposed to collect. Those who follow the law are placed at a competitive disadvantage in contrast to those who do not, and their reputations are harmed when they are lumped in with their competitors who engage in illegal activities.

When I was Ohio Attorney General, we had numerous headaches over debt collection. Sometimes the problems were jurisdictional. Sometimes the players were tiny, fly-by-night operators. Sometimes, they were larger companies. All too often, going after illegal debt collection activities felt like that old game at the carnival, "Whack a Mole." As soon as we got one, another popped up.

But nothing much has seemed to change. Debt collection remains one of the top sources of consumer complaints on the state and federal level. While debtors need to pay back their creditors, the methods used by some debt collectors are just unconscionable. Harassment. Inexcusable language and threats. Repeated late-night phone calls. Collectors erroneously telling relatives they are responsible for the debt of the deceased. Calling military superiors about a service member's debt and threatening their security clearance. Repeated efforts to collect debts from the wrong consumers. Some of this activity is downright illegal, and none of it comports with any proper vision of a civilized society.

You work on debt collection issues all the time at the state level. For example, General Swanson recently brought a case accusing one of the country's largest debt buyers with defrauding Minnesota's courts and citizens by filing robo-signed affidavits. You may have encountered the tactic known as "sewer service" — lawsuits filed on undocumented debt claims, leading to default judgments when service is not effectuated (with contested lawsuits usually being withdrawn). Yet often the same debt collectors magically are able to find the debtor once they have a judgment in hand, which they then collect on. These tactics harm consumers both directly and indirectly, by damaging their credit reports.

We also know of the yeoman's work the FTC is doing on the federal front to curb illegal debt collection. Over the past year, the FTC commenced seven debt collection cases, the highest number of debt collection cases that it has brought or resolved in any single year. In doing so, it obtained multimillion-dollar penalties as well as far-reaching injunctive relief. These victories represent great strides in attempting to rein in abusive debt collectors.

But even with the aggressive and creative work being done by the FTC and the states, I fear that some debt collectors view law enforcement merely as a cost of doing business. We can look back and find that many of us have sued the same parties at different times; they have paid their settlements or judgments, promised to sin no more, and gone right out to do the same things all over again.

If we can collaborate together towards a national strategic plan, we can address illegal debt collection more effectively. These practices affect all kinds of people — young and old, urban and rural, people of all races and religions — it can affect anyone who struggles with repaying a debt. The worst practices undermine our basic humanity, turning people into mere account ledger entries and spawning treatment that flatly disregards all common courtesy on the way to violating the law.

We intend to forge a strategic partnership with you and with our federal government colleagues in this arena — the FTC and the Department of Justice — to transform this situation in a more lasting way. Our goal is to help the honest debt collectors do their jobs responsibly and see that the rest are either rehabilitated or run out of business once and for all. Until we do so, we will be failing all those people who are counting on us to change the world for the better — including ourselves.

As we put our heads together to tackle this problem, the Consumer Bureau now has the benefit of those new tools I mentioned. Significantly, we recently issued a proposed rule to supervise all debt collectors in the United States with more than $10 million in annual receipts resulting from collection activities. Everyone in this room is familiar with enforcement actions, which will be an important part of addressing problems in this marketplace. But you may not be as familiar with supervision.

When this proposed rule becomes final, our supervision authority will then allow us to go onsite with debt collectors, examine their operations from the inside, and determine whether a collector is complying with the law. We will set forth our expectations through public examination procedures, encourage robust compliance programs, communicate expectations confidentially to the entity throughout the examination and rating process, and ensure appropriate corrective action where necessary. These supervisory efforts would cover more than 60% of market activities.

By comprehensively assessing large collectors, as well as many of the bank creditors who originate the debt, supervision would allow us to understand and address the systemic problems posing risks to consumers. By proactive coordination among federal and state law enforcement, we can help Americans dig themselves out of the residue of this financial crisis, without being plagued by the indignity of illegal debt collection tactics.

As U.S. Attorney General Robert Kennedy once said: "All of us might wish at times that we lived in a more tranquil world, but we don't. And if our times are difficult and perplexing, so are they challenging and filled with opportunity." In our day as in his, I say Amen to that assessment, and I thank you all for your much-needed service to the United States of America.

Chapter 16

The Consumer Financial Protection Bureau: The Solution or the Problem?

Brenden D. Soucy[1]

Introduction

In 2010, President Barack Obama signed the Consumer Financial Protection Act into Law[2] as a part of the Dodd–Frank Act.[3] This Act created the Consumer Financial Protection Bureau (hereinafter "CFPB"), which is an "independent bureau" that is "in the Federal Reserve System," but is to "be considered an Executive agency."[4] While the CFPB is a part of the Federal Reserve System, it is subject to very little oversight from the Federal Reserve. The CFPB does not report to the Board of Governors of the Federal Reserve, the Board has no power to override decisions of the CFPB,[5] and the Board does not have appropriations authority over the CFPB.[6]

---

[1] Florida State University College of Law, J.D. (2013), summa cum laude. This article was originally published in the *Florida State University Law Review*, 2013, 40(3), 691–720. It is reprinted with permission from the *Review*.

[2] Helene Cooper, *Obama Signs Overhaul of Financial System, N.Y. Times* (July 21, 2010), http://www.nytimes.com/2010/07/22/business/22regulate.html?_r=0.

[3] Dodd–Frank Wall Street Reform and Consumer Protection Act (Dodd–Frank), Pub. L. No. 111-203, 124 Stat. 1376 (codified in scattered sections of the U.S.C. (2012)).

[4] *Id.* §1011(a) (codified at 12 U.S.C. §5491(a) (2012)).

[5] *See infra* notes 94–98 and accompanying text (discussing how the only body with the power to override CFPB policy initiatives is the FSOC, which can only defeat CFPB regulations with a supermajority vote of its members).

[6] *See infra* notes 78–82 and accompanying text (discussing how the Federal Reserve is bound by statute to provide a specified percentage of its budget to the CFPB, at the discretion of the CFPB Director).

The Dodd–Frank Act was signed into law in the wake of the financial crisis, and the CFPB was meant to "protect consumers from unfair, deceptive, and abusive acts that so often trap them in unaffordable financial products."[7] According to the Senate report, "it was the failure by the prudential regulators to give sufficient consideration to consumer protection that helped bring the financial system down."[8] The report goes on to assert that "it was the organizations that promote consumer protection that were urging that underwriting standards be tightened for both consumer protection and safety and soundness reasons, and it was the prudential regulators who ignored these calls."[9]

To be sure, the prudential regulators' focus on encouraging home ownership — a goal which it pursued with blind zealousness while utterly failing to give sufficient consideration to consumer protection — contributed to the financial crisis. Predatory lending, and other abusive practices that could have been curtailed had sufficient consumer protection been in place, certainly enhanced the magnitude of the crisis,[10] but so did consumers that decided to strategically default on their mortgages.[11] Ultimately, as discussed in Part III.A, inadequate consumer protection was just one of many causes of the financial crisis, and it is unlikely that increased consumer protection alone would have significantly reduced the scale of the financial crisis.

That said, it is clear that prior to the creation of the CFPB consumers were not adequately protected, and the system designed to protect them was in need of substantial reform. Thus, at first glance, it appears that the creation of the CFPB is a positive development, and that with its creation consumers will finally have adequate protection. Unfortunately, the CFPB suffers from serious structural deficiencies that, if not reformed, may ultimately result in the CFPB harming the consumers it is meant to protect.

This Note begins with a discussion of the creation of the CFPB and its brief history in Part I.A, and then in Part II it assesses the structural deficiencies of the CFPB, comparing it to past regulatory agencies that failed. Part III provides an overview of the causes of the financial crisis and finds that the CFPB cannot prevent another crisis. As explained in Part IV, in order for the CFPB to avoid suffering from the same type of tunnel vision that made past regulatory agencies that were

---

[7] S. REP. NO. 111-176, at 11 (2010).

[8] *Id.* at 166.

[9] *Id.*

[10] *See infra* notes 119–122 and accompanying text (discussing the failures of the prudential regulators and abusive practices).

[11] *See infra* notes 124–125 and accompanying text (discussing strategic defaults).

similarly structured fail, the CFPB must be reformed. Most importantly, the CFPB should be: (1) made subject to congressional oversight,[12] (2) reformed to be led by a multimember commission instead of a single director,[13] (3) made subject to review by the Office of Information and Regulatory Affairs,[14] and (4) made subject to more meaningful review from the Financial Stability Oversight Council (FSOC) by reducing the vote needed to veto a CFPB action from two-thirds to one-half.[15]

The creation of the CFPB and the appointment of its first director

The architect of the CFPB, Elizabeth Warren, first proposed creating a new consumer financial protection agency in a short article published in 2007.[16] Warren proposed basing this new agency on the Consumer Product Safety Commission (hereinafter "CPSC"), which regulates the safety of consumer products, saying that "[f]inancial products should be subject to the same routine safety screening that now governs the sale of every toaster, washing machine, and child's car seat sold on the American market."[17] Despite the logical fallacies in basing an agency designed to protect consumers in credit markets off of one designed to protect them from dangerous appliances,[18] the Obama Administration published a "White Paper" in 2009 on financial regulatory reform which embraced Warren's idea and advocated for financial reform legislation including a new consumer financial protection agency modeled on the CPSC.[19] This paper provided the framework for the original version of the financial reform legislation,[20] which was introduced by Representative Barney Frank in July of 2009.[21]

---

[12] *See infra* Part IV.A.

[13] *See infra* Part IV.B.

[14] *See infra* Part IV.C.

[15] *See infra* Part IV.D.

[16] *See* Elizabeth Warren, Unsafe at Any Rate, DEMOCRACY J. 8, 16 (Summer 2007), available at: http://www.democracyjournal.org/article.php?ID=6528.

[17] *Id.* at 16.

[18] *See* Todd J. Zywicki & Stefanie Haeffele-Balch, Loans Are Not Toasters: The Problems with a Consumer Financial Protection Agency, MERCATUS ON POL'Y 1–2 (October 2009), available at: http://mercatus.org/sites/default/files/MOP_-60_Loans_are_not_Toasters_web.pdf (pointing out that while a dangerous product such as an exploding toaster is not useful to any consumer, virtually all consumer credit products, from payday loans to mortgages, are suitable and useful to some consumers in some situations).

[19] DEP'T OF THE TREASURY, FINANCIAL REGULATORY REFORM: A NEW FOUNDATION 55–63 (2009), available at: http://online.wsj.com/public/resources/documents/finregfinal06172009.pdf.

[20] *See* Todd J. Zywicki, The Consumer Financial Protection Bureau: Savior or Menace? 81 GEO. WASH. L. REV. 856, 860 (2013).

[21] H.R. 3126, 111th Cong. §112 (2009), available at: http://www.gpo.gov/fdsys/pkg/BILLS-111hr3126ih/pdf/BILLS-111hr3126ih.pdf.

In the originally introduced version, the new agency was to be led by a multimember commission[22] and funded by appropriations.[23] But in the modified version of the bill, which was enacted by the House of Representatives in December of 2009, the new agency was designed to be free from appropriations oversight, instead receiving 10% of the Federal Reserve System's total expense budget as guaranteed funds each year.[24] And by the time the legislation that ultimately became the Dodd–Frank Act was introduced in the Senate by Senator Christopher Dodd in April of 2010, the agency had been changed from a standalone agency to a bureau of the Federal Reserve, which instead of being led by a multimember commission was to have a single director.[25] Three months later, the Dodd–Frank financial reform legislation passed Congress over near uniform Republican opposition and was signed into Law.[26]

The creation of the CFPB was met with considerable criticism before the Dodd–Frank Act was even passed,[27] and it has been surrounded in controversy since its creation, including over the selection of its inaugural director.[28] Originally, it was expected that the first proponent of a new consumer protection agency, Elizabeth Warren, would become the CFPB's first director, but it eventually became clear that Warren would not be able to get Senate confirmation.[29] Consequently, Warren was never even nominated. President Obama ultimately nominated former Ohio Attorney General Richard Cordray to serve as the inaugural director of the CFPB.[30]

---

[22] *Id.*

[23] *Id.* §118.

[24] H.R. 4173, 111th Cong. §4109 (2009) (enacted), available at: http://www.gpo.gov/fdsys/pkg/BILLS-111hr4173ih/pdf/BILLS-111hr4173ih.pdf.

[25] *See* Sewell Chan, *Dodd to Unveil a Broad Financial Overhaul Bill*, N.Y. TIMES (March 14, 2010), http://www.nytimes.com/2010/03/14/business/14bank.html?pagewanted=all&_r=0.

[26] *See* Cooper, *supra* note 1.

[27] *See, e.g.*, Jessica Holzer, *Republicans Criticize Agency for Consumers*, WALL ST. J. (July 15, 2009), http://online.wsj.com/article/SB124758746553939621.html? KEYWORDS=consumer+financial+protection+bureau; Richard A. Posner, Op-Ed., *Treating Financial Consumers as Consenting Adults*, WALL ST. J. (July 22, 2009), http://online.wsj.com/article/SB10001424052970203946904574302213213148166.html? KEYWORDS=consumer+financial+protection+bureau (expressing concern that the agency has the power to "design 'standard' consumer financial products that will contain whatever 'features or terms [are] defined by the Agency for the product or service'").

[28] Damian Paletta, *Fight Over Consumer Agency Looms as Overhaul is Signed*, WALL ST. J. (July 22, 2010), http://online.wsj.com/article/SB10001424052748704746804575367502836650966. html? KEYWORDS=consumer+financial+protection+bureau+elizabeth+warren+director.

[29] *See* Binyamin Appelbaum, *Warren's Candidacy Raises a Partisan Debate*, *N.Y. TIMES* (July 25, 2010), http://www.nytimes.com/2010/07/26/business/26warren.html?_r=0; Paletta, *supra* note 27.

[30] *See* Binyamin Appelbaum, *Former Ohio Attorney General to Head New Consumer Agency*, *N.Y. TIMES* (July 17, 2011), http://www.nytimes.com/2011/07/18/business/former-ohio-attorney-general-picked-to-lead-consumer-agency.html?pagewanted=all.

Senate Republicans quickly announced their intention to filibuster any vote on confirmation of Cordray as director until structural reforms were made to the CFPB.[31] Most importantly, the Republicans advocated having the agency run by a multimember commission, making it subject to congressional appropriations authority, and giving the other financial regulatory agencies more oversight power over the CFPB.[32]

The Obama Administration was unwilling to agree to make any of these reforms, and the director position consequently remained empty until January 4, 2012, when President Obama named Cordray as CFPB Director, stating that he had the authority to do so under his power to make recess appointments, despite the fact that the Senate had gone less than three days without meeting.[33] This was the first recess appointment made during a break of fewer than 10 days since a 1993 opinion of the Justice Department which suggested that breaks of just a few days would not be sufficient.[34] House Speaker John Boehner referred to the action as "an extraordinary and entirely unprecedented power grab by President Obama that defies centuries of practice and the legal advice of his own Justice Department."[35] Senate Minority Leader Mitch McConnell stated that "[t]his recess appointment represents a sharp departure from a long-standing precedent that has limited the president to recess appointments only when the Senate is in a recess of 10 days or longer."[36] Senator McConnell expressed concern that "[b]reaking from this precedent lands this appointee in uncertain legal territory, threatens the confirmation process and fundamentally endangers the Congress' role in providing a check on the excesses of the executive branch."[37]

Even if the appointment is constitutionally valid, it may have been statutorily deficient, as the CFPB statute specifies that "the Director shall be appointed by the President, by and with the advice and consent of the Senate."[38] Thus,

---

[31] *See* John H. Cushman Jr., *Senate Stops Consumer Nominee*, *N.Y. Times* (December 8, 2011), http://www.nytimes.com/2011/12/09/business/senate-blocks-obama-choice-for-consumer-panel.html.

[32] *See Id.*

[33] *See* Jim Puzzanghera & Lisa Mascaro, *Obama Bypassing Senate to Appoint Richard Cordray Consumer Chief*, *L.A. Times* (January 4, 2012), http://articles.latimes.com/2012/jan/04/business/la-fi-obama-cordray-20120104.

[34] *See Id.*

[35] Helene Cooper & Jennifer Steinhauer, *Bucking Senate, Obama Appoints Consumer Chief*, *N.Y. Times* (January 4, 2012), http://www.nytimes.com/2012/01/05/us/politics/richard-cordray-named-consumer-chief-in-recess-appointment.html?pagewanted=all.

[36] Puzzanghera & Mascaro, *supra* note 32.

[37] *See Id.*

[38] 12 U.S.C. §5491(b)(2) (2012).

Cordray's status as Director remains unclear, but the CFPB has nonetheless begun exercising its authority, announcing its first enforcement action on July 18, 2012.[39] The constitutionality of Cordray's appointment has no bearing on the problems with the structure of the CFPB, but the issue does bring into sharp focus how unusual the structure of the CFPB is.

The Senators who blocked Cordray's Senate appointment did not do so because they did not think he was fit for the job — in fact, many of them praised Cordray's qualifications for the job.[40] But they pledged to prevent any candidate from being confirmed unless the CFPB was reformed, including changing its leadership from having a single director to a multimember commission.[41] The CFPB is unique in that, unlike other regulatory agencies, it is headed by a single director who is only removable for cause;[42] this anomaly and other structural deficiencies of the CFPB were daunting enough to convince 45% of the Senate to block the appointment of a highly qualified candidate and to refuse to appoint any candidate until the deficiencies could be addressed,[43] prompting the President to make the disputed recess appointment of Cordray.[44]

Repeating the mistakes of the past: The structural defects of the CFPB

Why past independent regulatory agencies failed

In the history of the United States, numerous regulatory agencies have been put into place, many of which were structurally designed to be independent so that they could be insulated from market and political pressures and freely pursue the "public interest."[45] The theory behind such agencies seems to be that insulating

---

[39] *See* Halah Touryalai, *Obama's Consumer Protection Agency Strikes: $210M Fine for Capital One*, FORBES (July 18, 2012), http://www.forbes.com/sites/halahtouryalai/2012/07/18/obamas-consumer-protection-agency-strikes-210m-fine-for-capital-one/.

[40] *See* Ylan Q. Mui, *Senate Blocks Richard Cordray Confirmation to Head Consumer Watchdog Agency*, WASH. POST (December 8, 2011), http://www.washingtonpost.com/blogs/2chambers/post/senate-republicans-block-cordray-as-obama-consumer-watchdog-nominee/2011/12/08/gIQA6j9BfO_blog.html.

[41] *See Id.*

[42] *See infra* notes 84–91 and accompanying text (discussing how other federal regulatory agencies are headed by multimember commissions or boards).

[43] *See* Mui, *supra* note 39.

[44] *See* Puzzanghera & Mascaro, *supra* note 32.

[45] *See* MAXWELL L. STEARNS & TODD J. ZYWICKI, PUBLIC CHOICE CONCEPTS AND APPLICATIONS IN LAW 44–46 (2009) (discussing the role of the "public interest" theory of regulation).

regulatory agencies from congressional oversight is the best way to ensure that policies are made absent any outside pressure and instead are made based on what is best for the public.[46] In the abstract, this view seems to make logical sense, but as became clear in the decades following the creation of agencies structured to be highly independent, having a government agency insulated from other government sectors can lead to disastrous regulatory policies.[47] While such insulation provides independence, it also results in isolation.

Insulation from outside pressures can be a good thing, but isolation from other agencies and the rest of the government is not, as it can lead to a conflicting and irrational regulatory scheme.[48] An isolated agency trying to achieve a desired result in one sector might unwittingly cause a disproportionally negative effect in another sector.[49] It was these types of concerns that led to the creation of the Office of Information and Regulatory Affairs (hereinafter "OIRA"), which was designed to create coherence among the often-conflicting directives of the various regulatory agencies and to try to balance the efforts of each agency so as to preserve broader interests — such as economic growth and national security.[50] When the OIRA discovers a position that is inconsistent with the overarching regulatory scheme, it can coordinate with the agency taking the outlier position to ensure that the overall regulatory scheme remains consistent and coherent.[51] Thus, the OIRA largely solved the problem of conflicting directives and helped to make the regulatory process more collaborative, in the process somewhat reducing the independence of the agencies subject to its jurisdiction.

The problems prompting the creation of the OIRA demonstrate why having agencies be completely independent is not ideal, but the OIRA cannot completely solve these problems, in part because independent regulatory agencies, including

---

[46] *See* Rachel E. Barkow, *Insulating Agencies: Avoiding Capture Through Institutional Design*, 89 Tex. L. Rev. 15, 42–44 (2010) (expressing concern that any agency subject to congressional appropriations authority will have its decisions improperly influenced by partisan considerations).

[47] *See infra* notes 60–72 and accompanying text (discussing how the Civil Aeronautics Board and the Interstate Commerce Commission created policies conflicting with other sectors and having results counterproductive to their purposes, leading ultimately to both agencies being abolished).

[48] *See* Stearns & Zywicki, *supra* note 44, at 363 (noting that a "potential problem for bureaucratic actors is a tendency toward 'tunnel vision,' meaning too narrow a focus on their particular regulatory agenda at the expense of alternative policy goals").

[49] *See Id.* ("[B]ureaucratic tunnel vision might create or exacerbate risks in one sector while seeking to eliminate or to reduce it in another.").

[50] *See Id.* at 366–367 (discussing the formation of the OIRA and its purpose); Barkow, *supra* note 45, at 30–31.

[51] *See* Barkow, *supra* note 45, at 30–31.

the CFPB, are exempt from OIRA oversight.[52] It is also important to note that while an agency can be free from direct political oversight, no amount of statutory independence can prevent the bureaucrats running the agency from pursuing their own ideological and political objectives.[53] Nor can it prevent special interest groups from exerting influence over the bureaucrats, some of whom will inevitably leave the agency to pursue careers in private practice in the fields that they were previously regulating.[54] Of course, this is not a problem limited to bureaucrats.

As subscribers to the public choice theory have long recognized, all actors in political life — including voters, legislators, bureaucrats, and even judges — "behave rationally to maximize or optimize some objective function (wealth, status, power)."[55] In regards to elected officials, the voters can, in theory, remove from office those that are acting contrary to the beliefs and views of the voters, thus providing an incentive for those officials to act at least to some degree with the interests of their constituents in mind.[56] This is one of the hallmarks of a representative democracy.[57] The same logic applies to unelected bureaucrats — when subject to congressional or executive oversight they would, in theory, act with some regard to input and concerns from the overseers, if only out of self-interest in maintaining their positions. That said, whether the possibility of removal actually results in the preferences of the person holding the power to remove significantly influencing the official's actions is questionable.[58] But the risk of

---

[52] *See infra* Part IV.C (arguing that the CFPB and other independent regulatory agencies should be subject to OIRA review).

[53] *See* Stearns & Zywicki, *supra* note 44, at 364–365.

[54] *See, e.g.*, *Dan Gallagher, Deputy Director of Trading and Markets, to Leave SEC and Return to Private Practice*, U.S. Securities and Exchange Commission (January 25, 2010), http://www.sec.gov/news/press/2010/2010-11.htm (announcing that SEC Deputy Director Gallagher was leaving the SEC to return to private practice); *FTC Bureau of Competition Deputy Director Barry Nigro Returns to Private Practice*, Federal Trade Commission (November 16, 2005), http://www.ftc.gov/opa/2005/11/nigro.shtm (announcing that FTC Deputy Director Nigro was leaving the FTC to return to private practice).

[55] Jerry Louis Mashaw, *Public Law and Public Choice: Critique and Rapprochement*, *in* Research Handbook on Law and Public Choice 19, 20 (Daniel A. Farber & Ann Joseph eds., 2010).

[56] *See Id.* at 21 (discussing how in an "idealist account" the problem of representatives acting contrary to the desires of a majority of the voters is cured by the dynamics of the system because "[o]ver time the voters can replace legislators whose preferences do not reflect those of their constituents").

[57] *See* Richard Bellamy, *The Political Form of the Constitution: The Separation of Powers, Rights and Representative Democracy*, 44 Pol. Stud. 436, 445 (1996), available at: http://papers.ssrn.com/sol3/papers.cfm?abstract_id=1531367.

[58] *See* Mashaw, *supra* note 54, at 21 ("The notion that voters' preferences control legislative action or that legislative action controls bureaucratic decision making is, [under the public choice theory,] a fundamental misdescription of U.S. government.").

self-interested behavior is especially great in the case of an agency that is structurally highly independent. As recognized by the public choice theory, an agency could never truly be independent because of the biases and preferences of the bureaucrats running it, and without any type of oversight there is little to stop such an agency from acting in accordance with those biases and preferences — favoring particular sets of ideological and political beliefs without giving due consideration to other views. This type of structure and the potential for decisions to be made in pursuit of a particular set of ideological beliefs without any substantive input from anyone with a different view[59] makes the agency much more likely to suffer the type of narrow-minded "tunnel vision" that results in conflicting policies and unintended consequences.[60]

Prior to the creation of the OIRA, there existed a number of agencies structured to be highly independent. The Interstate Commerce Commission (hereinafter "ICC") and the Civil Aeronautics Board (hereinafter "CAB") are classic examples of "independent" agencies gone wrong.[61] Both of those agencies were, like the CFPB, designed to be highly independent, and both of those agencies were ultimately abolished in a bipartisan effort to restructure or abolish government agencies which had, as a consequence of their extreme independence, created policies conflicting with other sectors and had created results counterproductive to their purpose.[62]

The ICC was created in 1887, making it the nation's very first independent regulatory agency.[63] The agency was originally put into place to regulate interstate rates charged by railroads, but its power was gradually increased by Congress to include numerous other aspects of interstate rail travel, including safety and racial discrimination.[64] Then, in the late 1970s through early 1980s, the Executive Branch began using its appointment power to fill the Board of Commissioners that ran the ICC with individuals "fervently dedicated to deregulation."[65] The ICC pursued deregulation with such narrow-mindedness and zeal that "courts ... found it necessary to remind the ICC that Congress' decision to enter into comprehensive regulation contravenes the ICC's apparent belief that

---

[59] *See infra* Part IV.B (discussing how no meaningful restraints exist on the CFPB's ability to make decisions without input from outsiders with different views and interests).

[60] *See* Stearns & Zywicki, *supra* note 44, at 363.

[61] *See Id.* at 326.

[62] *See Id.* (discussing the abolishment of the CAB and the ICC).

[63] *See* Paul Stephen Dempsey, *Transportation: A Legal History*, 30 Transp. L.J. 235, 265 (2003), available at: http://papers.ssrn.com/sol3/papers.cfm?abstract_id=1793331.

[64] *See Id.* at 265, 267–269, 315–316.

[65] *See Id.* at 347.

national policy unqualifiedly favors competition."[66] The United States Court of Appeals for the Sixth Circuit accused the ICC of "disregarding congressional intent by making decisions solely for the purpose of increasing competition."[67] Congress ultimately abolished the ICC in 1995.[68]

In 1938, Congress created the Civil Aeronautics Authority, which it then reorganized the subsequent year as the CAB, to regulate the airline industry, much as the ICC regulated the railroads.[69] The CAB was based off of the ICC; in fact, President Roosevelt had initially wanted to give the ICC the power to regulate the airlines rather than create a new agency, but that was avoided out of a concern that the ICC would protect railroad interests over aviation interests.[70] Like the ICC, the CAB began to suffer from narrow-minded tunnel vision in the 1970s, focusing on deregulation as the answer to all the airline industry's problems.[71] Congress ultimately abolished the CAB in legislation passed in 1978, though the CAB continued operating until it winded down in 1984.[72] The legislation passed with "overwhelming bipartisan support."[73]

Other agencies suffering from similar independence-related problems, such as the Federal Trade Commission (hereinafter "FTC"), were dramatically reformed to significantly increase congressional oversight.[74] Originally created in 1914, the FTC is charged with protecting consumers from fraud in the marketplace and "preventing anticompetitive business practices."[75] As it exists today, the FTC is run by "five Presidentially-appointed, Senate-confirmed commissioners," who each serve in seven-year terms.[76] At any given time, a maximum of three of the five commissioners may be members of the President's political party.[77] This type of structure, with a multimember commission as opposed to a single director, reduces the risk of narrow-minded behavior and inconsistent policies, but perhaps not

---

[66] *See Id.* at 349.

[67] *See Id.* (citing Argo-Collier Truck Lines v. United States, 611 F.2d 149, 155 (6th Cir. 1979)).

[68] *See Id.* at 350.

[69] *See Id.* at 289–290.

[70] *See Id.* at 290.

[71] *See Id.* at 333–336.

[72] *Id.* at 336.

[73] *Id.*

[74] *See* Zywicki, *supra* note 19, at 871–872.

[75] Spencer Weber Waller, Jillian G. Brady & R.J. Acosta, *Consumer Protection in the United States: An Overview*, Eur. J. Consumer L. 803, 805–807 (2011), available at: http://papers.ssrn.com/sol3/papers.cfm?abstract_id=1000226.

[76] *Id.*

[77] *Id.*

enough. Even adding congressional budgetary authority may not be enough; one of the most independent modern regulatory agencies is the Federal Reserve itself, which — while run by a multimember commission and subject to congressional budgetary authority, unlike the CFPB — has been guilty of focusing too narrowly on a particular goal, not taking into account the effect on the other government sectors and on the economy as a whole.[78] This highlights why, as discussed in Part IV, the CFPB should not only be subject to congressional budgetary authority and run by a multimember commission, but should also be made subject to review by the OIRA and subject to more meaningful review from the FSOC.

The structure of the CFPB ignores these lessons from history

The CFPB is structured in a way that completely ignores the lessons learned from the failures of past agencies. First, the CFPB is completely exempt from the congressional appropriations process, instead receiving guaranteed funds from the Federal Reserve, equal to "the amount determined by the [CFPB] Director to be reasonably necessary to carry out the authorities of the [CFPB] … ."[79] Thus, the CFPB Director has sole discretion in determining how large the agency's budget will be, subject to statutory limits. In 2011, the limit was 10% of the Federal Reserve's total operating expenses, with the limit increasing to 11% in 2012, and 12% in 2013, with the 12% rate applying to each year thereafter.[80] This resulted in the CFPB receiving $162 million in mandatory appropriations in 2011[81] and $344 million in 2012,[82] with a total of $522 million appropriated for the 2013 fiscal year.[83] Thus, during the 2013 fiscal year, the CFPB will be receiving more than half a billion dollars in mandatory appropriations with no budgetary

---

[78] *See* Steven A. Ramirez, *Depoliticizing Financial Regulation*, 41 Wm. & Mary L. Rev. 503, 548–550 (2000). Shortly after President Reagan's election, Congress enacted and the President approved $540 billion in tax cuts as a part of a fiscal stimulus meant to promote economic growth. *Id.* The Federal Reserve responded by allowing short-term interest rates to skyrocket up to 20.5% in pursuit of its desire to have tighter monetary policies; the Federal Reserve's actions conflicted with the efforts of Congress and contributed to a sharp increase in unemployment, along with a sharp decrease in the gross national product. *Id.*

[79] 12 U.S.C. §5497(a)(1) (2012).

[80] *Id.* §5497(a)(2)(A).

[81] Office of Mgmt. & Budget, The Budget for Fiscal Year 2013: Other Independent Agencies 1295, available at: http://www.whitehouse.gov/sites/default/files/omb/budget/fy2013/assets/oia.pdf.

[82] Office of Mgmt. & Budget, The Budget for Fiscal Year 2014: Other Independent Agencies 1205-06, available at: http://www.whitehouse.gov/sites/default/files/omb/budget/fy2014/assets/oia.pdf.

[83] *Id.*

oversight from Congress, the Federal Reserve, or anyone else outside of the CFPB. While this may be a reasonable cost to run an agency of the CFPB's size and magnitude, the concern is not just the amount of money but the fact that by having its appropriations guaranteed the CFPB is exempt from congressional appropriations authority, which leaves Congress without any meaningful way to oversee the actions of the CFPB.[84]

Second, the CFPB is led by a single director who is appointed for a fixed term of five years and can only be removed for "cause," meaning "inefficiency, neglect of duty, or malfeasance in office."[85] This differentiates the CFPB from most other federal regulatory agencies, which are led by multimember commissions or boards, including the CPSC,[86] which was "the inspiration for the [CFPB's] creation";[87] the FTC;[88] the Commodities Futures Exchange Commission;[89] the Federal Deposit Insurance Corporation;[90] the Federal Reserve;[91] and the Securities and Exchange Commission (hereinafter "SEC").[92] To be sure, many agencies are headed by a single director, but unlike the director of the CFPB these directors are almost always removable at the pleasure of the President or another specified official, and

---

[84] *See infra* Part IV.A (arguing that the CFPB should be subject to some degree of congressional oversight).

[85] 12 U.S.C. §5491(c)(1)–(3) (2012).

[86] *U.S. Consumer Product Safety Commission Organizational Chart*, U.S. Consumer Prod. Safety Comm'n, http://www.cpsc.gov/PageFiles/128975/orgchart.pdf (last visited May 10, 2013) (showing that the Commission is headed by a group of five Commissioners).

[87] Barkow, *supra* note 45, at 72.

[88] *Commissioners*, Fed. Trade Comm'n, http://www.ftc.gov/commissioners/index.shtml (last modified March 21, 2013) ("The Commission is headed by five Commissioners, nominated by the President and confirmed by the Senate, each serving a seven-year term.").

[89] *Commissioners*, U.S. Commodity Futures Trading Comm'n, http://www.cftc.gov/About/Commissioners/index.htm (last visited May 10, 2013) ("The Commission consists of five commissioners appointed by the President, with the advice and consent of the Senate, to serve staggered five-year terms.... No more than three commissioners at any one time may be from the same political party.").

[90] *Board of Directors & Senior Executives*, Fed. Deposit Ins. Corp., http://www.fdic.gov/about/learn/board/index.html (last updated March 5, 2013) (showing that the Corporation is run by a Board of five Directors).

[91] *About the Fed*, Fed. Reserve, http://www.federalreserve.gov/aboutthefed/default.htm (last updated Apr. 24, 2013) (showing that the Federal Reserve is headed by a seven-member Board).

[92] *Current SEC Commissioners*, U.S. Sec. & Exch. Comm'n, http://www.sec.gov/about/commissioner.shtml (last modified Apr. 11, 2013) ("The SEC has five Commissioners who are appointed by the President of the United States with the advice and consent of the Senate. Their terms last five years and are staggered ... . To ensure that the Commission remains non-partisan, no more than three Commissioners may belong to the same political party.").

they generally do not hold any significant policymaking responsibilities.[93] An example is the Food and Drug Administration, which is led by a single commissioner who serves at the pleasure of the Secretary of the Department of Health and does not wield any significant policymaking authority.[94]

Third, the CFPB is not subject to OIRA review,[95] and thus the safeguard against the historical problem of independent agencies creating policies conflicting with other government sectors or not coherently fitting into the overall regulatory scheme does not apply to the CFPB. The only body that can override decisions of the CFPB is the Financial Stability Oversight Council (hereinafter "FSOC"), which was created as a part of Dodd–Frank[96] to be a "collaborative body chaired by the Secretary of the Treasury that brings together the expertise of the federal financial regulators, an independent insurance expert appointed by the President, and state regulators" for the purpose of "identifying risks and responding to emerging threats to financial stability."[97] The FSOC has 10 voting members, made up of the heads of the 9 federal financial regulatory agencies and 1 independent member appointed by the President, who must have insurance expertise.[98] The FSOC can only override CFPB decisions by a two-thirds vote, and each member of the FSOC can only vote to set aside a regulation of the CFPB if the agency or department that the member represents has "made an official determination, at a public meeting where applicable, that the regulation which is the subject of the petition would put the safety and soundness of the United States banking system or the stability of the financial system of the United States at risk."[99]

The FSOC thus has very limited oversight authority over the CFPB; a regulation passed by the CFPB will still become effective even if a majority of the FSOC's members — who are some of the most knowledgeable people in the world when it comes to designing effective regulations — vote against it after the department or agency they represent has made an official determination that the regulation would "put the safety and soundness of the United States banking

[93] *See* Zywicki, *supra* note 19, at 873–874.

[94] *See* James T. O'Reilly, 1 Food & Drug Admin. §2:2 (2012).

[95] Hester Peirce, *Economic Analysis by Federal Financial Regulators* 5–6 (Mercatus Ctr., George Mason Univ., Working Paper No. 12-31, 2012), available at: http://mercatus.org/sites/default/files/FinancialRegulators_Peirce_v1-0.pdf.

[96] *See* 12 U.S.C. §5513 (2012).

[97] *Financial Stability Oversight Council: About FSOC*, U.S. Dep't of the Treasury, http://www.treasury.gov/initiatives/fsoc/about/Pages/default.aspx (last updated May 10, 2013).

[98] 12 U.S.C. §5321(b)(1) (2012).

[99] *Id.* §5513(c)(3).

system or the stability of the financial system of the United States at risk."[100] This is a virtually insurmountable standard, and an unreasonable one, considering that any one of these regulatory experts making such a determination should be enough to at least warrant a second look at the regulation so the dissenter's concerns can be considered.

Taken collectively, the above provisions may well make the CFPB the most independent agency in United States history,[101] and it is difficult to imagine an agency design more likely to result in the agency acting with the type of tunnel vision focus on its regulatory mission that led to conflicting and incoherent regulatory policies prior to the reforms of the 1970–1980.[102] For example, in an effort to protect consumers the CFPB might overly restrict access to mortgages and other financial products, resulting in otherwise qualified consumers, who would benefit from the financial products, being denied access. In addition to being a bad policy that would likely hurt more consumers than it would help, such a policy might conflict with efforts by other government sectors to help consumers purchase homes. These types of conflicting policies can lead to incoherent and inconsistent results, creating uncertainty for consumers.

The more independent an agency is the more likely it is that it will become isolated and will create policies with only its own goals in mind, not taking into consideration or understanding how the policies will affect other sectors or the financial system as a whole.[103] This risk is further amplified by the CFPB being led by a single director, who has broad authority to engage in rulemaking. The CFPB Director has no multimember commission to answer to, no higher authority to answer to in budgetary appropriations (in fact, the CFPB Director himself sets the agency's budget, subject to statutory limitations),[104] and any policy initiatives of the director and the agency as a whole are subject to oversight only by the FSOC, which can only defeat CFPB regulations with a supermajority vote of its voting members.[105] Moreover, the members of the FSOC cannot even vote against a CFPB regulation except in the extreme circumstance of a threat so severe that it "put[s] the [very] safety and soundness of the United States banking system or the stability of the [United States] financial system … at risk."[106]

---

[100] *See Id.*

[101] *See infra* Part IV (discussing how most other regulatory agencies are subject to congressional appropriations authority and are led by multimember boards or commissions).

[102] *See* Stearns & Zywicki, *supra* note 44, at 363.

[103] *See Id.*

[104] *See* 12 U.S.C. §5497(a)(1) (2012).

[105] *See Id.* §5513(c)(3)(A).

[106] *See Id.* §5513(c)(3)(B).

The CFPB's extreme independence is touted as one of its greatest virtues, but history has shown that while independence from political pressure can be a virtue, near total isolation is not. The CFPB must be reformed in order to effectively carry out its mission of protecting consumers, or it may well ultimately inadvertently harm the very consumers it was designed to protect.

Despite its broad power, the CFPB cannot prevent another crisis

The CFPB was put into place not just to protect consumers but also as a safeguard against a future crisis. According to the Senate report on the Dodd–Frank Act, "it was the failure by the prudential regulators to give sufficient consideration to consumer protection that helped bring the financial system down."[107] However, as discussed in the subsequent section, while a lack of sufficient consumer protection did contribute to the financial crisis, it was just one of a great many factors, and a fairly minor one at that. Thus, even assuming that the CFPB can succeed where other regulators have failed and provide for the optimum level of consumer protection without cutting potential borrowers off from the credit markets unnecessarily, the CFPB still would not be able to prevent another crisis.

Causes of the financial crisis

An in-depth analysis of what caused the financial crisis is outside the scope of this Note, but a general overview is needed in order to put into context the issue of consumer protection. A good place to start is the findings of the Financial Crisis Inquiry Commission (hereinafter "FCIC"), which was created as a part of the Fraud Enforcement and Recovery Act of 2009 to "examine the causes, domestic and global, of the current financial and economic crisis in the United States."[108] The FCIC was composed of a ten-member panel, six of which were appointed by the Democratic leadership of Congress and four by the Republican leadership.[109] The majority's report is over four hundred pages long,[110] which is an indication

---

[107] S. Rep. No. 111-176, at 166 (2010).

[108] *About the Commission: History of the Commission*, Fin. Crisis Inquiry Comm'n, http://cybercemetery.unt.edu/archive/fcic/20110310173617/http://www.fcic.gov/about (last visited May 10, 2013).

[109] *Id.*

[110] Nat'l Comm'n on the Causes of the Fin. & Econ. Crisis in the U.S., Fin. Crisis Inquiry Comm'n, The Financial Crisis Inquiry Report vi (2011), available at: http://cybercemetery.unt.edu/archive/fcic/20110310173545/http://c0182732.cdn1.cloudfiles.rackspacecloud.com/fcic_final_report_full.pdf.

of the complexity of the issue and the difficulty in determining what the root causes of the crisis were.

The FCIC found that "widespread failures in financial regulation and supervision proved devastating to the stability of the nation's financial markets," noting that while regulators had the power to protect the financial system, that power was not adequately exercised.[111] The government as a whole was not prepared for the crisis, and the various regulatory agencies did not respond in a consistent manner, which contributed to the crisis by creating uncertainty and panic.[112] This finding underscores the importance of a coherent and consistent regulatory scheme and the need for the regulatory agencies to be interconnected with each other and the rest of the government. A powerful independent agency such as the CFPB is even more likely to cause confusion and panic than the other regulatory agencies because it has a narrow focus, broad power, and it is nearly completely independent from the other agencies and the rest of the government.[113]

The FCIC next identified as a "key cause" of the crisis "dramatic failures of corporate governance and risk management at many systemically important financial institutions."[114] Many of these institutions either drastically misjudged the risk of mortgage-related securities built with subprime mortgages or were so focused on short-term gains that they ignored these risks.[115] Normally we would expect institutions that take such big bets and lose to simply fail and be swallowed up, but because these institutions are so intrinsic to the financial system as a whole they were considered TBTF.[116] This resulted in many of the financial institutions being "bailed out."[117] A related factor was executive compensation, which was often focused on short-term gain without proper regard for long-term consequences.[118] The compensation systems greatly incentivized taking highly risky actions because of the potential for huge profits on the upside and limited downside.[119] In fact, acting in

---

[111] *Id.* at xviii.

[112] *See Id.* at xxi.

[113] *See* Zywicki, *supra* note 19 at 872 ("[T]he institutional structure of the CFPB … [makes it] a virtual poster child for an agency design that eventually will be likely to manifest the bureaucratic pathologies that led to the disastrous regulatory policies that were abandoned in the 1970s.").

[114] Nat'l Comm'n on the Causes of the Fin. & Econ. Crisis in the U.S., *supra* note 109, at xviii–xix.

[115] *See Id.*

[116] *See Id.* at 37.

[117] *See Id.* at xxv.

[118] *See Id.* at xix.

[119] *Id.*

a prudent, risk-adverse manner was highly discouraged by such compensation systems.

Another cause identified by the FCIC was a race to the bottom in mortgage-lending standards prompted by an ever-increasing demand for mortgage-backed securities.[120] Many lenders "simply took eager borrowers' qualifications on faith, often with a willful disregard for a borrower's ability to pay."[121] These subprime mortgages often included an "option ARM" and other terms that made the payments backloaded, so that the payments would start out at an affordable level but gradually rise, sometimes by large percentages.[122] Some lenders and third parties went even further, engaging in predatory practices, with some of the more unscrupulous "openly stalking desperate families looking for a financial lifeline."[123] When the housing bubble popped and housing prices fell, many borrowers found themselves owing significantly more than the property was worth.[124] This was not limited to subprime borrowers; as the crisis deepened, even buyers who were well-qualified at the time they bought their home and who had put down reasonable down payments found themselves underwater on their mortgage, resulting in some middle class and even "rich" borrowers strategically defaulting.[125] Strategic defaults are themselves a contributory factor to the depth of the crisis; they did not cause the crisis, but they did widen its scope and slow the economic recovery.[126]

The credit-rating agencies also share in the blame; in the years leading up to the crisis, Moody's alone rated nearly 45,000 mortgage-backed securities with its coveted triple A rating, without which they would not have been nearly as

---

[120] *See* Id. at xxiii–xxiv ("We conclude collapsing mortgage-lending standards and the mortgage securitization pipeline lit and spread the flame of contagion and crisis.").

[121] *Id.*

[122] *See Id.*

[123] Christopher L. Peterson, *Foreclosure, Subprime Mortgage Lending, and the Mortgage Electronic Registration System*, 78 U. Cin. L. Rev. 1359, 1360 (2010).

[124] *Id.* at 1359–1360.

[125] *See* Curtis Bridgeman, *The Morality of Jingle Mail: Moral Myths About Strategic Default*, 46 Wake Forest L. Rev. 123, 123–124 (2011) ("The decision to default even when one can afford to make the payments may make financial sense if the homeowner bought or refinanced at the height of the market and now owes much more than the house is currently worth.").

[126] *See Id.* at 153 ("Those who engage in strategic default not only threaten the stability of the banking system and slow down the economic recovery; they also fail to live up to their obligations to each of us, leaving us to pay for the money they borrowed, and for no better reason than because they find it in their best interests to do so.").

marketable.[127] About 83% of these mortgage-backed securities were ultimately downgraded, but the damage was already done.[128] This leads to the question of how they could have been so wrong, and a large part of the answer is that they had little incentive to get it right. The credit-rating agencies compete with each other for business, and because of the relatively limited field of potential clients, with the major financial institutions constituting the majority of their business, the credit-rating agencies have a strong incentive to give the institutions the ratings they want.[129] The institutions and the credit-rating agencies knew that the marketability of the mortgage-backed securities depended on them receiving triple A ratings, and if a credit-rating agency did not give the securities the needed rating then the institution issuing them would likely have turned to one of the other agencies.

This list of causes is far from exhaustive but is sufficient to show that numerous factors contributed to the financial crisis, with the lack of sufficient consumer protection being but one small piece of the problem. But even if a lack of sufficient consumer protection was the root cause of the financial crisis, the CFPB still would likely fail in preventing a future crisis. The FCIC did not find that the failure of the regulators to adequately protect consumers and the financial system as a whole stemmed from it lacking the power to act; rather, it found that the regulators failed to effectively use their power.[130] Consequently, the creation of a new highly independent regulator with broad authority is not the answer. As discussed further in the subsequent section, no amount of regulatory power invested in a wholly independent consumer protection agency can prevent a financial crisis. It can reduce the effects of a financial crisis, but it could just as easily worsen the effects, or even trigger a financial crisis itself by overly restricting access to credit.

In order to avoid such a result, the CFPB must not be isolated from other parts of the government and free from any significant oversight. Effective regulation can greatly help to reduce the risk of a financial crisis, but only when the regulatory scheme as a whole is coherent. Without a multimember commission, budgetary oversight, or any meaningful oversight on its policy making, the CFPB will likely become overly isolated and make policies without duly considering interests outside of its own narrow focus. In order to successfully

---

[127] *See* Nat'l Comm'n on the Causes of the Fin. & Econ. Crisis in the U.S., *supra* note 109, at xxv ("Investors relied on [the credit ratings], often blindly, and [i]n some cases … were obligated to use them, or regulatory capital standards were hinged on them.").

[128] *See Id.*

[129] *See* John C. Coffee, Jr., *Ratings Reform: The Good, the Bad, and the Ugly*, 1 Harv. Bus. L. Rev. 231, 232–234 (2011).

[130] *See* Nat'l Comm'n on the Causes of the Fin. & Econ. Crisis in the U.S., *supra* note 109, at xviii.

protect consumers and protect against another crisis, the CFPB must act as a part of a whole, not as a completely independent entity with broad power and a narrow focus.

The CFPB cannot prevent another crisis

The CFPB has broad authority over transactions with consumers, including the authority to take action against a covered person or service provider who engages in "unfair, deceptive, or abusive act[s] or practice[s] under Federal law in connection with any transaction with a consumer for a consumer financial product or service, or the offering of a consumer financial product or service."[131] The CFPB also has the power to prescribe rules relating to any such conduct, including requirements imposed for the purpose of preventing such acts or practices from occurring.[132] The CFPB was granted this authority to further its purpose, which is to "ensure[ ] that all consumers have access to markets for consumer financial products and services and that markets for consumer financial products and services are fair, transparent, and competitive."[133]

The CFPB's broad authority over transactions with consumers cannot address many of the causes of the crisis, and inadequate consumer protection was not a significant enough cause on its own for improvements in that area to prevent another crisis.[134] The CFPB has a role to play in preventing a future crisis, but only if it acts in conjunction with the other regulatory agencies so that the overall regulatory scheme is coherent. The statute creating the CFPB purports to require that it coordinate with the other agencies, saying that "[t]he Bureau shall coordinate with the Commission, the Commodity Futures Trading Commission, the FTC, and other Federal agencies and State regulators, as appropriate, to promote consistent regulatory treatment of consumer financial and investment products and services."[135] However, because of the lack of any meaningful oversight of the CFPB's actions, this purported requirement has no force.

---

[131] Dodd–Frank Wall Street Reform and Consumer Protection Act (Dodd–Frank), Pub. L. No. 111-203, §1031(a), 124 Stat. 1376, 2005 (codified at 12 U.S.C. §5531(a) (2012)).

[132] *Id.* §1031(b) (codified at 12 U.S.C. §5531(b) (2012)).

[133] *Id.* §1021(a) (codified at 12 U.S.C. §5511(a) (2012)).

[134] Nat'l Comm'n on the Causes of the Fin. & Econ. Crisis in the U.S., *supra* note 109 (identifying numerous causes of the financial crisis in a majority report spanning more than 400 pages, with inadequate consumer protection just being one factor of many).

[135] Dodd–Frank §1015 (codified at 12 U.S.C. §5495 (2012)).

How to fix the CFPB

The CFPB must undergo significant reform in order to avoid it acting with the same type of tunnel vision that led to the abolishment of the CAB and ICC.[136] An agency should not act inside a vacuum; in fact, an agency should not be allowed to act with such a degree of independence that it could take actions in conflict with other government actors without Congress or anyone else having any meaningful way to prevent the action. The risks associated with the level of independence possessed by the CFPB far outweigh any corresponding benefits, and there is no legitimate reason why the CFPB should be structured so differently from the other regulatory agencies.

That is not to say that having an agency possess some level of independence is in no way beneficial. Some degree of political and financial independence can be valuable for an agency like the CFPB because such independence insulates it from outside pressures, potentially allowing it to take action when other sectors of the government fail to do so. A balance must therefore be struck between having enough autonomy to operate effectively and being subject to enough oversight to ensure that the overall regulatory scheme is consistent and that decisions are not made in an overly narrow-minded fashion. The CFPB's current structure gives it far too much independence, making the risk of it creating narrow-minded policies, potentially conflicting with the actions of other government sectors and thus making the overall regulatory scheme inconsistent and incoherent, far greater than any potential benefits of such a high level of independence. With some prudent reforms, the CFPB can maintain a useful level of autonomy while being subject to enough oversight to negate the risks posed by its current structure.

The CFPB should be subject to congressional oversight

As it is currently structured, the CFPB is virtually completely insulated from congressional oversight, with the only notable exception being the Senate's power to confirm the Director. However, this exception has not yet had much significance other than potentially delaying the appointment of the CFPB's inaugural director and dissuading President Obama from nominating Elizabeth Warren, since the CFPB's inaugural director has not actually been confirmed by the Senate.[137] In any event, the CFPB is free from congressional appropriations authority, or even

---

[136] *See supra* notes 62–72 and accompanying text (discussing the history and ultimate abolishment of the CAB and ICC).

[137] *See supra* Part I.A (discussing the appointment of CFPB Director Richard Cordray).

appropriations authority from the Federal Reserve, and appropriations authority is one of the most effective means of congressional oversight.[138]

Those against giving Congress appropriations authority argue that doing so would make the CFPB vulnerable to political influence.[139] To the extent that Congress is made up of individual members, each of whom holds his or her own political beliefs, subjecting the CFPB to congressional appropriations authority will subject the CFPB to some degree of political influence. But the same can be said for virtually every other expense of the government, including the budgets of all the agencies that are subject to the congressional appropriations process, which includes two of the other federal financial regulators: the SEC[140] and the Commodities Futures Exchange Commission.[141]

By giving Congress appropriations authority over the CFPB, Congress will at least have some mechanism of oversight over the CFPB, which could serve as a means of ensuring that the CFPB considers various different viewpoints and interests. And even if the balance between restricting autonomy and reducing the risks created by the CFPB's high level of independence was found, in the case of congressional appropriates authority, to weigh against granting that authority, the CFPB's current structure should not be retained. A less intrusive alternative to giving Congress direct appropriations authority would be to instead make the CFPB subject to appropriations authority from the Federal Reserve. Under this scenario, instead of the CFPB Director setting the agency's budget himself,[142] the seven-member Board of Governors of the Federal Reserve[143] would set the CFPB's budget based on its needs and the needs of the CFPB. This would at least subject the CFPB to some oversight authority, and would make it less removed from the congressional appropriations process since the CFPB budget would then be a part of the Federal Reserve's budget that could be changed by the Federal Reserve based on congressional input.

---

[138] *See* Barry R. Weingast & Mark J. Moran, *Bureaucratic Discretion or Congressional Control? Regulatory Policymaking by the Federal Trade Commission*, 91 J. Pol. Econ. 765, 767–769 (1983).

[139] *See* Arthur E. Wilmarth, Jr., *The Financial Services Industry's Misguided Quest to Undermine the Consumer Financial Protection Bureau*, 31 Rev. Banking & Fin. L. 881, 951 (2012).

[140] *Id.*

[141] *Id.*

[142] 12 U.S.C. §5497(a)(1) (2012) ("Each year … the Board of Governors shall transfer to the Bureau from the combined earnings of the Federal Reserve System, the amount determined by the [CFPB] Director to be reasonably necessary to carry out the authorities of the Bureau under Federal consumer financial Law … .").

[143] *See About the Fed*, *supra* note 90.

The CFPB should be headed by a multimember commission

The CFPB is unusual in that it is both an independent agency with rulemaking authority and it is led by a single director. This is made even more unusual by that single director being insulated from removal except for "cause," meaning "inefficiency, neglect of duty, or malfeasance in office."[144] Most other regulatory agencies are headed by a multimember commission or Board,[145] and agencies that are led by only a single director usually do not have any significant rulemaking authority and are removable at the pleasure of the President or another delegated official.[146] Combining near total independence with broad rulemaking authority and a single director that cannot be removed except for cause is a recipe for disaster; any possible benefits that could result from such a structure are far outweighed by the corresponding risks.

Notably, some scholars disagree with the above assertion and argue that the single director structure should be retained. Professor Arthur E. Wilmarth, Jr., Executive Director of the Center for Law, Economics and Finance at George Washington University School of Law,[147] laid out his arguments against changing the current leadership structure of the CFPB in a recent article.[148] The crux of Professor Wilmarth's argument is that "the factors of efficiency, stability, decisiveness and accountability argue in favor of retaining CFPB's single-Director model of governance."[149] Modifying the agency to be led by a five-member commission would, according to Professor Wilmarth, "likely produce more delay and less consistency in CFPB's decisionmaking … [and] would expose CFPB to the risk of leadership deadlock whenever a commissioner left office."[150] The problem with that line of argument is that it applies to literally every agency headed by a multimember commission that has any decisionmaking authority. Indeed, Professor Wilmarth seems to advocate for doing away with multimember commissions altogether.[151]

---

[144] 12 U.S.C. §5491(c)(3) (2012).

[145] *See supra* notes 85–91 and accompanying text.

[146] *See* Zywicki, *supra* note 19 at 873–874.

[147] *Faculty Directory: Arthur E. Wilmarth, Jr.*, Geo. Wash. U. L. Sch., http://www.law.gwu.edu/Faculty/profile.aspx?id=1732 (last visited May 10, 2013).

[148] *See* Wilmarth, *supra* note 138 at 919–924.

[149] *Id.* at 921.

[150] *Id.*

[151] *See Id.* at 922 ("[T]he lengthy vetting process for Presidential nominees and prolonged Senate confirmation battles have frequently resulted in persistent vacancies and policy deadlocks at agencies with multimember commissions.").

Having a single director as opposed to a multimember commission does, admittedly, streamline the decision-making process making it easier for the agency to operate, much like having a dictatorship would make the government much more efficient compared to our current government with its checks and balances. If a single individual controlled all aspects of the government, then policies could be created and implemented in much less time and that individual would be able to ensure that the government acts as a unified whole. An extreme analogy, but it illustrates the point that efficiency concerns should not be the key factor in determining the optimum agency structure. The value of discourse should not be understated; having a multimember commission of individuals with different ideological views could drastically improve the decision-making process.[152]

When a group of people with different ideological views must come to a decision, it forces the proponents of each course of action to articulate reasoned arguments supporting their view, which allows both sides to see the strengths and weaknesses of their positions, thus allowing them to reach an informed decision.[153] Of course, this may be a somewhat optimistic view. In some cases, views and positions are so divergent that no real middle ground can be found. But even in those instances, where the majority does not alter its position and takes action irrespective of strong objections by the minority, the existence of the minority still serves a valuable function as it can serve as a whistleblower to actions taken by the majority which have potentially serious ramifications.

Professor Wilmarth warns of a "threat of institutional paralysis" if the CFPB is headed by a multimember commission; a threat he argues will be heightened if any such commission is limited to only having three of the five members affiliated with the same political party.[154] However, other regulatory agencies have exactly that structure, including the FTC,[155] the Commodities Futures Exchange Commission,[156]

---

[152] *See* Stephen M. Bainbridge, *Why a Board? Group Decisionmaking in Corporate Governance*, 55 VAND. L. REV. 1, 12 (2002) ("[N]umerous studies have found that group decisions are not only superior to those of the average member, but also to those made by the very best individual decisionmakers within the group.").

[153] *See Id.* at 29 ("Although individuals may well be better at devising a brilliant plan, individuals often become wedded to their plans and fail to see flaws that others might identify.").

[154] *See* Wilmarth, *supra* note 138, at 921.

[155] 15 U.S.C. §41 (2012) (stating that the FTC "shall be composed of five Commissioners, who shall be appointed by the President, by and with the advice and consent of the Senate" and that no "more than three of the Commissioners shall be members of the same political party").

[156] 7 U.S.C. 2(a)(2)(A) (2012) ("The Commission shall be composed of five Commissioners who shall be appointed by the President, by and with the advice and consent of the Senate … . Not more than three of the members of the Commission shall be members of the same political party").

and the SEC.[157] These agencies have been creating policies and making decisions for decades without suffering from "institutional paralysis." There is no reason to expect that the typical structure of a five-member commission with a maximum of three members being from the same political party would not work for the CFPB when it has for so many other agencies, and having a multimember commission ensures that meaningful discourse will take place in reaching decisions.

As Professor Wilmarth points out, the director of the CFPB is currently statutorily required to consult with others before making major policy decisions.[158] While technically true, these requirements unfortunately ring hollow. Professor Wilmarth's first example is that the director must seek advice from the CFPB's Consumer Advisory Board.[159] The Dodd–Frank Act specifies that "[t]he Director shall establish a Consumer Advisory Board to advise and consult with the [CFPB] in the exercise of its functions under the Federal consumer financial laws, and to provide information on emerging practices in the consumer financial products or services industry … ."[160] Other than stating that appointments to the Board should be made "without regard to party affiliation" and that at least six of the members (the total number of which is not specified) must be appointed based on the recommendation of the regional Federal Reserve Bank Presidents, there is no constraint on the Director's power of appointment.[161] Nothing prevents the Director from simply filling the Board with individuals sharing the same ideological beliefs as himself, which would greatly limit how effectively it could meaningfully contribute useful feedback on proposed policies. Moreover, even if the Director did not have sole discretion in appointing the Board members, the Board would still have little effectiveness because the Director is under no obligation to actually listen to anything the Board has to say. The Board is supposed to "advise and consult" with the CFPB, but it has no power whatsoever; the Director is free to simply disregard everything that the Board members say.[162]

Professor Wilmarth points to the small business advisory panel as another example of how the Director must consider outside interests.[163] Unfortunately, the

[157] 15 U.S.C. §78d(a) (2012) (stating that the SEC shall "be composed of five commissioners to be appointed by the President by and with the advice and consent of the Senate" and that no "more than three of such commissioners shall be members of the same political party").
[158] *See* Wilmarth, *supra* note 138, at 923.
[159] *See Id.*
[160] Dodd–Frank Wall Street Reform and Consumer Protection Act (Dodd–Frank), Pub. L. No. 111-203, §1014(a), 124 Stat. 1376, 1974 (codified at 12 U.S.C. §5495(a) (2012)).
[161] *Id.* §1014(b) (codified at 12 U.S.C. §5494(b) (2012)).
[162] *See* Id. §1014(a) (codified at 12 U.S.C. §5494(a) (2012)).
[163] *See* Wilmarth, *supra* note 138, at 923–924.

small business advisory panel is even more ineffective than the Consumer Advisory Board. The panel only plays any role at all when the proposed regulation would have an impact on the cost of credit for small businesses,[164] and even then it plays only a minor advisory role.[165] As with the Consumer Advisory Board, the panel has no authority whatsoever over the CFPB; the CFPB Director is free to form a panel filled with individuals sharing his ideological views, and free to completely ignore any input provided from the panel.[166] Thus, neither the Consumer Advisory Board nor the small business advisory panel adequately compensate for the lack of a multimember commission.

Finally, Professor Wilmarth points to how the CFPB is required to consult with the other federal financial regulators before adopting major policies.[167] The Dodd–Frank Act specifies that the CFPB "shall consult with the appropriate prudential regulators or other Federal agencies prior to proposing a rule and during the comment process regarding consistency with prudential, market, or systemic objectives administered by such agencies."[168] If the consulted regulator formally objects to the CFPB's proposed rule and provides the CFPB with a written objection, then the CFPB must respond to that objection in its release of the rule and provide the basis for the CFPB's decision.[169] This is Professor Wilmarth's most compelling point, because the CFPB does at least have to respond to the objection and provide some basis for its decision to proceed irrespective of the objection, but in the end the CFPB is still free to proceed as it pleases regardless of how many objections it receives and how compelling those objections are.

Thus, even taken in the aggregate, these requirements that the CFPB consult with other parties is no substitute for having the agency headed by a multimember commission. None of these other parties has any control over what policies the CFPB puts into place, and the Director is largely free to simply ignore any input received. By contrast, in a multimember commission, each member gets an equal vote, and each member's concerns and advice must therefore be taken seriously. Even if a majority of the commissioners share a similar ideology and agree on most points, a multimember commission is still far more effective than any of the consultation requirements Professor Wilmarth points to because it better protects

---

[164]*See* Dodd–Frank §1100G(b) (codified as amended at 5 U.S.C. §609 (2012)).

[165]*See Id.* (When applicable, the CFPB shall "identify representatives of small entities in consultation with the Chief Counsel for Advocacy of the Small Business Administration [and] collect advice and recommendations from the representatives … .").

[166]*See Id.*

[167]*See* Wilmarth, *supra* note 138, at 923.

[168]Dodd–Frank §1022(b)(2)(B) (codified at 12 U.S.C. §5512(b)(2)(B) (2012)).

[169]*See Id.* §1022(b)(2)(C) (codified at 12 U.S.C. §5512(b)(2)(C) (2012)).

against shortsighted or irrational policies. The members of the commission would be much more knowledgeable about the CFPB's operations and about the goals and intentions behind any particular policy than any outside party, and they would thus be in a better position to raise concerns or objections to the proposed policy. Moreover, because each commissioner would get a vote, the members with the minority viewpoint would only need to convince one of the three members with the majority viewpoint that a given action is unwise, or that a suggested change would be beneficial, in order for the proposed policy to be rejected or revised. By contrast, with a single director, he does not have to seriously consider any outside advice (or even advice from others inside the CFPB for that matter) before taking action.

What makes the one director structure especially dangerous in the context of the CFPB is that the director cannot even be removed from office by the President except for cause. If the single director structure is retained, the position should at least be modified to subject the director to removal at the discretion of the President. This is an imperfect solution as the CFPB director would still possess the same broad power that he does now and would still be able to act with little regard for concerns raised by other parties, but at least the President would have some mechanism to ensure that the actions taken by the director conform with the overall regulatory scheme and do not conflict with actions taken by other agencies. Presidential removal power would give the Executive Branch a means of constraining a director who acts with too narrow of a focus or otherwise does not act in conformance with the best interests of society as a whole. However, because it would still leave too much power in a single director and would not be enough to ensure that meaningful discourse takes place in the decision-making process, reforming the CFPB to be headed by a multimember commission is a far better solution.

The CFPB should be subject to OIRA review

Since its creation, the OIRA has been relied upon to ensure that the overall regulatory scheme is coherent and that the various agencies coordinate with each other to produce sound policies.[170] Over the course of the last 30 years, the general rule has been that all agencies must submit proposed regulations to the OIRA

---

[170] *See* STEARNS & ZYWICKI, *supra* note 44, at 366 (discussing how the OIRA is the primary office tasked with solving the "chronic" issue of creating a coherent regulatory scheme).

along with a cost–benefit analysis of the regulation.[171] An exception applies to "independent agencies"; agencies that are listed as such in the Paperwork Reduction Act do not have to submit their regulations to the OIRA for review.[172] The CFPB is included in this list, along with other regulatory agencies such as the FCC and the SEC.[173] Thus, the exclusion of the CFPB from OIRA review is not surprising or unusual, but as a matter of efficient policy it is puzzling why such an organization would not be subject to OIRA review. Sally Katzen, who served as the Administrator of the OIRA during the Clinton Administration, highlighted how critical the OIRA's role as overseer is:

> The agencies focus like a laser, as they should, on their statutory missions — in the case of EPA, protecting the environment. The White House and OIRA take a broader view and consider how, for example, an environmental proposal will affect energy resources, tax revenues, health policy, etc. Stated another way, EPA is pursuing a parochial interest; OIRA is tempering that with the national interest, as it should.[174]

As a policy matter, the reasoning behind subjecting an organization like the EPA to OIRA review seems to apply at least as strongly to an organization like the CFPB. Perhaps the reason independent regulatory agencies have historically been exempt from OIRA review is that they are generally headed by a multi-member commission, and this is considered enough of a substitute for OIRA review.[175] If that is the case, then exempting the CFPB makes very little sense

---

[171] *See* Id. at 366 ("OIRA reviews all economically significant regulations proposed by executive branch agencies, and its central tasks have been supported by Presidents of both parties for the past thirty years."); Barkow, *supra* note 45, at 31 ("Every president since Ronald Reagan has used OIRA to require agencies under OIRA's jurisdiction to justify their proposed regulations using cost–benefit analysis.").

[172] *See* Barkow, *supra* note 45, at 32.

[173] *See* 44 U.S.C. §3502(5) (2012).

[174] Sally Katzen, *A Reality Check on an Empirical Study: Comments on "Inside the Administrative State,"* 105 MICH. L. REV. 1497, 1505 (2007).

[175] *See* Zywicki, *supra* note 19, at 892 ("It is not clear why independent agencies have been exempted from OIRA's reach, … but one possible pragmatic or policy justification is that independent agencies have alternative mechanisms of ensuring quality control in the production of rules and other outputs, which Executive Branch departments often do not have … . For example, independent agencies typically are headed by a multi-member commission, often bipartisan in composition, and the information and debate produced in the resulting deliberative process may provide a partial substitute for OIRA review.").

considering its current structure,[176] but even if the CFPB is reformed to be headed by a multimember commission it should still be subject to OIRA review. The OIRA is in the best position to ensure that the regulatory scheme as a whole is coherent and consistent, but it cannot fully fulfill its role when agencies such as the CFPB are exempt from having to submit their proposed regulations for OIRA review.

The FSOC should be given enhanced veto power over the CFPB's regulations

With the CFPB's current structure, the FSOC is the only entity that can actually prevent a CFPB regulation from taking effect. It provides some oversight over the CFPB, but it is much too limited, because the standard for the FSOC to override a decision of the CFPB is so high that it is virtually insurmountable. Only a two-thirds vote of the FSOC's ten voting members, consisting of the heads of the nine federal financial regulatory agencies and one independent member appointed by the President,[177] can override a decision of the CFPB.[178] The CFPB Director, as a voting member of the FSOC,[179] counts for one of the ten votes on whether or not the CFPB's regulation should be overridden. As a practical matter, it is extremely unlikely that the CFPB Director will ever vote to override a regulation of the CFPB, which could not have been issued in the first place without his approval; thus, in order for the FSOC to override a CFPB regulation, seven of the remaining nine voting members — roughly 78% — must vote to override the regulation. As if this weren't daunting enough, a member of the FSOC can only vote to set aside a regulation of the CFPB if the agency or department that the member represents has "made an official determination, at a public meeting where applicable, that the regulation which is the subject of the petition would put the safety and soundness of the United States banking system or the stability of the financial system of the United States at risk."[180]

In order for the FSOC's oversight of the CFPB to be meaningful, the standard for it to set aside a CFPB regulation must be reduced to a more reasonable level. If instead of a two-thirds vote of the voting members the standard was a simple

[176] *See supra* discussion in Part IV.B (discussing how the CFPB currently has a single director instead of a multimember commission).

[177] Dodd–Frank Wall Street Reform and Consumer Protection Act (Dodd–Frank), Pub. L. No. 111-203, §111(b)(1), 124 Stat. 1376, 1985 (codified at 12 U.S.C. §5321(b)(1) (2012)).

[178] *See Id.* §1023(c)(3)(A) (codified at 12 U.S.C. 5513(c)(3)(A) (2012)).

[179] *Id.* §111(b)(1) (codified at 12 U.S.C. §5321(b)(1) (2012)).

[180] *Id.* §1023(c)(3)(B)(ii) (codified at 12 U.S.C. 5513(c)(3)(B)(ii) (2012)).

majority of the voting members — excluding the CFPB Director — then the FSOC would be in a much better position to ensure that the CFPB does not pass regulations with harmful effects. This would still be a very high standard; five out of the nine remaining voting members — roughly 56% — would have to vote to set aside the regulation, and each member would still only be able to vote if their organization had determined the regulation "would put the safety and soundness of the United States banking system or the stability of the financial system of the United States at risk."[181] Thus, any concern that such a change would give the FSOC too much control over the CFPB is misplaced. This reform would simply give the FSOC the power to effectively perform its oversight function, which is to ensure that CFPB regulations do not threaten the United States banking or financial system.[182]

It is worth noting that there is one other way for a regulation of the CFPB to be invalidated — the courts can intervene when an agency neglects its statutory obligations and have shown a willingness to do so in challenges involving other regulatory agencies.[183] But while the courts can, and at times will, invalidate agency regulations that are arbitrary and contrary to the agency's statutory obligation,[184] this is far too limited and too uncertain of a check on the CFPB's power. Part of the reason that it is an insufficient safeguard is that the Court must wait for a challenge to be brought before it can review an action of the CFPB; thus, it cannot review all actions of the CFPB, nor can it prevent them from taking effect prior to its review. But even more fundamentally, the courts are not a sufficient safeguard because their power to invalidate regulations is too limited. A court cannot invalidate regulations because they are bad policy or conflict with other regulations; the court needs a valid statutory or constitutional reason for invalidating a regulation. Moreover, a court's review does not help in the policy

---

[181] *See Id.*

[182] *See Id.*

[183] *See* Bus. Roundtable v. SEC, 647 F.3d 1144, 1144 (D.C. Cir. 2011) (invalidating a rule of the SEC because, as summarized in the Reporter: (1) the agency "neglected its statutory obligation to assess economic consequences of [the] rule by not making tough choices about which of [the] competing estimates regarding proxy contests was most plausible or to hazard a guess as to which was correct; (2) [the] SEC relied upon insufficient empirical data when it concluded that [the] rule would improve board performance and increase shareholder value by facilitating [the] election of dissident shareholder nominees; (3) [the] SEC acted arbitrarily and capriciously by not conducting [a] serious evaluation of costs that could be imposed upon companies from use of [the] rule by shareholders representing special interests, particularly union and government pension funds; (4) [the] SEC arbitrarily ignored [the] effect of [the] final rule upon [the] total number of election contests; and (5) [the SEC's] discussion of [the] estimated frequency of nomination under [the] rule was internally inconsistent and therefore arbitrary").

[184] *See, e.g., Id.*

creation stage, because its review generally is not conducted until the policy has already been implemented. A court cannot simply make suggestions on how to improve the policy; it must decide whether it is valid or not.

Conclusion

The CFPB currently suffers from the same structural deficiencies that led to the incoherent regulatory scheme that plagued the nation prior to the massive reforms put into place in the 1970s–1980s.[185] During that time period, agencies with similar structures to the CFPB were either abolished or drastically reformed, yet the CFPB is structured very similarly to those failed agencies, ignoring the lessons from the past. In order to avoid a repeat of the agency failures seen leading up to the reforms of the 1970s–1980s, the CFPB must be reformed.[186] While OIRA review largely solved the problem of conflicting and incoherent policies, the CFPB (and other independent regulatory agencies) are currently not subject to it, making it an incomplete solution to the overall problem and no help at all in the context of the CFPB.[187]

Moreover, while a lack of consumer protection contributed to the financial crisis, it was a relatively minor cause in comparison to others.[188] The CFPB cannot prevent another crisis on its own; it needs to work in conjunction with the other government sectors, not operate in a vacuum in which the CFPB can do as it sees fit without regard to broader interests. In order to effectively perform its function, do its part in preventing another financial crisis, and avoid suffering from the same type of tunnel vision that made past regulatory agencies that were similarly structured fail, the CFPB must be reformed.

First, the CFPB should be made subject to some degree of congressional oversight. Subjecting the CFPB to the congressional appropriations process would be a prudent way to ensure that the CFPB does not act in a way that is detrimental to the broader interests of the country. Second, the CFPB should be reformed to be led by a multimember commission instead of a single director. A multimember commission is superior to having a single director for a number of reasons, not the least of which is the benefits of having discourse in decisionmaking.

---

[185] *See supra* notes 64–77 and accompanying text.

[186] *See supra* Part II.

[187] *See supra* Part II.

[188] *See supra* Part III.

Third, the CFPB should be made subject to review by the OIRA, as should other similar independent agencies. The OIRA serves a valuable function: it ensures that the overall regulatory scheme is coherent and that the various agencies coordinate with each other and other government sectors to produce sound policies. But the OIRA cannot adequately perform this function when agencies like the CFPB are exempt from its review. All agencies, the CFPB included, should be subject to review by the OIRA — only then will the OIRA be able to effectively prevent conflicting and narrow-minded policies from being enacted and ensure that the overall regulatory scheme is consistent and coherent. Lastly, the CFPB should be subject to more meaningful review by the FSOC by reducing the vote needed to veto a CFPB action from two-thirds to one-half. The way the FSOC is structured, a two-thirds vote is a virtually insurmountable standard; by reducing the requirement to a simple majority the FSOC's role as an overseer of the CFPB will actually be fulfilled. Taken in the aggregate, these reforms will ensure that the CFPB adequately performs its function, does not act in an overly narrow-minded fashion, and does not enact policies that are inconsistent with the overall regulatory scheme. The result will be a more effective agency that will not be doomed to fail because of structural defects, but instead should continue to fulfill its mission for generations to come.

PART VII

Was Dodd–Frank Necessary? Needed?

Part VII discusses whether the Dodd–Frank legislation, and associated regulatory reform, was necessary to enable authorities to achieve the stated goals. The first chapter was prepared by the staff of Congressman Barney Frank and explains the reasoning behind Dodd–Frank. Why was it needed? What issues does it try to address? Why was the 'old' regulatory framework ineffective? The chapter has somewhat of a political tilt and concentrates on the need for a revised failure resolution process, however it makes the basic arguments as to why the legislation, and the regulatory reform more broadly, was necessary to protect consumers and taxpayers. The authors also include a brief postscript to the chapter to update it to account for events since the piece was originally released.

Alternatively, the chapter by Peter Wallison argues that Dodd–Frank was not needed. Interestingly, the President's Financial Crisis Inquiry Commission was created to evaluate the causes of the financial crisis and to make recommendations that could direct the regulatory reform. However, the Dodd–Frank Act became law *before* the Commission presented its findings addressing the causes of the crisis. Wallison participated on the Commission and disagreed with the findings of the report. As a result, he wrote a dissent from the majority position. Most importantly for the evaluation of Dodd–Frank, Wallison argues, and explains why, "Dodd–Frank was not the appropriate response" to the financial crisis.

Chapter 17

The Financial Crisis and "Too-Big-To-Fail"

Barney Frank and the Minority Staff of the House Financial Services Committee[1]

At the height of the financial crisis in 2008, the Bush administration believed that it was forced to choose between doing two unprecedented and undesirable things: propping up large failing financial companies at taxpayer risk on the one hand, or on the other permitting such companies to go through bankruptcy, with potentially catastrophic results for an already weak financial system.

Bush administration officials in most cases judged the risks associated with not acting to be unacceptably high. The Federal Reserve first provided direct aid under Section 13(3) of the Federal Reserve Act to support and facilitate the acquisition of Bear Stearns. Bush administration officials then let Lehman Brothers fail, but that choice proved to be highly destabilizing because the abrupt cessation of the company's operations, combined with its interconnectedness with other financial firms, caused freezing up of financial markets in the United States and around the world. Because of these seriously damaging economic consequences, the Bush administration concluded that bankruptcy was not up to the task of dismantling a complex financial intermediary, and the Federal Reserve again used Section 13(3) to support AIG. At the urgent request of the Bush administration,

[1]This analysis was released on October 15, 2012, and explicitly stated that it was in response to assertions that the Dodd–Frank Act perpetuates 'too-big-to-fail' and taxpayer bailouts of large financial institutions. At the time the chapter was originally released, Barney Frank was a congressman from Massachusetts who served as chairman of the House Financial Services Committee. He was a co-sponsor of the 2010 Dodd–Frank Act. In January 2014, Congressman Frank updated the chapter for this part to include a new *Conclusion and Postscript*.

Congress created the Troubled Asset Relief Program (TARP) to support a number of banks during the crisis. Bush administration officials also invoked the systemic risk exception in the Federal Deposit Insurance Act to allow the Federal Deposit Insurance Corporation (FDIC) to create a loan guarantee program for banks.

That the government was forced to prop up troubled firms to avoid a systemic collapse clearly demonstrated that the regulators' tool kit for managing the failure of large, interconnected financial firms, much of which was put in place when the financial system was significantly simpler, was inadequate. The provision of extraordinary government support blurred the line between liquidity support and solvency support and perpetuated the belief that some financial firms were "too-big-to-fail" (TBTF).

Wall Street reform addresses the TBTF problem at its roots

The Wall Street Reform and Consumer Protection Act addresses the TBTF problem at its roots by protecting the financial system without protecting the existence of any individual financial firm. It accomplishes this result through two basic means — first, by providing a set of tools to ensure that large, complex financial firms and the financial system in which they operate are more stable and transparent, and that regulators can supervise the financial system and its constituent parts more effectively; and second, by ensuring that a failing financial firm can fail in a fashion that minimizes risks to the financial system without any ultimate cost to taxpayers. As former Treasury Secretary Hank Paulson has made clear, if these tools had been in place before 2008, spillover effects of the crisis could have been managed with much less disruption in the economy and with no direct burden on the taxpayers.

Requiring companies to better manage risks and absorb losses, and giving regulators necessary tools to supervise The Wall Street Reform and Consumer Protection Act ensures that the largest, most interconnected firms are less likely to fail, not by preventing them from taking risks, but rather by making sure that they manage risks prudently and are capable of absorbing losses when they make mistakes. To that end, the law automatically places bank holding companies (BHCs) with assets of $50 billion or more under enhanced prudential supervision by the Federal Reserve,[2] and empowers the new Financial Stability Oversight

[2]Section 165, codified at 12 U.S.C. 5365. A BHC that received financial assistance under TARP and that subsequently divests it bank cannot escape stricter regulation unless it appeals to the FSOC and 2/3 of that body, including the Treasury Secretary, affirmatively vote to grant that appeal. See Section 117, codified at 12 U.S.C. 5327.

Council (FSOC) to designate nonbank financial companies for such supervision.[3] Enhanced supervision includes heightened capital, liquidity, and risk-management requirements; resolution plans, also known as "living wills," which demonstrate how a company could be resolved in an orderly fashion under the bankruptcy code; and rigorous stress tests.[4] These requirements will help companies to understand and manage their risk profiles more fully, and will allow regulators to target their attention more precisely on problem areas.

The Wall Street Reform and Consumer Protection Act empowers regulators to address a financial firm's size and activity mix in the event that these cause problems, but it does not assume that large size and certain activity combinations will always be problematic.[5]

The Wall Street Reform and Consumer Protect Act also strengthens the broader system within which the financial firms operate by giving the financial regulators a mandate and the necessary tools to address the health of the entire financial system, not just the safety and soundness of individual firms.[6] The FSOC, backed by an Office of Financial Research,[7] monitors the system for risks and can respond to identified threats not only by placing nonbank financial firms under Federal Reserve supervision, but also by providing for stricter regulation of systemically destabilizing activities and practices wherever they occur.[8] This will allow regulators to address, for example, destabilizing situations that are created not by the action of one firm, but by the collective action of many firms.

---

[3] Section 113, codified at 12 U.S.C. 5323.

[4] Section 165, codified at 12 U.S.C. 5365.

[5] The law allows regulators to require a company to downsize or to limit certain activities if necessary to prevent grave threats to the financial system, or if the company fails to produce a credible living will in a timely manner. See Section 121, codified at 12 U.S.C. 5331, and Section 165(d)(5), codified at 12 U.S.C. 5365(d)(5), respectively. An often-overlooked component of the Volcker Rule prevents the largest financial firms from growing through acquisitions of other firms after they reach certain limits, although it does not prevent their organic growth or prevent them from acquiring a failing firm. See Section 622, codified at 12 U.S.C. 1852.

[6] See generally Title I, Subtitle A, codified at 12 U.S.C. Sections 5321–5333; see also Section 604, codified within various banking laws, which requires regulators to consider the impact on financial stability as a factor when acting upon applications for structural changes and activity expansions.

[7] Title I, Subtitle B, codified at 12 U.S.C. 5341–5346.

[8] Section 120, codified at 12 U.S.C. 5330. This authority does not empower the FSOC to regulate systemically destabilizing activities directly, but rather allows the FSOC to provide for stricter regulation by making recommendations to the relevant primary regulator(s), which must either implement the recommendation or explain the failure to act to the FSOC. If a company engaged in a systemically destabilizing activity did not have a primary regulator, the FSOC could designate it for enhanced prudential supervision by the Federal Reserve in order to bring it within the scope of Section 120.

This authority, had it been in place before 2008, could have allowed regulators to prevent poor mortgage underwriting practices and the shedding of all associated risk through securitization. In addition, the Volcker Rule prohibits banking entities from making proprietary bets that could result in losses that, if severe and widespread enough, could cause the failure of one or more banking entities and create systemic problems.[9]

Some have claimed that the new supervisory tools discussed above are not workable because they leave too much to regulators, and because many key provisions, such as the Volcker Rule, do not draw bright lines. These critics should ask themselves two questions. First, would it be appropriate for Congress to write detailed rules that address many complex considerations and that need the capacity to evolve as facts and circumstances change? The answer to that clearly is "no." Second, is there any precedent for statutory provisions that involve general concepts that must be fleshed out by the regulators or courts over time? The answer to that clearly is "yes," as demonstrated by provisions such as securities disclosures based on "materiality," antitrust laws, and OSHA's recognition of "functionally equivalent" standards. All these provisions involve facts-and-circumstances tests that nonetheless have resulted in clear sets of expectations on the part of the regulated.

Others have claimed that the Wall Street Reform and Consumer Protection Act caused the largest financial firms to get bigger. This confuses correlation with causation and ignores the likely effects of the law. Some firms got bigger before the law was enacted because they acquired other large firms that were on the brink of failure. These mergers were done at the urging and with the cooperation of Bush administration officials, who felt that, given the tools available at the time, these mergers reduced taxpayer exposure. That result was compelled precisely because we did not have something like Wall Street reform in place to guard against weakness but also to allow the weak to fail. The requirements in the Wall Street Reform and Consumer Protection Act's new supervisory regime should result in firms naturally rationalizing their structure and perhaps downsizing, although it is not realistic to expect these changes overnight.

Providing a clear path to failure while protecting the financial system and taxpayers

In spite of the aforementioned tools designed to minimize the odds of failure, a financial firm still could fail. In that event, the Wall Street Reform and Consumer

[9] Section 619, codified at 12 U.S.C. 1851.

Protection Act provides the government with a clear, definitive path to ensure that the insolvent financial firm fails instead of being put on taxpayer-financed life support. The law recognizes that bankruptcy will remain the failure mechanism for the vast majority of nonbank financial firms and BHCs.[10] To address the rare situations in which the operations of a nonbank financial company or BHC are too complex or important to go through bankruptcy without significantly disrupting the entire financial system, the Wall Street Reform and Consumer Protection Act provides a new Orderly Liquidation Authority (OLA) as an alternative path to failure.[11] Having such an alternative ensures that the government never again will face the choice that it did in 2008 between propping up a failing firm or letting it fail at the risk of unacceptable systemic consequences.

The OLA has been the subject of substantial, and repeated, mischaracterizations by some, who claim that it entrenches TBTF, when in fact it does exactly the opposite. Below is a detailed discussion of how OLA would work in reality, based on the statutory framework and the FDIC's implementing rules.

The bar to use the OLA is very high

The Federal Reserve, the appropriate federal agency for the largest subsidiary of the failing firm, and the Treasury Secretary, in consultation with the President, must conclude that the company is failing and that its failure would cause serious adverse effects in the financial system.[12] If that determination were made, the FDIC would be appointed as receiver,[13] and would have many of the same powers it has had for many years when it liquidates failed banks, and which no legitimate critic has ever accused of being used to provide a "bailout."

The FDIC as receiver would be required to liquidate the firm within 5 years.[14] In the course of doing so, the FDIC would be required to fire culpable management

[10] Section 202(c), codified at 12 U.S.C. 5382(c).

[11] Title II, codified at 12 U.S.C. 5381–5394. The OLA preserves existing federal and state insolvency regimes as the resolution mechanism for any insolvent part of the failing company that already is subject to them, including banks subject to resolution under the FDI Act, broker–dealers that are SIPC members, and insurance companies that would be resolved by their state insurance regulator. See the "covered broker–dealer," "covered financial company," "covered subsidiary," and "financial company" definitions in Section 201, codified at 12 U.S.C. 5381. See also Section 203(e), codified at 12 U.S.C. 5383(e), and Section 205, codified at 12 U.S.C. 5385.

[12] Section 203(a)–(b), codified at 12 U.S.C. 5383(a)–(b).

[13] Section 202, codified at 12 U.S.C. 5382.

[14] Section 202(d), codified at 12 U.S.C. 5382(d). The only purpose for which a receivership may be extended beyond 5 years is to allow for the completion of ongoing litigation.

and directors, and to ensure that shareholders and unsecured creditors bear losses consistent with their first and second loss positions, respectively, in the statutory list of payment priorities.[15] The FDIC has authority to place some or all of the firm's assets in a bridge company, and the FDIC has indicated that it will use this authority.[16] It may do this, however, solely for the purpose of preserving financial stability during the liquidation, and it may not take any action to resuscitate the failed firm.[17] Use of the bridge authority will allow the FDIC to liquidate the firm's assets in a manner that does as little systemic harm as possible, and will occur in furtherance of, and be entirely consistent with, the statutory mandate that the firm be liquidated within a finite time.

In recognition that a failed firm's inability to honor any of its financial contracts could have cascading and far-reaching effects throughout the financial system, the OLA empowers the FDIC to pay some financial contracts, in whole or in part, to prevent a financial meltdown. The FDIC is authorized to transfer qualified financial contracts to a solvent financial institution, subject to specific requirements regarding notice, timing, and preservation of counterparty contractual rights.[18]

Counterparties to qualified financial contracts that are not transferred would stand in line with other unsecured creditors under priority-of-payment rules. These rules allow the FDIC to pay some unsecured creditors more than others similarly situated, or to pay some unsecured creditors more than the liquidation value they would have received in bankruptcy, but the FDIC may make such payments only for the purpose of minimizing "covered financial company," "covered subsidiary," and "financial company" definitions in Section 201, codified at 12 U.S.C. 5381. See also Section 203(e), codified at 12 U.S.C. 5383(e), and Section 205, codified at receivership losses or enabling the continuation of functions essential to the receivership.[19] The FDIC's implementing rule, however, provides that such payments cannot be made to shareholders, subordinated debt holders, and longer-term debt holders.[20]

To continue functions essential to the receivership and to pay creditor claims while the liquidation is in progress, the FDIC likely will need access to temporary

---

[15] Section 206, codified at 12 U.S.C. 5386.

[16] Section 210(h), codified at 12 U.S.C. 5390(h).

[17] See Section 206(1), codified at 12 U.S.C. 5386(1).

[18] Section 210(c)(8)–(12), codified at 12 U.S.C. 5390(c)(8)–(12).

[19] Sections 210(b)(4), (d)(4), and (h)(5)(E), codified at 12 U.S.C. 5390(b)(4), (d)(4), and (h)(5)(E), respectively.

[20] See the FDIC's rule implementing the OLA at 12 CFR Part 380, particularly §380.27; see also the Federal Register notice explaining that final rule, at 76 FR 41626 (July 15, 2011).

funding. For this reason, the Treasury Department is authorized to lend to the FDIC, but not until the FDIC has presented a plan acceptable to Treasury regarding how the FDIC actually will use the money.[21] The FDIC is authorized to use such borrowed funds solely for the purpose of taking actions that stabilize the financial system and explicitly is prohibited from taking any equity interest in the failing firm.[22] There are two statutory limits on the amount that Treasury can lend to the FDIC. First, Treasury can lend only up to a percentage of the failing company's assets.[23] While this is a legal maximum, the actual amount of Treasury lending to the FDIC would be substantially lower than this, because Treasury's transactions with the FDIC are public debt transactions and thus are limited by the debt ceiling.[24] In contrast, some of the extraordinary assistance provided to financial institutions in 2008, such as the Federal Reserve's lending under Section 13(3), was not subject to specific amount limits or the debt ceiling. In combination, the safeguards in the OLA's funding mechanism definitively show that there is no basis to claims that the OLA could be used to lend trillions of dollars to, or to save, a failing firm.

Claims that taxpayers will bear the cost of an Orderly Liquidation similarly are not based on the statute, which explicitly rules out the possibility that taxpayers ultimately will lose money.[25] First, the FDIC and the United States are the first creditors in line for repayment from the proceeds of the sale of the firm's assets.[26] Second, if the proceeds of the liquidation are insufficient to repay the

[21] Sections 204(d) and 210(n)(9), codified at 12 U.S.C. 5384(d) and 12 U.S.C. 5390(n)(9), respectively.

[22] Sections 204(d), 206(1), and 206(6), codified at 12 U.S.C. 5384(d), 12 U.S.C. 5386(1), and 12 U.S.S.C. 5386(6), respectively.

[23] Section 210(n)(6), codified at 12 U.S.C. 5390(n)(6), provides that, during the first 30 days of the receivership, the aggregate amount of outstanding debt that the FDIC issues or incurs in connection with an orderly liquidation cannot exceed 10% of the company's total consolidated assets based on the most recent financial statements available (unless the FDIC already has determined the fair value of the company's total consolidated assets that are available for repayment); after the first 30 days, or such earlier time as the FDIC determines the fair value of the company's total consolidated assets that are available for repayment, the amount of outstanding debt that the FDIC issues or incurs cannot exceed 90% of the fair value of the company's total consolidated assets that are available for repayment.

[24] Section 210(n)(5)(E), codified at 12 U.S.C. 5390(n)(5)(E).

[25] Section 214, codified at 12 U.S.C. 5394, specifically prohibits taxpayer funds from being used to prevent liquidation, requires that all taxpayer funds expended during a liquidation be recovered from the assets of the failed firm or through industry assessments, and provides that taxpayers shall not suffer losses from the exercise of the OLA.

[26] See Section 210(b)(1)(A)–(B), codified at 12 U.S.C. 5390(b)(1)(A)–(B), Section 204(d), and 12 CFR Part 380.

government, then the FDIC is required to claw back any payments it previously made to creditors beyond the liquidation value of their claims.[27] Finally, if those sources in combination were inadequate to repay the full amount of the temporary funding, then the FDIC would be mandated to impose risk-based assessments on financial firms with total consolidated assets of $50 billion or more to recover the remaining shortfall.[28] The statute thus unequivocally requires that the temporary funding Treasury provides be fully repaid, and no further congressional action is needed to ensure that result.

The Wall Street Reform and Consumer Protection Act affirms the value of liquidity support but ensures that it cannot turn into solvency support

Although the Wall Street Reform and Consumer Protection Act ends the need for solvency support, it recognizes that liquidity support may be entirely justified to enable healthy financial firms to withstand periods of systemic stress. The law therefore preserves liquidity tools but include safeguards to ensure that they do not become a backdoor through whichsolvency support could be provided. The Wall Street Reform and Consumer Protection Act amended Section 13(3) of the Federal Reserve Act so that the Fed now may provide emergency liquidity only to solvent firms, and only through facilities that have broad-based eligibility.[29] The law also ensures that the FDIC can establish a loan guarantee program only for solvent banking entities, which must pay a guarantee fee and are subject to backup assessments to ensure that the program pays for itself and there is no cost to taxpayers.[30]

---

[27] Section 210(o)(1)(D)(i), codified at 12 U.S.C. 5390(o)(1)(D)(i). The FDIC is required to establish rules, in consultation with the Treasury Secretary, regarding how to carry out the assessment authority in Section 210(o), including the creditor claw backs discussed here and the industry assessments discussed below.

[28] Section 210(o)(1)(D)(ii), codified at 12 U.S.C. 5390(o)(1)(D)(ii). These assessments would be determined using a risk matrix, developed by the FDIC in consultation with the FSOC, that takes into account, among other factors, the risks an assessed firm presents to the system and whether the firm or any of its subsidiaries pays into other insolvency regimes, such as the DIF, SIPC, or the state insurance guaranty system.

[29] Section 1101, which amends 12 U.S.C. 343. The Wall Street Reform and Consumer Protection Act did not amend the Federal Reserve's "discount window" authority, which was before the crisis, and remains, a lender-of-last resort authority under which the Fed charges above-market rates for fully collateralized loans to solvent banks.

[30] Section 1105, codified at 12 U.S.C. 5612.

The law also removes authority for the FDIC to provide open bank assistance to failing banks.[31]

The clearer distinction that the Wall Street Reform and Consumer Protection Act draws between solvency support and liquidity support would, if in effect in 2008, likely have eliminated the need for a program such as TARP, which blurred that distinction. Some have argued that, under the Wall Street Reform Law, the banking agencies and the Treasury nonetheless would rescue a failing firm, but, as former FDIC Chairman Sheila Bair recently has pointed out, they would be breaking the law if they did so. Similarly, Adair Turner, Head of the United Kingdom's Financial Services Authority, has acknowledged that US law no longer permits taxpayer funds to be used to provide support on an entity-specific basis.[32]

Empirical evidence suggests that the Wall Street Reform Act ends TBTF

The markets have affirmed that being subject to enhanced prudential supervision is not a guarantee of being TBTF in several important ways. Enhanced prudential supervision seems to be the gift that no one wants. In multiple congressional hearings, Democratic members of Congress have asked regulators how many nonbank firms have asked to be designated for heightened supervision; the answer consistently has been "none," and in fact some such firms actively have sought to avoid designation.[33] In addition, the rating agencies have downgraded many large financial companies, in part on the theory that extraordinary government support of the kind provided during and in the wake of the 2008 crisis is no longer likely.[34] At least 1 large bank CEO has indicated that, when one takes into

---

[31] Section 1106, which amends 12 U.S.C. 1823(c)(4)(G).

[32] See Adair Turner speech, entitled "*Reforming finance, are we being radical enough?*," dated February 18, 2011.

[33] See Rep. Frank's questioning of the government panel at a hearing held by the Oversight & Investigation subcommittee of the House Committee on Financial Services on April 14, 2011; see also Rep. Maloney's questioning of the government panel at a hearing held by the Financial Institutions and Consumer Credit subcommittee of the House Committee on Financial Services on June 14, 2011. In addition, many large BHCs have sought, through their comments on regulatory proposals, to minimize the consequences of automatically being subject to enhanced prudential standards.

[34] See, e.g., the Moody's rating action dated September 21, 2011. Moody's recognized that some forms of government support could remain, but opined that Wall Street Reform decreased the probability of the extraordinary support of the type extended during the crisis and increased the likelihood that the government might allow a large financial institution to fail because the contagion of such a failure could be contained. Some forms of ongoing "government support" for banking entities of all sizes

consideration the mix of assets and liabilities, funding costs for his firm are comparable to those of other financial firms, and are higher than those of nonfinancial companies.[35] This same CEO has indicated clearly that he thinks the Wall Street Reform and Consumer Protection Act provides the tools to end TBTF.[36] In the wake of the crisis, we witnessed the market turn against Bank of America, which saw its costs in the bond market increase more than its similarly-sized competitors in response to its deteriorated condition. All of the above-mentioned factors indicate that, because of the passage of the financial reform law, the long-assumed "funding advantage" of the largest financial firms is a thing of the past.

In addition to reactions here in the United States, policymakers in other countries, who similarly are attempting to end the need to rescue failing firms, are looking at the same sets of issues that Wall Street Reform addresses and taking similar actions. The Basel III accord among the G20 countries affirms the importance of higher capital, lower leverage, and improved liquidity coverage, and holds the largest, internationally-active banking entities to higher standards in these areas. The Financial Stability Board has proposed a resolution framework that its member countries should enact, which closely tracks OLA and starts to address the cross-border issues that no country can solve in isolation. In Great Britain, the ring-fencing proposal advocated by the Vickers Commission is designed to prevent commercial banks from taking risks that threaten their safety, which is similar in intent to the Volcker Rule. More generally, policymakers in other countries, including Adair Turner, have spoken favorably about US financial reform efforts.[37]

The Republicans' "modified bankruptcy" alternative during financial reform missed the mark badly

As the Lehman Brothers failure amply demonstrated, existing bankruptcy laws are inadequate for unwinding a complex financial intermediary without causing significant contagion within the broader financial system. During development of

include deposit insurance and discount window access, but neither of those mechanisms can be used to save a failing firm. The discount window exists to provide backup liquidity to solvent banks, and deposit insurance exists to enable a bank to fail without precipitating runs or creating other systemic disruptions.

[35] See Jamie Dimon's testimony before the House Committee on Financial Services on June 19, 2012.

[36] *Id.*

[37] See Adair Turner speech, entitled "*Reforming finance, are we being radical enough?*," dated February 18, 2011. See also Adair Turner interview with *Prospect Magazine*, dated December 14, 2011.

the Wall Street Reform and Consumer Protection Act, Republicans on the House Committee on Financial Services repeatedly offered a "modified bankruptcy" proposal intended to end TBTF.[38] As even a Republican witness at a 2011 hearing on TBTF indicated, any regime for unwinding a financial intermediary needs two things, speed and liquidity, that current bankruptcy laws lack.[39] The bankruptcy modifications that the Republicans proposed for financial institutions would have exacerbated, not mitigated, the problems inherent in existing bankruptcy laws with respect to those critical elements, and, had they been in effect in 2008, likely would have made the Lehman bankruptcy more disruptive, not less so.

The Republican alternative would have slowed the bankruptcy process down and potentially frozen the claims of many creditors, both of which would precipitate runs on the failing firm and exacerbate damaging effects within the financial system. The Republican plan generally would have required a pre-bankruptcy consultation process that would have delayed commencement of bankruptcy by at least 10 days.[40] The apparent intent of this was to avoid the need for bankruptcy by encouraging creditor forbearance, or alternatively to pave the way for a more orderly bankruptcy proceeding. The more likely effect, however, would be to alert creditors of the firm's failing state and encourage them to pull their funds during the consultation period, which would make a destabilizing failure more certain. The Republican alternative also would have allowed the bankruptcy court, upon the motion of the debtor, to subject counterparties to qualified financial contracts to an automatic stay on their contractual rights. Many of these creditors currently enjoy a statutory exemption from the automatic stay, in recognition of the interconnected nature of financial contracts and the importance of their fulfillment or

---

[38] Reps. Capito, Bachus, Neugebauer, Biggert, Hensarling, and Garrett offered an amendment in the nature of a substitute, which included the modified bankruptcy language among other provisions, during a markup to Title I of the House bill in November 2009. Modified bankruptcy language appeared again in a more comprehensive amendment in the nature of a substitute that these same Republicans offered during floor consideration of the House bill in December 2009. Reps. Capito and Smith (of Texas) offered bankruptcy modifications as an alternative to Title II of the Wall Street Reform Act during the conference committee proceedings on June 17, 2010.

[39] See the written and oral testimony of Stephen Lubben at a hearing held by the Financial Institutions and Consumer Credit subcommittee of the House Committee on Financial Services on June 14, 2011. Although Professor Lubben was not uniformly supportive of the OLA, he did commend its speed and liquidity features and opine that they were an improvement over existing bankruptcy.

[40] The proposal would have allowed the institution, its functional regulator, and a Market Stability and Capital Adequacy Board, in consultation with any agency charged with administering an insolvency regime for any component of the firm, to certify that an immediate filing is necessary "in the interest of justice." It is unclear, however, how quickly this determination could be made, or whether it would allow an immediate filing for the purpose of avoiding systemic problems.

prompt liquidation to keeping financial markets running. Merely the threat of these contracts being subject to the stay would incentivize a run on the failing firm, and, if the authority actually were exercised, financial intermediation could grind to a halt with serious systemic consequences.

The Republicans' "modified bankruptcy" also would have provided no alternative to existing private debtor in possession (DIP) financing and specifically would have prohibited any federal funding to facilitate a modified bankruptcy, which would severely constrain liquidity options instead of improving them. DIP financing, which is used to sustain a firm's activities during its liquidation or restructuring under current bankruptcy law, is critical to a successful bankruptcy — without it, the firm's operations are effectively shut down immediately, without regard to the value of the firm or the importance of its operations to the financial system. DIP financing was not readily available during the financial crisis, however, and similarly would not be available in the future if a complex financial institution failed during a period of economic stress and illiquid markets.[41] It is unlikely that DIP financing could be arranged even in good times in a sufficient amount and within a sufficiently short time to facilitate a controlled bankruptcy that does not have broader systemic effects.[42]

Although the Republican proposal likely would have exacerbated the systemically destabilizing aspects of a bankruptcy involving a large, complex financial intermediary, it did not recognize, let alone explicitly protect taxpayers from, these destabilizing spillover effects.

Conclusions and Postscript (January, 2014)

The Wall Street Reform and Consumer Protection Act clearly established a framework that allows large financial firms to fail while preventing catastrophic harm to the broader economy. It effectively ends "too-big-to-fail" and specifically outlaws future taxpayer bailouts of a failing financial institution.

Since the original release of this summary, the implementation of the law's provisions designed to reduce systemic risk has moved significantly toward completion. The FDIC has finished much of the work on its resolution process for large, complex institutions, creating a "single point of entry" regime that

---

[41] Professor Lubben's written testimony at the June 14, 2011 subcommittee hearing, referenced above, acknowledged these points.

[42] Again, Professor Lubben concurred with this assessment in his written testimony at the June 14, 2011, hearing.

minimizes potential risk to taxpayers. These rules have substantially clarified the process for resolution; affirmed that the OLA is designed to be used only in the most extreme circumstances, with conventional bankruptcy as the preferred initial alternative; and is serving as a model for resolution rules being adopted in Europe and elsewhere internationally. The FSOC has begun designating some of the largest nonbank financial companies as systemically significant, bringing them under FSOC and Federal Reserve oversight for the first time. New requirements for much higher levels of capital, the most important shield against losses and potential failure in a crisis, have been imposed pursuant to both the Wall Street Reform and the multilateral Basel III accords. These have already forced institutions to raise substantial capital and/or rethink their lines of business.

In December 2013, the federal financial regulators issued a final version of the "Volcker Rule" prohibiting proprietary trading by insured financial institutions, forcing them to divest their proprietary trading desks and permitting only a very narrow range of trading on behalf of their customers under strict new guidelines. Similarly, the Commodities Futures Trading Commission has released a series of tough new rules to bring much-needed transparency and accountability to trading in the types of derivative instruments that served as fuel for the fires of the 2008 crisis. Each of these regulatory actions has set off a firestorm of criticism, particularly from large institutions, and lawsuits against the agencies are already underway. As noted above, these tough new rules are "gifts that nobody wants," indicating that they will substantially curtail banks' ability to take risks that would previously have left taxpayers on the hook, provide a clear path to the closure of troubled institutions, and put an end to government bailouts.

Given the pace of the regulatory implementation and the need for experience under the new rules, market observers have moved carefully in adjusting expectations and pricing to reflect the strength of the new restrictions and the end of government support for these institutions. These changes are, however, now occurring. On November 14, 2013, Moody's Investors Services made a major announcement to this effect, stating that in "rating actions reflecting strengthened US bank resolution tools, prompted by the Dodd–Frank Act, which affect Moody's assumptions about US government support," the rating agency has "removed all uplift from US government support in ratings for BHC debt."[43] While the impact of the new rules on bank funding costs is still evolving, Brookings Institution scholars Martin Baily and Douglas Elliott stated in a recent paper that "recent evidence does indicate that the interest rates paid on bonds

[43]"Rating Action: Moody's concludes review of 8 large US banks," Moody's Investors Service Global Credit Research release, November 14, 2013.

issued by large BHCs have risen as markets realize the new risks these bonds face."[44] In addition, a recent Goldman Sachs Global Market Institute review of large BHC debt concludes "first, that a significant bond funding advantage for the largest banks would *not* have been unusual or surprising, even if TBTF did not affect funding costs, and second, that the actual observed advantage has been quite small over time, and has been a *dis*advantage since the crisis abated. This strongly suggests that the market is not pricing in any government assistance that would benefit the largest banks' bondholders."[45]

The financial crisis of 2008 devastated our economy and resulted in massive losses of jobs and household wealth. It would have been irresponsible for Congress not to have addressed the root cause of the crisis and end the TBTF problem that was so central to it. As the foregoing analysis shows, the Wall Street Reform and Consumer Protection Act accomplishes both goals by combining tools to prevent financial firms from failing with tools that allow a financial company to fail without causing collateral damage to the system if a failure nonetheless occurs. Arguments to the contrary ignore the provisions and structure of the financial reform law, the practical evidence regarding the law's impact, or both.

[44]"A New Chapter Begins in 'Too-Big-To-Fail'," Martin Neil Baily and Douglas J. Elliott, Brookings Institution, November 19, 2013.

[45]Steve Strongin, Amanda Hindian, Sandra Lawson, Jorge Murillo, Koby Sadan and Balakrishna Subramanian, "Measuring the TBTF Effect on Bond Pricing," Goldman Sachs Global Markets Institute, May, 2013.

Chapter 18

A Dissent From the Majority Report of the Financial Crisis Inquiry Commission

Peter J. Wallison[1]

As many of you may know, I was a member of the Financial Crisis Inquiry Commission, a 10-member group set up by Congress to find and report the causes of the great financial crisis of 2008.[2] The Commission finished its work and released its report in late January. I dissented from the majority report. A copy of my dissent can be downloaded from the AEI website.[3] In this talk today, I'd like to explain not only why I dissented but why this dissent was necessary.

If you have had an opportunity to read the Commission's report, you know that it did not do a thorough study. Among the issues that were not covered were the following:

— What information persuaded the rating agencies that subprime mortgages were unlikely to fail in numbers that would eat into the AAA tranches?
— What role did the partial repeal of Glass–Steagall play in the failures of commercial banks and investment banks?
— Most important, why did mortgage underwriting standards decline so precipitously through the 1990s and into the 2000s?

---

[1] Peter J. Wallison is the Arthur F. Burns Fellow in Financial Policy Studies at the American Enterprise Institute. The text resulted from a speech delivered at the 47th annual Conference on Bank Structure and Competition. It was originally published in the *Proceedings of a Conference on Bank Structure and Competition*, Federal Reserve Bank of Chicago, May 2011, Chicago.

[2] This was a great mystery at one time. I once participated in a 2008 academic conference where one of the papers had this title — "WTF" (If you don't know what that means, you're showing your age).

[3] See http://www.aei.org/papers/economics/fiscal-policy/dissent-from-the-majority-report-of-the-financial-crisis-inquiry-commission-paper/.

There were many other unanswered questions. Instead of pursuing a thorough study, however, the Commission's majority used its extensive statutory investigative authority to seek only the facts that supported its initial assumptions — that the crisis was caused by "deregulation" or lax regulation, greed, and recklessness on Wall Street; predatory lending in the mortgage market; unregulated derivatives; and a financial system addicted to excessive risk-taking.

The Commission did not seriously investigate any other cause and did not effectively connect the factors it investigated to the financial crisis. In the end, the majority's report turned out to be just a story *about* the financial crisis, rather than a report on what *caused* the financial crisis. That, however, is not the only reason I dissented.

What caused the financial crisis?

George Santayana is often quoted for the aphorism that "Those who cannot remember the past are condemned to repeat it." Looking back on the financial crisis, however, we can see why the study of history is often so contentious and why revisionist histories are so easy to construct. There are always many factors that could have caused a historical event; the difficult task is to discern which, among a welter of possible causes, were the significant ones — the ones without which history would have been different.

Using this standard, I believe that the *sine qua non* of the financial crisis was U.S. government housing policy, which fostered the creation of 27 million subprime and other risky loans — half of all mortgages in the United States — which were ready to default in unprecedented numbers as soon as the massive 1997–2007 housing bubble began to deflate. If the U.S. government had not chosen this policy path, the great financial crisis of 2008 would never have occurred.

With this background, I want to take you through the logical process that I followed in coming to the conclusion that it was the U.S. government's housing policies — and nothing else — that caused the 2008 financial crisis.

This position has been called monocausal or simplistic. That doesn't make it wrong.

A child playing with matches can burn down a house. The fact that the child was left alone in the house, that the house did not have a security system that reported the fire, and that the fire department's truck broke down on the way to the fire are not other causes. If the child had not been playing with matches, the house wouldn't have burned down.

The inquiry has to begin with what everyone agrees was the trigger for the crisis — the so-called mortgage meltdown that occurred in 2007. That was the relatively sudden outbreak of delinquencies and defaults among mortgages, primarily in a few states — California, Arizona, Nevada, and Florida — but to a lesser degree, everywhere in the country.

No one disputes that the losses on these mortgages and the decline in housing values that resulted from the ensuing foreclosures were the precipitating cause of the crisis. These mortgage losses weakened and caused a loss of market confidence in Bear Stearns, Lehman, WaMu and Wachovia. The Fed rescued AIG because it wrote credit default swaps on portfolios of private mortgage-backed securities (MBS) backed by subprime mortgages.

The great housing bubble of 1997–2007

Between 1997 and 2007, the U.S. experienced what was by far the largest housing bubble in its history. Figure 1 was derived from Robert Shiller's calculation of real home prices since 1890.

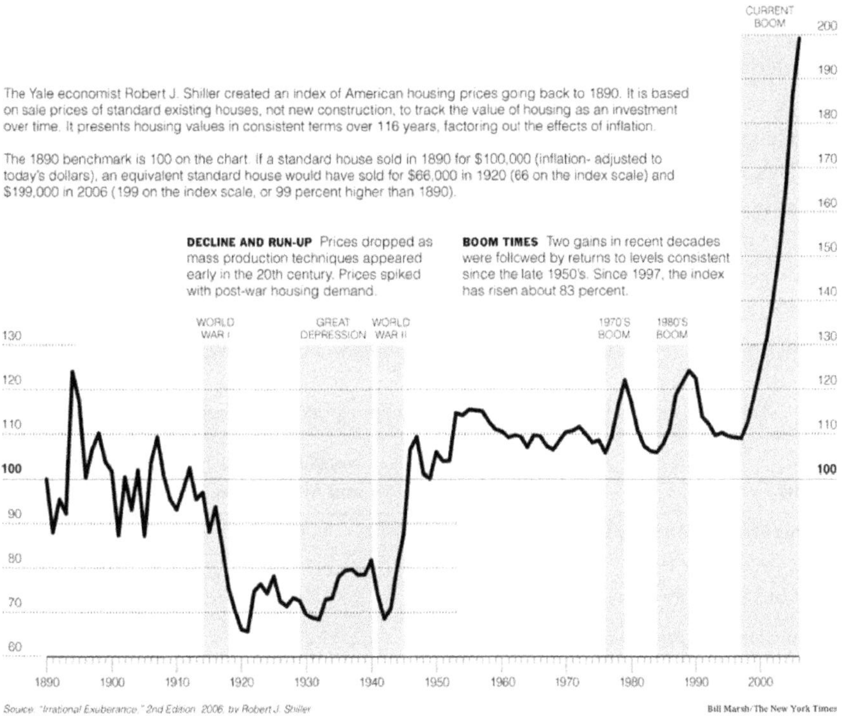

Figure 1. A History of Home Values.

Why was an international financial crisis triggered by the collapse of a housing bubble in the U.S.? The U.S. had had housing bubbles in the past. Since the Second World War, there had been two — beginning in 1979 and 1989 — but when these bubbles deflated, they had triggered only local losses.

Why was the deflation of the housing bubble in 2007 so destructive? The Commission's answer was that there were weaknesses in the financial system — failures of regulation and risk management, excessive leverage and risk-taking — that were responsible for the ensuing devastation.

This is like the fire truck breaking down. The truck would not have been on its way to the fire if the child had not been playing with matches.

The Commission ignored the obvious reason for the meltdown's destructiveness — the quality of the mortgages in this bubble. As I noted earlier — and as the Commission never acknowledged or disputed — by 2008, half all mortgages in the U.S. — 27 million — were subprime or otherwise risky loans. Table 1, drawn from my dissent, shows the subprime and Alt-A mortgages outstanding before the financial crisis in 2008.

This was unprecedented. In prior housing bubbles, the number of low-quality nonprime loans never exceeded a few percent. As I will show, it was the unprecedented number of delinquencies and defaults among these low-quality loans that drove down housing values, caused the collapse of the market for MBS, and weakened financial institutions in the U.S. and around the world.

This fact raised two key questions — Why were there so many weak and risky loans in this bubble? And what had happened to mortgage underwriting standards in the preceding years that caused such a serious deterioration in mortgage quality?

The Commission completely ignored these questions, but the answer lay in plain sight — beginning in 1992, U.S. housing policy sought to increase home

Table 1. Entities Holding Credit Risk of Subprime and Other High-Risk Mortgages.

Entity	No. of Subprime and Alt-A Loans	Unpaid Principal Amount
Fannie Mae and Freddie Mac	12 million	$1.8 trillion
FHA and other Federal	5 million	$0.6 trillion
CRA and HUD Programs	2.2 million	$0.3 trillion
Total Federal Government	**19.2 million**	**$2.7 trillion**
Other (including subprime and Alt-A Private MBS issued by Countrywide, Wall Street and others)	7.8 million	$1.9 trillion
Total	**27 million**	**$4.6 trillion**

ownership in the United States by reducing mortgage underwriting standards in order to make mortgage credit more readily available to low-income borrowers. Indeed, home ownership rose from 64% — where it had been for 30 years — to 69% in 2004.

The affordable housing goals and the deterioration in underwriting standards

The turning point came in 1992, with the enactment by Congress of what were called "affordable housing goals" for Fannie Mae and Freddie Mac. These two firms, which were shareholder-owned, had been chartered by Congress more than 20 years earlier to operate a secondary market in mortgages. The original idea was that by purchasing mortgages from originators, Fannie and Freddie would provide them with the cash to make more mortgages.

Fannie and Freddie's congressional charters required them to buy only mortgages that would be acceptable to institutional investors — in other words, prime mortgages. A prime mortgage at the time was a loan with a 10–20% downpayment, made to a borrower with a good credit record who had sufficient income to meet his or her debt obligations after the loan was made. Fannie and Freddie operated under these standards until 1992.

The 1992 affordable housing goals required that of all mortgages bought by Fannie and Freddie in any year, *at least 30%* had to be loans made to borrowers who were at or below the median income in the places where they lived.

Over succeeding years, the Department of Housing and Urban Development (HUD) increased this requirement — to 42% in 1996, 50% in 2000, and finally to 56% in 2008. Table 2, prepared by the Federal Housing Finance Agency, shows the years in which various increases went into effect.

At this level, Fannie and Freddie had to acquire at least one goals-eligible loan for every prime loan that they acquired and since not all subprime loans were goals-eligible, Fannie and Freddie were in effect required to buy many more subprime loans than prime loans to meet the goals.

As a result of this process, by 2008 Fannie and Freddie held the credit risk of 12 million subprime or otherwise risky loans. But this was not all. HUD took Congress's enactment of the affordable housing goals as an expression of a congressional policy to reduce underwriting standards so that low-income borrowers would have greater access to mortgage credit.

As outlined in my dissent, by tightening the affordable housing goals, HUD put Fannie and Freddie into competition with Federal Housing Administration (FHA),

Table 2. GSEs' Success in Meeting Affordable Housing Goals 1996–2008.

	1996	1997	1998	1999	2000	2001	2002	2003	2004	2005	2006	2007	2008
Low & Mod Housing Goals	**40%**	**42%**	**42%**	**42%**	**42%**	**50%**	**50%**	**50%**	**50%**	**52%**	**53%**	**55%**	**56%**
Fannie Actual	45%	45%	44%	46%	50%	51%	52%	52%	53%	55%	57%	56%	54%
Freddie Actual	41%	43%	43%	46%	50%	53%	50%	51%	52%	54%	56%	56%	51%
Special Affordable Goal	**12%**	**14%**	**14%**	**14%**	**14%**	**20%**	**20%**	**20%**	**20%**	**22%**	**23%**	**25%**	**27%**
Fannie Actual	15%	17%	15%	18%	19%	22%	21%	21%	24%	24%	28%	27%	26%
Freddie Actual	14%	15%	16%	18%	21%	23%	20%	21%	23%	26%	26%	26%	23%
Underserved Goal	**21%**	**24%**	**24%**	**24%**	**24%**	**31%**	**31%**	**31%**	**31%**	**37%**	**38%**	**38%**	**39%**
Fannie Actual	25%	29%	27%	27%	31%	33%	33%	32%	32%	41%	43%	43%	39%
Freddie Actual	28%	26%	26%	27%	29%	32%	31%	33%	34%	43%	44%	43%	38%

which had an explicit mission to provide credit to low-income borrowers, and with subprime lenders such as Countrywide, that signed up for a HUD program to reduce underwriting standards. Moreover, these organizations were joined by insured banks and S&Ls, which were required under the Community Reinvestment Act to make mortgage credit available to borrowers who are at or below 80% of the median income in the areas where they live.

As a result of this government-induced competition, as shown in Table 1, by 2008, 19.2 million out of the total of 27 million subprime and other weak loans in the U.S. financial system could be traced directly or indirectly to U.S. government housing policies.

Of course, it is possible to find borrowers who meet prime loan standards among low-income families, but it is far more difficult to do this than among middle-income groups. Among the more obvious problems, low-income borrowers don't generally have downpayments, their FICO credit scores are often below average, and debt to income ratios are often very high.

And when Fannie, Freddie, FHA, subprime lenders, and insured banks and S&Ls were all competing to find loans to borrowers in the low-income category, they had to reduce their underwriting standards in order to find the mortgages they were required to make. So underwriting standards deteriorated as the affordable housing goals rose. For example, in 1990, one in 200 mortgages involved a downpayment of 3% or less; but by 2007, 40% of all mortgages made that year had a downpayment of 3% or less.

The securitization of subprime loans

What about the additional 7.8 million low-quality mortgages labeled as PMBS in Table 1? These were subprime and other risky mortgages securitized by the private sector and held by financial institutions around the world. They were less than one-third of the total number of subprime and other risky loans outstanding, but they are the reason that banks and loan originators generally have been blamed for the financial crisis in the media, in most books about the financial crisis, and of course by the government, which is seeking to avoid its own culpability.

How were these mortgages related to U.S. government housing policy? The large-scale securitization of subprime and other risky loans was also a new phenomenon in the housing bubble that ended in 2007, and it was a direct result of the extraordinary growth of the bubble itself.

As shown in Figure 1, most bubbles in the past lasted for 3 or 4 years. This is because in that time delinquencies begin to appear and the inflow of the necessary speculative funds begins to dry up. The bubble that deflated in 2007, however, had an unprecedented long 10-year life. The reason was that the money flow into that bubble was not from private speculators looking for profit, but primarily from the government pursuing a social policy by directing the investments of companies it controlled. The government was not concerned about growing risk.

Housing bubbles tend to suppress delinquencies and defaults. As housing prices rise, people who can't meet their obligations can sell the house for more than they paid, or can refinance, so defaults are limited.

By 2002, five years into the bubble that began in 1997, investors were noticing that subprime and other risky loans — which usually carried higher than normal interest rates because of their risk — were not showing commensurate defaults. In other words, the data suggested that these securities were offering unusually high risk-adjusted yields.

This stimulated the development of a private market in securitized subprime loans — called private-label or private mortgage-backed securities — something that had never been seen before. This market was about 4% of all mortgages made in 2002 — about $130 billion. For comparison, in the same year, Fannie and Freddie had already acquired almost $1.2 trillion in subprime and other risky loans, including $206 billion in 2002 alone. The market kept growing through 2005 and 2006, but completely collapsed in 2007, when the 10-year bubble finally topped out and began to deflate.

The extraordinary speed of this collapse is shown in Figure 2. Thus, the 7.8 million subprime and other risky loans that were securitized by the private sector during the 2000s and still outstanding in 2008 were also the *indirect* result of U.S. government housing policies, which had built an unprecedented bubble in the late 1990s.

The bubble created the necessary conditions — a long run of subprime loans without the expected losses — for the growth of a huge securitization market in subprime and other risky loans in the mid-2000s. Thus, government housing policies, which created and prolonged this bubble, were also responsible for the development and growth of the huge private label securitization market in the 2000s.

Before leaving this subject, I'd like to deal with an issue that comes up again and again — whether Fannie and Freddie followed Wall Street into subprime lending or Wall Street followed Fannie and Freddie.

From what I've just said, it should be obvious that Fannie and Freddie led Wall Street. Still, those who want to protect the government won't give up. The FCIC,

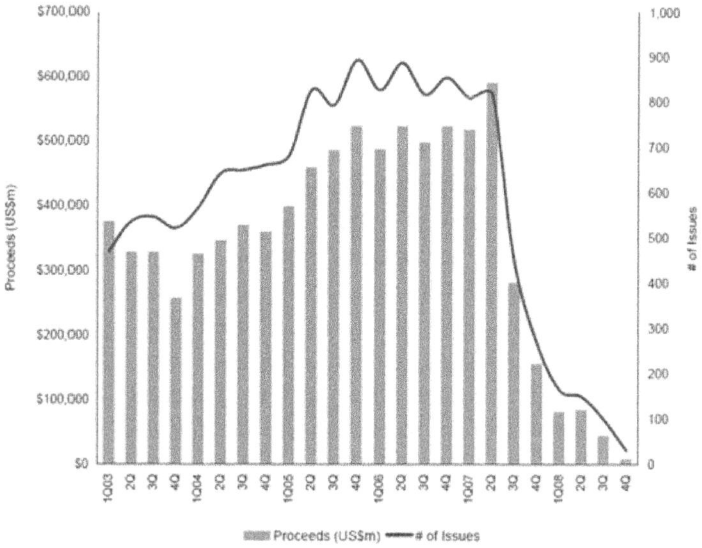

Figure 2. Quarterly Residential ABS, MBS & CDO Volume.

without any evidence at all, said in its report that Fannie and Freddie followed Wall Street into subprime loans for market share or for profit — that the affordable housing goals were not responsible. This is simply false. Here's a quote from Fannie's 2006 10-K:

> [W]e have made, and continue to make, significant adjustments to our mortgage loan sourcing and purchase strategies in an effort to meet HUD's increased housing goals and new subgoals. These strategies include entering into some purchase and securitization transactions with lower expected economic returns than our typical transactions. We have also relaxed some of our underwriting criteria to obtain goals-qualifying mortgage loans and increased our investments in higher-risk mortgage loan products that are more likely to serve the borrowers targeted by HUD's goals and subgoals, which could increase our credit losses.

This language, which confirms that Fannie bought subprime and other risky loans to comply with the affordable housing goals, somehow never made it into the Commission's report.

Subprime and other risky loans cause the financial crisis

With half of all mortgages weak and low quality by late 2007, the financial crisis was a foregone conclusion. No financial system could withstand the huge losses that occurred when the delinquencies and defaults associated with 27 million subprime and other risky loans began to appear.

As shown in Figure 2, alarmed by these unexpected and unprecedented numbers of these delinquencies and defaults, investors fled the multi-trillion dollar market for MBS, dropping MBS values — and especially those MBS backed by subprime and other risky loans — to fractions of their former prices.

Mark-to-market accounting then required financial institutions to write down the value of their assets — reducing their capital and liquidity positions and causing great investor and creditor unease. In this environment, the government's rescue of Bear Stearns in March of 2008 temporarily calmed investor fears but created significant moral hazard; investors and other market participants reasonably believed, after the rescue of Bear, that all large financial institutions would also be rescued if they encountered financial difficulties.

However, when Lehman Brothers — an investment bank even larger than Bear — was allowed to fail, market participants were shocked; suddenly, they were forced to consider the financial health of their counterparties, many of which appeared weakened by losses and the capital write-downs required by mark-to-market accounting. This caused a halt to lending and a hoarding of cash — a virtually unprecedented period of market paralysis and panic that we know as the financial crisis of 2008.

Conclusion

In brief, my dissent shows that the financial crisis was not caused by lack of regulation, or by private sector greed, but by misguided government housing policy. The policy implication of this is that Dodd–Frank was not the appropriate response.

The Financial Crisis Inquiry Commission was correct that the 2008 financial crisis could have been prevented. However, that could have been done simply by changing U.S. government housing policy. There was no need to saddle the U.S. economy with new regulations.

Index